D086530?

PSYCHOSOCIAL CAPACITY BUILDING IN RESPONSE TO DISASTERS

GEORGIAN COLLEGE LIBRARY

$45.52
GEOR-BK

PSYCHOSOCIAL CAPACITY BUILDING IN RESPONSE TO DISASTERS

JOSHUA L. MILLER

Library Commons
Georgian College
825 Memorial Avenue
Box 2316
Orillia, ON L3V 6S2

COLUMBIA UNIVERSITY PRESS   NEW YORK

COLUMBIA UNIVERSITY PRESS
Publishers Since 1893
New York   Chichester, West Sussex
cup.columbia.edu

Copyright © 2012 Columbia University Press
All rights reserved

Library of Congress Cataloging-in-Publication Data
   Miller, Joshua (Joshua L.)
    Psychosocial capacity building in response to disasters / Joshua L. Miller.
      p. cm.
    Includes bibliographical references and index.
    ISBN 978-0-231-14820-7 (cloth : alk. paper) — ISBN 978-0-231-14821-4 (pbk.) —
ISBN 978-0-231-51976-2 (electronic)
    1. Disaster victims—Psychology.   2. Disasters—Psychological aspects.
3. Stress (Psychology)   I. Title.
   HV553.M55 2012
   363.34'86—dc22   2011012294

Columbia University Press books are printed on permanent and durable acid-free paper.
This book was printed on paper with recycled content.
Printed in the United States of America
c 10 9 8 7 6 5 4 3 2 1
p 10 9 8 7 6 5 4 3 2 1
References to Internet Web sites (URLs) were accurate at the time of writing. Neither the author
nor Columbia University Press is responsible for URLs that may have expired or changed since
the manuscript was prepared.

PREFACE

AFTER HURRICANE KATRINA STRUCK the Gulf Coast in late summer 2005, the landscape was shattered almost beyond recognition. The winds and floodwaters had tossed objects and structures haphazardly across the countryside: large fishing boats were stranded on hills or snagged in the branches of trees and houses had been blown into the streets. Glass, wood, metal shards, downed power lines, and contaminated mud made walking and driving hazardous. In the hot, sultry air, swarms of love bugs stuck to clothing and flesh.

A few days after Katrina made landfall, what I saw in coastal Missis-sippi—particularly, Biloxi—as a Red Cross mental health counselor was overwhelming for even the most seasoned of responders. Many houses were completely destroyed or severely damaged. At first glance, neighborhoods appeared to be deserted but often were in fact behind hills of rubble—soggy sofas, moldy carpets, water-stained dolls and stuffed animals, mildewy clothing—deposited on front lawns. There were signs of life indicated by makeshift tents, tarps, shelters, and even open hammocks. The homes left standing had Xs painted on their exterior walls, around which numerals tal-lied the occupants and the deceased.

Those residents who remained, camping inside or outside of their dam-aged homes and apartments, were stunned and shocked, isolated from their families, friends, and neighbors. They surveyed the destruction but did not know how to respond. All essential services had been disrupted. The water supply was so badly contaminated it was not only undrinkable but risky for bathing. A power outage meant residents had no fans or air conditioning to counter the oppressive heat. The remaining supermarkets, banks, stores, and ATMs were closed down or inoperable, leaving residents without food or money. Near the beach, steel girders that had once framed office buildings or large chain stores were all that was left standing.

The hurricane shattered support systems and communications. There was no public transportation, no telephone or cell phone service, no Internet connections or e-mail. Schools, set to open for the fall semester, were either too damaged to open or were being used as shelters. Senior centers, civic organizations, and social services were no longer operating; doctor's and dentist's offices had been destroyed. Driving was curtailed for lack of gas and, for those fortunate enough to have a gasoline source, there were no working traffic lights. Dodging debris and downed power lines while gingerly nosing through intersections made every excursion a jaw-clenching ordeal. Most people had fled to other parts of the state or country while others were in shelters run by the Red Cross and other charities.

For many first responders, the only analogs to the landscape of destruction were scenes from World War II movies, such as *The Pianist*. Veterans of the Iraq and Afghanistan wars were reminded of the aftermath of bombings in Baghdad and Kabul. Volunteers and workers from the Red Cross and myriad other organizations, including FEMA (Federal Emergency Management Agency) and similar government responders, found themselves sleeping in churches, makeshift shelters, and, a lucky few, in rooms at local military bases that had withstood the most destructive aspects of the storm and where generators provided electricity.

In addition to those representing government entities or large formal charities, hundreds of private citizens had driven down to the disaster site to deliver clothing or to cook food in their own campers, some vehicles serving as jury-rigged diners in parking lots. Police officers from other communities and states stationed themselves at major intersections and directed traffic.

Despite an influx of donated goods, distribution was difficult. Piles of clothing accumulated outside of shelters and relief staging areas, with dazed residents picking through them under a fierce and unyielding sun. Eventually, rain transformed much of what lay on the ground into an unusable textile soup.

Schools and churches that had sustained minimal damage were used as shelters, often managed by the Red Cross. Displaced families would camp on the floor, forming microcommunities around their cots, self-segregated by race and ethnicity—whites in one hallway, African Americans in another. Yet a third segregated group was young Latino men who worked during the day at construction jobs and returned to the shelters at night to eat and sleep. Most spoke only Spanish, while shelter volunteers and other residents spoke only English. Announcements and notices were sporadically translated. Celebrities—such as Gloria Estefan, Jimmy Smits, Daisy Fuentes, and Andy Garcia—would periodically visit shelters to cheer up the residents. Feelings toward the Latino residents ranged from anger and resentment to gratitude. They were resented for having jobs unavailable to others and yet appreciated for saving lives during the storm and for rebuilding broken communities.

Conspicuously absent from the shelters were the Vietnamese people who had settled along the Gulf Coast. Many worked in fishing or in casinos or operated small businesses. Having endured wars in Vietnam, arduous and dangerous crossings to the United States—often in fragile boats—and then prolonged stays in refugee camps, Vietnamese families, friends, and neighbors tried hard to stay together. Many did not speak English, and most storm warnings and subsequent relief notices were not translated into Vietnamese. The porches of Buddhist temples and Catholic churches became de facto shelters, with people setting up camp there. And it was at these places of worship where the Red Cross and other charities distributed food, clothing, and cooking supplies. Marines from Mexico unloaded essential goods there, such as bottled water. Vietnamese American doctors set up makeshift health clinics in the temples.

This is a snapshot of a typical working environment for a Red Cross mental health volunteer after a massive disaster. Although every disaster is unique, they have some common threads: physical damage and destruction, social dislocations, chaos, fear, and numbness. The lattice of social networks, public spaces, civic organizations, and socioeconomic supports is left torn and shattered. The social ecology of the disaster—history, culture and social structures, and the dynamics of privilege, power, and oppression—can be seen in the way people respond, such as the segregation within shelters and decisions by Vietnamese residents to stay in their devastated community, resisting another diaspora. Prejudice survives (as expressed by a white man donating clothing: "as long as it doesn't go to those Vietnamese, 'cause they'll just resell them") but may be held temporarily in abeyance (as an African American woman expressed to me: "There is still a lot of racism along the Gulf Coast, but when times are hard, people will pull together and help each other out").

Social and economic inequities are both heightened and ironed out by disasters. People and communities with more resources are better able to take preventive measures to rebuild and recover. Those who lack opportunity, assets, and social and economic capital because of racism, severe poverty, and linguistic and cultural marginalization are more vulnerable to the effects of storm surges, exploitation by politicians, and neglect by relief agencies that are staffed by predominantly white middle-class people. And yet suffering can also bring people together, if only momentarily.

Disasters are stories of communal destruction and collective loss, as well as individual and family anguish, but they are also narratives of personal and collective strength and resiliency. One story in the wake of Hurricane Katrina is about a Vietnamese couple taking refuge on a dock along a river. The man, in his fifties, was a fisherman whose boat was damaged by the storm. He was concerned that the listing vessel would be looted and ransacked, so he kept an around-the-clock vigil on a nearby dock. His wife was in her thirties and five months pregnant with twins. Neither of them spoke fluent English. The water surrounding the dock was made septic and toxic by the storm. Behind the dock was a field from which chemicals had leached. The U.S. Coast Guard made daily trips to the dock, bringing water and sometimes food. They were concerned about the couple's health, particularly the pregnant woman's, but the man was adamant that neither of them would leave the dock.

The Red Cross asked me to visit the family and assess the situation. With the help of the Coast Guard (which provided a translator), I was taken to the dock with two Red Cross public relations personnel. The trip by boat up the river was surreal as we passed many beached or damaged boats, some resting on land and others with their noses in the water. The Coast Guard cautioned us to avoid being splashed by any water because of possible contamination.

The dock was about fifteen feet above the water table and we ascended a rusty ladder to meet the couple. They had established a camp with tarps, bedding, cooking utensils, and food supplies from the Coast Guard. The woman, Nguyen, seemed cautiously glad to see us, while the man, Van (both names are pseudonyms), was watchful and appeared to be uncomfortable. As we conversed, Van made it clear that he would not leave the dock because of his concern for his boat. The couple had lived in a Vietnamese neighborhood that was severely damaged by the storm, and their house had been destroyed. After lengthy discussion about the risks to Nguyen's pregnancy, he agreed to let her visit a doctor if the Red Cross promised to bring her back to the dock, no matter what was found.

The next day, the same Red Cross contingent, this time traveling on land and minus the Coast Guard translator, drove across the chemically contaminated field to the rear of the dock. Nguyen was ready to leave, while a wary Van said, "Promise bring back?" After reassuring Van, we drove to a local obstetric clinic that was one of few in operation. Nguyen could only tell us that her regular doctor was Dr. Morgan. The only doctor with that name no longer had an office and there was no phone service. Nguyen understood a little English, but communication was challenging. She appeared to be nervous and, when walking from the Red Cross van to the office, held my hand tightly.

The three Red Cross workers were male, as was the obstetrician. The nurses were female. After examining Nguyen and conducting an ultrasound, the doctor asked to speak with me. "She's not pregnant. The ultrasound shows no sign of any fetus." I explained that Nguyen was supposed to be five months pregnant with twins. "She might have been, but she isn't now," he responded. I asked if he could conduct another test, such as a urine sample, to be sure, and although he complied, the result was the same. He did not want to tell Nguyen the news on his own and asked if I would stay in the room with him. I asked Nguyen if she minded, and she agreed to let me be present.

Nguyen appeared to grasp what the doctor told her and started sobbing. The doctor left us alone in the consulting room, and she again took my hand and squeezed it. A nurse came in and mentioned that Nguyen had described some vaginal bleeding a few days before and suggested that this might have been a miscarriage. I told Nguyen that I was sorry for her loss and asked her what she would like to do. She asked to be taken to her house. We went out to the lobby, rejoined the other two Red Cross workers, and drove to her old neighborhood.

The frame of her house was still standing, but the inside had been scoured out by the storm—windows were missing, and walls had collapsed or disappeared. All the furniture and other belongings were ruined. Nguyen began crying again. She again held my hand and asked if I could take her to a staging area in the community to get emergency food and provisions.

Many people were gathered at the relief area. While Nguyen was collecting supplies—rice, water, fuel for the cooking stove—a Vietnamese woman approached me. She pointed to Nguyen and, out of earshot, said, "She not pregnant, she not pregnant," gesturing with her hand in a circle pointed at her head. "She crazy," the woman said and then walked away. When

Nguyen returned to me, she started to sob. Another Vietnamese woman asked me in English why she was crying. Nguyen said something in Vietnamese. I said in English that she had lost a lot. The woman then spoke sharply to Nguyen in English, saying, "What are you crying for? We all lost everything."

As we drove her back to the dock with her supplies, Nguyen asked me in broken English if I was going to tell her husband what the doctor had said. I reassured her that her medical information was private and that she was in control of who she told and what she said. When we returned to the dock, a grim-faced Van was waiting. Nguyen called to him, "Doctor say everything okay," and she waved to us to leave, which we did.

As a Red Cross mental health volunteer, I had many other assignments. I ended up working in the Vietnamese neighborhood where Nguyen and Van had lived. We (I along with other dedicated Red Cross workers, including a nurse, supply specialist, and one of the men who had accompanied me with Nguyen) tried to get the neighborhood some desperately needed supplies—tarps, tents, cots, rice, and cookers. Vietnamese monks, priests, doctors, and many volunteers were trying to help the community recover, even though their own buildings and houses had been damaged. Many people could not call the Red Cross and FEMA assistance numbers because they did not speak English, and even when a translator was available, the lines were often busy. After a few days, the supervisors of the other Red Cross workers reassigned them to other neighborhoods, insisting that they not spend too much time helping any one group of people.

I was more fortunate and was given support for trying to devise culturally responsive services for this neighborhood. As with much of disaster mental health work, I engaged in psychological first aid (see chapter 6), which included a lot of networking, advocacy, and arranging for the provision of concrete services. The local Buddhist temple and Vietnamese Catholic church appeared to be the central point of indigenous responses to the disaster—coordinating distribution of supplies, providing translators, opening ad hoc medical clinics—and equally as important, serving as places where people could gather to socialize, discuss their losses, talk about rebuilding, and identify those in need of special help. I tried to support their efforts, accessing supplies and services when possible and following their lead about who needed help.

While I was working in the neighborhood, the Coast Guard translator called to ask me what had happened with Nguyen and Van. I was not able to share any details with him other than to say that I had taken her to the doctor. He was clearly concerned about the couple and unhappy with my circumspection. We were able to talk about how the Red Cross might help the couple get funds so that Van could salvage his fishing boat, and I made some phone calls to start this process.

Toward the end of my two-week stint, when I was preparing to return to my family, job, and community, I drove by the dock with another Red Cross worker who had just arrived for a two-week tour of duty. Nguyen and Van were both there, and the situation had not changed. I tried to explain about the calls that I had made about assistance in repairing the boat. Nguyen was smiling and repeated, "Doctor said everything okay." I introduced them to the new worker, and she agreed to visit them again in a few days.

As I drove away, I realized that I still had no idea what had happened and would probably never know. Had Nguyen been pregnant? If so, what had happened? Was it related to the storm and the conditions on the dock? If she was not ever pregnant, what was the meaning of that? Was it a false pregnancy? Was she concerned that her husband, who was in his fifties and wanted descendants, would leave her if she did not bear him children?

As with much disaster mental health work, I had no idea whether I had been helpful to Nguyen and Van. I did not know how many Red Cross workers followed in my footsteps, working with them or with the community to help it recover from the hurricane. Did they remain in their community? Did they even remain together as a family? Are they still grappling with the psychological, social, and economic effects of the hurricane? What enabled them to continue with their lives? These and many other questions remained unanswered.

However, I was able to return to Biloxi two years later in the role of researcher. As described in chapter 3, my colleague Yoosun Park and I worked with Bao Chau Van, a Vietnamese-speaking social work master's student, to interview Vietnamese people living in the neighborhood where I had responded immediately after Katrina (Park, Miller, & Van, 2010). We were interested in understanding their lives before Hurricane Katrina, their experience of the hurricane, and what had happened to them since. The respondents and key informants we interviewed reported that only about half the families that had been living in the neighborhood had returned. There were still many vacant lots and significant numbers of people were still living in FEMA trailers. Many had lost their homes, businesses, and belongings. The costs of rebuilding were prohibitive, and casinos were gobbling up land, offering high prices to induce selling. Government support for rebuilding was minimal and inadequate. The fishing industry was severely depressed, but this had less to do with Katrina and more to do with the low price of shrimp and the high cost of fuel. Many had fled the area immediately after the storm and had been scattered throughout the United States. The loss of extended family and community left many of them feeling empty and alone. Many of those who returned were still fearful about the consequences of another storm.

Yet a majority of the hurricane survivors were rebuilding their lives and felt positive about the future. They had worked hard, earned money, and reconnected their family networks. Many were engaged in new jobs, often at casinos, or were starting new businesses, such as restaurants. Some had returned to their neighborhoods, while others were living in outlying areas. What was striking was the importance of the old neighborhoods in their lives. People were attending the Catholic church and Buddhist temple, both of which had been central in the recovery effort, offering material, social, and spiritual resources. Social networks had been reconfigured but also reconstructed. Whether the community will continue to be viable as an ethnic enclave is not clear, with many social, political, and economic forces at play. But in the short term, there was evidence of the intersection of individual, familial, and community resiliency.

So although I never knew what happened to Nguyen, and many other people to whom I offered psychological first aid, I was fortunate to witness how a community responded to a major disaster over time—something that eludes most responders who spend only a few weeks working in the early aftermath of a calamity. I learned that despite the ways disaster disrupts lives, overwhelms families, and fractures and shatters communities, people and their communities manage to find many sources of strength and resiliency to help them recover. Yet most clinicians responding in the early phases after a disaster are organized to focus on providing psychological first aid, crisis intervention, and acute mental health services to individual survivors. The work of reconstructing community is often viewed as separate and distinct, the province of public health workers, government officials, and community workers, most of whom do not have clinical training or skills.

This is an artificial dichotomy. Individual and family healing and recovery from disaster are intricately linked to the reconstruction and resurrection of community. Community resilience and individual resilience are intertwined. Approaching disaster from the standpoint of having a social ecology calls for a unified model—what is referred to in this book as *psychosocial capacity building*—in which the work of disaster mental health clinicians is informed by a person-in-environment perspective. This approach is described throughout. It is contrasted with the more Western, Eurocentric paradigm of disaster mental health services that has dominated the field in the United States and Europe. This prevailing model, with a strong *trauma* orientation to disaster response, has helped and assisted millions of people throughout the world for many years and there is much value in retaining some of its methods and practices. But it has also imposed an individualistic, culturally biased model on much of the world's populations, particularly those living in the developing world, and it runs the risk of producing iatrogenic effects. These effects can turn those being helped into victims who require professional assistance, and they can focus too much on the micro level (individuals and families) while paying inadequate attention to the mezzo and macro contexts in which people's lives are inextricably embedded.

Through my international work in Sri Lanka after the tsunami; northern Uganda in the wake of a twenty-year civil war; Sichuan Province, China, after the Wenchuan earthquake of 2008; and Haiti following the earthquake of 2010, as well as in responding to many large-scale and local domestic disasters, I have witnessed the tension between these two approaches. Increasingly, in non-Western countries or with non-Western populations, those affected by disaster and the indigenous professionals helping them to recover often resist counseling and psychotherapeutic interventions. I have heard many concerns voiced about how Western-style therapy is inappropriate, and even how it disempowers and pathologizes. Also, there are professionals who believe that trauma is rampant and that more therapy and counseling are indeed what is required. This dynamic is further complicated in that some indigenous professionals were trained in the West or exposed during their professional training to theories of human behavior and counseling that originated in Europe and the United States. Whatever one's position in this discourse, it is generally accepted that developing non-Western nations never have enough clinicians on the ground to provide counseling to even a small fraction of affected people. And bringing in outsiders always raises issues about the lack of cultural responsiveness and linguistic barriers to effective communication. Clearly, something more is needed.

Culture is never monolithic or static; there are differences within cultural groups (constituting an array of microcultures) and there are tensions between traditional cultural beliefs and practices and the increasingly wired, interdependent world. Therefore, in many instances, helping communities to rebuild is enhanced by drawing on traditional cultural practices—these are wellsprings of wisdom and contain narratives of how people have encountered and survived catastrophic events in the past. Large-scale disasters often disorient people, disconnecting them from their traditional cultural practices. Part of the work of disaster recovery is to reconstruct cultural resiliency with the knowledge that the reconstituted culture will never be what it was before the disaster. The disruptions from the disaster event, the changing landscape of the social ecology, and the cultural influences of those who respond from the outside lead to a new set of circumstances facing individuals and communities, as faced by Nguyen and Van and Little Saigon after Hurricane Katrina. Thus, people must reconnect with the stories, lessons, and traditions of the past while also forging a new vision of the future—one that incorporates the past, acknowledges the losses and disruptions stemming from the disaster, and looks forward to a life that contains some measure of hope and meaning.

The charge of disaster responders is not only to acknowledge the vulnerabilities and wounds of disaster-affected communities and their residents, supporting them with evidence-based practices that may involve professionals, but also to recognize the strengths and sources of resiliency that can be nurtured through a psychosocial capacity-building approach. Responders need to respect the inherent strength and wisdom of local communities while also helping to repair the tattered strands of social networks that overwhelmed local leaders are often unable to restore on their own. In some communities in China after the Wenchuan earthquake of 2008, huge numbers of cadres—local governing units essential to the civic functioning of rural Chinese villages—were lost or had themselves lost children, partners, and parents. Given the scale of this disaster, cadres neither were able to respond effectively on their own nor did they have the knowledge, skills, or resources to help their communities recover. Yet it is unimaginable that earthquake-devastated areas in China could be reconstructed without rebuilding the network of cadres; they are essential local leaders and civil servants.

In this book, I integrate the range of models and approaches to helping people recover to offer a comprehensive model of disaster response grounded in an understanding of the social ecology of disaster. Nguyen and Van's losses as well as their potential sources of strength and well-being cannot be separated from their family and community. There is no one way to help *all* the diverse communities of the world to respond to disasters, although we are continuously developing a knowledge base of strategies and best practices to at least inform and guide our efforts. I write this book in this spirit, with awe and gratitude for all the people who have demonstrated strength and resiliency in their recovery from disaster and for all the people who have helped them in this process.

ACKNOWLEDGMENTS

I HAVE HAD MANY TEACHERS in my education as a disaster responder. My first disaster response team was the Community Crisis Response Team of Western Massachusetts, and I am grateful to my teammates for helping me get my feet wet. The American Red Cross trained and deployed me to national disasters, while the Western Massachusetts Emergency Medical Services team trained me and regularly uses me to debrief uniformed responders.

The Center for Peace Building and Reconciliation (CPBR) worked devotedly to help people in eastern and southern Sri Lanka recover from the tsunami, and I was privileged to work alongside its volunteers. I particularly thank Dishani Jayaweera and Jayantha Senevirathne for their friendship and inspiration. Joanne Corbin has worked with survivors of the armed conflict in northern Uganda. I am indebted to her for including me in one phase of her psychosocial capacity building project. I learned a great deal from my Ugandan colleagues, particularly Father Remigio and social worker Stella Ojera. Dr. Ann Markes, Dr. Matt Kane, Eileen Giardina, David LaLima, Dr. Mwaki Amos Deo, and Okello Patrick Onguti were all cherished collaborators in a medical capacity building project in northern Uganda. In China, I have been privileged to work alongside Dean Xiulan Zhang, Braven Zhang, and Xiying Wang of Beijing Normal University and Cecilia Chan of Hong Kong University, and with my many other Chinese colleagues. Recently, I was fortunate to be able to work with CapraCare, a small Haitian NGO, and I thank its executive director, Jean Pierre-Louis; creative director, Laurie Pillow; local field captains, Smith and Janine; and the many volunteers with whom I worked. I would also like to mention Pere Daniel Felix of Fonfrede, Haiti, who works tirelessly on behalf of his community. Jeff Grabelsky and K. C. Wagner of the Cornell School of Industrial and Labor Relations and their colleague, psychologist Lorraine Beaulieu, did impressive work to help construction workers with their psychosocial reactions after 9/11, which is described in this book.

Many of my colleagues at Smith College School for Social Work have influenced me over the years. The Clinical Research Institute has funded a number of projects that supported both interventions and evaluations of those efforts, which are described in this book. My thanks to Dean Carolyn Jacobs and Associate Dean Susan Donner for encouraging and supporting me in my disaster response work and giving me the time to do it! Yoosun Park has been an important collaborator, particularly in the development of the concept of psychosocial capacity building. Bao Chau Van was a valued student collaborator in our work. And Kay Naito and Daphne Nayar were great help as research assistants on a number of psychosocial capacity building projects.

There are always those in the field who serve as inspiration, and I would like to mention a few. Bill Yule and Atle Dyregrov of the Children and War Foundation have been generous with their time and resources. I have great admiration for their work. Charles Figley, Kay Saakvitne, and Laurie Pearlman have done much to help many of us who have suffered the secondary consequences of responding to disaster. I have appreciated their writing, talks, and in Laurie's case, friendship. Ervin Staub, Paula Green, and Olivia Drier have all helped me better understand the dynamics of intergroup conflict, peace building, and healing. I have appreciated their friendship and collegiality. I particularly acknowledge my close friend Adin Thayer, who tirelessly helps war-affected communities recover in Africa. My thanks go to Tracy Kidder for his work on behalf of Partners in Health and for putting me in touch with Bepe Raviola, who was very receptive to my ideas about psychosocial capacity building. There are many other mentors whose works are listed in the references of this book. Although I have not met all of them personally, they have strongly influenced my thinking.

Students are great teachers, and I have learned tons from them while teaching courses about psychosocial capacity building and disaster at Smith College, Beijing Normal University, and Hong Kong University. I would like to thank the thousands of volunteers with whom I have worked at disaster sites in the United States and internationally in China, Haiti, Sri Lanka, and Uganda. Also, I appreciate how many friends have informally debriefed me over the years.

I owe a special debt to a woman who was murdered in London in the 1970s, whom I have written about as "Violet." She was my client when her husband killed her. Her life and death have had a strong influence on all my work. I am very fortunate to have ongoing relationships with her children and grandchildren. Also, I learned a great deal of professional wisdom in my younger years from Irving and Helen Miller, Sidney Miller, Alex and Naomi Gitterman, Stanley Ofsevit, Richard Cloward, Frances Fox Piven, Ann Hartman, and Mitchell Ginsberg. Abby Miller and Melanie Suchet have supported my work through the years.

Lauren Dockett and the staff at Columbia University Press have been a pleasure to work with. Two anonymous reviewers offered helpful feedback and criticism. I am very grateful to Frank Citino of Smith College, who has been a wizard with most of the book's diagrams. I particularly acknowledge Eileen Dunn, an editorial alchemist who reviewed an early draft of the manuscript; she consistently transforms rubble into gold. I also thank Merrill Gillaspy, my copy editor, who pruned and strengthened the manuscript. And last, my love and gratitude to my family—Davina, Lucy, Corina, and Sophie—whose love, support, and efforts in the world make my life meaningful and my work possible.

PSYCHOSOCIAL CAPACITY BUILDING IN RESPONSE TO DISASTERS

1

THE SOCIAL ECOLOGY OF DISASTERS

A HURRICANE SWEEPS across the Florida Keys, damaging homes, businesses, and roads, injuring and killing people. In northern Uganda, a civil war rages for more than twenty years, resulting in many deaths, maimings, and the forcible abduction of children as soldiers and concubines. The majority of the population is relocated to internally displaced persons camps (IDPs). In Sichuan Province, China, an earthquake levels villages, collapses schools, and triggers avalanches, leaving nearly one hundred thousand people dead and many more displaced. The Asian tsunami kills nearly a quarter million (World Health Organization, 2005) in more than ten countries, some at peace and others enduring ongoing armed conflicts.

After a high school senior prom, a car accident kills four students. Another survives but is left partially paralyzed. In a small city, a fire destroys an apartment building and twenty-five residents are displaced, losing their belongings and, in some instances, their pets. A man murders his estranged wife and then kills himself outside a courthouse after she obtains a restraining order against him.

What is a disaster? Most would agree that the natural disasters and Ugandan civil war cited here constitute disaster, but what about the other examples? If all of the examples fall into the category of disaster, then what qualities and attributes do they share? What is *not* a disaster?

And how do we respond to disasters? Who responds? What activities do they engage in? What are the consequences of disasters, and what helps individuals, families, and communities to recover from them? How universal are these reactions, and how are they influenced by culture and social structures? Are there interventions that are harmful or that make things worse? Can the same people, using the same skill sets, respond to all kinds of disasters, no matter what they are?

These are among the questions that this book seeks to explore. It considers a range of disasters and applies a variety of concepts and techniques to illustrate how professionals and volunteers in the helping professions (social workers, community psychologists and psychiatrists, teachers, counselors, clergy, and public health workers) can work effectively with individuals, groups, and communities to support them in their recovery from disaster. This book focuses not on rebuilding physical structures, such as homes and businesses, but rather on restoring people (reconstructing meaning, reconnecting people with one another, revitalizing hope), linking life before the disaster with the consequences of the disaster, and looking to the future. This is not to say that the repairing of infrastructure is distinct from the renewing of psyches, spirits, and a sense of collective community efficacy— using a social ecology framework, I emphasize how interconnected these processes are. But the primary focus of this book is how people responding to disaster can effectively work to develop the psychosocial capacity of those living and working in the affected community. In so doing, responders can help those affected by disaster help themselves and others to feel empowered and to regain control over their lives, as they rekindle hope for their futures.

DEFINING DISASTER

Disasters come in many sizes, some affecting entire regions or nations, others upsetting small communities or subcommunities. Some disasters are considered acts of God, or natural events, such as earthquakes, tsunamis, and floods, while others are the result of either bad intentions (terrorism, war) or incompetence and human error (chemical explosions, mining disasters, train crashes). The length or duration of disasters varies considerably—some occurring in the tremor of an earthquake or flash of a gunshot, others staggering on for years, such as an ongoing civil war.

Rosenfeld, Caye, Ayalon, and Lahad (2005) have identified the following six characteristics of disasters. While these characteristics are relevant and helpful, they still raise a number of questions and merit further investigation.

1. *Has a footprint of a certain size.* Loss of life and destruction of property are certainly hallmarks of a disaster. But how does scale factor into the

characterizing of disaster? If a one-family home burns to the ground and the inhabitants are displaced to temporary housing in an otherwise unaffected community, is this a disaster? Does the situation change if an entire apartment building or a nursing home burns? What about an entire block? Does it matter if the fire was caused by a faulty fuse box or a bomb?

2. *Has an identifiable beginning and end, occurs suddenly, and has long-lasting effects.* When does a disaster begin or end? With Hurricane Katrina, for example, did it begin with the hurricane gathering force over the Atlantic Ocean and Gulf of Mexico? Did faulty engineering and maintenance of levees sow the seeds of the disaster? What about the risk factors amplified by racism, which left many low-income African Americans living in areas of higher risk than wealthier white residents? These social and group vulnerabilities have a history that extends back hundreds of years (Park & Miller, 2006).

3. *Negatively affects large numbers of people.* The examples presented in the first part of this chapter clearly involve large numbers of people. But what of those mentioned that are not natural disasters or atrocities of war? If an adult dies in a single car crash because of icy conditions, is this a disaster? Does it matter if the driver was drinking? What if the car hits a group of schoolchildren waiting for the school bus? How many people need to be affected directly, or indirectly, for something to be deemed a disaster?

4. *Affects more than one family in a public arena.* Is the boundary between private and public always that clear? If a child's parent dies of natural causes, is this a public event? What if the child needs to be taken into custody by the Department of Social Services because there is no other caretaker? Does it matter if the parent was a drug user? What if the parent was the victim of domestic violence? What if many children in a neighborhood are taken into custody? At what point does a private tragedy become a public disaster?

5. *Is out of the realm of ordinary experience.* This is an important, although subjective, criterion. Disasters are not everyday occurrences, although their impact is mediated by many factors, such as culture, beliefs, spiritual practices, and other value systems. The varied experiences of people determine whether an event or series of events is outside of the realm of ordinary experience. People living in hurricane zones or tornado alleys are more familiar with powerful storms than those living in less tempest-prone areas. Even acts of terrorism are more usual for some and abnormal for others.

6. *Has the power to induce stress and trauma in anyone who experiences the event.* This statement heralds one of the most controversial debates in the

field of disaster mental health. When there is a disaster, do many people experience stress that is clinically considered trauma? Those trained in Western psychology are more likely than non-Westerners to answer this question in the affirmative, although there is not a consensus on this. One question that the trauma criterion raises is this: If the majority of those who experience the event do not develop severe stress and trauma, can it still be considered a disaster?

I return to many of these questions in chapter 3 and explore them in greater depth. Although it is important to define a disaster, both for the purposes of planning responses and for researchers studying this phenomenon, what constitutes a disaster is contested terrain. Some researchers would not see the small-scale set of examples as disasters but rather as "emergencies," while also viewing very large-scale disasters as "catastrophes" (Quarantelli, 2006). Conceptual clarity is always helpful, but I have found in my practice that there are areas of similarity and overlap between small- and large-scale events, as well as differences, and that the realities of practice involve the existence of some measure of ambiguity in what is always or sometimes present in a disaster.

CRITICAL INCIDENTS

A concept related to disaster is that of a "critical incident" (Mitchell, 1983). Although this notion originally evolved from a peer-driven movement to assist emergency responders, such as police, firefighters, and ambulance drivers (Armstrong, O'Callahan, & Marmar, 1991; Bisson, McFarlane, & Rose, 2000; Conroy, 1990; Everly & Mitchell, 2000; Mitchell, 1983; Mitchell & Bray, 1990; Solomon, 1995), its application was widened to include many different kinds of populations (Dyregrov, 1997, 2003; Miller, 2000, 2003; Raphael, 1986) and many of the responses of affected people, and suggestions about how to help them overlap with disaster mental health. A critical incident, like a disaster, leads to strong reactions and makes it difficult for a person to continue to exercise normal responsibilities and functions (Mitchell, 1983) and results in a heightened sense of vulnerability and loss of control (Solomon, 1995). Critical incidents are sudden and unexpected and may involve one's life being threatened. They can lead to psychological and emotional wounds, undermine one's sense of how the world works and of what is fair and normal, and challenge a person's sense of self-worth (Solomon, 1995), all of which have been described in the disaster mental health literature (Halpern & Tramontin, 2007; Rosenfeld et al., 2005).

THE COLLECTIVE CONTEXT OF DISASTERS

An important dimension of disaster is, what happens to individuals and families occurs within the context of collective wounds and losses as well as public policies. As Kaniasty and Norris (1999, p. 26) have put it: "Individual suffering unveils itself within the parameters of other people's suffering." It is in the nature of disaster that there is a collective context for individual suffering and a public dimension of private loss.

Thus, the example of the car crash after the senior prom, with multiple deaths, involves personal and private losses, but the crash also has public consequences. The incident may overwhelm other students in the school who were about to graduate, as well as the school personnel who taught the students or who were chaperoning the prom. Law enforcement officers may feel a sense of guilt and inadequacy over having failed to check for alcohol and drugs before the students left the prom in their cars. First responders may have a particularly strong reaction to being called to a scene where a number of young people have died. Other families who knew the teenagers may be devastated, and the event may trigger evocative reactions for parents or siblings who have suffered similar losses in the past. But there are also policy issues that arise from such events. Should the school continue to hold a prom? Are there psychoeducation programs that can reduce the inclination of teenagers to drink and drive? Are there cultural norms about drinking that need to be interrogated? Is this a community in which tragic events are more likely to happen?

The interaction of individual and collective, private and public, also applies to a large-scale disaster, such as 9/11. There are those who are directly affected, such as families who lost loved ones or those who escaped from the World Trade Center. First responders have a strong sense of fraternity and camaraderie, which was put to the test with 9/11, where there were massive casualties and injuries, particularly among firefighters. Rippling out from this core were numerous other affected groups: eye-witnesses, children evacuated from schools, residents cleared from their neighborhoods, and neighbors living in communities that lost residents in the attack. Local businesses in adjacent neighborhoods as well as workers who served the World Trade Center were also affected. Construction workers who responded to Ground Zero, both in the immediate aftermath and in the long months of clearing the debris, subjected themselves to health and mental health risks (Miller, Grabelsky, & Wagner, 2010). Schools that served children who lost parents were impacted, and thousands of therapists absorbed painful and tragic stories that put them at risk for disaster distress, compassion fatigue, or secondary trauma. New York City as a collective entity was affected in many ways, ranging from the cordoning off of streets and neighborhoods to the collective loss of safety, self-esteem, and a sense of basic trust in the world. At the time, people did not know whether this was a single attack or the beginning of a series of assaults. As we now know, the attacks led to two wars—in Iraq and Afghanistan—and many other military encounters and skirmishes and attempts at future terrorism.

In Washington, DC, similar processes were at work, as they were in Boston and Newark from which the planes had departed, and in Shanksville, Pennsylvania, where one of the planes crashed. Airline employees were distraught, as were travel agents who had sold tickets to passengers on the airplanes. Modern media brought scenes of the disaster into millions of living rooms, and people all over the nation and the world watched the coverage of the events. Among those most at risk from this exposure were people with their own psychological vulnerabilities and especially those who had previously experienced terrorism or armed conflict. Both the initial attacks and subsequent responses involved policy decisions at many levels of government and between many state and nonstate actors.

Did the disaster of 9/11 end after the initial attacks? It certainly did not for the people of Afghanistan and Iraq or for the soldiers and their families. Should the subsequent bombings in London and Mumbai be seen as a continuation of this disaster or as new and discrete disasters? There are many different perspectives on and social constructions for the 9/11 disaster. In many ways, this disaster is still in process ten years after the original event, although the specific phases and the impact of these on individuals and communities have varied over time. And was 9/11 the opening salvo in this disaster or were there earlier events that are part of this disaster narrative? The answer depends on one's social and political positioning and accompanying disaster narratives, a theme that is explored in subsequent chapters.

The examples illustrate the contingencies and instabilities involved when trying to define disaster. Any disaster narrative comprises numerous perspectives and diverse and varied players. What is most salient for disaster responders is having an understanding, within a sociocultural context, of the subjective experiences of individuals, groups, and collectivities that have lived through disaster and recognizing the many stories, meanings, reactions, and needs engendered by a specific disaster.

We can therefore say that certain qualities constitute a disaster, but they are contingent and subjective criteria and need to be applied flexibly and situationally. While a disaster contains an event, or series of events, that affects multiple people, groups, and communities and has a public dimension as well as private suffering, it is more helpful to think of a disaster as a process (Oliver-Smith, 2002). A disaster *does not* always have a clear beginning or end, and, yet, it is socially constructed as an event outside of ordinary experience that overwhelms a group's individual and collective coping capacities, destabilizing and disrupting everyday life and normal functioning. Disasters lead to horizontal and vertical disruptions. They interrupt social connections and relationships. They sever people and their communities from past sources of strength and wisdom and from their vision of a hopeful future. And whether or not disasters lead to traumatic reactions, they are stressful events involving losses and evoking powerful responses.

Thus, my working definition of disaster is *a process that encompasses an event, or series of events, affecting multiple people, groups, and communities, causing damage, destruction, and loss of life. There is a public and collective dimension to a disaster, as well as individual suffering. The disaster process is socially constructed (at least by some) as being outside of ordinary experience, overwhelming usual individual and collective coping mechanisms, disrupting social relations, and at least temporarily disempowering individuals and communities.* And by using this definition, I believe that the similarities between the large-scale and small-scale examples given earlier, particularly when considering the activities of responders engaged in disaster mental health and psychosocial capacity building, outweigh the differences. It is a theme that is developed further in chapter 3. This is particularly true when working from a social-ecology perspective, in which there is an integration of micro, mezzo, and macro factors and disaster is viewed not as an event but as a process. Rather than viewing something purely as a disaster or nondisaster, the book considers the spectrum of disasters, ranging from small to large, local to international.

THE SOCIAL ECOLOGY OF DISASTERS

Disasters are contextualized and are formed and shaped by history, culture, social structures and processes, and political economies. Every disaster has a unique social ecology that influences perceptions and experiences before, during, and after the disaster (Park & Miller, 2006, 2007). The social ecology includes the history of how people arrived in certain geographic areas and the patterns of relationships among ethnic groups in these areas. It encompasses social and economic disparities as well as differential access to resources and services. Unequal power, status, and social capital are part of the social ecology as are different cultural beliefs and practices; sociopolitical factors interact with geographic and geological forces—they are inseparable. Figure 1.1 illustrates how the process of disaster involves the interaction between a precipitating event and the affected people and their community within the context of a social ecology.

Because of the social ecology of disaster, families and groups are differentially affected by the same disaster and often develop different narratives of the disaster and its consequences. Such narratives not only reflect the disaster experience but construct and shape its meaning. Thus, understanding

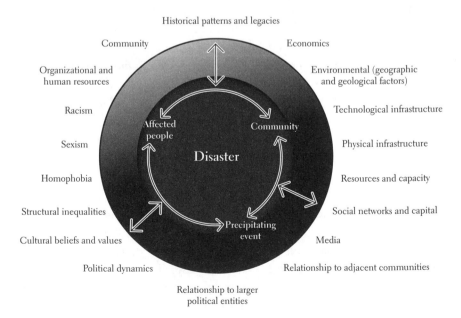

FIGURE 1.1 Social Ecology of Disaster

the social ecology of a given disaster has implications for who needs help and how to respond, as well as who is best positioned to respond.

Hurricane Katrina was a "natural" event, but because of the social ecology of the Gulf Coast, it had a differential impact. White middle-class people living in New Orleans suffered terribly during the storm but lost fewer lives and less property—and recovered more quickly—than poor African Americans living in the same city (Kates, Colten, Laska, & Leatherman, 2006). These inequalities did not just emerge during the storm; they were present for centuries before Hurricane Katrina. However, they were amplified during the storm and further augmented afterward. The Lower Ninth Ward, a predominantly low-income African American area, is a neighborhood that still has not been rebuilt. The same is not true of the whiter and more affluent Garden District and the French Quarter. Government policies and private market factors, such as who had home insurance and who did not, interacted with political agendas (reducing public housing for poor African Americans, for example) to contribute to the situation (Dreier, 2006; Frymer, Strolovitch, & Warren, 2005; Green, Bates, & Smyth, 2007; Masozera, Bailey, & Kerchner, 2007; Sommers, Apfelbaum, Dukes, Toosi, & Wang, 2006).

When the Asian tsunami struck on December 25, 2004, it killed more than two hundred thousand people in Asia and Africa, particularly in Indonesia, Sri Lanka, India, and Thailand. The relief agency Oxfam estimated that in many areas, up to four times as many women as men were killed because they were either on the beach waiting for fishermen to return or at home caring for their children (British Broadcasting Corporation, 2005). One of the hardest hit countries was Sri Lanka, where more than thirty thousand perished, mostly on the eastern and southern coasts. But the social ecology of Sri Lanka meant that these two regions experienced very different trajectories for rebuilding. The south of Sri Lanka is dominated by ethnic Sinhalese and has not experienced armed conflict based on ethnicity. (The south of Sri Lanka was the site of political and social conflict in the past but not at the time of the tsunami.) For more than twenty years, eastern Sri Lanka had been in a civil war. Three major ethnic groups live there: the Sinhalese, who are Buddhist; the Tamils, who are Hindu; and Muslims, who speak Tamil but are regarded as a distinct ethnic group. The civil war was between the Sri Lankan government and two separatist organizations— the Tamil Tigers, whose stronghold was in northern Sri Lanka, and Colonel Karuna's breakaway faction that had greater strength in the east. The army, which had a large presence in the area, is dominated by the Sinhalese.

The government at the time, under the leadership of Chandrika Kuma-ratunga, worked out a cease-fire with the Tamil Tigers, and foreign governments and nongovernmental organizations (NGOs) were able to provide immediate relief. Even during this period, there was mistrust and tension between the three ethnic groups as well as between the Tamils and the army. And over the course of six months, there were daily assassinations in the east, culminating in the assassination of the foreign minister (one of the few Tamils in the government) in Columbo by the Tamil Tigers. This was followed, in 2005, by the election of Mahinda Rajapaksa as president, who had pursued ultranationalist policies favoring the Sinhalese and aggressively fought to pacify and to finally eliminate the Tamil Tigers. After his ascension to power, the region devolved into all-out war. Consequently, post-tsunami rebuilding and reconstruction slowed, and many NGOs and representatives from foreign governments withdrew. On top of the dislocations caused by the tsunami, there are now many Tamils living in refugee camps as a result of the final (and successful) push by the government to eliminate the Tamil Tigers. The International Crisis Group, a nonpartisan NGO, has alleged that there were massive war crimes committed by the government against Tamil citizens and has called for further investigation ("Atrocities Against Tamils," 2010).

This contrasts strongly with southern Sri Lanka, where there is a clear Sinhalese majority and no war. Rebuilding from the tsunami has continued at a much faster clip, and there are far more resources. While the south witnessed a resurgence in tourism since the tsunami, the east became an isolated, violence-plagued zone, where few outsiders dared enter. The differing fates of two regions within the same country hit by the same natural disaster illustrate how the social ecology profoundly affects the arc of recovery after the storm. All this has occurred within an international context where there have been pressures from investors to use the storm as an opportunity to open up prime beachfront, previously inhabited by poor families, to hotel and tourism development (Klein, 2007). Thus, the social ecology of disaster has, like many things, become globalized.

TREATING TRAUMA OR PSYCHOSOCIAL CAPACITY BUILDING?

DISASTER MENTAL HEALTH

A field known as disaster mental health has coalesced over the past twenty-five years (Halpern & Tramontin, 2007). It has its roots in crisis intervention, which evolved after World War II in response to such disasters as fires in nightclubs and airline crashes (Halpern & Tramontin, 2007; Roberts, 2005). In the 1980s, debriefings and other group-oriented measures were used to help emergency personnel and others directly or indirectly impacted by disasters (Armstrong et al., 1991; Curtis, 1995; Mitchell, 1983; Raphael, 1986). Organizations such as the American Red Cross, the National Organization for Victim Assistance, and the International Organization for Victim Assistance used these methods on a large scale, over time adapting and amending them based on information gained from research and practice. The International Critical Incident Stress Foundation became the center for training hundreds of emergency management teams set up to serve firefighters, police officers, ambulance drivers, and other first responders around the nation. Over time, controversy emerged over the use of debriefings (Bisson et al., 2000; Chemtob, Tomas, Law, & Cremniter, 1997; McNally, Bryant, & Ehlers, 2003; Miller, 2003; Raphael, Meldrum, & McFarlane, 1995) and a more complex range of disaster response services was developed, often using some form of cognitive behavioral method (Halpern & Tramontin, 2007; Rosenfeld et al., 2005; Ritchie, Watson, & Friedman, 2006).

The disaster mental health complex usually involves psychologists, psychiatrists, and social workers from the United States or Europe, or practitioners from other parts of the world who are trained in the West. The application of disaster mental health methods increasingly expanded from the United States and Europe, and soon they were used in responding to disasters all over the world. Although practitioners within this paradigm may value clients' resiliency (Watson, Ritchie, Demer, Bartone, & Pfefferbaum, 2006), there is a tendency to emphasize trauma as a common disaster response, particularly post-traumatic stress disorder (PTSD). Schlenger (2005) has reviewed studies of adults immediately after 9/11. His results found that 44 percent had at least one PTSD symptom. Although some of the studies bear out that these symptoms decreased over time, other research cited by Schlenger found 7.5 percent of adults in New York City had PTSD two months following the 9/11 attack. Somasundaram (2005) mentions a study in northern Sri Lanka that found 25 percent of children had PTSD and 57 percent were unable to deal effectively with daily life because of the stress of the war. Many more studies, too numerous to summarize here, have found high rates of PTSD.

Trauma reactions, particularly PTSD, have informed the dominant paradigm used to organize the efforts of professionals who seek to help people recover from disaster (American Red Cross [ARC], 2006; Gist & Lubin,

---

BOX 1.1

COMPARISON OF DISASTER MENTAL HEALTH AND PSYCHOSOCIAL CAPACITY
BUILDING

Disaster Mental Health

- Universal biophysical reactions
- Psychological consequences
- Pathology
- Trained professionals
- Individual recovery

Psychosocial Capacity Building

- Strength and resiliency
- Family, social groups, and communities
- Self-healing versus medicalization
- Empowerment of indigenous people
- Mutual aid and self-help groups
- Cultural responsiveness
- Gender, race, ethnicity, and social class
- Human rights and equity
- Wariness of iatrogenic effects

1999; Halpern & Tramontin, 2007; Lystad, 1988; Ritchie, Watson, & Friedman, 2006; Rosenfeld et al., 2005). The assumptions for this approach are summarized in box 1.1 and are accompanied by discussion.

UNIVERSAL BIOPHYSICAL REACTIONS   It is assumed that people have similar biophysical reactions to disaster. The nature of disaster, its impact, and the history of each individual all interact to influence what the reactions will be. There is some recognition that the nature of the community (its social capital and networks) has some bearing on the outcomes. Culture is seen as a variable determining how trauma reactions are expressed, but it is secondary to the universal human response to disaster.

PSYCHOLOGICAL CONSEQUENCES   This approach emphasizes the psychological, emotional, and biophysical reactions to a disaster. Although the impact on families, groups, and communities is acknowledged, this is usually secondary to the individual's psychological reactions.

PATHOLOGY   Disaster mental health professionals have emphasized, more than most mainstream clinicians and therapists, that an individual's strengths and resources are foundational for his or her recovery. And these professionals put an admirable emphasis on "normalizing" reactions. A common mantra is that "these are normal reactions to an abnormal event"; yet, much of the literature concentrates on the adverse consequences of disaster and the need for psychological first aid and crisis intervention in the early stages (Everly, Phillips, Kane, & Feldman, 2006; Halpern & Tramontin, 2007; Watson, 2007), moving to counseling and treatment for those who continue to experience symptoms months, and even years, after the disaster (Gist & Lubin, 1999; Halpern & Tramontin, 2007; Lystad, 1988; Ritchie, Watson, & Friedman, 2006; Rosenfeld et al., 2005; Ursano, Fullerton, Weisaeth, & Raphael, 2007; Yule, 2006).

TRAINED PROFESSIONALS   A logical outcome to this is that there is a need for trained professionals—psychologists, counselors, social workers—to help individuals recover from disaster. Cognitive behavioral approaches are viewed as being most efficacious in helping people to recover once psychological first aid has been applied (Halpern & Tramontin, 2007; McNally, Bryant, & Ehlers, 2003; Ritchie, Watson, & Friedman, 2006). As disaster often overwhelms the capacity of local professionals to respond, outsiders are generally called in. When the focus eventually turns to helping the helpers, particularly uniformed responders (fire, police, ambulance workers), there is more of an emphasis on training peers to debrief their fellow responders (Everly & Mitchell, 2000; Miller, 2000, 2003, 2006a; Mitchell, 1983)—yet even this model has the expectation that a clinician will be a part of the debriefing team.

INDIVIDUAL RECOVERY   Many early disaster mental health interventions focused on using groups, such as debriefings, particularly for uniformed responders. In recent years, debriefings have been de-emphasized and psychological first aid and cognitive behavioral treatments encouraged (Halpern & Tramontin, 2007; McNally, Bryant, & Ehlers, 2003; Ritchie, Watson, & Friedman, 2006). What has been implicit in all of these approaches is that the target of recovery is the psychological well-being of the individual, which is consistent with most Western notions of mental health intervention. This is not to say that there is not also concern for improving social functioning and interpersonal relationships, but these are usually secondary to the recovery of the individual.

PSYCHOSOCIAL CAPACITY BUILDING

Although these assumptions have dominated the disaster mental health field for many years, there has been concern about the field's Western focus on the individual, the tendency to "pathologize" reactions to disasters, and a response system primarily predicated on professionals (Ager, 1997; Kleinman & Cohen, 1997; Strang & Ager, 2003; Summerfield, 1995, 2000; Wessells, 1999; Wessells & Monteiro, 2006). This has been reinforced by the Inter-Agency Standing Committee (IASC) (2007) guidelines for mental health and psychosocial services when there are emergencies. This organization has the backing of the United Nations and many major NGOs. It has international participation and recognition for setting standards in response to all kinds of disasters. According to the IASC, it is wrong to assume most people develop significant psychological problems in response to disaster. An emerging paradigm is that of psychosocial capacity building. The assumptions of this model are summarized in box 1.1 and accompanied by discussion.

STRENGTH AND RESILIENCY Although all individuals feel consequences in a disaster, psychosocial capacity building moves a person's strengths and sources of resiliency to the forefront. People are viewed as being inherently durable and resilient and capable of recovering from disaster, often using their own or local resources (Mollica, 2006).

FAMILY, SOCIAL GROUPS, AND COMMUNITIES This approach does not assume that individuals are the fundamental focus of intervention. Families (including extended families and clans), tribes, and other social group categories; cadres (for example, trained local government units in Chinese villages, comparable to civil service employees in the West); and communities are often seen as the fundamental units of psychosocial rebuilding after a disaster. This method places a greater emphasis on collective capacity and how to strengthen and reconstruct it after a disaster. Individual recovery is inextricably linked to collective recovery (Farwell & Cole, 2002; Landau & Saul, 2004; Saul, 2000) as well as economic recovery (Weyerman, 2007).

SELF-HEALING VERSUS MEDICALIZATION Critics of a disaster mental health model (Farwell & Cole, 2002; Reyes & Elhai, 2004; Summerfield, 1995; Wessells, 1999) are wary of Western tendencies to overly medicalize social phenomena and to work with individuals in a decontextualized way that is not culturally and socially grounded. Although professionals have a role in psychosocial capacity building, it is more often as consultants in creating the conditions that allow people to self-heal (Mollica, 2006) and using training-of-trainers models (Corbin & Miller, 2010; Miller, 2006a).

EMPOWERMENT OF INDIGENOUS PEOPLE Psychosocial capacity building is predicated on the reconstruction and restitution of collective life—the social threads and braids that connect people and give their lives meaning. Rebuilding collective capacity relies on the empowerment of local people who know their culture, community, and one another. Local participation in planning and decision making is essential (IASC, 2007). This is not always straightforward, as there are schisms and struggles within communities and between groups (Wessells, 1999). This makes peace and reconciliation work (see chapter 9) a particularly critical component of psychosocial capacity building, especially when there have been political struggles or armed conflict, but also when there are ongoing social catastrophes, such as endemic racism or religious persecution.

MUTUAL AID AND SELF-HELP GROUPS Narratives—individual, familial, and collective—are an essential part of acknowledging loss, mourning death and destruction, and reconstructing hope and meaning. They are important ingredients of both disaster mental health and collective capacity building approaches. But whereas many disaster mental health activities rely on conversations (often versions of talk therapy or crisis intervention), psychosocial capacity building places a greater emphasis on self-help and mutual aid groups. Such groups often engage in activities, whether they are recreational, social, or psychoeducational, frequently aimed toward mourning and memorializing or geared toward reconstructing social connections and networks or meaning-making systems—narratives are enacted as well as spoken.

CULTURAL RESPONSIVENESS Disaster challenges our sense of what is normal, fair, and possible, and it can cause great pain and sustained losses. How we make sense of this and what we see as being helpful (or unhelpful) greatly depends on our cultural values and worldviews. Culture is not static. Generally, a variety of cultural traditions exist before a disaster. Once disaster strikes, it disrupts cultural traditions and ties with ancestors (Landau, 2007). Frequently, a postdisaster temporary culture then forms, perhaps among people living in shelters or refugee camps. Although people yearn for a return to their vision of their lives before the disaster, things are rarely the same. A central question is how can people reconnect with their cultural past while acknowledging the losses sustained by the disaster—and how can they then draw on these cultural practices and traditions to face a changed landscape while sustaining a sense of efficacy and hope? Disasters, and war, often disrupt traditional cultures with information and influences from the outside. Disaster response workers are often the ambassadors of these external stimuli, particularly if they are imposing models and techniques that reflect *their* cultural assumptions rather than those of the people affected by the disaster. Thus, cultural responsiveness is a key principle of psychosocial capacity building.

GENDER, RACE, ETHNICITY, AND SOCIAL CLASS   Disaster does not strike everyone in the same way. A lack of resources, whether it is economic, social, or personal, affects the vulnerable and their capacity to recover. Social identity—how a person constructs his or her race, gender, class, and so on, as well as how others socially construct that identity (Miller & Garran, 2008)—has profound consequences before, during, and after a disaster. Everyone suffers when disaster strikes, but women, due to their social roles and identities, are more vulnerable to assaults, social marginalization, and physical and economic exploitation. Their lack of access to external sources of social support and economic security, as well as the burden of their caretaking responsibility, contribute to their vulnerability during disaster. In many societies, certain ethnic and racial groups have fewer privileges and less access to resources than other groups, which heightens their risk for negative outcomes. Also, they may be socially constructed as less worthy, as were African Americans in New Orleans during and after Hurricane Katrina, which not only dampens public support for their plight but can lead to their treatment as social outcasts and even criminals. Social identity and social oppression are major factors in many of the disasters that serve as case examples in this book—9/11, Hurricane Katrina, the Asian tsunami, and armed conflicts in many parts of the world—and paying attention to them is central to a psychosocial capacity building approach.

HUMAN RIGHTS AND EQUITY   Respect for the human rights of all is essential to a psychosocial capacity building approach (IASC, 2007). Given the inequities that are amplified during any disaster, an important principle of psychosocial capacity building is that all people affected are entitled to humane and equitable treatment by those who are responding (IASC, 2007). Although this is a principle that most responders would assume as part of their professional ethics, it is easier to imagine than to implement. Predisaster inequities were often very entrenched and there are vested interests among those with social privilege for maintaining social hierarchies and divisions. Thus, disaster responders may find themselves in conflict as they seek support and resources from those with greater social and political power, while also advocating for those who had the least, have lost the most, and face the greatest challenges to recovery.

WARINESS OF IATROGENIC EFFECTS   Medicine is always alert to well-intentioned interventions that lead to unintended negative consequences. The same holds true for responding to disaster. For example, resettling people in refugee camps where they have food and shelter is often essential, but this can isolate people from their jobs, social networks, and geographical communities. Offering aid and assistance directly addresses emotional and psychological needs; however, this can create dependency and reliance on outside professionals who eventually must leave. Thus, when responding to disaster, it is always important to consider what unintended harm can come from "helpful" interventions (IASC, 2007; Wessells, 2009), and for outsiders, a clear exit strategy should be part of any intervention (Wessells, 1999).

INTEGRATING THE TWO APPROACHES

These two broad approaches, disaster mental health and psychosocial capacity building, have important areas of difference, yet they are not irreconcilable. They are not either/or poles of a dichotomy. Mental health approaches focus more on the psychological responses, while psychosocial capacity building places a greater emphasis on the social aspects of recovery. However, both are intended to promote greater psychosocial well-being (IASC, 2007). While psychosocial capacity building was developed, in some part, as a response to unexamined assumptions implicit in a disaster mental health approach, this does not mean that there is no validity or utility in employing some of the methods of disaster mental health work. And those trained as disaster mental health responders can adapt their intervention styles and philosophies to respect the important principles inherent in a psychosocial capacity building approach. There is of course great stress and trauma in the wake of disaster and clinical interventions can be helpful. But it is important to conceive of these interventions in the context of a local culture and society and for those people from affected communities to have leadership roles in the planning, implementation, and evaluation of those efforts.

AREAS OF DIFFERENCE

When trying to integrate these approaches, it is helpful to consider three points of divergence (Ager, 1997). The first is the generalizable versus unique axis. What is common to all human beings and what is unique, contextualized, and culturally grounded? Psychological theories are more likely to stress what all people have in common, while psychosocial models stress what is local and distinctive. Summerfield (2004) cautions that even if a behavior seems to occur in different cultural contexts, it should not be assumed that it has the same meaning and resonance for all people. A second area of divergence is the balance between bringing in outside experts with technical expertise versus relying on the capacity of local indigenous people. Local people will continue to live in an area, are local experts, and can interact with many more people than can outsiders. They simply lack the skills of professionals. This is not an either/or situation and many projects have used outside experts to train local professionals, who in turn work to develop the capacity of local nonprofessionals. (This approach is discussed in subsequent chapters.) The third question is whether to try to reach a broad population or to target vulnerable people. Most public health models grapple with this question. The IASC (2007) has developed an intervention pyramid to illustrate how a mental health and psychosocial model can be integrated along this dimension (see figure 1.2). In the pyramid, basic services and security for all represent the widest swathe, followed by community and family support, whereas focused and specialized interventions are part of the intervention spectrum but reach a much smaller number of people.

Other helpful areas to consider are differences in cultural orientation—that is, divergent worldviews and values between cultures in some core areas

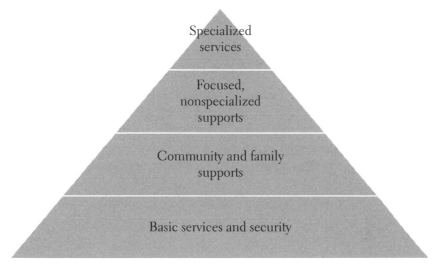

FIGURE 1.2 Inter-Agency Standing Committee (IASC) Intervention Pyramid

(see box 1.2). Nisbett (2003) has identified a number of areas in which Asians and Westerners differ in how they think and view the world, which is interactively connected with differences in history, social structure, and customs. Although it is important not to generalize about gross differences between cultures, as there are also similarities between and variations within cultures, his schema highlights important issues to consider. For instance, many collectivist Asian cultures place a greater emphasis on relationships, while in the West there is more of a tendency to view people as being independent and freestanding. Thus, there is also more of a belief in the East that context matters, while in the West there is a greater inclination to look for logical patterns that are universal and intrinsic. Nisbett also found that Westerners tend to see progress and recovery as a more linear process than Easterners, who may view patterns in a more cyclical fashion. Another continuum is stability versus flux: Is the world basically a place where things are fixed and constant (Western) or always flowing and changing (Eastern)? And how much agency (Western) do we have when preventing or recovering from disaster, and how much is fate and karma (Eastern)?

It is prudent to be wary of painting group differences with broad brushstrokes. Nisbett (2003) does not claim that these patterns are absolutes, and there is increasingly cross-fertilization and hybridization as cultures and nationalities interact, migrate and immigrate, and study and work in multiple

---

BOX 1.2

DIVERGENT CULTURAL ORIENTATIONS

1. Are objects and people freestanding or always embedded in larger networks?
2. Do people have personal agency or are they subject to an external locus of control in the form of beliefs such as karma or fate?
3. Is progress linear or cyclical?
4. Is the set point of normal stability or flux?
5. Do events have a self-contained intrinsic logic or are they part of larger patterns and processes?
6. Should we strive to reduce contradictions or embrace paradox?
7. Is behavior more attributable to personality traits or situational factors?
8. Is it safe, healthy, and healing to talk about thoughts and feelings with others, particularly painful or negative reactions?
9. Have our ancestors died and departed or are they with us at this moment?

NUMBERS 1 THROUGH 7 FROM NISBETT, 2003.

---

settings—but these patterns represent tendencies that have implications for how to structure, design, and implement disaster responses.

I have found two other areas of divergence between Western and non-Western cultures, which have significant implications for disaster response. One is whether it is both safe and helpful to share feelings. A fundamental assumption of Western psychological counseling is that it is helpful to talk about feelings. "Ventilation" is often a goal in disaster mental health, whether it is in the early stages or in the mid- to long-term phases of response (Dyregrov, 1997; Halpern & Tramontin, 2007; Miller, 2003, 2006a; Ritchie et al., 2006; Rosenfeld et al., 2005). It is seen as being useful and cathartic to share feelings, including distressing or sad feelings. However, in non-Western cultures, there is often less of a tradition of sharing feelings with others, let alone with professionals or strangers. The expression of negative feelings may lead to negative outcomes, karma, or consequences. In Balinese culture, expressing bad feelings can even leave one vulnerable to harm from others (Wikan, 1989). When I responded to the tsunami in eastern Sri Lanka, I found that many Tamils smiled when relating very sad or tragic events (Miller, 2006a). When I inquired about this, I was told that it is not considered socially appropriate to share one's sadness publicly.

A second area of major departure is the relationship between ancestors, being, and time. Most Westerners view ancestors as existing in the past, perhaps to be remembered, but they are not seen as having an actual presence. When I have conducted workshops and asked participants if they believe that their ancestors are in the room, right at this moment, most white Westerners are surprised at the question and look confused. But if they are participants from Africa, the Caribbean, Asia, and from other non-Western parts of the world, the answer can be "of course they are!" In Chinese cultures, there is a more active sense of the presence of ancestors than in most Western traditions (Chan et al., 2005). Differing beliefs about the temporal presence of ancestors has implications for grieving, mourning, and recovery, which is discussed in subsequent chapters.

THE WHEEL OF RECOVERY: AN INTEGRATED MODEL

Mollica (2006) has made an explicit link between psychological and social interconnectedness, particularly when there is armed conflict or disaster. He considers the neurological consequences of disaster and distinguishes between declarative and emotional memory, which are stored in different parts of the brain. Like many who work with trauma (Ochberg, 1988; Van der Kolk, 2002, 2006), he describes how traumatic memories (emotional) are stored in the amygdala, whereas rational words and narratives are declarative memories stored in the prefrontal cortex. Emotions are often overwhelming and it can be difficult to understand why the emotions are occurring. Thus, people "lose their capacity to use emotions as guides for effective action" (Van der Kolk, 2006, p. 5). This helps to explain why traumatic memories can be triggered by sights, sounds, and smells that are logically not at all the same as the sensory stimulation from the disaster and yet can evoke a panicked, physiologically overwhelming response. For example, after 9/11, those who escaped from the World Trade Center towers often experienced burning smells or sounds of airplanes and intrusive and evocative physical flashbacks of what they sensed and how they felt when they were fleeing the towers.

But Mollica (2006) links this traumatic focus with a psychosocial approach by stressing the power of self-healing—a formulation that supports an empowerment-based outlook. He goes further, linking neurological healing with social connectedness, altruism, and spirituality. Wilkinson and Pickett (2009) cite studies of how certain neurological and endocrinological processes foster social cohesion and connection, but the reverse is also true: social interactions benefit neurological processes, leading to positive physiological consequences. Van der Kolk (2006) also cites research showing that not only does meditation aid in self-awareness but it also leads to a thickening of parts of the brain associated with "attention, interoception, and sensory processing" (Van der Kolk, 2006, p. 12). Thus, the social and spiritual activities suggested by a psychosocial capacity building approach foster neurological changes that lead to self-healing and recovery. This is similar to the findings that skilled practitioners can "rewire" their brains through meditation and achieve neurological and endocrinological changes that lead to less anxiety and a greater sense of calm and well-being (Goleman, 2003; Wallace, 2007). There is a recursive interconnectedness between the plasticity of our neurological wiring and conscious thoughts, social interactions, and spiritual practices.

Figure 1.3, The Wheel of Recovery, attempts to illustrate some of these connections. It diagrams a strengths-based model of recovery for communities struck by disaster, emphasizing collective capacity while also acknowledging the need to respond to stress, trauma, and bereavement. Surrounding

FIGURE 1.3 The Wheel of Recovery

the circle are entities—NGOs, self-help groups—that can support a community struck by disaster, offering resources and interventions in ways that respect the cultural and social integrity of the community. The bottom part of the circle describes the strengths and resources that individuals, families, and communities had before the disaster struck and that can serve as sources of wisdom and hope if this well of the past can be uncovered from the debris of the disaster. Resources antedating the disaster include wisdom gained from direct life experiences as well as lessons passed down from previous generations. The horizontal band in the middle of the circle describes the reactions and dislocations caused by the disaster. Above this band are a variety of postdisaster tasks and activities that contribute to collective and individual healing and recovery, incorporating ideas and interventions from both disaster mental health and psychosocial capacity building. And at the top of the circle are the three most important things for a community to strive for in the wake of disaster: a sense of hope, social connectedness, and constructing meaning forged from the font of the past and the ashes of the disaster. As this wheel turns, the social touchstones mentioned in the predisaster part of the circle meld with the postdisaster processes and become the new "normal" for people and their communities.

TRUTH AND PERSONHOOD

When professionals respond to help the people who have experienced disaster, they pack a suitcase full of assumptions, beliefs, and values about how people react and how to help them to recover. Summerfield (2004) notes that this baggage is often unexamined and culturally biased; the practitioner's worldviews are applied universally and in a decontextualized, ahistorical fashion. Every historical period and culture has meaning-making systems to understand phenomena and human behavior. Living as a temporal and cultural insider leads to taking for granted these perceptual and conceptual lenses—they attain the status of truth. Those with greater power are in a better position to establish what is normal, valid, and meaningful, and those with differing understandings are often subordinated and repressed (Foucault, 1984). There are "battle[s]" for establishing "truth" as well as the rules for verification of truths (Foucault, 1984, p. 74). Given the world's history of racism, class conflict, and colonialism, many truths about human behavior have been contested politically, economically, and militarily.

Doctors, psychologists, social workers, public health workers, and other non-governmental players have often been the social foot soldiers in attempts to impose some truths as being better than others, installing certainty over subjectivity, legitimacy over folklore. When disaster workers respond, they are not neutral players but rather embodied and embedded political actors in a world of colonialism or, at best, neocolonialism. We are not ever neutral, even when we actively strive to be.

Thus, in the Victorian era, a doctor responding to an upper-class white English woman, who had experienced the disaster of sexual abuse as a child and who was hypervigilant and emotionally labile after a rape attempt, might attribute the patient's reactions to "hysteria." If attending to a poor or working-class woman, however unlikely this would have been in this historical and social epoch, he (most doctors during this period were male) might have seen the woman's reactions as further evidence of "social degeneracy." And if by some freak of circumstance that same doctor were evaluating a refugee from (what is now) Kenya or Zimbabwe, he might conclude that this was a manifestation of superstitions carried by genetic inferiors. A doctor practicing today, whatever race and gender, would probably reject (or certainly criticize) all of these formulations. A female doctor from Kenya, however, would likely acknowledge the legacy of patriarchy and colonialism in both her assessment and responses. Helpers are always historically situated and politically positioned.

Given this, it might be advisable for disaster responders to be cautious about making assumptions and rather ask some questions about the nature of personhood. Summerfield (2004) defines personhood as the way that a person exists in the world—how an individual responds to adversity and risk in life. Summerfield suggests a number of questions, which are included in box 1.3. The answers to these questions help to map out the diverse and shifting parameters of personhood for dissimilar populations facing unusual situations in distinctive cultures and societies at different points in time.

ESSENTIAL ELEMENTS OF DISASTER RESPONSE

It is critical to understand social constructions of reality and sociopolitical and cultural factors when responding to disasters. It is also important to be guided by empirical confirmations ("evidence" is too strong a term, implying objective truth) about what helps and what does not. Hobfoll and his

BOX 1.3

QUESTIONS ABOUT PERSONHOOD

1. What kinds of risk can be faced?
2. What kinds of adversity can be managed?
3. When are people likely to be fatalistic?
4. When are people likely to feel hopeful?
5. What constitutes a grievance?
6. What is normal and abnormal behavior?
7. What are acceptable reactions after a disaster?
8. How is distress expressed?
9. How is help-seeking behavior expressed?
10. What constitutes reconciliation?
11. What serves as just compensation?

ADAPTED FROM SUMMERFIELD, 2004.

nineteen colleagues (2007) have done an excellent job of reviewing the empirical studies of immediate and midterm mass trauma intervention and have found that five intervention principles are empirically supported. The research team constitutes many of the world's leading experts on disaster response and recovery, and they are culturally, racially, and nationally a diverse group. There were also many responses to their research published in the same issue of the original journal article. Many, if not most, of the authors have probably been trained in Western traditions of psychotherapy, and this should be taken into consideration when weighing their recommendations. But their research offers some of the most clear-cut guidelines presented about how to help people recover from disaster. (See box 1.4, which shows the original five principles and three that I have added—grieving and mourning, a sense of place [Prewitt Diaz & Dayal, 2008], and reestablishing a link to the past.) Their recommendations for intervention and my additions are incorporated in subsequent chapters that examine how responders can best intervene. The areas that they have identified are closely linked with one another, and interventions directed at one domain are likely to have an impact on other domains. What follows is a brief summary of the importance of the five areas.

PROMOTING A SENSE OF SAFETY When people feel unsafe, it is difficult to access strengths and resources. Acute or chronic insecurity saps resiliency

BOX 1.4

ESSENTIAL ELEMENTS WHEN RESPONDING TO MASS TRAUMA

1. Promoting a sense of safety.
2. Encouraging a sense of calm.
3. Inspiring a sense of self and collective efficacy.
4. Promoting connectedness.
5. Instilling a sense of hope.
6. Allowing for grieving and mourning.
7. Establishing a sense of place.
8. Reestablishing a link to the past.

NUMBERS 1 THROUGH 5 ADAPTED FROM HOBFOLL ET AL., 2007.

and fosters hypervigilance, stress, and possible trauma. People feel unsettled and are unable to regroup, rebuild, and rebound from disaster. It is also difficult to grieve under such circumstances. A person is often left with severe reactions, such as high anxiety or deadening numbness.

Hobfoll et al. (2007) point out that lack of safety particularly undermines the relationship between children and caretakers, as safety of offspring and other dependent people is one of the major tasks for caretaking adults. The researchers also stress the physiological consequences of living in an ongoing state of danger, particularly neurological and endocrinological reactions. Social support is weakened and fear and anxiety can be amplified by media saturation and overexposure.

It is important to stress that responders cannot wait for conditions to improve to help engender a sense of safety for affected people. Many dangerous situations—such as the armed conflicts in northern Uganda and eastern Congo, northern and eastern Sri Lanka, and the Middle East—persist for a long time. And there is a recursive relationship between a sense of safety and ongoing disaster, particularly disaster involving armed conflict. When people feel more threatened, they are less likely to heal and more likely to harm others. When people and communities feel empowered, they are able to face and confront threats and contribute to creating the conditions that allow for even greater safety. One of the important questions to consider when we move to discussing psychosocial capacity building and mental health interventions is: how can children and caretakers attain a sense of safety while living in zones of violence, resettlement, and uncertainty?

ENCOURAGING A SENSE OF CALM Feeling unsafe is related to high states of physiological and emotional arousal. As Hobfoll et al. (2007) point out, this can lead to disruptions in routines—such as eating and sleeping—which are essential for healthy functioning. Even normal breathing can be disrupted. Anxiety, stress, and tension make it more challenging to maintain meaningful and supportive social relationships. Heightened levels of fear and anxiety can distort perceptions and lead to avoidance.

Hobfoll et al. (2007) draw on many studies of rape and other forms of personal assault that correlate with PTSD as an analog for disaster-induced trauma. This body of literature focuses on using mindfulness and meditation, body scans and awareness, guided imagery, as well as cognitive-behavioral and stress inoculation techniques that focus on perceptions, meaning-making, and behaviors. Fostering positive emotions is a related strategy, as are problem-solving and coping methods. Psychoeducation can normalize and render understandable the reactions people are having and lead to a greater sense of efficacy and control.

INSPIRING A SENSE OF SELF AND COLLECTIVE EFFICACY There is a reciprocal relationship between self and collective efficacy—the sense that one, or one's group, can effectively respond to and cope with threats and challenges (Landau & Saul 2004; Miller, 2001; Samson, Raudenbush, & Earls, 1997). When individuals and families feel empowered, they act in ways that make their communities safer (supervising children in public places, for example), and safer communities lead to more people feeling secure, calm, and empowered. This interconnectedness means that interventions directed at the individual/psychological level, such as psychological first aid, counseling, and therapy, as well as those targeted at the community level, such as psychosocial capacity building, will complement and reinforce one another. This domain is a good example of how a disaster response approach that is both psychological and social is preferable over interventions that exclusively focus on only one of these dimensions.

PROMOTING CONNECTEDNESS Disasters displace and affect many people, yet they leave people feeling isolated and alone. The paradox of mass casualties leading to profound isolation hinders recovery from disaster. This has both social and psychological components. Socially, people are often scattered, loved ones are missing or dead, transportation and communication networks are severed, and public and social spaces are damaged and even erased. The disaster of Hurricane Katrina exemplified this process. People who have been resettled to temporary living quarters or are besieged by armed conflict experience even greater social isolation. Hobfoll et al. (2007) cite research that confirms that terrorism and death make people more suspicious and mistrustful. Psychologically, they often become numb, feel alienated from others, and may even carry a sense of guilt and responsibility, fostering shame, all of which creates a deepening sense of loneliness and separation. Thus, activities that foster connectedness, whether they target a person's inner processes or ruptured social networks, or preferably both, are essential building blocks of resiliency and recovery.

Hobfoll et al. (2007, p. 296) cite the substantial weight of research confirming the human need for "sustained attachments to loved ones and social group[s] in combating stress and trauma." Even if one is not using a trauma formulation, social connectedness is a process, goal, and outcome of psychosocial capacity building. Social connections move in many directions (for example, vertically between parents or caretakers and children and horizontally between friends, colleagues, and extended family) and social connections are recursive (giving leads to receiving, which encourages more giving). Hobfoll et al. state that while social connectedness is the most empirically substantiated of their five principles, the interventions that foster it are less articulated than they are in the other realms. Subsequent chapters describe ways of fostering social connectedness, particularly when considering group interventions, collective activities, psychoeducational responses, the use of the media, community organizing, and collective mourning and memorializing.

INSTILLING A SENSE OF HOPE All professionals and volunteers who engage in clinical work or community organizing know that instilling hope is an indispensable and vital part of helping people and communities. Hopelessness closes the doors to social connection and shutters windows to the future. Frankl (1997) has written extensively about how hope was vital for surviving the most gruesome and degrading of situations—living in concentration and death camps. When facing challenging social inequities, such as racism, sexism, and homophobia, hope is necessary for sustained engagement (Miller & Garran, 2007). Hope is indispensable for constructing generative meaning. Hope leads to a sense of efficacy and social agency (Hobfoll et al., 2007). But hope is often the first casualty of disaster. Threats lead to fear, destruction can cause trauma, and loss can lead to grief (Weyerman, 2007). How can hope be instilled?

Here, the cultural sensitivity of psychosocial capacity building is critical. In some cultures, hope is achieved through action or problem solving. In others, meditation or religious beliefs, or faith in the tribe, clan, or even in the national government may be fundamental (Hobfoll et al., 2007). Instilling hope is located at the nexus of disaster mental health and psychosocial capacity building—it is achieved through the interaction of internal beliefs, values, and emotions with social, economic, and political rebuilding. This can often take time and may be difficult to come by. While effective disaster intervention may focus on stress, trauma, loss and grief, and social alienation, all roads in disaster recovery need to lead to hope.

WHAT DO WE NEED TO KNOW?

This chapter serves as a conceptual foundation to this book. Subsequent chapters erect the scaffolding, by focusing on what disaster responders can do and presenting case examples to support the suggestions. Chapter 2 focuses on the various roles that professionals and volunteers play when responding to disaster, and chapter 3 builds the walls that elucidate a conceptual understanding of disaster. Using a disaster mental health framework, chapter 4 describes the many ways that disaster responders help people recover from disaster. Special attention is paid to the twin (and at times opposing) tasks of coping and grieving and mourning. The different phases of disaster recovery are described.

The book then focuses on a psychosocial capacity building approach: the political, sociocultural, and global issues and the kinds of activities that need to be taken into account. Ways of integrating disaster mental health and psychosocial capacity building are considered and then applied to specific situations, such as armed conflict, working with specific populations (children, women, the elderly). As well, activity-oriented approaches are used that foster social connectedness, efficacy, and hope. The final chapters focus on linking memory and memorializing—the losses of the past with the promise of the future—and conclude with recommendations for self-care of disaster workers.

The key concepts introduced in this chapter are developed throughout the book: the social ecology of disaster, fostering empowerment and resiliency, respecting and responding to cultural differences, and integrating psycho-social capacity building with disaster mental health. The recursive relation-ships between individual recovery and collective recovery and among psy-chosocial healing, peace, and social justice are also central themes; these are dynamic relationships and cannot be separated. Individual recovery without collective recovery is at best partial and incomplete, and with-out peace and social justice, psychosocial healing is stymied or truncated. Conversely, when individuals feel empowered, communities can develop a sense of collective efficacy; when psychosocial wounds are healing, the bonds of human connection can be reconstituted. Then hope, forgiveness, and justice become enduring possibilities.

MINDFULNESS EXERCISE: BREATHING

Responding to disaster is stressful work. Mindfulness techniques constitute an important self-care strategy. Even reading about disaster can lead to an internalized sense of discomfort and unease; the act of empathically imag-ining the consequences of disasters can cause mirror neurons to resonate and lead to physiological, cognitive, and emotional reactions. Thus, there is a simple mindfulness exercise at the end of each chapter. Not only can these exercises help the reader tolerate any affect generated by the material, but they can offer a range of portable responses that can be carried into the field. They come from my own work with disaster and teaching about disaster; they are gleaned from many sources.

The most basic thing we do is constantly and continuously breathe. It is usually in the background as our awareness shifts elsewhere, unless it is dis-rupted and we find ourselves gasping for breath or breathing rapidly, such as when we experience a sense of panic. However, there are times when we might not notice that our breathing has become constricted or shallow, especially during deep engagement with stressful situations.

Try to find a location that is not overly noisy or filled with distractions, such as people talking or traffic whizzing by. Over time, this exercise can be done anywhere, even in frenetic places. Sit in a comfortable, upright posi-tion, either in a chair or on a cushion; good posture is important to good breathing. Either close your eyes or fix your gaze on the floor, whichever works best for you. You might want to try doing this with your eyes open and then closed to see which you find most effective.

Focus on your breath. It sometimes helps to concentrate on a specific body part—such as your lungs as they fill with air and deflate or your nose as air enters and leaves. Do not try and control your breath—simply observe it. If you hear sounds or other distractions, do not try and push them away. Simply note them and return to your breath. If you find yourself becoming distracted or thinking about something, merely notice it and return to your breath without judgment, self-criticism, or editorializing.

It can help to start small—do the exercise for three minutes. If it seems to be helpful, you can expand the time to fit with your own needs and schedule. Some people find that counting each breath helps them to stay focused. If you use this method and lose count or become distracted, just start over again. If you have an alarm on your watch or cell phone, it can free you from having to focus on the time. However this exercise works for you is fine; there is no standard or goal to measure yourself by. It becomes your own way of practicing mindfulness, wherever you are and whenever you want—deriving whatever benefit this activity offers you.

2

RESPONDING TO DISASTERS
THE FIELD OF DISASTER MENTAL HEALTH AND
THE ROLE OF HELPING PROFESSIONALS

EVEN THE MOST RESILIENT among us feel overwhelmed in the aftermath of disaster, when resources are lost or destroyed, routines disrupted, and social networks frayed. Along with experiencing physical reactions and behavioral alterations, individuals often have confused thinking and overwhelming affect. This is evident in large-scale disasters, such as those described in the preface and chapter 1, when infrastructure is destroyed and the social fabric shredded, and also true of smaller, more localized disasters, such as a fatal car accident, homicide, or fire resulting in the death of many residents.

In the immediate wake of a disaster, normal coping mechanisms are often inadequate and the usual and trusted support systems unavailable. When an elementary-school child dies in an automobile accident, teachers, students, and parents are shocked and distressed. But so are the principal and guidance counselors, the very people who may ordinarily offer consolation and support. When a major disaster strikes, the disruptive impact is further magnified, as bridges go down, power is cut off, and offices and homes are lost. Even areas with strong and resilient communities and organizations require some sort of outside intervention. How help can be offered without undermining natural support systems is an important consideration, which is discussed in subsequent chapters. This chapter focuses on the specific helping professionals who respond to a disaster and the auspices under which they serve. A brief review of the history of disaster mental health response is also presented so that the work of disaster responders today can be viewed in a historical context. In addition, consideration is given to the types of interventions available to disaster mental health professionals and the questions raised about the limitations of this approach.

HELPING PROFESSIONALS AND DISASTERS

There are a range of professionals from an array of disciplines and with a multiplicity of skills who respond to disasters. When hurricanes strike the Florida Keys, first responders—law enforcement, paramedics, firefighters, civil defense workers, and even, at times, the military—are deployed to ensure safety, evacuate and rescue people, and maintain social order. (Solnit [2009] questions whether members of the military are really needed to maintain social order and suggests that this may be repressive rather than responsive, but in large-scale disasters they are often sent out.) Civil engineers check levees and dams and work to control flooding. During a hurricane and immediately after, the most pressing needs are to ensure safety and mitigation of the disaster's effects. In the United States, Federal Emergency Management Agency (FEMA) workers and American Red Cross (ARC) volunteers help to shelter, feed, and clothe people and eventually help them find temporary shelter and rebuild their damaged homes. Medical personnel attend to physical and medical needs. Thus, there is a mélange of government agencies (local, state, and federal; civilian and military), nongovernmental organizations (NGOs; ranging from international, to national, to local), established institutions (hospitals, medical centers), ad hoc organizations, and independent and informal volunteers. The exact mix of these entities varies, depending on the nature and scale of the disaster, where it occurs, and social, cultural, and political factors. While immediate needs must be prioritized, such as providing shelter, food, and water and reuniting people with family members, even during the first hours and days of a disaster, clinical services are quickly added to the mix of emergency services.

CLINICAL PERSONNEL

Social workers, psychologists, counselors, clinically trained chaplains, and psychiatrists are often deployed in response to disasters in countries and areas where they are available. Although training may vary among the different disciplines, the core clinical skill set has many commonalities, particularly if the clinicians have been specifically trained in disaster mental health. This includes offering psychological first aid, crisis intervention, group interventions, and brief assessment and treatment. Well-known brief training programs for licensed clinicians include those run by the ARC, which has a two-day training program for disaster mental health workers who are deployed within the ARC system, and the International Critical Incident Stress Foundation (ICISF), which focuses more on critical incident stress management. The ICISF training is used by many emergency medical services (EMS) in the United States. It offers debriefings and other critical-incident stress-management interventions for uniformed personnel (police officers, firefighters, emergency medical technicians [EMTs]).

The Green Cross, whose motto is "helping the traumatized through education, certification, and deployment" offers more in-depth training, lasting nearly a year for "experts" in the field of "traumatology" (Green Cross, 2009). The organization had focused on training and counseling only in the United States but has recently expanded its training sites and deployment targets to worldwide sites. In addition to traumatology, the Green Cross works to protect and support clinicians who face emotional contamination and "compassion fatigue" in their work with traumatized people (see chapter 12).

Other programs focus on responding to armed conflict or helping refugees, such as the Harvard Program in Refugee Trauma (HPRT), which has extended training programs for clinicians (Harvard Program in Refugee Trauma, http://www.hprt-cambridge.org). The HPRT endeavors to integrate indigenous healing systems, primary care, and a community organization approach when responding to trauma caused by conflict and natural disaster worldwide.

In the United States, many communities have local teams that respond to a range of disasters and other traumatic events. These teams often include a mix of clinical professionals and laypeople who are trained through a curriculum developed by the teams, often tailored to the needs of the community being served. Larger agencies, such as hospitals or community mental health centers, may have their own crisis response teams. These serve staff or programs within the agency or are available to other groups in the community. While the primary focus of this book is geared toward clinical responders, there are other responders whose efforts are closely related and therefore explored as well. The categories are not discrete; there is much overlap between them.

CLERGY, TRADITIONAL HEALERS, AND SPIRITUAL LEADERS

A profound consequence of disasters is often a loss of meaning and a questioning of one's spiritual, philosophical, and religious beliefs. A common reaction is, If there is a God, how could this have happened? Many emergency response teams have members who are clergy, some of whom have been trained in disaster mental health work. For example, there were chaplains available to construction workers toiling at Ground Zero in New York after 9/11. Chaplains are usually part of EMS teams serving uniformed personnel. Religious personnel of many denominations were deployed in countries affected by the Asian tsunami. In war-affected areas—such as northern Uganda—priests, ministers, and faith healers have been actively responding to distressed communities and individuals.

PUBLIC HEALTH WORKERS

Clinical services are often viewed as being part of a public health response to disasters. A public health model assesses the health and mental health needs of populations and has strategies that range from intervening with all people living in an affected area to targeting specific vulnerable groups, such as orphans, those who lost family members, and elderly people requiring assistance (de Jong, 2002; Mollica, 2006). Prevention is usually part of any public health approach to disaster, such as hurricane preparedness campaigns, as is triage work and prioritizing after a disaster strikes. Public health workers who are not specifically trained as clinicians may work alongside clinicians as the needs of affected families and communities are studied, assessed, and mapped out.

PUBLIC OFFICIALS

Alongside public health workers and clinicians are public officials charged with responding to disasters. In the United States, on a national level, this includes officials from the Department of Homeland Security and FEMA. It is FEMA's mission to help communities prepare for, prevent, and respond to national emergencies, which includes disasters. It works collaboratively with other organizations, including other federal agencies, state and local agencies, and the ARC. After 9/11, it was subsumed under the auspices of the Department of Homeland Security, a move that was frequently criticized after the inept and inadequate government response before and immediately after Hurricane Katrina.

Locally, there are key players, such as mayors, police and fire chiefs, and school superintendents and principals. For example, after a gang incident in which one adolescent murders another, a meeting with local residents may include the chief of police, who outlines the status of the criminal investigation and efforts at prevention of further violence, alongside a clinician, who offers psychoeducation by explaining common reactions to the event, suggesting self-care and mutual support activities and providing information about follow-up and referrals. In China, cadres (trained local government officials) were critical players in helping communities recover socially from the Wenchuan earthquake in 2008. Clinicians may advise public officials about vulnerable populations or offer suggestions about ways to reassure and comfort people.

Internationally, the United Nations (UN) has a number of organizations, such as UNICEF (United Nations Children's Fund), that respond to the needs of specific affected people when there are disasters. UNICEF offers disaster and refugee assistance, particularly for children and their families. Children's health is a particular focus and there are psychoeducation programs as well as efforts to improve sanitation and clean water sources.

NONGOVERNMENTAL ORGANIZATION (NGO) PERSONNEL

NGOs encompass large international organizations, such as Doctors Without Borders, the International Red Cross, Oxfam, and Save the Children, as well as local nonprofit organizations, local social service agencies, and mutual aid and self-help groups, such as the organizations staffed by formerly abducted children in northern Uganda, which worked to help support and reintegrate newly returning abductees. International/intergovernmental organizations, such as the United Nations, are sometimes referred to as IGOs (Halpern & Tramontin, 2007). Some NGOs, including the Children and War Foundation based in England, offer direct services to children exposed to conflict and natural disaster as well as indirect support—for example, in the funding of other programs and local NGOs engaged in this type of work. They, like other NGOs, evaluate programs to gain a sense of best practices and to guard against unintended harmful effects of interventions. While NGOs may have clinical personnel in attendance, many of the workers are career NGO administrators and planners and development workers, as well as volunteers and other community helpers. Some NGOs, like the

ARC, have special charters empowering them to be the central organizations responding to a disaster. Large domestic and international NGOs are often adept at fund-raising and, consequently, well staffed and resourced. This can be problematic as they have been criticized for using donations intended for disaster victims to further their organizational aims. Large NGOs often provide their own disaster response training programs to staff. Smaller NGOs are constantly struggling to make ends meet and to garner the necessary resources to fulfill their missions.

Those working for NGOs are usually greeted by local people with gratitude for their efforts and services. They build houses for affected populations; ensure safe drinking water; and offer clothing and food, medicine, and health services, as well as provide counseling and other clinical services. However, there are times when NGOs are perceived by communities and their members as being officious, imperious, and overbearing, and failing to engage in sufficient consultation with indigenous people or work from a stance of partnership and humility. These were frequent charges made by local survivors after the Haitian earthquake of 2010, along with concerns that donations were being used to support organizational infrastructure rather than going directly to people in need. It is particularly delicate when the NGO comes from another country, particularly if the country offering assistance was at one time a colonizer of the nation being helped. This was also a dynamic in the support offered to Haiti from the United States and France after the earthquake. Some large NGOs act as if they know best how to help people, despite their insensitivity to local cultures and customs. It can be particularly galling to people living in refugee camps along dirt roads, where the main means of transportation is walking or cycling, when they are forced to scatter as huge SUVs rumble by, bearing NGO flags, carrying people who are there to "help" as they leave those who are being helped in a cloud of dust.

PEACE AND RECONCILIATION WORKERS

Some disasters involve armed conflagration, interethnic or religious conflict, or war and the dislocation of civilian populations. At times, natural disasters occur in locations where such conflict is occurring, as in the Banda Aceh district of Indonesia and the eastern coast of Sri Lanka, both areas where long-term civil wars were raging when the Asian tsunami struck. In

New Orleans and Biloxi, two areas hit hard by Hurricane Katrina, chronic and endemic racism and social injustice were simmering conflicts that interacted with the "natural" disaster. As considered in chapter 10, there is a very close, recursive relationship between psychosocial healing and peace and reconciliation. Some clinicians, such as social psychologists and specially trained psychologists and social workers, have skills in mediation, reconciliation, and the resolution of intergroup tension and conflict. There are also peace workers who are not clinicians but whose efforts at peaceful understanding and resolution have as much if not more impact on healing and recovery as do counseling and therapy.

COORDINATION

As can be seen, there are many different players and entities who respond to disasters. When they work well together, their different skill sets and resources are woven into a web of assistance and relief. In many complex disaster situations, however, there is often duplication or omission of services (a lack of coordination, in other words) and turf battles and power struggles among the various helpers and responders.

ORIGINS OF DISASTER MENTAL HEALTH

The field of disaster mental health is relatively new—the term "disaster mental health" is not regularly found in scholarly databases until the 1990s (Halpern & Tramontin, 2007). The field is a result of the confluence of a number of different contributing streams—among them stress and trauma studies that deal with reactions to war and the response to the consequences of natural and technological disasters. Another example is the field of crisis intervention. A century ago, Sigmund Freud reflected on the notion of "unbearable situations" and his colleague Pierre Janet found that such events could lead to disassociation and hysteria (Halpern & Tramontin, 2007; Smelser, 2004). While this interest initially came from clients who had experienced childhood trauma or sexual abuse, there were questions about how large-scale events, such as war, could lead to overwhelming reactions (Jacobs, 1995). The "shell shock" experienced by WWI soldiers was a disorder pointing to a relationship between devastating events and severe psychological decompensation. The British army identified eighty thousand combatants suffering from the disorder (Halpern & Tramontin, 2007). Smith College School for Social Work in the United States was specifically established in 1918 to serve this population.

This pattern of soldiers responding to combat with decompensation continued in subsequent wars, the psychological reaction at times being called "combat fatigue" and, during the Vietnam War, "battle fatigue" in the United States (Halpern & Tramontin, 2007). U.S. veterans returning from Korea and Vietnam were coming home from unpopular wars where atrocities had been committed. They were not viewed as heroes in the way the WWII "greatest generation" had been, which compounded the stresses and adjustments to civilian life. Films like *Coming Home* describe the potential for the retriggering of fight-or-flight responses in soldiers safely at home who encounter situations that remind them of combat. Also, around the time of the Vietnam War, there was an increasing awareness of domestic violence, directed at both children and women (sometimes by returning Vietnam veterans), as well as behaviors such as hypervigilance and a range of anxiety and stress disorders. By 1980, the American Psychiatric Association's *Diagnostic and Statistical Manual of Mental Disorders* listed post-traumatic stress disorder (PTSD) as a clinical syndrome and, in 1994, acute stress disorder was listed as well (Friedman, Ritchie, & Watson, 2006; Halpern & Tramontin, 2007).

On the domestic front, industrialization and advances in technology were intertwined with the development of the field of disaster mental health. Industrialization and urbanization brought people into denser living and work situations. Therefore, when there were disasters, such as fires or earthquakes, the damage and casualties were all the more extensive. The ability to extract minerals and natural resources aided by technology placed people in situations prone to disasters, such as the collapse of deep-sea oil rigs and coal mines. Plants producing toxic substances led to disasters such as the meltdowns of the Chernobyl nuclear facility in Russia and the Three Mile Island reactor in the United States. When the Union Carbide plant exploded in Bhopal, India, which was near a high population center, the disaster caused high numbers of casualties. Recent "natural" disasters, such as Hurricane Katrina, led to the leaching of chemicals and other toxic waste because of flooding, while the Tohoku earthquake of 2011 in Japan unleashed a devastating tsunami and led to the meltdown of the Fukushima nuclear power plant. There is even a hypothesis that the Wenchuan earthquake in China may have been triggered by the building of a huge reservoir on the earthquake fault line (LaFraniere, 2009).

Other theoretical and practice streams that led to the field of disaster mental health were grief and bereavement studies and the development in the 1960s of the community mental health movement in the United States, which led to the provision of telephone crisis lines and crisis intervention services (Halpern & Tramontin, 2007). The field of disaster mental health also drew on the work of Abraham Maslow with his emphasis on attending to a hierarchy of needs and Viktor Frankl's focus on the construction of meaning as people experience traumatic events (Halpern & Tramontin, 2007).

The field of crisis intervention is a forerunner, if not close cousin, of disaster mental health. Three basic tenets of crisis intervention are that crises occur episodically, disturb a person's homeostatic balance, and overwhelm the usual mechanisms for coping (Roberts, 2005), which are also assumptions in the field of disaster mental health. Both crisis intervention and disaster mental health share a similar emphasis on identifying the acute, precipitating problem and working out a concrete plan of action. Roberts developed a seven-step model of crisis intervention: (1) conduct an assessment, (2) establish a relationship and rapport with the client, (3) identify the major problems and precipitators, (4) deal with feelings and emotions, (5) generate and explore options and alternatives, (6) formulate an action plan, and (7) establish a follow-up plan. All of these activities are consistent with a disaster mental health approach. In James and Gilliland's (2001) six-step model, ensuring client safety and offering support are also mentioned as important interventions, and these steps fit with a disaster mental health orientation as well. Crisis intervention, as with disaster mental health, views an acute event as both a threat and an opportunity (James & Gilliland, 2001).

Crisis intervention, as a field, also evolved from the response to disasters. In 1943, there was a fire in the Coconut Grove nightclub in Boston that killed 493 people (Jacobs, 1995; Roberts, 2005). Erich Lindemann and Gerald Caplan, two of the founders of crisis intervention, found that many of the survivors experienced somatic distress, preoccupation with images of the deceased, guilt and anger, and changes in their behavior patterns (Roberts, 2005). Airplane crashes were other events that fueled an interest in both crisis intervention and disaster response. While disaster mental health is predicated on responding to people and communities affected by external public events, crisis intervention has a broader application and is an approach that can be used to respond to internal psychological processes (the panic that ensues after failing an exam) and domestic events (an acute breakdown of communication in a marriage). Crisis intervention is a foundational block in the architecture of disaster mental health, although the disaster mental health field has become both more specialized and broader in scope; it is more specific in its focus on crises distinctively engendered by disasters. Within this frame, the field has also considered group and public interventions, such as debriefings and community informational sessions, which goes beyond the more traditional microfocus of crisis intervention.

As was mentioned earlier, the ARC in the United States has a special role in the provision of services in response to disasters, including mental health services (Halpern & Tramontin, 2007; Jacobs, 1995; Park & Miller, 2007). Local EMS teams offer debriefings and other forms of critical incident stress management to police officers, firefighters, and emergency medical personnel. EMS teams use the model of critical incident stress management pioneered by Jeffrey Mitchell in the early eighties (Mitchell, 1983) and developed for uniformed responders, with training provided by the International Critical Incident Stress Foundation. This model was adapted by the ARC from the 1990s through 2001 for use in civilian populations. However, it was overused in response to 9/11—in some organizations it was nearly mandatory for all employees and sometimes foisted on people—and has been dropped by the ARC as a means of responding to disasters (Miller, 2003, 2006a). This was in part because of concerns about not only the effectiveness of this intervention in preventing long-term trauma reactions but also possible harmful effects, such as emotional contagion, in which people who were previously coping became stirred up by others in the group who were emotionally overwhelmed (Friedman et al., 2006; McNally et al., 2003). (Chapter 7 covers debriefings in greater detail.)

WHAT HELPING PROFESSIONALS OFFER IN RESPONSE TO DISASTERS

Disaster mental health responders offer different responses depending on a number of factors: the nature of the disaster, the timing of the intervention, and the particular organizational auspices overseeing the response. The specific types of interventions are considered in detail in subsequent chapters, while a brief overview of what helping professionals can offer in response to disaster is summarized here.

The field of disaster mental health describes different phases of disaster response, each of which calls for a different intervention that carries a distinct name and term (Alexander, 2005; Halpern & Tramontin, 2007; Rosenfeld et al., 2005; Vernberg & Vogel, 1993). The first phase is typically viewed as the predisaster preparation stage. It includes planning by officials and providers, offering information about risks and consequences to families and communities, and educating and mobilizing potential responders (Vernberg & Vogel, 1993). When a disaster is impending, fear and arousal can be primed prior to the event, which can accentuate the depth of stress and trauma reactions once it occurs, so advanced preparation and normalization of reactions can be helpful (Halpern & Tramontin, 2007; Rosenfeld et al., 2005).

When disaster strikes, there is the disaster impact phase (Alexander, 2005; Rosenfeld et al., 2005; Vernberg & Vogel, 1993). Using Maslow's hierarchy of needs, physical safety and security is of the utmost importance at this time. People also need shelter, food, clothing, and comfort. They are often in a state of psychological shock, ranging from numbness and immobilization to frantic attempts to flee or heroic efforts to respond, which can involve helping others (Halpern & Tramontin, 2007). The type of intervention responders offer at this stage constitutes psychological first aid (Alexander, 2005; Halpern & Tramontin, 2007; Vernberg & Vogel, 1993) and this includes offering information and connecting people with loved ones and resources (Orner, Kent, Pfefferbaum, Raphael, & Watson, 2006).

Following this phase is what is known as the short-term adaptation phase, which can last from twenty-four hours to three months (Vernberg & Vogel, 1993). Alexander (2005) calls this the recoil phase, while Halpern and Tramontin (2007) term it the honeymoon phase, focusing on how people come together. Although the immediate impact of the disaster is over, the loss, destruction, and dislocations are inescapable realities confronting individuals, families, and communities. People may be living in temporary shelters or trailers and are sometimes relocated to different communities, some far away from their homes. Services, community networks, and social supports are still disrupted, as are routines. During this period, the types of disaster mental health interventions include psychosocial identifying, validating, and normalizing of reactions, often with small groups, families, or children, for whom natural settings such as classrooms are deployed, if they are back in operation (Rosenfeld et al., 2005; Vernberg & Vogel, 1993). This is a time when critical incident stress management activities can be applied as well as crisis intervention techniques with individuals, families, and groups (Rosenfeld et al., 2005).

The next phase is often known as the recovery phase (Alexander, 2005) or long-term adaptation phase (Rosenfeld et al., 2005; Vernberg & Vogel, 1993) and disillusionment phase (Halpern & Tramontin, 2007). Acute reactions should have moderated or subsided by this time with the exception of the minority of people with severe reactions (Rosenfeld et al., 2005). While during earlier phases there can be a sense of pulling together and responding to challenges with fortitude and heroism, this level of energy is difficult to sustain and the hard realities of what it takes to rebuild can be dispiriting. There is an interaction between the concrete realities on the ground and the perceptions of what can actually be accomplished. The impact of the disaster alone can foster despair, despondency, and depression. But there are also the collective and individual meanings that mediate the concrete effects of the disaster. Was the disaster a low point and is there an emerging narrative that sees hope and progress down the road? If not, then resignation and despair can set in. Narratives of efficacy and hope can sustain communities even when there are long-term losses. But pessimism is fueled by inadequate government and NGO responses, particularly when there is large scale confusion, incompetence, and corruption, all of which occurred in the aftermath of Hurricane Katrina. Can people see visible signs that progress is being made or are they consistently frustrated, encountering barriers to their recovery, not being given the tools and resources to rebuild? It is during this period that disaster mental health interventions are targeted more toward individual, family, and group therapy (Rosenfeld et al., 2005) while a psychosocial capacity building approach focuses more on the social, economic, and political aspects of reconstruction (IASC, 2007).

The length of the reconstruction phase varies, depending on many variables. In eastern Sri Lanka, in 2009, five years after the tsunami, there were still many widows facing economic insecurity, people living in temporary housing, and children struggling with anxiety, fear, insecurity, and lack of social connection. There was much greater drug use among children than before the tsunami—with children as young as twelve drinking to excess. The age of marriage plummeted, with weddings of people as young as thirteen. Community workers were alarmed as the young couples having children lacked the maturity to be parents. Recovery from the effects of the tsunami was hampered by long-standing ethnic tensions among Tamils, Sinhalese, and Muslims in the region and an escalating conflict between the Sinhalese-dominated government and the rebel organization, the Liberation Tigers of Tamil Eelam (LTTE), known in the West as the Tamil Tigers. NGOs found their relief efforts stymied and were wary of working in a war zone. The government appeared to be more intent on suppressing the LTTE than on rebuilding the area. Roads and communications, which are essential to rebuilding, were severely compromised (Miller, 2006b).

Since Hurricane Katrina in 2005, the city of New Orleans had far from recovered nearly five years later. A combination of the devastation from the storm, poverty, long-standing racism, economic decline, and remarkable government incompetence and indifference, at all levels, has been crushing to attempts at recovery. Historical and comparative research indicates that when cities are ascendant, the disaster recovery process moves in a positive direction. The opposite is true for cities in decline; the disaster interacts with the community's predisaster trajectory (Kates et al., 2006). New Orleans had already been losing population before Katrina, down from a high of 627,525 in 1960 to 437,186 in July 2005: estimates in 2006 put the city's population at 158,253 (Kates et al., 2006). This trend appears to have reversed recently, with the population growing by 13.8 percent from July 2006 to July 2007 (U.S. Census Bureau, 2009). But there has been uneven economic recovery, with those with more resources rebuilding more easily. Thus, for both eastern Sri Lanka and New Orleans after major storms, the recovery/long-term adaptation phase continues half a decade later.

Disaster mental health activities during this phase typically focus on helping individuals to improve their coping mechanisms and relationships and revise their life goals and values (Alexander, 2005). Deeper reflective work can occur when there is greater stability and safety. This can include individual and family therapy and play therapy for children (Rosenfeld et al., 2005). However, as in the two case examples previously described, where there is ongoing conflict or long-term social oppression, the negative impact of the disaster continues well beyond the initial point of impact. The combination of terrible losses brought on by the disaster, particularly loss of life, home, and community (Halpern & Tramontin, 2007), along with a social ecology of continuing barriers to recovery, mean that recuperation could be a long-term if not lifelong process. This is difficult for many people to accept, as they often long for life as it was before the disaster, a longing that might never be fulfilled.

Phase models of disaster recovery are overly linear. Recovery can be idiosyncratic and its trajectory does not move in a straight line. While most people and communities recover over time, this is not true for all. There are relapses and ebbs and flows. It is also important to recognize that the categories are not discrete. For example, part of recovery and reconstruction can be planning for prevention, which is an empowering activity for survivors of disasters. In southern Taiwan, there are frequent typhoons with consequent landslides and flooding. Disaster recovery stations engage local people in planning the prevention of losses in the future, which helps them to feel less vulnerable and at the mercy of the elements. Thus, the phases of disaster recovery in this region can be viewed as being more cyclical than linear and less distinct and hierarchical than the way they are presented in many disaster mental health models.

It is important to consider memorializing the losses (described in detail in chapter 11) sustained because of the disaster through all phases of disaster recovery, although conditions are more favorable for this process when there is peace, stability, and progress toward recovery. It is difficult for people to adequately grieve when they are expending a lot of energy on survival. Anniversary dates are good times to have memorial rituals and ceremonies. Memorializing is covered in detail in chapter 11, but it is important to note that this is not a straightforward course of action. It is a process with individual, family, and collective dimensions, which do not always mesh well. Some in a community may want to move on and avoid reliving the pain of the disaster, while others feel drawn to memorializing as part of their process of grieving, mourning, and healing. Collective memorializing can remind people of social divisions, pinpointing those who are still struggling as it reveals those who have recovered most easily. Yet this process has the potential for unifying people and connecting the past, present, and future. Rituals and ceremonies can mark the transition from the social role of victim to that of survivor.

When designing collective memorials, it is important to have an inclusive, participatory planning process that includes as many sectors and stakeholders in an affected community as possible. Examples of collective memorializing include installations, commemorative plaques, books, photographic exhibits, artistic displays, and quilts. Other types of memorials are more future oriented, such as projects and programs to prevent or mitigate future disasters or to ease the suffering of survivors. The group Mothers Against Drunk Driving is an example of this. Another was the presence of New York firefighters responding to communities along the Gulf Coast after Hurricane Katrina. On the anniversary of 9/11, while responding to Katrina, they and all other relief workers momentarily ceased their activities and observed a moment of silence to commemorate the earlier disaster, and in so doing, responders linked communities from different parts of the country in remembering the past while responding to the present.

The town of Hanwang in Sichuan Province, China, is at the juncture of the Sichuan plains and the beginning of the Himalayan plateau. It was near the epicenter of the Wenchuan earthquake that struck in May 2008. Many people died, including children attending school, and the town was rendered uninhabitable. Residents were resettled in temporary housing and slated to occupy a new, government-built Hanwang in 2011, a few miles from the original site. There were informal and formal attempts at memorializing the catastrophe. In the center of the town, the clock tower is still standing with the clock reading 2:28, the moment that the earthquake struck. Soon after the earthquake, a small wreath of dried flowers was placed at the base of the tower in the shape of a heart, attached by cellophane tape, an ad hoc contribution toward a collective memorial. The reason that the damaged clock tower was not bulldozed is that the government decided to keep the town ruins as a memorial to the earthquake, open to former residents and the public at large. Two years after the event, walking through the shell of the old town, one can see into the eviscerated apartments, revealed by the gaps where external walls were peeled away—a torn curtain still hanging by a broken window, an empty flower pot on the veranda, a bed dangling over a shattered floor—reminders of the lives that were lived and lost. Without much fanfare, there are small signs along the road with simple messages: "Ruins generate hope. Purify your mind and take a look at the disaster area."

CRITIQUE OF THE DISASTER MENTAL HEALTH MODEL

The field of disaster mental health is a growing and evolving discipline. Over the past decade, there has been an expansion of clinical interventions in response to disasters, an increase in training programs, and an emphasis on research, evaluation, and evidence-based intervention. Professional associations of psychiatrists, psychologists, and social workers have special divisions, training programs, and symposia dedicated to this field. The number of books and scholarly articles focused on this topic has increased.

Many individuals, families, and communities have been helped by the efforts of clinicians responding to disasters. Although some research has indicated that early intervention does not appreciably lower the risk of long-term consequences (McNally et al., 2003), the vast majority of studies confirm that people receiving disaster mental health services appreciate the intervention and often feel better, at least in the short term. The range of people offered such services has expanded considerably. Peer-oriented debriefing teams serving uniformed personnel exist throughout North America. There are clinicians attached to Red Cross services all over the world. Thousands of students and teachers in schools have received some form of disaster mental health intervention. People living in war zones, refugees, and displaced individuals, and survivors of ethnic cleansing and attempts at genocide have all been exposed to services within the disaster mental health continuum, as have survivors of earthquakes, floods, fires, tsunamis, hurricanes, and landslides.

Despite the range and scope of intervention, and the short-term (and possibly long-term) value for many who receive such services, it is important to apply a critical lens in the spirit of improving the services that people receive and to ensure that good intentions do not inadvertently lead to poor outcomes or unintended disempowerment. My critique broadly falls into two categories: sociopolitical and cultural.

SOCIOPOLITICAL CRITIQUE

The field of disaster mental health has been essentially a European and North American project from the beginning. The centers of knowledge production have been in universities, institutes, foundations, and agencies in the Western world. This is not to say that there have not been major contributions from non-Western professionals in this discipline—there have been many—but the locus of influence and power has been in the West. Many non-Western practitioners have studied or trained in the West. The level and depth of this sociopolitical imbalance permeates all levels of this line of work.

Disaster mental health is akin to an industry, albeit one often run by government entities and nonprofits. The product is the implementation of disaster mental health services, and the manufacturing of both the hardware and software necessary for this enterprise comes mostly from the West. Although there are international organizations involved with planning and coordination, such as the United Nations and Inter-Agency Standing Committee, the major players come from Western nations. The West is where the centers of training are located, where the majority of practitioners live, and where the corporate headquarters exist for the major international NGOs responding to disasters (International Committee of the Red Cross [ICRC], Oxfam, Save the Children, World Vision International, CARE International) Médecins Sans Frontières [Doctors Without Borders], Catholic Agency for Oversees Development [CAFOD], ActionAid, UNICEF). The sanctioning bodies for practitioners are mostly housed in Western locations.

There are many reasons for this geographic imbalance and dominance by one sector of the globe, including wealth, resources, levels of education and training, and the depth and breadth of the professionalization of clinical services in the West. There are also historical factors at play, such as colonialism. Another factor is the emphasis on psychology as the major area of focus when responding clinically to disasters, which is a priority more in the West and where there are more professionals to deliver such services. Most psychological theories emanated from Western thinkers and this has spawned a sprawling mental health industrial complex—where professionals and training programs shape the social construction of need and response. The psychologizing of need is amplified by media discourses and insurance programs that pay for people receiving such services in response to a range of bio-psycho-social issues and problems. Also, there is an assumption of psychological universality. As Summerfield (2004, p. 243) has written, the same symptoms and even syndromes do not necessarily have the same meaning across cultures: "There is no one definitive psychology."

A focus on psychology is not inherently problematic—all cultures and societies have mechanisms for responding to certain behaviors, feelings, and adjustments and challenges to living. But the disaster mental health industry is situated in a world that has experienced centuries of Western dominance through colonialism and neocolonialism in countries where racism has privileged white European-descended citizens over people of color. Is there a risk that the field of disaster mental health perpetuates these systems of privilege and inequality? Is the field potentially using the "soft power" of psychological treatment to serve as agents of social control even if this is not the intent? Does the disaster mental health complex serve the interests of its members, who are predominantly white and of European descent?

These questions are not meant to be provocative or to undermine the good intentions of most disaster mental health organizations and their practitioners. They are raised because all beneficence has its limits and potential negative consequences. As Ira Glasser (1981, pp. 145–146), former executive director of the American Civil Liberties Union, puts it: "Every program designed to help the dependent ought to be evaluated not on the basis of the good it might do, but rather on the basis of the harm it might do." There have been numerous studies that review the efficacy of certain psychological interventions, such as critical incident stress debriefings (Bisson et al., 2000; Chemtob et al., 1997; Gist & Woodhall, 2000; McNally et al., 2003). But the fundamental assumptions about the frameworks for evaluating need and response remain mostly unexamined. Such assumptions include the centrality of professional clinicians, whether employed or in a volunteer capacity, when helping people recover from their psychosocial challenges. They also include viewing trauma as predominantly a psychological reaction to overwhelming events that is suffered by individuals. This assumption is shared by many, if not most, Western-trained clinicians, but trauma can also be constructed as a collective response to socially constructed meanings, offering multiple frames for understanding events (Smelser, 2004). How trauma is interpreted has much to do with the conceptual lens of the interpreter, which in the field of disaster mental health is most often a Western-trained clinician who tends to privilege the psychological over the social and the individual over the collectivity when responding to disasters.

Disaster mental health responses cannot be separated from who is offering the services, how problems are conceptualized and constructed, or what organizational interests are vested in doing things in certain ways. As well, responses cannot be set apart from the historical circumstances preceding the disaster or the personnel who are trained to respond and what they are trained to see, hear, and do. Even the research that confirms what works and does not work is saturated with social, political, and cultural assumptions so that empirically grounded evidence-based practices often reflect the value systems and conceptual lenses of both the researcher and practitioner. A closer examination of some of the cultural assumptions of the disaster mental health project forms the second part of this critique.

CULTURAL CRITIQUE

There are a number of key cultural assumptions implicit in disaster mental health models that are by no means universally shared by ethnic and national groups. Four significant ones are the notion of change, reliance on clinically trained professionals to offer talk therapy or related interventions, the focus of intervention, and how much control people have over their lives.

The first assumption is the concept of change. In most disaster mental health approaches, there is a linear trajectory that projects how change occurs, as illustrated by the phases of disaster described previously. It is assumed that most people go through a process of change that includes loss and then steps toward recovery. There is a starting point and a goal, or end point. This model does not mesh well with cultures that have a more cyclical view of change and of growth and destruction. Many millions of people in the world who are Hindus and Buddhists view change as being part of a continuing cycle of creation and annihilation (Ross, 1966). In Sri Lanka, where more than 90 percent of the population is Hindu and Buddhist, the notion of a terrible event that is an overwhelming exception and a path of recovery that is a straight line of progress is inconsistent with the cultural worldview of the majority of its citizens. Certainly, people are emotionally affected by events like the tsunami or armed conflict, and they have reactions that are deemed to be socially abnormal or a shift from previous expectations of social behavior. Most affected people want to return to "normal." But the metaphors employed by disaster mental health models, particularly those of a critical incident and phases of recovery may be inconsistent with the worldviews of most people affected by the events. Are there ways the disaster mental health model can be recast according to the non-Western worldview that embraces wheels of suffering and cycles of creation and destruction?

The second problem with the disaster mental health model is dependence on professionals. Reliance on professionals with clinical training is in itself a cultural assumption, as there are cultures that do not privilege such people to help others in times of crisis. There may be reliance on spiritual or faith healers or other community members vested with special privileges. Related to this is the assumption that talking to someone about one's symptoms of distress is helpful, which is alien to many cultures and in some is seen as actually dangerous, opening oneself up to negative consequences, such as bad spirits or karma as well as social ostracism (Wikan, 1989). This is also more than a cultural issue, as in many parts of the globe, there simply are insufficient numbers of helping professionals to make a significant impact. Even if there are social workers, psychiatrists, counselors, and psychologists in the country, they are often clustered in large cities and do not live and work in regions where the disaster has occurred. In such situations, professionals are always outsiders who are not part of the community and will not remain in the community, which raises the critical question of what will happen after they leave? Using outsiders who are professionals as the main vehicle of intervention and change creates social distance between the community and families being helped and those who are doing the helping. It reduces reactions to disaster to symptoms requiring professional attention, which can undermine feelings of efficacy and empowerment by those being helped. Having experts as guides to recovery reinforces the social role and status of affected people as victims. Ways of overcoming this dilemma are considered in the discussions about psychosocial capacity building and the use of training-of-trainers (TOT) model.

A third assumption in the disaster mental health approach is that the focus of intervention is on the individual and at times the family or work group, but seldom the community. This is consistent with the Western emphasis on the autonomous individual that informs an approach to mental health and the treatment of emotional and psychological problems. Thus, this approach makes sense for most Western or Western-trained practitioners. In more collective societies and cultures, however, this emphasis on the individual can be experienced as dissonant and difficult to understand and respond to. The very notion of the individual in relation to the collectivity varies considerably, and intervention and research models that assume the individual as the main unit to help and measure progress against may be missing the point for many nations and social groups. Thus, a pure disaster mental health model, as is practiced in the West, may be incomplete or inappropriate for people living in non-Western countries and often for non-Western people living in Western countries with more of a collective orientation.

As the IASC (2007) has concluded, this is not an either/or proposition and a combination of disaster mental health approaches with psychosocial capacity building frameworks is both possible and advisable in many situations. Many practitioners are focusing on the sociopolitical-cultural contexts in which trauma and recovery take place and recognize that individual psychological reactions, such as trauma, cannot be separated from the shattering of social bonds and structures (Farwell & Cole, 2002; Mollica, 2006; Wessells, 1999; Wessells & Monteiro, 2006). Weyerman (2007, p. 83) has rightly called for "linking economics with emotions," meaning that economic and emotional well-being are intricately related. Individual and collective recovery are similarly linked. There is a concerted movement among professionals responding to disasters, particularly those involved in armed conflict situations, to broaden the prevailing disaster mental health focus on the individual to that of the collectivity and cultural traditions and patterns.

More work also needs to be done in examining how to best help people where individual autonomy and differentiation is not extolled as a psychological virtue and embeddedness in family does not necessarily mean that a person is enmeshed, or not "individuated," which is a decidedly Western spin on non-Western families. Many cultures have a sense of self that is much more interdependent than in the West (Miller & Garran, 2007; Yeh & Hwang, 2000). This also pertains to cultures in which extended family structures are the norm and individuals are very connected to cousins, nieces and nephews, godchildren and parents, as well as their communities.

Cultural patterns interact with sociopolitical policies and structures. The one child per family policy in China meant that many families lost their only child in the Wenchuan earthquake. All parents are bereft when their children die in a disaster, but when a family loses its only child, this is particularly devastating. In rural China, families invest many of their hopes for a secure future in their children, aspirations that were shattered by the earthquake. In some villages, such as Hanwang and Beichuan, cadres suffered high casualties, leaving a gaping hole in the local civil service structure at a time when it was most needed. Those cadres that survived felt an enormous sense of responsibility to help their villages, despite the fact that many of them had directly lost children, other family members, friends, and colleagues. These people worked ceaselessly to help their fellow villagers, and as a result, many suffered from acute stress disorders (Wang Xi Lu, personal communication, April 3, 2010). These examples illustrate how the psychosocial impact of the Wenchuan earthquake had different repercussions and implications for response than would a comparable earthquake in Lincoln, Nebraska.

As the roots of disaster mental health evolved from responding to local disasters, often in Western nations (floods, fires, mine disasters, airplane crashes), *and* the foundations for disaster mental health were being laid down at a time when individual treatment had more currency than family interventions, much emphasis was placed on treating individuals. Another factor that supported this tendency was the ascendance of critical incident stress debriefing (Mitchell, 1983) to treat uniformed responders—a situation where individuals were viewed more in relation to their work groups than their families—which, although recognizing the importance of team support, emphasized the individual over the family. Moreover, many if not most of the early theorists and practitioners in the field were white European-descended professionals who perhaps viewed the focus on the individual, rather than family, as normative and consistent with their own cultural perspectives and worldviews.

The fourth assumption, related to the third, embedded in many disaster mental health models, is that of personal agency and autonomous action. Consistent with this assumption are the notions that we are responsible for our own fates and are capable of pulling ourselves up by our own bootstraps. We can be and do whatever we want, as the Western sporting-goods giant declares: "Just do it." These are very Western notions, consistent with the philosophy underpinning capitalist economic systems. Not surprisingly, these beliefs and values are very much a part of Western psychology and therefore underlie much thinking in the field of disaster mental health. An assumption is that individuals should find within them the means for change and take the responsibility for enacting that change. Different cultures have different beliefs about where the locus for change and responsibility is situated (Sue & Sue, 2003). Many cultures see individuals as having less control or less responsibility for their fates. The notion of karma and a belief in prior lives can lead to a very different construction of the meaning of disaster and what one should do to recover compared with the Western concept of natural disaster and phases of recovery. Also, there are differences between Western and non-Western views of authority, one's place in society, the role of gods and spirits, and therefore constructed meaning about who is responsible for healing and recovery.

One way to approach this is to consider the differences between worldviews and values. Worldviews are how we see and comprehend the world. They are naive psychologies embedded in culture and handed down by families that inform what is common sense and taken for granted about life. Values are the principles and standards that tell people how to live their lives (Miller & Garran, 2007; Reiss, 1981; Sue & Sue, 2003). Many North Americans and Europeans share cultural values that emphasize a belief in the equality of individuals; the goodness of humanity; the value of action, work, and materialism; and the advantage of interactional styles that are direct and proactive (Katz, 1985; Miller & Garran, 2007). And yet notions of privacy, independence versus interdependence, gender roles, children's roles, sickness and health, ways to express respect, views of authority, and time and punctuality vary considerably across cultures (Miller & Garran). As in the discussion of "personhood" considered in chapter 1, there is no cultural consensus about the implications for managing risk, adversity, or grievances. And there is no overall agreement as to how various cultures go about seeking help, responding to loss, and finding resolutions to disaster (Summerfield, 2004). Disaster mental health models and protocols often do not consider this spectrum of difference in meaning-making and social behavior, and a task for the West is to decenter Western Eurocentric assumptions in the disaster mental health project.

This chapter provides a brief overview of the field of disaster mental health, particularly focusing on its history, the roles of service providers, and a sketch of what they do. Subsequent chapters provide more detailed consideration of the effects of disasters and how to help people recover.

My critique of this model of intervention, particularly in its traditional forms, has focused on Western assumptions about the phases of recovery from disaster, the separation of psychological reactions and needs from sociopolitical contexts, the emphasis on the individual more than families and communities, and the cultural assumptions about worldviews and values. As mentioned in chapter 1, my goal is not to reject the field of disaster mental health, which has much to offer in response to disasters, but rather to offer a constructive critique in the interest of improving its effectiveness and also trying to open it up so that it is not solely a project of Western professionals. Also, I offer a critique that promotes only those psychosocial capacity building approaches that focus on the social to the exclusion of the psychological, and throughout the book, I attempt to integrate both of these approaches.

MINDFULNESS EXERCISE: PERSONAL SPACE AND EYE CONTACT

As this chapter has considered cultural assumptions, worldviews, and values, I offer a simple exercise that helping professionals may use to reflect on two very basic cultural components of social interaction: personal space and degree of eye contact—where one rests the eyes when engaging with another person. Both of these components tend to have been taught at a very early age and are often reinforced by one's culture. Gender and social class are also important variables, as is personal experience, such as having been subject to domestic violence (E. Dunn, personal communication,

2010). Direct eye contact, while respectful for some, may be interpreted as being threatening or disrespectful by others.

People who have lived and worked cross-culturally may have noticed some major differences in how people manage these activities and have adjusted their approaches accordingly. Both of these subtle, often unconscious, components of interaction have implications for trust, comfort, intimacy, and for expressing respect and disrespect, which are all important factors when working with people after disaster. This exercise is best done in small groups with people from different cultural and/or economic backgrounds, but it can be done with just two people or can serve as a template for reflecting on how these differences play out in one's experience with others in the world.

If in a small group, form two parallel lines with every person facing another person. Label the lines A and B. Ask the people in line A to find the ideal space between them and the person across from them and to move forward or backward to achieve that distance. Then, ask the people in line A to rest their eyes where they feel most comfortable. Repeat the exercise with line B. Then ask each pair to discuss their thoughts and feelings while doing the exercise. Then ask them to reflect on what they were taught—either explicitly or implicitly—about personal space and eye contact from their families. Ask them as well if they have ever been in situations or had relationships in which these areas were problematic or had to be negotiated. Then open up for group discussion the different perspectives on what is the most comfortable distance between people and the different issues that arise around gaze. What are the contextual factors that influence these decisions?

After doing this exercise, it can be helpful to be mindful of how space and eye contact are managed as you go through your day. What are the subtle interactions and dances that negotiate these basic methods of human contact and interaction? It can be helpful to notice patterns, but it is also important to be cautious about making generalizations about cultural patterns based on only a few encounters.

To illustrate the power of physical space and eye contact, I offer some brief examples.

A friend and colleague who is Puerto Rican American and was a school superintendent related a story to me about when he was in grade school and was confronted by a teacher about something. He had been taught by his family, who were poor at the time, to look down at the floor and to not make eye contact with adults, particularly adults with power and prestige—it would be disrespectful to look such an adult directly in the eyes. The teacher, an American of European descent, became angry with him and kept asking him to look at her while she spoke. When he refused, she insisted that his parents come to school, which was a shameful experience for both the child and his parents.

In one of my classes, there was an echo of this when I conducted the above exercise in which a Mexican American woman was paired with a Jewish American woman. The Mexican American woman felt a great deal of tension when the Jewish American woman kept looking her directly in the eye from a distance of about two feet away, while the Jewish American woman initially felt alienated when her partner stood farther away and did not make eye contact.

When I was responding to the tsunami in eastern Sri Lanka in 2005, I would sometimes walk on the beach. I began to notice that if there was just one other person on the beach, he or she would soon walk over to me, stand quite close to me, and at times sit and talk with me. At first, I felt as if my space and solitude were being impinged on by these encounters, until I discussed this with my Tamil colleagues. They explained that it would be considered antisocial, if not rude, not to make an attempt at contact.

In conclusion, personal space and eye contact are two of the most basic methods of communicating and interacting between people, and yet they are insufficiently analyzed by clinical practitioners. There are cultural and social class differences, as well as personal differences, in the management of these dimensions and it is important not to generalize about entire cultural and social groups. Mindfulness and awareness by practitioners of these often taken-for-granted aspects of human connection are helpful when responding to any disaster.

3

CONCEPTUALIZING DISASTERS

HAVING PROVIDED an overview and critique of the field of disaster mental health in chapter 2, I consider the *nature* of disasters, particularly different categories of disasters, in this chapter. Classic typologies group disasters into at least two categories, natural and human caused, with the latter often being subdivided into categories with titles such as technological, complex, terrorism, armed conflict, mass violence, and acts of omission and commission (Halpern & Tramontin, 2007; Rosenfeld et al., 2005; Van den Eynde & Veno, 1999). What do these categories mean and what are the implications for responders? Are they valid conceptual baskets? Is it valuable and helpful to think of disasters this way? These are some of the questions considered in this chapter. Before exploring them, it is helpful to review the definition of disaster. After considering and critiquing the categories used to describe disasters, I present a framework that dynamically elucidates key parameters of disasters, which can be used by responders when evaluating the needs of individuals, families, groups, and communities.

ASSUMPTIONS ABOUT THE NATURE OF DISASTER

In chapter 1, I review Rosenfeld et al.'s (2005) six characteristics of disaster: (1) has a footprint of a certain size; (2) has an identifiable beginning and end, occurs suddenly, and has long-lasting effects; (3) negatively affects large numbers of people; (4) affects more than one family in a public arena; (5) is out of the realm of ordinary experience; and (6) has the power to induce stress and trauma in anyone who experiences the event. I raise questions with each of these aspects to illustrate the contingent, subjective, and socially constructed nature of disaster and offer a definition of disaster: *A disaster is a process that encompasses an event, or series of events, affecting multiple people, groups, and communities, and causing damage, destruction, and loss of life. There is a public and collective dimension to a disaster, as well as individual suffering. The disaster process is socially constructed (at least by some) as being outside of ordinary experience, overwhelming usual individual and collective coping mechanisms, disrupting social relations, and at least temporarily disempowering individuals and communities.*

By using this definition, I am making a number of assumptions and assertions. One is that a disaster is more than an event; it is how the event is perceived and socially constructed (Echterling & Wiley, 1999; Van den Eynde & Veno, 1999). A given hurricane can be terrifying and overwhelming for a community (or certain people within that community) or perceived as a seasonable event to grumble about and take precautions for, but it is not a disaster. Related to this, disasters are contingent and contextual events. The meaning they have for individuals and communities cannot be separated from what has gone before and what is happening elsewhere; the notion of disaster is always in relation to nondisaster. There is also the dimension of time. While some disasters affect an entire community from the same moment (9/11, Oklahoma City), other disasters affect different groups at different times. For example, an armed conflict moves from fighting among rebels and the government in one area of the country (northern and eastern Sri Lanka) to another region where there are suicide bombers killing civilians (predominantly Sinhala regions of Sri Lanka). The ongoing disaster for Tamils in the war zone then spreads to a disaster leading to deaths, injury, and destruction in other parts of the country, directly affecting the majority ethnic group living outside of the conflict zone.

A second assumption is that in addition to how the event is perceived and constructed, the consequences are important. By consequences, I mean not only material consequences, although these are important, but also psychosocial consequences. Using the same example of the hurricane, a small town may live in a hurricane corridor and need to rebuild on an almost annual basis. Some hurricanes may even inflict severe damage—destroying roads, homes, and businesses—but can still be experienced as within the range of normal life, without major psychosocial implications. Residents might view this as part of the normal cost of living on a beautiful island or in a beachfront community. Another example of differential psychosocial consequences with similar events is a blizzard. Major snowstorms and icc storms arc regular cvcnts in the northeastern and midwestern United States. Power lines are downed and electricity eventually restored. Roads are plowed and sanded, and schools and businesses remain open. In Seattle, however, two inches of snow can shut down the city. Besides having an ecology that includes very steep hills, the city does not have sanders and snowplows, and residents are not used to coping with driving, walking, and living in an area where it snows. An event that would receive little notice in Minnesota or New Hampshire becomes a major test of fortitude and resilience in Seattle.

But in the example of snow in Seattle, probably few people would die and there would not be lingering and lasting effects. But if a school bus slides down a hill and collides with a freight train, resulting in a large number of casualties, this would be considered a disaster, as it would in any community in the world. It may not be a large-scale or catastrophic disaster—communication systems would not be damaged, people would not be left homeless, for example—but for a significant number of people in the community, it would be outside of everyday experience, overwhelming, sudden, and shocking; it would result in loss of life, shaken community trust, and many psychosocial reactions. The physical consequences of an event in which homes collapse or people sustain injuries arc mediated by prior cxperience, social expectations, cultural values and beliefs, and the social meaning of the event and its effects. However, some events, like a lethal school bus accident, would be experienced as a disaster in any place, at any time, in any culture or society.

Two other assumptions implicit in the definition are covered in chapter 1. One is that there is a public dimension to the event and its consequences; it is socially constructed as having meaning for unrelated individuals, families, and groups within a community, in interaction with the other criteria. When my father died of a heart attack, it caused grief for my family and his friends. It may have been distressing to people in the nursing home where he was residing. But it was not outside of the course of normal events for someone his age or for the nursing home. However, if a nurse poisoned residents in the nursing home, causing a number of them to die of cardiac arrest, this would be considered a local disaster because of the malevolent intentions, the scale, the breach of trust, and the breakdown in social organization (law and order) within the institution. If a tornado struck the nursing home and killed ten residents, even though this is viewed as an act of God, it would still be experienced as a disaster by many residents, staff, family members, and people in the community—its range of impact would extend beyond the usual level of mourners described in the example of my father's heart attack.

Another assumption in the definition is that people feel at least temporarily disempowered. This is another type of psychosocial consequence. Whether the impact is disrupted social arrangements (attending school) or psychological and emotional reactions (numbness or intrusive thoughts and memories), individuals, groups, and communities do not feel as competent and in control when a disaster strikes as they usually feel in their lives. Of course, some people find they feel chronically overwhelmed and disempowered, and this does not constitute a disaster unless it is combined with the other criteria mentioned in the definition.

In summary, disasters are socially constructed, fluid, and contingent processes, which raises questions about the typical categories used to differentiate between different types of disasters. Figure 3.1 illustrates the relationship between concrete events and the perceptions and constructed meanings of those events within a social ecology.

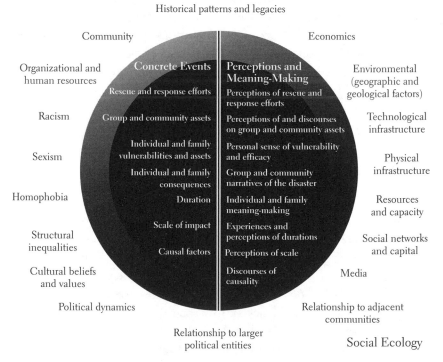

FIGURE 3.1 Dimensions of Disaster

TYPES OF DISASTERS

The first major divisions when classifying disasters are natural and human-caused disasters.

Natural disasters are viewed as events that are caused by forces of nature, or acts of God (Rosenfeld et al., 2005). These include earthquakes, floods, hurricanes, tsunamis, fires, prolonged droughts, and winter storms. Pandemics are often included in the category of natural disasters. If a disaster is the result of natural causes, rather than human actions, then it is more difficult to assign blame or direct anger when it occurs (Halpern & Tramontin, 2007; Rosenfeld et al., 2005).

Human-caused disasters are those disasters that are attributable to human actions and behaviors, whether they are a result of neglect and incompetence (omission) or direct actions (commission) (Van den Eynde & Veno, 1999). Rosenfeld et al. (2005) use the terms "technological" and "complex" to distinguish between these kinds of disasters. Technological disasters include such events as oil and chemical spills, nuclear power plant meltdowns, transportation accidents, and contaminated food products. Although the disaster is unintentional, there is often a great deal of strong affect directed toward finding a source to blame for the inept actions that contributed to the disaster.

The category of complex disasters, as defined by Rosenfeld et al. (2005), refers to terrorism, community violence, armed conflict, and war. What is common to all of these examples is that malevolent human intention is both the cause of the disaster and its consequences. Often the perpetrators of the events believe they are acting for the good of a group, in reaction to an untenable sociopolitical situation and in response to provocations or to exact respect or revenge. However, the targets of such actions are likely to have very intense reactions—fear, panic, rage, hatred—which often lead to cycles of retaliation and revenge. Halpern and Tramontin (2007) note that such disasters often occur without warning and that the scale of the disaster is often large, with loss of life and carnage. The events cause fear and uncertainty, which is what the perpetrators intended, as it is not clear when these events will end (suicide bombings) or who or what will be targeted next (commercial airplanes). People living in combat areas must function knowing there are people who want to hurt or kill them.

Sometimes complex disasters are caused by weapons of mass destruction. There are various types of disasters that fall within this category, including nuclear weapons as well as exposure to radioactivity and biological and chemical agents (Pastel & Ritchie, 2006). Just the *threat* of using weapons of mass destruction can sow the seeds of panic, stress, and even trauma.

Armed conflict, another subcategory of complex disasters, has some unique features. The conflict can last for many years, such as the twenty-year-old civil war in Uganda. It can also ebb and flow, and there can be ceasefires and then resumption of hostilities. Armed conflict often results in large numbers of civilian casualties and massive displacements, with entire communities and even tribes needing to be resettled into internally displaced persons (IDP) camps. Often the camps are not safe and residents may face threats from the side that attacked them as well as from the forces sent to protect them. For example, many Acholi people of northern Uganda, living in refugee camps as a result of attacks from the Lord's Resistance Army (LRA), were threatened by further attacks from the LRA. At the same time, they were brutalized, and women were raped by the government forces—usually soldiers from a different tribe—who were sent to protect them. Globally, children are increasingly being conscripted by armed forces, and women are always at risk for sexual assault and other forms of physical and psychological humiliation. Armed conflict can also lead to ethnic cleansing and genocide, the most extreme forms of complex disaster.

Another way of conceptualizing disasters is by time. Some disasters are acute while others are recurring or long term. On the surface, a natural disaster usually has a clear and sudden onset—a hurricane making landfall or the moment of impact of an earthquake. Certain disasters, such as mud slides, floods, typhoons, or brush fires in residential areas, occur at certain times of the year or under certain conditions (heavy rain, drought), often year after year, creating a cycle of disaster. An armed conflict or civil war frequently lasts for many years. It can be difficult to ascertain exactly when the conflict becomes a disaster, as there may have been raids or isolated attacks before the struggle approaches the level of full-scale armed conflict.

Quarantelli (2006) argues that it is important to make the distinction between everyday emergencies, disaster, and catastrophe. While everyday emergencies involve accidents or unplanned-for events, he reasons that disasters are on a larger scale, affecting more people and a greater diversity of groups. With a catastrophe, the scale is such that there is an overwhelming impact: infrastructure is destroyed, capacity and social capital are diminished, everyday routines grind to a halt, local leaders and responders cannot meet the challenges, and even nearby communities cannot adequately

respond to the scale of need. As mentioned earlier, the psychosocial consequences of all three of Quarantelli's levels of calamity bear enough similarity to one another, as well as to the types of responses called for by those
who help, that I have included all three within the framework of disaster for
the purposes of this book.

THE CONTINGENCIES OF DISASTER CATEGORIES

Presumably, a reason for trying to categorize disasters is to be able to anticipate common consequences, dynamics, and reactions that are linked
to a given category. It also gives professionals a sense of conceptual clarity and can offer parameters for conducting research (Van den Eynde &
Veno, 1999). One of the biggest distinctions made is that when disasters are
human caused, whether by omission or commission, there is accompanying
anger, a sense that the disaster could have been prevented, and the feeling
that someone is responsible and/or culpable, while with natural disasters
people may feel there is less blame or liability. Shultz, Espinel, Galea, &
Reissman (2007) find, in their review of research, that intentional and technological disasters lead to more serious psychological consequences than
natural disasters. Terrorism leaves people feeling deliberately targeted and
undermines their sense of safety and security. A millennial flood may shake
the security of those affected by it, but they know that other people are not
trying to hurt them. However, even those who have used these categories
as conceptual guidelines for scholarship raise many issues of consideration,
particularly when using a social ecology framework.

Rosenfeld et al. (2005) note that with natural disasters, poor people and
those with fewer resources usually suffer greater losses and damage, a point
made by other disaster scholars (Ager, 1997; Farwell & Cole, 2002; Halpern & Tramontin, 2007; Kaniasty & Norris, 1999; Kleinman & Cohen, 1997;
Park & Miller, 2006, 2007; Reyes & Elhai, 2004; Shultz et al., 2007; Strang &
Ager, 2003; Van den Eynde & Veno, 1999). Rosenfeld et al. (2005) identify
a number of reasons for this: inadequate and poorly constructed housing,
preexisting vulnerabilities because of poor health and nutrition, isolated living, political instability leading to disrupted response efforts, urbanization
and overcrowding, and the lack of an adequate safety net. Park and Miller
add that social targeting, because of racism or by virtue of gender discrimination, places certain populations at greater risk for negative consequences

before, during, and after the disaster. And there are vast differentials in resources to help people recover from natural disasters.

A number of writers question how "natural" a natural disaster is (Halpern & Tramontin, 2007; Park & Miller, 2006; Van den Eynde & Veno, 1999). Where people live and what they are living in is not "natural," and yet this increases risks for negative consequences from natural phenomena (Park & Miller, 2006). When an earthquake strikes, the collapse of certain buildings is a result of not only the force of the earthquake but the quality of the structures (Halpern & Tramontin, 2007). Despite tight government control over the discourse surrounding the Wenchuan earthquake in Sichuan Province, China, in 2008, many Chinese families and intellectuals are questioning whether the high mortality rate for children was linked to the faulty construction of schools (Barboza, 2009). When there is a natural event accompanied by human error or inaction—such as the Vaiont Dam disaster in the Italian Alps in 1963, where a dam was built in an unstable area and after repeated landslides eventually burst, killing more than twenty-five hundred people (Van den Eynde & Veno, 1999)—it raises the question: Was this a natural disaster or a technological one?

The Tohoku earthquake in Japan in 2011 illustrates the complexities of categorization. The earthquake that struck near Sendai, north of Tokyo, caused a massive tsunami that killed at least 13,000 people, with the numbers expected to rise (Osawa, Dvorak, Wakabayashi, & Sekiguchi, 2011). The tsunami disrupted the cooling systems at the Fukushima Daiichi nuclear power plant, about 150 miles north of Tokyo, leading to fuel meltdowns in three reactors (Tabuchi, 2011, May 24) and posing a radiation risk to nearby residents, the scale of which remains to be determined. This "natural" disaster spawned a secondary disaster that killed many people and in turn led to a technological disaster. At one point, three hundred thousand people were displaced by the cascading disasters (Fujimura & Nishisawa, 2011). All of this created an economic disaster, as Japan was thrown into recession (Tabuchi & Wassener, 2011). A growing social mistrust was further fueled by poor communication and misinformation on the part of the government as well as the owners of the nuclear power plant about the extent of the nuclear meltdown and the long-term risks posed to children and families (Tabuchi, 2011, May 25).

Another example is pandemics, often viewed as natural disasters. Overcrowding and poor sanitation and social practices (such as unprotected sex) can contribute to epidemics. While heat waves have historically resulted in the deaths of many elderly people, when this occurred in the Chicago heat wave of 1995, critical factors were, in addition to a lack of access to air-conditioning, the kinds of dwellings in which people lived as well as their social practices, which left many isolated elderly people spending a lot of time inside poorly ventilated buildings (Klinenberg, 2003). Different social conditions—such as greater congregating outdoors—might have led to fewer deaths.

There is always a sociohistorical context that is part of any disaster, including a natural disaster, which contributes to the social ecology of the event. Hurricane Katrina had a huge impact on the entire city of New Orleans when it struck in 2006, and the city's location by a major river at one of the lowest elevation points in Louisiana (and the United States) placed it at particular risk (Masozera, Bailey, & Kerchner, 2007)—this in itself is a major human factor interacting with a natural event. However, the storm disproportionately affected poor people and people of color for a variety of reasons. The location of housing was one source of vulnerability, and the Lower Ninth Ward, which was predominantly an African American neighborhood, was hit especially hard: it was located near levees that broke, sustaining extensive damage from the massive flooding (Green, Bates, & Smyth, 2007). There were other vulnerabilities for neighborhoods such as the Ninth Ward, including the quality of housing stock, which was less resilient in the face of the storm (Masozera et al., 2007). Also, New Orleans is one of the nation's poorest cities, with some of the worst social and economic inequality among races (Masozera et al., 2007). All these factors contributed to the social ecology of this disaster.

As some have argued (Dreier, 2006; Frymer et al., 2005; Park & Miller, 2006), these racial disparities have a long history, going back to the era of slavery, the Civil War, and the failure of Reconstruction in the South. The pattern of segregation and economic inequality has its roots in racism and the structural inequalities that are its legacy and are still in place. The pattern is also part of racialized social discourses, law enforcement biases, and differential access to resources such as education, transportation, and health care. This meant that not only were African Americans, other people of color, and other low income people more vulnerable when the storm broke, they were severely impeded in their ability to evacuate and achieve safety during the storm (Masozera et al., 2007). Also, African Americans were stigmatized: they were portrayed negatively in the local and national media, which made them more vulnerable to hostile and compassionless treatment. This stigmatization impeded rescue efforts and African Americans' own ability to have agency in their response and recovery (Lee, 2006; Sommers et al., 2006). And since the storm, their ability to rebuild has been severely impeded by many factors. There has been less access to neighborhoods such as the Ninth Ward and greater resistance to allowing people to rebuild, amplified by media discourses mistakenly describing the neighborhoods as "unsalvageable" (Green et al., 2007). Even public housing projects that were not severely damaged by the storm were slated for demolition, perhaps an example of "disaster capitalism": the use of disasters to further political agendas (Klein, 2007) or taking advantage of the disaster to "ethnically cleanse" the city of poor African Americans (Davis, 2005). When considering the social ecology of New Orleans, it is very difficult to conceptualize the disaster of Hurricane Katrina as strictly a natural disaster.

One reason given for distinguishing between different types of disasters is that people may respond differently to natural disasters than to human-caused disasters, particularly because of the sense of culpability that comes with technological and complex disasters (Halpern & Tramontin, 2007; Rosenfeld et al., 2005). And yet this argument betrays some cultural assumptions. For instance, in cultures where worldviews are heavily saturated with the notion of karma, this distinction might not be helpful or useful. Karma, in many Eastern religions, is the belief that what happens to a person, good or bad, is the result of earlier acts and deeds (and their consequences), even actions taken in previous lifetimes (Fleischman, 1999; Ross, 1966). Thus, whether a disaster is considered natural or human caused, it may be interpreted as the consequences of bad karma. Therefore, the sense of causality and the impact of the meaning of this for psychosocial recovery is independent of whether the disaster is considered natural or human caused.

NONDISASTERS?

Considering what *is* a disaster and the different ways of categorizing disasters raises the question of what is *not* a disaster. Uneventful everyday living, following routines, living in a community that is functioning—this is clearly not a disaster. Referring back to the definition of disaster, if I slip on the ice as I walk to work and twist or break my ankle, this is not a disaster because this event has no public dimension.

But what about chronic racism or endemic poverty afflicting a community—is this a disaster? Chronic racism can lead to people living in socially isolated, segregated communities, where there is a loss of jobs, poorly funded schools, and deteriorating housing stock that is declining in value. Because of racism, the police may be excessively brutal or, conversely, callously disengaged. This in turn can open the way for an increase in gang activity with attendant violence and perhaps illegal drug sales. As a result of the violence, there may be an increase in injury and death. As a consequence of drug use, there can be overdoses and unprotected sex, which leads to a spike in HIV rates. If there is poor access to health care, infant mortality rates may increase.

Over time, the casualties of poverty and racism resemble the victims of disaster: higher death and infant mortality rates, isolated neighborhoods, and a fragmentation of community cohesion. Psychologically and emotionally there are also similarities. People may experience a sense of despair and hopelessness. There can be self-blame or feelings of guilt, anger, or rage. If there has been gang violence or police brutality, residents may feel unsafe going outdoors and be hypervigilant, easily startled, emotionally wound up, and on edge.

What differentiates the consequences of severe, persistent racism from a disaster? Some argue that this *is* a disaster (Miller & Garran, 2007). It is a social disaster (C. Robertson, personal communication, August 2009). But in the field of disaster mental health, this is not considered a typical disaster scenario. It is sometimes mentioned as background or context when a disaster occurs, but it is not a disaster in its own right. This perhaps is a function of the chronic nature of the situation. However, armed conflicts, which are often viewed as disasters, can be chronic situations. And in the hypothetical situation described above, the neighborhood may have at one time been thriving or at least stable, with a reasonable degree of social cohesion. The neighborhood's decline probably was not sudden or triggered by a critical event but happened gradually.

There is no clear-cut distinction between disasters and other social phenomena that cause widespread suffering and pain. Every definition of disaster has its limitations, as certain events are excluded from the frame of disaster. Categories used to distinguish between different types of disasters lack precise conceptual clarity and are subject to theoretical questions and challenges. What we can do, at best, is roughly frame the contours of disaster, recognizing that because of the contingent, subjective, socially constructed nature of the concept, it is more helpful to consider the unique social ecology of each situation and to approach each one with a certain degree of flexibility, considering relative factors and dimensions rather than absolute airtight boundaries. The next section considers what some of the important dimensions are.

DIMENSIONS OF DISASTERS

The social ecology of disaster includes many interacting variables—social capital and cohesiveness, power dynamics, economic factors, historical legacies, and political realities. All should be mapped out for the sake of their unique and specific attributes. Doing so helps responders understand who needs help, what assets and liabilities exist in the community, what barriers there are to recovery and change, what cultural traditions exist to draw on, and what available pathways there are on which to move forward. More specifically, there are certain dimensions of disasters that trace the contours and form the parameters of a particular event or series of events, which can be helpful for responders to consider: scale, duration, causal factors, consequences and cascading effects, circles of vulnerability, community complexities, resources available for recovery, and the rescue, response, and recovery efforts.

SCALE

As has been previously mentioned, the scale of a disaster varies considerably depending on the event. Smaller-scale disasters are more localized and affect fewer people. Some examples of these are severe car accidents, suicides and homicides, accidental deaths of children, snowmobiling accidents, apartment fires, and bank and store robberies. Although small in scale, such disasters can have a deep and penetrating impact on individuals, groups, organizations, and an entire community. When a school bus accident results in the accidental death of a child, the family grieves and mourns. But there is also a profound impact on the school bus driver and the driver's colleagues, in addition to friends of the child and students who knew the child. Also impacted are teachers and administrators who worked with the child and the firefighters and police who responded at the scene. In a small community, such an event may also lead to collective grief and mourning.

Examples of more midsized disasters are small-city train derailings involving toxic cargo, river floods that prompt evacuations and cause damage to residential areas, and clashes between rival gangs that leave a number of people seriously wounded or dead. Large-scale disasters include many already discussed events—hurricanes, earthquakes, and mass shootings and acts of terrorism. Armed conflicts, wars, and other disasters requiring a humanitarian response, such as prolonged drought, ethnic cleansing, and genocide, are among the most far-reaching of disasters.

The scale of a disaster will indicate how many people have been affected and the resources needed to respond. A large-scale disaster can devastate an entire community, region, or nation. Large-scale disasters tend to overwhelm governmental and civic organizations and structures and have the capacity for tearing apart social fabrics and inhibiting cultural practices. Thus, there are often fewer available resources for recovery and there is a collective sense of hopelessness and despair in addition to the suffering of many individuals and families. Conversely, huge disasters can attract regional, national, and even international compassion, aid, and assistance.

DURATION

Despite efforts to conceptualize disaster as having a clear beginning and ending, the start and end points are anything but clear. Certain events or moments, such as when a hurricane makes landfall, stand out as significant, critical incidents, punctuating the life course of a disaster, but they are often part of a process that has many antecedents and rippling consequences. What is striking about disasters is not only that they have long-lasting consequences, but once the event has occurred, people revisit and rethink what led up to it. The familiar "would have, could have, should have" thinking is a normal cognitive process that seeks to make meaning of what led up to a disaster and also apportions (often unfairly) blame and responsibility. Moreover, it serves as a way of coping with the disaster as people and collectivities try to make sense of what happened in order to take steps to avoid future reoccurrences.

Having said this, there are certainly differences in the duration of different disasters. It is not so much that a given event, or series of events, occurs, but that awareness and attention are drawn to an event, constructing meaning from it. It is part of the narrative process for people to fashion a beginning and end. So there are at least two dimensions when considering the duration of disaster—the facts on the ground and the stories that people tell themselves and others to explain what has happened. Some disasters are clearer cut than others, with more obvious points of acceleration and deceleration. This can facilitate the narrative process of loss, grieving and mourning, and healing and recovery. Disasters that tend to drag on, or seem to have no end point, often lead to prolonged feelings of depression, helplessness, and hopelessness and a sense of chronic disaster fatigue. For those intervening, a chronic, long-lasting disaster can present more logistical and psychosocial challenges than a shorter, more defined disaster. Conversely, over time, people and communities can adjust and adapt to long-standing disasters, developing coping skills and forming ad hoc social networks and support systems. One of the consequences of surviving long-lasting disasters, particularly if they involve prolonged resettlement, is that the interim solutions have repercussions for recovery, such as resistance to yet more change and upheaval, even when this is presented as "returning to normal life." An example of this is opposition to the destruction of an internally displaced housing community formed in response to an earthquake or armed conflict. Temporary societies, cultures, and routines can be difficult to give up when it means experiencing more change, even when it is beneficial to have more long-term resolution.

CAUSAL FACTORS

The difficulty in clearly distinguishing between natural and human caused disasters has been discussed. What is more helpful than using an absolute typology is to consider what has led to the disaster. Again, there are two dimensions to this: the interaction of concrete variables and forces that contribute to a disaster as well as how people perceive causality. The importance of understanding the first set of factors—the interaction of geophysical forces with the social ecology and precipitating events and actions—is manifold. It aids planning for the prevention of other disasters. Understanding the social ecology makes it possible to map out vulnerable populations, key groups and players in disaster recovery. This reminds responders not to ignore certain people while overhelping others. Recognizing the contributions of social factors, such as racism and poverty, or, say, a complex immigration history for an affected group, can alert responders to social patterns, cultural styles, and prior and current grievances that interact with the disaster's impact.

Perceptions of causality have a profound influence on the experience of disaster, its meaning, and efforts to help people recover. The public narrative about the causes of a disaster influences how victims are perceived (worthiness of help) and how governmental and NGO entities respond. For example, declaring a situation a "natural disaster" can lead to certain types of state and local aid and involve different players than a disaster deemed to be a chronic situation (homicides in a high-crime neighborhood) or one that is constructed as resulting from "terrorism," which might activate a strong law enforcement and military response. The social constructions of causality framed by individuals, families, and groups influence how guilty or responsible people feel and how overwhelmed they are, and they affect other reactions, such as anger, depression, resignation, equanimity, and hope. Religious, philosophical, and cultural beliefs shape how affected people construct causality and lead to conclusions about the meaning of the disaster, individual and public responsibility, and implications for how to respond.

CONSEQUENCES AND CASCADING EFFECTS

What are the consequences of a disaster? How much damage has been done, how much property lost? How many people have died? These are important questions to consider when responding to a disaster. The common wisdom is that the more catastrophic the event—with the greater loss of life and deeper extent of damage—the greater the impact and potential for overwhelming stress and trauma (Halpern & Tramontin, 2007; Rosenfeld et al., 2005; Shultz et al., 2007). The scale of the destruction is in itself distressing. This is heightened when there are large numbers of casualties, particularly children (which is further considered in the next chapter, about the reactions people have to disasters).

While there is a great deal of truth in the belief that the greater the scale and nature of disaster casualties, the more negative the consequences, there are also caveats. Large-scale destruction and loss can lead to psychic numbing, which, although detrimental in the long run, can help people survive in the short term. Large-scale casualties can also unite survivors through their common bonds of suffering and grieving. And such consequences can put smaller losses in greater perspective and, at times, help people reevaluate their values and priorities in a meaningful way.

But it is not only the scale of a disaster that influences its consequences. The social ecology of disaster implies an interaction between an event, or series of events, with a sociopolitical-ecological set of environmental factors. Thus, the consequences, during and after the disaster, are heavily influenced by the social ecology of the disaster. One consequence of disaster can be cascading effects—an interaction of the various aspects of the social ecology that magnify and amplify the consequences of a disaster.

Little Saigon, the Vietnamese neighborhood in Biloxi I describe in the preface, offers an illustration of cascading effects. Park, Miller, and Van (2010) conducted ethnographic and phenomenological research with residents of the neighborhood in 2008 to understand the impact of Hurricane Katrina on individuals, families, and the overall community. The neighborhood had been a font of community resources and support for an immigrant population that had endured an arduous migration to the United States, often by boat and via long stays in refugee camps. Many residents did not speak English and were employed in the shrimp fishing and processing industries. Some worked for nearby casinos. The neighborhood was an ethnic enclave with businesses, stores, and restaurants run by Vietnamese residents and primarily serving this neighborhood. When the storm hit, many residents lost their homes, businesses, and fishing boats. They had to evacuate to locations all over the United States. This left many people feeling isolated and without their family, social, and community supports, a source of great pain and sorrow. For another group, less reliant on the resources of an ethnic enclave, this temporary diaspora might have been less distressing.

Upon returning to Little Saigon, months after the storm, residents faced daunting challenges. Many were renters or owners without flood insurance, so losses were extensive and rebuilding a costly enterprise. Stores and businesses no longer existed. Many housing lots remained empty. FEMA trailers were distributed by lottery and not all received them. Some who did receive trailers were rehoused outside of the neighborhood. Nearly two years after Hurricane Katrina, only about half of the original population from the neighborhood had returned.

Shrimp processing industries were destroyed. Because of a cluster of global factors, the cost of fuel oil rose while the price of shrimp dropped, leaving those who had repaired or intact boats little economic incentive to fish. Soon, casinos became one of the few sources for jobs. The ability or inability to speak English influenced the kinds of casino jobs that were available, with English speakers able to work as hostesses or dealers and non–English speakers relegated to maintenance, food production, and janitorial positions.

The disaster opened up an opportunity for the nearby casinos, which until this time had been confined to operating offshore, to move inland as regulations and ordinances were changed. With Little Saigon being located near the casinos, the land, which had been primarily residential, became valuable to the casinos for expansion and redevelopment. The value of property went up, offering incentives for landowners who had lost houses and belongings to sell to casinos. With fewer rental units and the higher value of land, rents went up.

In summary, there were tremendous losses of homes and property. There was the devastation of the shrimp fishing industry, the decimation of a neighborhood, and the encroachment by casinos. It is unclear whether this neighborhood will regain its viability and vibrancy as an ethnic enclave or instead become a condoized theme park for casino customers. For many residents, this is a source of loss, pain, and sorrow, and there is fear that without the neighborhood's capacity to offer resources and social buffering, their ability to achieve economic and social well-being in the larger society is also uncertain.

Park et al. (2010) find that there were differences in psychological reactions and that some who had harrowing experiences during the storm, such as almost drowning, exhibited signs of acute stress disorder or possibly even post-traumatic stress disorder. Others found the hurricane to be "no big deal" in comparison to their prior experiences of war and migration. But if the focus of the impact of the storm is only on the psychological reactions of individual survivors without taking into account the social ecology and collective impact of the disaster, then the consequences are viewed in narrow, individualized terms, which is only part of the picture. Thus, the consequences of a disaster should be evaluated socially and collectively to gain a more complete sense of its meaning for those directly affected by it.

CIRCLES OF VULNERABILITY

Rosenfeld et al. (2005) describe circles of vulnerability that radiate out from a disaster. This is a helpful metaphor and the authors use it to describe physical vulnerability as well as psychological and social vulnerability. The basic tenet is that the most vulnerable people, both physically and psychosocially, are those closest to the epicenter of the disaster. Rosenfeld et al. (2005) identify four groups radiating out from the center of the circle of physical vulnerability: (1) people who were directly exposed to the disaster; (2) witnesses or people who narrowly avoided the disaster; (3) people who could hear, smell, or feel the disaster but did not witness it; and (4) people who were outside of the disaster area but nevertheless were concerned about what happened. For psychological and social vulnerability, they describe three circles: (1) close family and friends of those who directly experienced the disaster, (2) those who knew disaster-affected people but were not close friends, and (3) those who identify with the disaster's victims. Rosenfeld et al. also discuss circles of risk and of support. The risk model has people who have experienced similar trauma in the past at the core, moving outward to those with current life challenges and crises, and then eventually to the far outer layers, where there are people who are acutely sensitive (children) but who did not directly experience the disaster or have preexisting personal vulnerabilities. The circles of support have family and close friends at the core, moving outward through those in the community who can be helpful to the outer layers of outside helpers moving in.

The circle metaphor usefully elucidates which groups of people are potentially vulnerable to disasters. The physical circle focuses on literal proximity to the event, which is certainly a very significant variable. The model also identifies the importance of prior vulnerabilities and attempts to map out sources of support. There is recognition that known local support systems are more central than the work of outside responders.

While these metaphors are very helpful, they are incomplete. Absent are cultural systems of meaning-making. Closeness to the event is rightfully stressed but the mediating meaning-making systems that shape how people socially construct the significance of the event are not highlighted. Prior exposure to traumatic incidents is certainly a vulnerability factor, but there are other factors as well. The model tends to use individuals and families as the unit of analysis. But the sociopolitical standing of a group can strongly influence how people who identify as members of that group experience a disaster. It is not only the internal vulnerabilities that individuals (and groups) bring to the disaster, it is also how the responses to the disaster reinforce social marginalization and inequities, as the examples given about Hurricane Katrina illustrate. Thus, circles of vulnerability need to also include vulnerability to social exclusion, exploitation, and outright oppression as further consequences of disaster. And such circles should not be universal circles—the specifics and dynamics of different disasters will vary, depending on the social ecology of the disaster. Therefore, the models of circles of vulnerability need to be separately and contingently drawn for each disaster.

Also, it is important to be aware of cultural and clinical assumptions made when mapping circles of vulnerability. While Rosenfeld et al. (2005) place prior exposure to trauma in the center of the circle of risk, there are exceptions to this. For example, the Vietnamese community in Biloxi had endured war, arduous and perilous sea crossings, years in refugee camps, and a painfully long diaspora before coalescing as a community in Biloxi, where they subsequently encountered Hurricane Katrina (Park et al., 2010). Many in this community reported that their travails *strengthened* them in their ability to withstand the impact of Katrina rather than making them more vulnerable.

The metaphor of circles of vulnerability is a useful tool for mapping the needs of disaster survivors, but for it to be realistic and nuanced, it should not be a universal, formulaic model but rather one that is incorporated into a social ecology framework in which the unique factors of a specific disaster interact with the psychosocial-cultural qualities of potentially affected groups.

COMMUNITY COMPLEXITY

Community complexity is both a subjective and a relative concept. I am using the term to mean how diverse, intricate, and socially variegated a given community is when struck by disaster. There are various ways in which a community is diverse and multifaceted. In some communities, there are high degrees of social stratification based on social class or because of racism or ethnic or religious prejudice. Some communities have an ethnically homogenous population while others are quite varied. The stability of population groups fluctuates, with some communities having large numbers of immigrants or refugees. The range of professions and occupations differs considerably between a traditional rural community and a densely populated urban area. The history of some communities has been relatively peaceful, with change occurring incrementally and over time, while other communities have been the site of ongoing conflict or have experienced seismic socioeconomic changes, such as industrialization or deindustrialization.

A given disaster interacts with the complexity of a community. One central aspect of this is how easy or difficult it is for the community to pull together in response to disaster. People help other people out of a sense of compassion. Compassion involves a certain degree of empathy and identification with the people being helped, which is easier to muster when there is greater community homogeneity. If there is tension, competition, or conflict among different community groups, then such tensions can be exacerbated by a disaster. If there are preexisting prejudices, these lessen compassion in the face of adversity. There were examples of this when African Americans were being turned away from white communities as they fled New Orleans after Hurricane Katrina, sometimes by the police, and also in the descriptions of them as "refugees" and "looters" in the media (Frymer et al., 2005; Sommers et al., 2006). When I responded as a Red Cross volunteer to mostly white rural communities in coastal Mississippi after Katrina, neighbors were checking in with and supporting one another with food, clothing, and even shelter. However, when I was stationed just outside of Biloxi (a more racially and ethnically diverse community), a white man in a truck pulled up with a load of clothes to donate, asking me to promise, as I mention in the preface, not to give them to "those Vietnamese, 'cause they'll just resell them to make some money—that's the way those people are." Thus, in more complex communities, there is greater potential for more complicated dynamics between groups as the community struggles to recover from a disaster. There are often perceptions of unequal or preferential treatment, which leads to resentment and even overt conflict.

Complex communities often have more resources to recover from disasters, particularly if there is socioeconomic diversity. There is likely to be a wider range of skills, assets, and social capital in the community. Yet when there is severe socioeconomic inequality between groups, there is less social trust (Wilkinson & Pickett, 2009).

As with all the dimensions of disaster, each community is unique, and the level of complexity is not always a predictor of how groups of people will respond. After 9/11, New York City, which is a very complex and diverse community, rallied in a very cohesive way. Responders, and even long-term residents, were struck by how friendly people were in public places, in contrast with the stereotype of New York as blasé and detached. There were many instances of people of different races and ethnicities interacting in a helpful and supportive way with one another. However, there are always exceptions, and those who were Arab, Muslim, or were socially constructed by others as looking Arab or Muslim were subject to harassment and even violence.

Turners Falls, Massachusetts, has a mostly white population living in a deindustrialized former mill town. It is a small, fairly homogenous community. When there was a fight between two teenagers, one white and the other black, resulting in the death of the white teenager, the community was devastated. It was also divided, as some families supported the victim and a smaller number the survivor of the fight. Although there were efforts to help the community heal and come together, this was challenging because of the nature of the incident and the different social meanings that people took away from what had happened. All of this was particularly trying for a small and ethnically homogenous community. Even when most of the community came together in its grieving and memorializing, some within the community felt left out and marginalized.

Thus, community complexity is always a factor that shapes how a community responds to a disaster, but how this interaction evolves depends on the particulars of the disaster and the unique social dynamics of the affected community.

RESOURCES AVAILABLE FOR RECOVERY

Resources available before a disaster beget resources for withstanding and recovering from disaster. As Kaniasty and Norris (1999, p. 35) put it: "Past resources influence the acquisition of future resources." The converse is also true. Masozera et al.'s (2007) review of the literature on the relationship between poverty and disasters found that the poor are more likely to die, suffer injuries, sustain higher material losses, have higher incidences of psychological trauma, and face greater hurdles in all phases of response, recovery, and reconstruction. In their study of Hurricane Katrina's disproportionate effects based on socioeconomic status, they found that "preexisting socioeconomic conditions play a significant role in the ability of particular economic classes to respond immediately to the disaster and to cope with the aftermath" (p. 299). Those with fewer resources are also aware of the contrast between themselves and others with greater assets (Kaniasty & Norris, 2007), which can impact both their sense of meaning and sense of fairness as they strive to recover. Social distance between classes exacerbates many negative outcomes for everyone—poorer health and mental health, higher rates of crime, and fewer social connections (Wilkinson & Pickett, 2009).

Resources available for recovery differ from household to household, between different ethnic and socioeconomic groups, and between communities, but the principle of "more means more" holds at all levels of analysis.

On the individual and family level, the ability to leave the Gulf Coast before the onset of Hurricane Katrina was heavily influenced by the possession of resources. These included having a car or access to a car as well as a place to go to. Theoretically, in a flood area, any fleeing family can find a shelter. However, those with second homes, available friends, or the money to pay for a hotel or motel are more likely to make the decision to leave. Another resource is the ability to speak English. Many evacuation warnings were not in languages such as Vietnamese. Therefore, many people in Biloxi's Little Saigon stayed in their homes, not understanding the gravity of the situation and how powerful Katrina was (Park et al., 2010).

The same pattern held true for Tamil families living in the northern and eastern Sri Lankan war zones. People with more money and resources were able to evacuate before heavy fighting occurred, while the vast majority of civilians living in the area lacked the means to relocate and were trapped in the heavy fighting between government troops and the LTTE.

During the phases of recovery, those with more resources are able to rebuild with much greater ease. Owning homes, with home insurance, serves as a hedge against losses, although many people with home insurance were unable to use it with Hurricane Katrina because their policies lacked flood insurance. Still, renters are more prone to losses that are not recoverable. If they lose their residences and properties during a storm, they are less able to receive compensation. If it is a large-scale disaster, such as a hurricane or major earthquake, there are losses of low-income housing stock, and rents rise when people try to return to the area, which is what Park et al. (2010) found in the Little Saigon neighborhood of Biloxi. People with greater resources have more rebuilding capital, personal savings, credit, and available money to expend on rebuilding (Green et al., 2007, p. 326). Another related factor is that people with resources have greater fluency and facility when navigating the complex labyrinths of bureaucracies available to help people rebuild after a disaster (Masozera et al., 2007).

On the group level, those with more social capital have tremendous advantages over those with less. Whether advantages are based on income, social status, or racial and cultural privileges, they will position certain groups to receive more aid and assistance than others. Homes and properties of higher value and in "safer" neighborhoods attract more loans at lower interest rates. Prejudice, whether overt or covert, leads to neglect and mistreatment of vulnerable groups when disaster strikes (Frymer et al., 2005; Sommers et al., 2006). The interaction of institutional racism (with barriers to access to resources) with inner biases and prejudices, often unconscious, leads to differential treatment of and responses to racial and ethnic groups of color in the United States (Henkel, Dovidio, & Gaertner, 2006; Miller & Garran, 2007; Park & Miller, 2007) and to ethnic minorities in other countries, such as the Tamils in Sri Lanka (Ferks & Klem, 2005; Miller, 2006b).

The resources of entire regions can result in a greater capacity to rebuild. Such resources involve political assets as well as economic capital. The contrast between the speed at which Mississippi was able to rebuild after Hurricane Katrina and the speed at which New Orleans recovered is a function of many complex factors. It may be significant that more than half of the population of New Orleans at the time of the storm was African American, while coastal Mississippi is predominantly white. Also, in Mississippi, there was greater cooperation among local, state, and federal officials and Republican governor and former GOP chairman Haley Barbour, who could exercise his political capital through access to a Republican president and lawmakers (Adams, 2007; "Mississippi's Failure," 2009). But even in Mississippi, the poor received less than their share of relief, as the Bush administration granted Governor Barbour a waiver, allowing him to withhold the usual mandatory 50 percent of Community Block Development funds for the poor, resulting in much more aid going to affluent communities and residents (Eaton, 2007). Four years later, the coastal communities of Mississippi had used the storm as an opportunity to move development projects forward, such as the expansion of casinos in Biloxi, and much of the aid had not found its way to poor people and people of color ("Mississippi's Failure," 2009).

Chapter 5 describes sources of individual and collective resiliency. It is important to note in this section, however, that resources to recover from disaster also include less tangible assets, such as prior experiences, wisdom gained from confronting adversity, and access to cultural traditions and practices that can serve as sources of support. Thus, any evaluation of the impact of a disaster should examine the tangible resources that advantage and disadvantage different individuals and communities as well as other sources of personal, social, and cultural capital that can help people rebuild and thrive.

RESCUE, RESPONSE, AND RECOVERY EFFORTS

When disasters occur, there is usually an organized, collective response by governments and NGOs to protect and assist people and to help them recover. There are two significant aspects to such efforts: (1) the concrete, material impact on the well-being of affected people, and (2) the social construction of the significance of the rescue and recovery effort and the different meanings it has for both affected and nonaffected people. The first facet is more observable and easier to measure. If people have lost homes, are they able to rebuild them? If there was a mass evacuation, have people been able to return to their homes? If schools closed down, have they been reopened? If many people are displaying the symptoms of acute stress and trauma, are these indicators abating over time? Have the government and NGOs offered assistance in a timely, respectful, and helpful manner?

The second factor is more subjective and open to interpretation. This involves perceptions about whether what is being done is responsive, useful, equitable, and just. These interpretations are constructed by individuals, but there are also collective representations and narratives that evaluate the disaster response. Examples of these include media reports, organizations engaged in reconstruction, and institutions in a community (churches) with moral and social capital. If individuals feel that as much is being done for them as is possible, that people and organizations really care about their well-being and are trying to help them to recover, this encourages feelings of strength, efficacy, and resiliency. When these sentiments find their way into a collective narrative, this reinforces a positive sense of identity and social solidarity. The converse is also true. In 2011, one year after the Haitian earthquake, much rubble remained on the streets of Port-au-Prince, hundreds of thousands of people still lived in tents and camps, cholera had broken out, and the domestic political process had broken down. The public perception by many Haitians was that little had been done to assist people in need. Haitian colleagues wrote to me describing a sense of pessimism and sadness.

The way a disaster is framed shapes the needs that are identified and the response that is called for (Echterling & Wylie, 1999). If people are socially constructed as victims, framed as individuals experiencing trauma, then the response will be counseling and therapy. Every well-intentioned intervention has the potential for unintended consequences (Kaniasty & Norris, 1999), and when responders conclude that many people in a community require counseling, this can undermine a collective sense of self-efficacy (Echterling & Wylie, 1999). People not only appraise how they are doing from their own sources of self-evaluation but are buoyed by collective narratives of empowerment or deflated by being assigned the social role of victim. Media discourses amplify feelings of hope or hopelessness depending on what is emphasized, whose stories are told, and how they are related.

An important component of the disaster response is leadership. Leadership occurs at many levels. Some is emergent as the disaster unfolds and the community is faced with a collective crisis, while other leadership falls to people with ascribed roles and responsibilities. President Ronald Reagan was perceived as helping a nation grieve and mourn the tragedy of the crash of the *Challenger* space shuttle (Zinner, 1999), an event that had symbolic meaning on a national level as well as local resonance for communities and organizations directly connected with the victims. I have worked with police and fire chiefs after local disasters who have been able to reassure the public, convey empathy, and project a willingness to listen and be responsive to public concerns.

In contrast, after 9/11, many in the United States felt proud to be Americans and initially viewed the government, particularly President George W. Bush, as offering positive leadership, which increased their confidence and shored up a shaken sense of security. But after the invasion of Iraq, the fighting of two foreign wars, revelations about domestic spying, and the possible use of torture, public opinion about the government response became more mixed. When the same administration's response to Hurricane Katrina was widely perceived as inept, unfair, and uncaring, confidence in the president's leadership waned and faith in the government plummeted.

Effective leadership realistically and transparently acknowledges the extent of losses while also offering a vision of hope. Effective leaders offer an empathic grasp of suffering while providing reassurance. They are able to bring other organizations and people to work effectively together. They are able to craft an inclusive vision of recovery, one that recognizes divisions and inequalities in the community while encouraging people to work collaboratively and collectively to recover, without leaving any behind.

In this chapter, I review the traditional ways in which disasters are classified and categorized and raise questions about the validity of these classifications as constructs to guide psychosocial responses. As an alternative, I suggest a number of dimensions of disaster that can be considered when attempting to assess needs and map out responses: scale, duration, causal factors, consequences and cascading effects, circles of vulnerability, complexity of the community, resources available for recovery, and rescue, response, and recovery efforts.

Clinicians responding to disaster, public health officials planning for it, and social scientists and other researchers trying to evaluate the impact of disaster or the effectiveness of postdisaster interventions all seek order, predictability, and meaningful categories to organize thinking and data collection. When the field of disaster mental health is more "scientific," then it is easier to plan, train, respond, and evaluate. It also guides government and nongovernmental funding sources in deciding what should be supported and invested in. With scientific order, there is a greater chance that best practices will be used, that harmful practices will be discouraged, and that codes of ethics for practitioners and researchers will be improved and enforced. These are admirable goals and worth striving for.

Yet disaster is the apotheosis of disorder. Although some disasters are predictable, such as hurricanes, according to season and path of a given storm, the impact and consequences will almost always produce unanticipated effects and surprises. The varieties of cultural worldviews and the vicissitudes of experience are healthy reminders that when helping people with their psychosocial needs, scientifically guided interventions must be combined with the art of responding to emergent and unpredictable reactions and the often chaotic processes that are part of collective planning, decision making, and acting. If an empowerment philosophy guides response efforts, local people need to be given an essential role in the recovery process, which means less control for central planners and outside interveners.

These are not only healthy tensions but unavoidable ones. Thus, the parameters for understanding disasters presented in this chapter are but contingent and often subjective ways of understanding what affected people and those trying to help them are grappling with. In the next chapter, I consider the kinds of reactions that disasters can cause, continuing to link the individual with the collectivity.

MINDFULNESS EXERCISE: BODY SCAN

This chapter delved into the dimensions and contours of disasters. Reading about this involves imagining destructive and catastrophic events, such as hurricanes, tsunamis, armed conflict, and terrorist acts. Whether we are directly experiencing a disaster, responding to one, or reading about it, our body can, often unconsciously, hold the stress and tension that results as we conjure images of destruction. The following exercise is a body scan adapted from Jon Kabat-Zinn (1990).

This can be done either sitting or lying down. It helps to be in a place where there are minimal distractions from noise or interruptions. It can be done alone or in a group. It can help to reestablish contact with the body, enhance awareness of places holding strain, and facilitate the release of tension. The scan can be done slowly, for thirty minutes or more, although it is still useful to do an abbreviated body scan of, say, five minutes.

- Close your eyes.
- Focus on contact points—where your body is touching the floor or a chair, and notice this boundary between you and what is outside of you.
- Feel the envelope of your body as a whole entity.
- Start by focusing on the toes of one foot and direct your breath to that area.
- Feel any and all sensations of that toe. If you do not feel anything, notice that as well.
- Try to channel your breathing to that area.
- Slowly move your attention up one leg to your pelvis, directing your breath in and out of each region you are focusing on.
- Do the same thing with the other leg.
- Continue moving your attention up through your torso, covering the lower back, abdomen, upper back, chest, and shoulders, directing your breath to those areas as you scan. If you have time, try to do this systematically.
- Then go to the fingers of both hands and focus simultaneously up both arms, ending with the shoulders.
- Move your attention through the neck, throat, all regions of the face, the back of the head, and the top of the head.
- When completing the exercise, engage your body slowly, possibly by moving your hands and feet a bit.

- If you are lying down, be careful about standing up too quickly.
- If time is short, rather than systematically scanning your entire body, notice where there are places of tension, tightness, or pain. After noticing where these areas are, direct your breath to these areas and linger for a few breaths before moving to another area.

4

THE PHENOMENOLOGY OF DISASTERS
THE IMPACT ON INDIVIDUALS, FAMILIES, AND COMMUNITIES

WE HAVE CONSIDERED the role of the helping professional in response to disaster and how we can conceptualize disaster; this chapter examines its impact, focusing on the psychosocial effects. This exploration involves reviewing research that classifies reactions, such as stress reaction or post-traumatic stress disorder (PTSD)—in a sense, reviewing the epidemiology of different bio-psycho-social responses. However, as should be clear by now, the presumption of universal reactions should not be taken for granted, and I interrogate the social and cultural filters that mediate experiences of disasters. Also, it is crucial to consider the subjective/phenomenological experiences of people in response to disasters and the meaning they make of these experiences.

Meaning is constructed by individuals, families, social and cultural groups, communities, and societies. Meaning-making occurs at these multiple levels when disaster strikes. The understandings that individuals take away from a disaster contribute to collective stories and narratives of disaster, and, conversely, collective narratives shape, liberate, and constrain the sense that individuals make of an event. So, although I discuss individual, family, and community responses to disasters in separate sections in this chapter, in reality the different levels of reactions, all of which include knowledge construction and meaning-making, are intricately related to one another and should not be treated separately. They are part of the same circle of the social ecology of disaster, and the strategies for responding to disaster, covered in chapters 6 through 12, link them together.

THE IMPACT OF DISASTER ON INDIVIDUALS

A mantra when working with people exposed to disaster is "these are normal reactions to abnormal events." Implicit in this statement, however, is that the "normal" reactions are not experienced as normal by the affected person. On the contrary, most people recovering from disasters feel as if their world has been dramatically altered and that they are having strange, unpleasant, and often overwhelming responses. It is also difficult to generalize what reactions people will have because they vary considerably. Some of this variation is a result of differences in vulnerability, resiliency, social support, and how the disaster fits or does not fit with prior experiences. Differential reactions can reflect disparate cultural frameworks for constructing the meaning of the disaster and relating this to what has happened in the past as well as to what is envisioned for the future. Also, a given individual often goes through different phases of reactions to the disaster—such as moving from a sense of numbness and unreality to increasingly intrusive and recurring images stemming from the disaster. Another question, explored in the next section, is when are a person's responses considered "normal" as opposed to debilitating, destructive, and possibly pathological? Related to this question is what is needed for a person to heal and recover? This is explored more fully in subsequent chapters.

This section reviews clusters of reactions that researchers and practitioners have often found in response to disasters. The following section considers more extreme reactions and diagnostic and treatment issues, particularly the distinctions between stress, traumatic stress, and PTSD. After considering how disasters affect families, this chapter covers the important area of grief and bereavement. While this chapter explores negative consequences of disasters, the next chapter focuses on sources of strength and resiliency.

There are various ways to group or organize common reactions to disasters. Rosenfeld et al. (2005) have a model that they call the BASIC Ph model. This paradigm groups reactions into six categories—beliefs and values, affect, social behaviors, imagination, cognitive, and physiological. Halpern and Tramontin (2007) organize reactions into four categories— physical/bodily, behavioral, emotional, and cognitive. However they are ordered, the reactions described in the different categories tend to cover the same ground. Yassen (1995) uses six areas of categorization to describe the consequences of disaster for those responding to primary victims—physical, cognitive, emotional, behavioral, spiritual, and interpersonal. I have found

---

BOX 4.1

COMMON STRESS REACTIONS IN RESPONSE TO DISASTER

Physical—shock, sweating, somatic reactions, impaired immune system, palpitations, jumpiness, fatigue, decreased sexual drive
Cognitive—distraction, confusion, disorientation, meaninglessness, self-doubt, rumination, obsessive thinking
Emotional—anxiety, guilt, fear, numbness, sadness, anger, hostility, vulnerability, helplessness, feeling overwhelmed, feeling depleted
Behavioral—irritability, hypervigilance, sleep disturbances, nightmares, appetite changes, drug use, self-harming behaviors
Spiritual—questioning life's purpose and meaning, questioning religious beliefs
Interpersonal—withdrawal, isolation, decreased intimacy, intolerance, increased dependency, domination

ADAPTED FROM YASSEN, 1995.

---

that these categories also work well for recognizing disaster consequences for those within the inner circles of exposure and vulnerability. Moreover, I have found them to be useful, helpful, and meaningful during psychoeducational discussions with a range of people who have encountered disasters. Thus, I describe Yassen's framework and add to her list findings from other researchers and practitioners. Stress and trauma syndromes are considered separately, in the next section.

I have organized Yassen's schema in box 4.1. In this formulation, again, there are six major areas of impact on an individual in the immediate aftermath of a disaster: physical, cognitive, emotional, behavioral, spiritual, and interpersonal. This reflects a Western orientation, as there are many cultures where these divisions are not normative. For example, in some cultures, there is no division between physical and emotional stress (Kirmayer, 1996). With that caveat in mind, I describe the typical reactions within these socially constructed categories.

PHYSICAL IMPACT

A disaster poses a physical threat to a person's well-being and can cause injury and even death. The physical events of a disaster can include explosions, landslides, collapsing buildings, colliding vehicles, and rising water levels. Surviving a disaster often involves having faced the threat of death and severe harm. When confronted by such threats, there are physiological reactions that seem to be intrinsic to all human beings—such as the activation of the autonomic nervous system that leads to the fight-or-flight response (Halpern & Tramontin, 2007; Rothschild, 2006)—although the specific ways that such deep neurological responses are manifested differ considerably from person to person and across cultures. Facing such threats is physically stressful and depleting.

During the actual encounter with the disaster, the sympathetic nervous system, which is the body's alarm mechanism, is activated, increasing blood flow to muscles and vital organs, mobilizing energy, but at the same time minimizing the influence of the prefrontal cortex, where conscious rational thought occurs (Smith, Katz, Charney, & Southwick, 2007). There is an increased heart rate and rapid breathing (Halpern & Tramontin, 2007). Also, this results in endocrinological changes, including the release of cortisol, which replenishes energy but also leads to hyperarousal and hypervigilance (Smith et al., 2007). Too much cortisol over a period of time can raise hypertension and lower immunity. Moreover, cortisol depletion is associated with PTSD; thus irregular cortisol levels, whether high or low, can be associated with distress (Miller, Kulkarni, & Kushner, 2006; Smith et al., 2007). High levels of adrenaline, which is also released when a person feels threatened, can lead to digestive problems and excessive fear and anxiety. Ultimately, fatigue and exhaustion can set in as neurotransmitters are depleted (Halpern & Tramontin, 2007). Children and adolescents are even more vulnerable to this process of arousal and depletion, as their bodies are still developing. Also, they have less experience against which to measure the event and fewer words and concepts to help them comprehend what they are experiencing.

Other physical reactions to disaster include headaches, sweating, and decreased sexual libido (Yassen, 1995). Muscle tension and physical fatigue also are frequent reactions (Halpern & Tramontin, 2007). I have heard stories of people feeling detached from their bodies, as if they were less physically centered and grounded. This sort of experience illustrates the difficulty of separating reactions into strictly defined spheres, as this is a combination of physical, cognitive, and emotional responses.

An unanswered question is whether there are universal autonomic responses affecting all people who are in situations that they perceive as threatening or destructive. Or do different ethnic and cultural groups literally have different physical experiences to the same types of events (Jenkins, 1996). Some experts are convinced that the neurobiological reactions are the same across cultures, particularly when they lead to the diagnosis of PTSD (Marsella, Friedman, Gerrity, & Scurfield, 1996; North, 2007), while others (Kirmayer, 1996; Miller et al., 2006) believe that the idioms of stress are so culturally contingent that the physical reactions to disaster differ considerably across ethnic groups. Wilson (2007) argues that while traumatic stress is universal, culture shapes the meaning, expression of symptoms, and most important, the best remedy for the afflicted person.

COGNITIVE IMPACT

Physiological reactions can affect how people think. As the noradrenergic pathway is set in motion and the locus coeruleus part of the brain is active, as well as the amygdala, there is heightened arousal, hypervigilance, jumpiness, and fear. During this process, deliberative thinking is deactivated (Benedek, 2007; Smith et al., 2007), which has a major impact on cognition (Halpern & Tramontin, 2007; Yassen, 1995). Concentration, other than on the disaster, can suffer as executive functions of the brain are compromised. Fear and arousal may contribute to obsessive-compulsive thinking and rumination. The ability to plan, think through, and make sense of events suffers, leading to confusion and disorientation (Halpern & Tramontin, 2007; Yassen, 1995).

I have often heard people report that they either cannot remember the events of the disaster and anything immediately afterward or that they can vividly recall every second of a sequence, as if it were happening in slow motion. There is sometimes the sense of detachment that I mention in the previous section, as if the event were happening to someone else. The metaphors of "being in a dream" or "like in a movie" often come up. People directly exposed to the disaster may have a hyperawareness of senses such as smell, sound, and taste. I heard a lot about that when working with survivors of the World Trade Center disaster on 9/11 in New York—with people recollecting the sounds of airplanes, sirens, screaming, and even the thud of elevators crashing in their carriage beds. The smell of burning or of gasoline was frequently mentioned. Because of these sensory associations, sounds and smells similar to those experienced during the disaster can easily trigger the sensation of the disaster anew. Therefore, people can find themselves having a severe stress response without consciously understanding the source of it. This is why debriefings often ask people to mention their sensory recollections in an effort to bring this into greater awareness and consciousness (Miller, 2003, 2006a; Mitchell, 1983; Mitchell & Bray, 1990; Young, 1997).

EMOTIONAL REACTIONS

Emotional reactions are closely linked to physiological and cognitive reactions. Emotions have a somatic basis and, when they are cognitively labeled, are known as feelings (Rothschild, 2006). Among the typical emotional/feeling reactions identified by Yassen (1995) are anxiety, fear, anger, and hostility, which are manifestations of the fight-or-flight syndrome mentioned previously. The depth and persistence of these emotions can lead to feeling overwhelmed, numb, and depleted. Over time, this can deepen to feeling depressed and despondent. When there has been loss of life, grieving and mourning shape many emotional reactions, which I discuss shortly. There is also sadness and remorse about loss of property. A woman whom I counseled after she escaped from the World Trade Center during 9/11 in New York, who was a manager in a financial services firm, began to weep as she recalled losing her office. She missed the physical space where she had spent so much of her waking time and all of the objects, mementos, and artifacts that had surrounded her. Another woman whom I met wandering the streets of D'Iberville, Mississippi, shortly after Hurricane Katrina had struck, could not stop thinking about the total destruction of her grandparents' home: "I used to spend weekends there when I was a child—I feel as if I my childhood was destroyed." Places and things are symbolic receptacles of aspects of self and identity (Csikszentmihalyi & Rochberg-Halton, 1981; Miller, 2001a).

Over time, more immediate, primal emotions give way to more complex feelings, such as guilt and remorse. It is very common for people to ruminate over steps or actions that they might have taken to prevent or mitigate against their experience of the disaster: "If only I had not let her drive to work" or "I could have moved to avoid this" or "Maybe I just have bad karma." These are examples of the kind of thinking saturated with feelings of guilt, shame, and regret that occur after disasters. Also, there are people who experience survivor guilt: "Why was I spared when so many others died?"

Feelings and emotions shape how we think—if we are feeling sad and depressed, we often have pessimistic, negative, and morbid thoughts. Conversely, cognitions and the ways that we construct the meaning of an event engender emotions. As has been discussed earlier, it is the meaning and sense that people attribute to events that influences their emotional and even physiological reactions. This is where culture, experience, and collective and individual differences have a profound impact on what people feel in response to disasters. This also shapes how people express what they feel, what is considered socially acceptable and unacceptable, and how these expressions are received by others. Related to this is what are considered legitimate and illegitimate grievances after a disaster (Summerfield, 2004) and whether or not these grievances are acknowledged and responded to. And expressing or not expressing certain emotions can in turn contribute to positive and negative biophysical reactions (Kirmayer, 1996).

BEHAVIORAL RESPONSES

Our physical state, cognitive appraisals, and emotional reactions contribute to how we behave in response to disasters. As part of the fight-or-flight dynamic, people often react behaviorally, both consciously and unconsciously. For example, after having experienced a disaster, people may become more alert and watchful. Consciously, this may involve scanning the environment for further threats or sources of help and relief. Unconsciously, particularly when there is acute or post-traumatic stress, this can be an unconscious reaction, a state of hypervigilance. The consequences of this are that a person cannot relax or let go, which increases stress levels and causes the person to feel depleted and exhausted. Hypervigilance can invade sleep, either because the person does not allow himself to sleep because he feels the need to remain awake and alert, or through distressing nightmares that disturb sleep. The costs of being in a heightened state of alertness are exhaustion, depletion, and even distorted thinking and reality testing.

Other common reactions are irritability (Yassen, 1995), a general state of unease, and even anger and hostile behavior. Conversely, some people behave in a withdrawn fashion. A Vietnamese American social service worker in Biloxi's Little Saigon described some people behaving like "turtles" (withdrawing into themselves) in response to the aftermath of Hurricane Katrina. This has interpersonal implications, which are discussed in the next section.

People may lose their appetite after a disaster (Everly & Mitchell, 2000; Halpern & Tramontin, 2007; Mitchell & Bray, 1990; Yassen, 1995) or conversely overeat or seek "comfort foods," craving salt and/or sugar. Another possible behavioral consequence is drinking or drug use (Everly & Mitchell, 2000; Halpern & Tramontin, 2007; Mitchell & Bray, 1990). In addition to trying to numb reactions through alcohol and drugs, affected people can become self-destructive (resorting to self-cutting, excessive risk taking) or even suicidal (Halpern & Tramontin, 2007; Mitchell & Bray, 1990; Yassen, 1995).

SPIRITUAL IMPACT AND MEANING-MAKING

Many researchers and practitioners have described the crisis of faith and meaning that may occur in people who have encountered disasters (Everly & Mitchell, 2000; Halpern & Tramontin, 2007; Miller et al., 2006; Mitchell & Bray, 1990; Rosenfeld et al., 2005; Yassen, 1995). This is often more profound with disasters that are attributed to human error or intentional harm than with disasters viewed as acts of God (Halpern & Tramontin, 2007; Rosenfeld et al., 2005). When I was counseling survivors of the World Trade Center, people frequently asked how this could happen if there was a God, although a minority of people felt that this brought them closer to their faith. Another reaction that several people had after 9/11 was to reevaluate what was important in their lives. Some people were considering changing careers or retiring, while others vowed to spend more time with families and friends.

In contrast to this, in my research with Vietnamese American families in Little Saigon three years after Hurricane Katrina, many people saw the impact of the storm as being part of things that just happen (Park et al., 2010). In this community, there was almost no loss of life but a great deal of property and economic damage so that the consequences of the storm were different than for survivors of 9/11. But it was also interesting to hear how many people felt that the storm was "not a big deal" when compared with the impact of the U.S.-Vietnam war on their lives. Thus, the meaning of the storm was very much influenced by collective past experiences as well as cultural beliefs and values. Being able to place the storm in a larger context and relate it to other disasters enabled people to regain their traction and move forward with their lives.

SOCIAL AND INTERPERSONAL REACTIONS

All of the above reactions contribute to changes in social interactions. After a disaster, people may become socially withdrawn, isolating themselves from others (Halpern & Tramontin, 2007; Yassen, 1995). Shame, humiliation, fear, and numbness can all contribute to mistrust and wariness of others. After disasters, people may need more social support and act in a more dependent way than usual. Perhaps related to this, some people become very controlling in their relationships (Halpern & Tramontin, 2007). There may be intensification in interpersonal violence, which can be amplified if a person is drinking or using other drugs. There can be increased tensions between partners, as well as between parents and children, at a time when family members and close friends are in need of interpersonal support. This not only happens at home but can become a pattern in the workplace after a disaster as well, when safety is compromised, routines disrupted, communication frayed, and trust shattered (Vineburgh, Gifford, Ursano, Fullerton, & Benedek, 2007). Social support is a buffer against prolonged trauma reactions, such as "losing it" emotionally, which has adverse consequences; social withdrawal disconnects people from what can be thought of as a natural debriefing process (Ursano et al., 2007).

Disasters can also bring people closer, particularly people who have gone through the same event together. This can happen in many domains—in the family, in friendships, in social and spiritual organizations, and in the workplace. There is often a sense of having experienced similar tragedies or of having survived something together.

Help-seeking is behavior associated with all cultures, although the form that this takes varies considerably. For cultures that are more collectively structured and interpersonally embedded, having others to relate to can be a major buffer against distress and a form of resiliency. However, losses of family members, including extended family, can be particularly devastating.

Interpersonal effects of disaster are not only the result of internal, psycho-emotional reactions. Interpersonal relationships are often disrupted by disasters because of the damage caused to a community, inhibiting the opportunities for social interaction (Park et al., 2010). This is considered in more detail in the next section.

SEVERE REACTIONS

All the previously discussed domains interact and can lead to stress and trauma responses. Some practitioners focus on full-blown psychiatric disorders, such as PTSD (Friedman & Marsella, 1996), while others emphasize the range of normal stress reactions to abnormal events (Kirmayer, 1996). As described in chapter 1, diagnosing reactions to disasters using a trauma lens is more prevalent in Western cultures and this tendency has been criticized as being Eurocentric and pathologizing (Ager, 1997; Keane, Kaloupek, & Weathers, 1996; Miller et al., 2006; Pupavac, 2004; Reyes & Elhai, 2004; Summerfield, 2004). In this section, I first sketch some typical diagnostic categories used by Western practitioners and then apply a critical analysis. Later in the chapter, I consider grief reactions.

Disasters cause stress reactions, but when do these reactions become trauma? Are there distinct clinical syndromes or is there a stress spectrum where, for example, PTSD is part of a continuum rather than a categorically distinct syndrome (Kirmayer, 1996)? And are there different types of trauma reactions beyond the diagnostic categories of the *Diagnostic and Statistical Manual* (*DSM-IV*) of the American Psychiatric Association? Kira (2001) has broken down trauma by its impact on different areas of individual functioning: attachment, autonomy/identity/individuation, interdependence/disconnectedness, achievement/self-actualization, and survival. Much has been written about traumatic syndromes and trauma reactions; for the purposes of this book, I summarize some that are most frequently found in Western disaster discourses.

POST-TRAUMATIC STRESS DISORDER

PTSD is usually not diagnosed until at least one month after a disaster because of the similarity of symptoms to acute stress disorder (ASD—discussion to follow) (Halpern & Tramontin, 2007; Perrin-Klinger, 2000). The first criterion for PTSD is its occurrence in response to a catastrophic event—disaster, armed conflict, torture, or sexual or physical assault (Friedman & Marsella, 1996). In the *DSM-IV* (1994), this is known as the stressor event.

The second criterion for PTSD, Criterion B, is the uncontrollable re-experiencing of the traumatic event through intrusive thoughts, recurring dreams, flashbacks, and other experiences of reliving the extreme distress of the event (American Psychiatric Association [APA], 1994). While many memories are processed and eventually metabolized, traumatic memories are like a stuck record that keeps replaying. Many of the physiological responses described earlier accompany intrusive memories. The third criterion involves determined efforts at avoidance, such as trying to suppress intrusive thoughts, avoiding places or events that trigger reactions, and experiencing memory deficits and constricted affect. The fourth criterion involves high rates of arousal, often referred to as hypervigilance, which can lead to sleeping disorders, difficulties with concentration, angry outbursts, and a low startle threshold. There is a variation of PTSD known as delayed onset. This type occurs at least six months after exposure to disaster (APA, 1994; Friedman & Marsella, 1996). Two other forms of PTSD are acute, which lasts for three months or less, and chronic, which has a duration of more than three months (Benedek, 2007).

ACUTE STRESS DISORDER

Acute stress disorder (ASD) is very common after exposure to a disaster and has many of the symptoms associated with PTSD but lasts only from two days to four weeks (APA, 1994; Benedek, 2007; Perrin-Klinger, 2000). The symptoms can be so similar—traumatic exposure, intrusive reexperiencing, avoidance—that the only sure way to distinguish between PTSD and ASD is its duration. ASD has criteria that include dissociation (numbing, detachment, depersonalization), which is not part of the official PTSD criteria (Benedek, 2007). The most important distinction between ASD and PTSD is that ASD usually resolves on its own, without the need for treatment, while PTSD is much more intractable.

OTHER PSYCHOLOGICAL DISORDERS

Some people have what are considered long-term stress disorders. These are not as debilitating as PTSD but render a person prone to "triggering," or periods in which the individual relives the event, such as during anniversaries of the event, increased media coverage, and court trials related to the disaster (Everly & Mitchell, 2000). There is also cumulative stress, which is the buildup of long-term exposure to stress-inducing situations that can lead to depletion and burnout (Perrin-Klinger, 2000). Nonspecific stress reactions can include shattered trust and assumptions, shame and guilt, and a sense of helplessness, but these do not have the magnitude or functional impact of PTSD (Perrin-Klinger, 2000). Depression is another consequence of exposure to disaster (Benedek, 2007).

Wilson (2007) finds that traumatic stress is ubiquitous across the globe, having a range of cultural manifestations. I agree with this. Traumatic stress is a concept that can incorporate (but is not limited to) PTSD. It is a more adaptable, fluid concept than PTSD, and while this makes it more difficult to study, it opens up more space for culturally responsive interventions.

SECONDARY PTSD, VICARIOUS TRAUMA, AND COMPASSION FATIGUE

Workers providing direct services are vulnerable to absorbing the stress and trauma of those with whom they are working. This includes first responders (emergency workers deployed immediately after a disaster), uniformed responders (police, fire, ambulance, National Guard), construction and maintenance workers, and health and mental health providers. These workers and volunteers often confront very distressing scenes of death and destruction with varying degrees of preparedness. Uniformed responders have been trained to manage crises and emergencies but are vulnerable to stress and trauma reactions when their lives are in danger, such as police officers who have been shot at. Uniformed responders are also vulnerable to feelings of guilt and a sense of failure, as when firefighters see civilians die in a fire or a chemical plant explosion. The police and military, in particular, exist in cultures of toughness and masculinity, which are internalized by all workers, including women. And although useful if not necessary for doing their jobs, this sense of toughness can make it difficult to acknowledge, express, tolerate, and receive help for distressing or overwhelming reactions. On the other hand, there is often a strong bond among fellow workers, fostering peer support and receptivity to group interventions that emphasize mutual aid and self-care.

Construction workers, for the most part, are not trained in emergency responses and are unprepared for the emotional toll of working on sites where there is mass destruction, bodies and body parts, and threats to their own safety. Like uniformed workers, they too have cultures of hardiness, where emotional expression or seeking therapy can be a sign of weakness. Trade unions have a tradition of mutual aid and support for their members. After the attacks on the World Trade Center in 2001, there were "workshops" designed and implemented by trade unions to offer psychosocial interventions to construction workers assigned to Ground Zero (Miller et al., 2010) (see chapter 8).

Clinicians are always prone to absorbing stress and trauma reactions through work with clients who have experienced trauma and tragedy. This is called countertransference and it involves identifying empathically with clients' suffering and having accompanying emotional reactions. In empathy, the brain's mirror neurons are deployed (Allen, 2001; Rothschild, 2006), reflecting the physio-emotional experiences of the client so that therapist and client can literally feel similar sensations. However, this can lead to "emotional contagion" (Adams, Figley, & Boscarino, 2007; Rothschild, 2006), in which the therapist internalizes the expressed emotion of the client.

Various terms may be used to describe these processes—secondary trauma and PTSD, vicarious traumatization (VF), compassion fatigue (CF), and burnout (Adams et al., 2008; Canfield, 2005; Pearlman & Saakvitne, 1995; Tosone, 2007; Tosone & Bialkin, 2003). There is overlap between these concepts, and there is still work being done to refine and test their validity (Adams et al., 2008). They are considered in greater detail in chapter 12, which looks at the risks for helpers and responders and strategies for self-care.

CRITIQUE OF A TRAUMA FOCUS

There is some value in having discrete diagnostic categories, such as PTSD. Treatment protocols can be developed, it is easier to conduct research about the effectiveness of different interventions, and there is a checklist of symptoms that can be used by practitioners to understand and conceptualize what has happened to a person after a disaster. And, in fact, there are now cognitive behavioral therapy (CBT) interventions that are very promising in their ability to treat PTSD (Allen, 2001; Bonanno, 2004; Friedman & Marsella, 1996; McNally et al., 2003). Another promising intervention strategy is known as somatic experiencing, which because of the nonverbal, noncognitive nature of trauma, "target[s] the way that posttraumatic responses have been stored or patterned in the body" (Leitch, Vanslyke, & Allen, 2009). Somatic experiencing has shown promise in studies with social service workers after Hurricanes Katrina and Rita (Leitch et al., 2009) as well as with tsunami survivors in India (Parker, Doctor, & Selvam, 2008).

Yet even those who study PTSD find that it occurs in a minority of people after a disaster. Friedman et al. (2006) cite research showing 95 percent of people exposed to a "traumatic event" developed post-traumatic psychological distress, but of these, only 29 percent were viewed as being clinically "serious." Ursano et al. (2007) found that between 50 and 70 percent of the U.S. population were exposed to traumatic events but only 5 to 12 percent developed full-blown PTSD. Clearly, there are many factors that foster resilience in people exposed to distressing events (considered in the next chapter), which are minimized if traumatic reactions to disasters are the main focus of attention.

One critique of the extensive use of a trauma lens is that it reflects more the cultural biases and mind-set of Western psychotherapists than the needs and experiences of people affected by a disaster (Chakraborty, 1991; Miller et al., 2006; Pupavac, 2004). PTSD is a diagnosis that flowered in postindustrial individualistic societies (Pupavac, 2004). PTSD theory, measurement, and research has been conducted by Westerners (Marsella, Friedman, & Spain, 1996). Not surprisingly, with a trauma lens, the focus is more on individual symptoms than on collective and communal consequences (Pupavac, 2004). There are many implicit assumptions with trauma that are Eurocentric (Kirmayer, 1996). These include suppositions about what are normal and abnormal affective reactions and expressions of distress and help seeking. As Chakraborty (1991, p. 1204) puts it, "A central pattern of (western) disorders is identified and taken as the standard by which other (local) patterns are seen as minor variations."

Trauma-focused approaches tend to take a universalistic, positivistic stance toward health and distress (Chakraborty, 1991; Miller et al., 2006). Yet an essential aspect of trauma is the shattering of what is known and expected, a crisis of meaning. As meaning is constructed in a social context, culture is an important part of this process (Pupavac, 2004; Wilson, 2007). All behavior occurs in a cultural context, which determines what is viewed as normal and abnormal (Chakraborty, 1991). Even when there are similar presentations of symptoms, these do not necessarily have the same meaning within different cultural contexts (Keane et al., 1996; Kleinman & Cohen, 1997; Miller et al., 2006; Summerfield, 2004). Thus, even if it is true that certain types of events result in traumatic reactions, wherever they occur (and this is still contested territory), the nature of these reactions—how individuals make sense of what happened to them, how their groups and communities narrate this process, and what interventions are helpful—depends on local, situational, and cultural contexts. By focusing on individual pathology instead of cultural idioms, we overlook important questions (Miller et al., 2006; Summerfield, 2004). What is the genesis of the problems? How do individuals seek help? Who do they turn to for assistance? Is it safe and socially acceptable to talk to others, including counselors, about one's feelings? What interventions are socially understandable and acceptable? Another aspect of trauma, particularly when there is armed conflict or terrorism, is that it is often a breach of relationship, a rupture of attachment (Allen, 2001). By focusing on treating the individual, Western psychological and psychiatric interventions do not sufficiently take into account the social resources that may be available as a source of strength for individuals. These resources may well have been ruptured, in which case an intervention should also focus on repairing social bonds and connections. Connectedness as well as altruism and spirituality are all relational processes with positive neurological consequences (Mollica, 2006).

Lastly, there is a political dimension to a trauma critique. Trauma categories were not only developed in the West but have been used by Westerners with non-Western populations to make sense of reactions to disasters and to guide therapeutic interventions. As Chakraborty (1991, p. 1205) states, "Attempts at an international classification of psychiatric disorders has always been a battleground." There is a huge trauma industry that supports these efforts (Kirmayer, 1996) and manufactures the knowledge used to support this formulation through research and publications, funded by Western foundations and government agencies. Given the history of Western colonialism, it is not surprising that there is resistance to the imposition of a Western-dominated psychology on non-Western populations. Not only is an individualistic psychotherapeutic approach problematic because of cultural assumptions and a privileging of an individual treatment focus over a collective recovery orientation, but there is another concrete difficulty: there often are not enough trained therapists on the ground to treat PTSD, even if this were an efficacious intervention (de Jong, 2002, 2007). The cost of being trained to use trauma-focused and somatic interventions is often prohibitively high for practitioners from poor countries or regions. There is always a political dimension when help is offered and the trauma industry is not politically neutral.

IMPACT ON THE FAMILY SYSTEM

Disasters have a profound impact on families and children. Chapter 6 considers unique factors to be taken into account when working with children. Most adults and children are actively part of family systems when disasters strike. In this section, I briefly consider some common dynamics and reactions.

When discussing families, there is an infinite range of possibilities. Family theorists have tended to emphasize Western, heterosexual, two-parent families with biologically related children as the archetypal family. However, there are many gay and lesbian families, single-parent households, and families without children. Many families with children are blended families, with children from prior relationships or children in foster care or who have been adopted. Some families are formed within a specific cultural-ethnic group while others are cross-cultural and/or multiracial. The meaning of extended family varies considerably from culture to culture and family to family, as do gender roles, expectations of parenting, and perceptions of older people and the elderly. The postmodern family is a shifting, varied enterprise that warrants caution when generalized about.

Within any family, however, there are ways of conceptualizing certain core processes. All families have meaning-making systems that help members to construct maps of reality (Reiss, 1981). There is a family structure, which is never frozen, constantly being renegotiated, and co-constructed and reconfigured over time and in differing contexts. There are communication patterns and styles influenced by culture, immigration, generation, gender, and other sociocultural variables, as well as role expectations. Relational patterns and how emotions and intimacy are experienced and expressed vary from family to family, but each family has patterns and norms for this. The boundary between who is considered to be "family" and "non-family" and how this boundary is managed differs among families, but for all families, there are boundaries to be maintained. There are also boundaries within the family, and every family manages them differently. Within all families, there are routines. Economic and social security are important for all families, although the contours and specifics of this vary. There is also a history of how the family came together and how it has changed and transformed over time. Within any given family, a unique life cycle is in motion. All of these processes are affected by disasters.

Meaning-making is a shared enterprise within families, and as discussed throughout this book, disasters often result in a crisis of meaning. There may be a crisis in what is assumed and believed about the world and the nature of reality. Shared belief systems can be strained as family members try to make sense of the catastrophe and sort through existing schisms. For example, some in a family may become more devout in their religious practices, while others may lose faith in their spiritual beliefs and reject the deeply held worldviews of others in the family.

When there is a disaster, family structure can be temporarily altered by separations or permanently changed by death. Some family members may never be able to function in the same way as before, which impacts roles and responsibilities. Also, structural changes may occur by virtue of postdisaster divorce or relational breakups. In a family in which male adults are the traditional breadwinners, others in the family may need to become economic providers if traditional sources of employment are no longer available. If jobs are lost, then some family members may have to move to a new locale. After Hurricane Katrina devastated Little Saigon in Biloxi, there were many short-term separations of family members (Park et al., 2010). There were also reports of relational breakups blamed on the stress of the disaster. While parents who spoke only Vietnamese tried to remain in Little Saigon, many of their English-speaking adult children were forced to move elsewhere to find work, causing further sorrow and distress.

As has been discussed previously, disasters have emotional consequences. Families have expectations about and patterns of emotional expression, often with an equilibrium having been established. When confronted with disaster, the family can be a refuge and safe harbor for processing and holding complex emotional reactions. However, emotions may be felt more strongly and expressed more forcefully, which may or may not have an impact on relational patterns and the ability of family members to respond empathically to one another. This is compounded by the tendency of disaster-related stress to lower the reservoirs of compassion in the family's emotional caretakers. If family members withdraw emotionally, become depressed, use drugs and alcohol to self-medicate, or become more aggressive and violent, relationships can become estranged or even ruptured.

Boundaries within the family and between the family and the outside world are often strained and tested by disaster. Staying and sleeping with relatives, friends, and neighbors or in shelters shifts privacy arrangements and places people in closer proximity, impinging on personal space. Sexual intimacy between partners is often compromised. Family routines are difficult to maintain, and the ability to eat customary food and engage in recreational activities is hampered.

Families offer material and economic support to members, and disasters threaten this capacity. Jobs are lost, offices destroyed, tools ruined, and access to food, clothing, money, transportation, and other resources that family members pool and share are often unavailable. Inability to provide for family members adds additional burdens and pressures on parents and caretakers who are already in a vulnerable space.

Family life cycles and roles are disrupted by disasters (Rosenfeld et al., 2005). Members may regress and become more dependent than previously or may be rapidly moved to confront new developmental challenges at an early age. When I was working in northern Uganda, I encountered children, as young as ten to twelve, who had become the heads of their households and were caring for younger siblings because of the loss of their parents during the civil war, which also meant that they had to drop out of school. Disasters also cut families off from the sources of their history and traditions. This can happen in many ways: elders are no longer accessible; pictures, documents, heirlooms, and other objects connecting families with their past are lost or destroyed; and family dwellings are rendered uninhabitable. Cultural traditions, practices, and routines that families had appropriated and reworked to make their own may no longer seem valid or applicable to the set of life challenges being faced postdisaster. Over time these can become lost or difficult to access.

The loss of resources and disruption of routines makes it difficult for adults to parent effectively. When feeling overwhelmed, parents are less able to care for their children. The mere fact that a disaster penetrates the family's sense of stability and security may serve to undermine the confidence parents have in themselves and their ability to keep their children safe. Losing homes and neighborhoods removes important containers and holding environments parents rely on. When schools are closed and friends and recreational resources no longer available, children lose their routines and social networks, leaving them in a more vulnerable position and creating even more responsibility for already depleted caretakers. This is compounded by children experiencing developmental regression and strong behavioral reactions.

With their community networks, resources, and capacities shattered, families are left without the context and social nest they have relied on to thrive and survive. Some of the most profound consequences of disaster for families are separation, loss of health and well-being, and the grief and bereavement that comes from the death of loved ones.

COMMUNITY CONSEQUENCES OF DISASTERS

One of the most striking aspects of large-scale disaster is the debilitating effect it has on the functioning of the community, at least in the short term. Sometimes there is a neighborhood at the epicenter of the disaster—lower Manhattan in 9/11, downtown Oklahoma City in the bombing of the Alfred P. Murrah Federal Building. Although the infrastructure of the local area was destroyed and the entire community affected by the losses (including the deaths of people who worked in the devastated area), the larger community is still able to function. Hurricane Katrina, however, devastated an entire region—a large swath of cities, towns, and rural areas. The Buffalo Creek flood in West Virginia in 1972 ravaged a number of small towns clustered in a coal-mining region. After heavy rains, a dam holding a reservoir of coal slurry burst. In a few minutes, 125 people were killed, 1,100 injured, more than 4,000 people left homeless, and 1,000 cars and trucks destroyed (Rosenfeld et al., 2005). These were poor communities with little social and economic capital. They were dependent on one industry, whose negligence was seen as having led to the disaster.

Small-scale disasters, such as the death of teenagers in a car crash, leave a social and emotional footprint in communities while the main engines of community life continue to churn. Large-scale disasters, such as a civil war, are overwhelming emotionally, socially, economically, politically, and culturally for years to come. Thus, when considering the community consequences of disasters, it is important to remain aware of these differences in scale and domains of functioning.

It can be helpful to consider the collective consequences of disaster as being both horizontal and vertical. What I mean by horizontal is the effect of the disaster on economic functioning, daily routines, social networking, and collective mood and spirit. These effects are both direct—loss of electricity, homes, phones, ATM machines, gathering places, transportation, medical services—and indirect, as told by collective narratives and discourses, which shape how the disaster is perceived and understood. There is often a collective sense of disempowerment (Weyerman, 2007).

To understand the vertical consequences of disaster it is helpful to use a metaphor that has been developed by Landau (2007, p. 353), which is the disruption of "transitional pathways," the "psychological connection between past, present and future." This happens on all levels—individual, family, and community. When disaster strikes, connections with the past are literally severed by the destruction of buildings and landmarks and the loss of mementos and other artifacts of the past. This has symbolic resonance, as in the case of the woman on the street in D'Iberville after Hurricane Katrina, crying that she had lost her childhood when her grandparents' home was destroyed. Links to past social and cultural practices are also lost, as with the Acholi people with whom I worked in northern Uganda. Because of the long-term civil war, at one point 90 percent of the population were living in internally displaced person's camps (IDPs), where they were unable to sustain themselves economically and were also unable to employ clan-based rituals that had provided meaning and social bonding in the past. They felt they had lost not only their connection with their history and ancestors but their collective sense of pride, worth, and meaning as well.

When a community or collectivity loses its connection with its past, this usually interferes with its vision for the future. Hope rests on the foundation of a present that is grounded in connection with the past. There are, of course, historical moments and periods when individuals and collectivities consciously seek to break with the past—such as when people reject repressive practices and policies that oppress women or target specific racial and ethnic groups. Modernization and technical innovation represent a breaking with the past. Also, when the children of immigrants seek to assimilate and shed the trappings of their parents' culture and ethnicity, they are distancing themselves from the past. Such shifts are not only the choices of individuals but reflect social, economic, technological, and political changes as well. They are often socially and economically disruptive and can lead to nostalgia (for happier times), ambivalence, and even conflict.

What distinguishes the discontinuities caused by a disaster from such social shifts is the suddenness of the change or disruption, often the scale of the change, and a sense that it is involuntary, which can contribute to a collective sense of inefficacy, or helplessness. Collective efficacy fosters collective trust (Samson et al., 1997), and a lack of efficacy can contribute to social mistrust. This in turn can lead to feelings of pessimism and hopelessness about the future. This is further compounded by the fraying of civic associations and public institutions that braid families into the community and to one another (Miller, 2001a). Such organizations, along with public places, offer spaces and sites for people to congregate, connect, and relate to one another, which are trust-building enterprises, so the loss of these social opportunities can alienate individuals and families from one another and their community. Existing social divisions in communities can widen and deepen as collective efficacy ebbs.

Disasters also undermine social norms and social roles for community residents by taking away jobs, disrupting routines, and impeding associational opportunities (Wessells & Monteiro, 2006). Economic growth can be hampered for years (Nakagawa & Shaw, 2004), which can also constrict social opportunities. Trust in leaders diminishes, raising questions about their competency and authority in their social roles. Social roles give people a sense of purpose and meaning and depend on the transitional pathways linking the past, present, and future.

GRIEF AND BEREAVEMENT IN RESPONSE TO DISASTER

When considering the processes of grief, bereavement, and mourning in response to disasters, it is helpful to review some major theoretical formulations about death and dying and then examine what is unique and distinct about the recovery process in the context of loss in disaster. It is also important to reflect on how culture determines the course of grieving and mourning by disaster-affected people as well as how culture shapes the way that responders and researchers interpret and understand what they are witnessing. Another important consideration is how bereavement intersects with stress, resiliency, and the will toward recovery.

Grief, bereavement, and mourning are often used interchangeably by disaster responders. However, Halpern and Tramontin (2007) define grief as the emotional reaction to loss and bereavement and mourning as the processes of relinquishing and adapting that survivors undergo in the wake of destruction, death, and dying. Although this is helpful, what is meant by relinquishing and adapting can vary considerably across individuals and cultures. Psychologist Paul Ekman has mapped universal emotions and feelings across cultures and concluded that sadness and anguish over loss is universal (Goleman, 2003). In all cultures, there are practices and rituals that work with these feelings and help survivors to create meaning out of what has happened and to assimilate the loss of loved ones with the lives of the living. Yet the specifics of these expectations and practices vary across cultures.

Three major ways that Western theoreticians have conceptualized the processes of bereavement and mourning are stage theories, phase theories, and task theories (see table 4.1). Stage theories, building on the pioneering work of Elisabeth Kübler-Ross, have tended to view bereavement as a sequential, developmental process with a linear trajectory. A grieving person can move through or become stuck in a particular stage, beginning with shock and denial and culminating in some form of adjustment and acceptance. For example, McKenna has postulated a six-stage model (Gilliand & James, 1996). The first stage is one of shock, sadness, and isolation. During this stage, people are stunned and in need of help and support from others for even daily tasks and routines. The second stage is one of intense sadness, as the reality of the loss sinks in. There can be powerful emotional release during this stage. The third stage, loneliness, can be characterized by anxiety, sleeplessness, and loss of appetite. The fourth stage, anger and guilt, may involve a lot of rumination about the deceased—what might have been—sometimes laden with feelings of personal responsibility, such as not having been attentive enough to the deceased in life. Depression colors the fifth stage, as the finality of the loss for the survivor has deeper meaning. McKenna's sixth and final stage is characterized by refocusing on the future, where there is integration of the loss, reestablishment of equilib-

TABLE 4.1 Comparison of Grief Models

KÜBLER-ROSS'S STAGE THEORY	MCKENNA'S APPLIED STAGES OF SURVIVOR GRIEF	HOOYMAN AND KRAMER'S SIX PROCESSES OF GRIEVING	WORDEN'S TASK MODEL	OCHBERG'S TASKS
1. Shock and denial	1. Shock, sadness, anxiety and isolation	1. Recognizing and accepting the reality of the loss	1. Accept reality of loss	1. Expression of affect
2. Anger and resentment, guilt	2. Sadness	2. Reacting to, experiencing, and expressing the pain of separation	2. Work through pain of grief	2. Understand meaning
3. Bargaining	3. Loneliness		3. Adjust to new environment	3. Elucidate ambivalence
4. Depression	4. Anger and guilt	3. Reminiscing	4. Emotionally relocate deceased	4. Recathect with others
5. Adjustment and acceptance	5. Depression	4. Relinquishing old attachments		
	6. Refocus on the future	5. Readjusting		
		6. Reinvesting		

From Gilliand & James, 1996; James & Gilliand, 2001; Hooyman & Kramer, 2008; Ochberg, 1988; Worden, 2008.

rium, and the ability to move forward and experience moments and periods of joy and happiness.

It is not particularly helpful to place time frames on the stages, as this puts value on a certain pace and speed for moving through the bereavement process. Unfortunately, human service workers sometimes conclude that a client's unique process of bereavement is taking too long, focusing on how they have become "stuck," as if there is only one way to go through this process. It is also questionable whether all people move through all of the stages sequentially and whether people from different cultural traditions would use the same terms and concepts when describing their processes of grief and mourning.

Phase theories focus more on the processes that people go through after a loss. Although the phases may occur sequentially, they can also be experienced in a more elliptical, recurring manner. A person may go through a period of relinquishing attachments and then find that something provokes a recurrence of the deep pain of attachment and separation. Some phase theorists suggest that aspects of different phases can occur at the same time and are not mutually exclusive. Hooyman and Kramer (2008) have identified six processes of grieving. Their process formulation is more active and interactive than the way that grief is described by stage theorists. Their language focuses on verbs more than nouns—recognizing, accepting, reacting, reminiscing, relinquishing, readjusting, and reinvesting. This captures the relationship between the survivor and deceased and current relationships and activities in the survivor's life.

Another way to approach this is to examine the tasks that survivors should negotiate and resolve as part of their process of bereavement. Worden (2008) has identified four tasks: (1) accept the reality of the loss, (2) work through the pain of the grief, (3) adjust to the environment without the deceased, and (4) emotionally relocate the deceased and move on.

Sudden or violent death, as with disaster, can result in what is called "traumatic loss," which leads to "traumatic grief" (Halpern & Tramontin, 2007, p. 90). Under such circumstances, bereavement can be an extended process. Ochberg (1988) has identified four tasks that must be undertaken when there has been traumatic loss: (1) expressing affect, (2) understanding the meaning of the loss, (3) articulating and integrating ambivalence over the lost person, and (4) recathecting with others.

Grief and bereavement are often more complicated when there has been an ambivalent or complex relationship with the deceased. They are also more complicated when they are ambiguous. Boss (2006) describes ambiguous loss occurring when bodies are not recovered and survivors are left to mourn without absolute certainty that the person is deceased. Another type of ambiguous loss is when a person is irrevocably changed by an event; the individual has survived but is no longer the same person. An example of this would be a person who sustains a serious head injury in a terrorist attack. The individual has almost no memory or the ability to connect with others. The parents, partner, or children are left with the task of mourning the loss of the individual they knew, and yet this person is not dead. Anything that complicates grief makes the tasks of bereavement more challenging and resolutions more elusive.

In general, disaster makes grief more complicated. Deaths and injuries often occur in a context where there have been numerous deaths and losses. This can both intensify the sense of loss as well as deplete available local resources to help people through their grief. Yet sharing the event with others can also be a source of support. Zinner (1999) describes this as "group survivorship." Another complicating factor with disaster is that people may be fighting for their own survival at a time when they have lost others, which makes it difficult to grieve properly; there is tension between the need to survive and cope and the pull toward engaging in bereavement (Halpern & Tramontin, 2007). Disasters often engender and intensify feelings of guilt and shame, magnifying what mourners already are prone to.

Specific types of disasters raise unique issues when it comes to the process of mourning. Spiritual beliefs are questioned or challenged by natural disasters at a time when people most need to access them. With technological disasters, feelings of anger and rage about irresponsible actions or inadequate safeguards often become part of the mix. Complex disasters bring the elements of fear and revenge, which can divert and misdirect the grieving process. Victims of war and terrorism feel disempowered and vulnerable, but they can also become perpetrators as they seek retribution as a means of expressing (or displacing) their grief (see chapter 10). There is tension between the desire to heal and the thirst for justice or restitution. Because of the intensity and scope of disaster-induced losses, feelings of grief can easily be retriggered by anniversaries or other events that are evocative of what occurred at the time of loss.

Culture plays a central role in grieving and mourning. Beliefs about the causes of death and what death entails; the handling of bodies; the expression of emotion—be it public or private; the nature of the rituals and funerals; the expectations for extended mourning; and the social roles during bereavement pertaining to the survivors and their relationships to one another are all culturally shaped and determined. In Japan, after the earthquake and tsunami of 2011, there were so many casualties that bodies were buried in mass graves rather than being cremated, which is the more traditional practice (Nishikawa, 2011). Many bodies were never recovered, further complicating cultural processes of grieving and mourning (Magnier, 2011). Beliefs about whether the dead are gone or still present with the living also differ considerably across cultures.

An example of culturally specific beliefs about death and bereavement that contrast with many Western assumptions comes from a study of Hong Kong Chinese people experiencing grief and mourning over the loss of a loved one (Chan et al., 2005). More than half of the study's respondents attributed death to fate, and many invoked the notion of karma. Other causes of death were "sick qi" (p. 931), which is negative life energy often from having attracted bad spirits, as well as bad feng shui (lack of harmony in aspects of one's living environment). Additionally, death was seen as an outcome of "clashes of fate" (p. 931) between the deceased and survivors.

When it came to evaluating whether the person suffered, respondents in the study focused on the expression on the corpse's face. Survivors scan faces carefully because there is a great deal of emphasis on wanting people to die a good death. Failure to have achieved a good death can lead to guilt and remorse for survivors, which is salient when deaths are caused by disaster. Many people believed in an afterlife or in reincarnation. Respondents also expressed the notion that the bond with the deceased continues after death and that communication is often initiated by the deceased. Photos are very important and people described having conversations with photographs of the deceased. Many of these beliefs seem to undermine some of the stages, phases, and tasks in Western theories of bereavement in which the survivor is expected to relinquish old attachments and recathect with new relationships; this relinquishing and recathecting does not adequately convey what the survivors in Chan et al.'s (2005) study were working on. Additionally, widows were seen as bringing bad luck and were often shunned by family members and excluded from celebrations, such as weddings, which has social implications for how people recover and heal.

I have summarized these points from Chan et al. (2005) to illustrate how culturally contingent grieving and mourning are and to raise questions about the universalistic or formulaic use of models of mourning and be-reavement—be they stage, phase, or task. What is clear is that disasters lead to grief and bereavement, but exactly how people grieve varies considerably across cultures and families, and disaster responders should approach this process with an open, nonjudgmental mind.

Disasters involve collective loss and group survivorship, and as with in-dividuals and families, there are community-level processes of grieving and mourning. Disaster legacies include material losses, social disruptions, and a sense of collective doubt and vulnerability. Communities and smaller group units, such as workplaces, also have tasks and go through phases of bereavement. There is a public dimension to the private losses sustained by individuals and families and often a desire for collective commemoration.

Collective memorializing occurs informally and through official action. An unofficial example is the crosses with flowers and mementos that dot the sides of U.S. highways at the sites of fatal car crashes. One example occurred on Cherry Street in Seattle, where a spontaneous shrine emerged after a respected community member was murdered there in 2009. The shrine, located on the sidewalk where the victim died, included pictures, notes, and artistic expressions of grief and loss. After 9/11, an installation quickly emerged on Canal Street, a few blocks from the World Trade Cen-ter. It incorporated candles, poems, notes, pictures, and even a mini replica of the Statue of Liberty. In eastern Sri Lanka, a group of Tamil women developed a dance to portray the losses from the tsunami. Haitian volun-teers in the town of Fonfrede planned a town memorial (featuring a list of the victims' names) following the 2010 earthquake. There is a human need, cutting across cultures, to express grief and sadness, to share and find meaning—and memorialize loss—after disaster (collective memorializing is covered in detail in chapter 11).

Disasters have an impact on individuals, families, groups, and communities. There are material and physical losses, and these elicit a variety of feelings and engender a range of responses in the search for meaning. Disasters af-fect individuals physically, cognitively, behaviorally, spiritually, socially, and interpersonally. There can be severe reactions for some people—notably, acute stress disorder, post-traumatic stress disorder, and depression. As the meaning of disaster is socially constructed, cultural and social differences influence expressions of distress and modes of help seeking. These differences also influence what is considered normal and abnormal, what is seen as being helpful, and whose role it is to offer support.

Disasters may rupture attachment between people and connectedness with one another and communities. For families, routines and relationships are disrupted, economic security threatened, and roles and boundaries re-negotiated. In communities, there can be a sense of collectively feeling overwhelmed, and as schisms rupture transitional pathways (Landau, 2007), there is a loss of collective efficacy (Samson et al., 1997) and challenges to sustaining a hopeful vision of the future.

Grief and bereavement are common consequences of disasters in all societies and cultures and occur at the individual, family, organizational, and collective levels. There are many ways of conceptualizing these processes, with stage, phase, and task theories being three major frameworks employed to describe and understand these processes. All three have their roots in Western society, and because grieving and mourning are socially and culturally constructed, these models must be interrogated for cultural biases and assumptions. The suddenness and scale of disasters, as well as the confusion and disagreement over causes and responsibility, can make the process of bereavement more complex than usual. A legacy of disasters is the public, collective dimension to grieving and memorializing, which has the potential to deepen alienation and pessimism or to transform and transcend losses.

While this chapter highlights many of the harmful consequences and problems resulting from disaster, what is remarkable is how resilient people and communities are in the face of terrible losses. Workers responding to disasters need to understand the complications and challenges that disasters pose for survivors but should also be mindful of how people survive such events and the inner and natural resources that they draw on in their recovery. The next chapter considers the sources of resiliency.

MINDFULNESS EXERCISE: LOVING-KINDNESS MEDITATION

Disasters can leave people feeling bereft and with complicated feelings of guilt and self-blame. Christopher Germer's (2009) practice of loving-kindness, or metta, can be a useful exercise in such situations.

Assume a comfortable sitting position and spend a few minutes focusing on your breathing. After finding your concentration, visualize yourself sitting and, on each out-breath, say the following phrases:

- May I be safe.
- May I be happy.

- May I be healthy.
- May I be at ease.

Try to really direct each of the thoughts—safe, happy, healthy, at ease—to yourself. It helps to repeat the phrases a few times and to really concentrate on what you are directing to yourself. If a phrase does not work, find one that does. For example, you can substitute "secure" for "safe" if that has greater resonance, or if you are very self-critical, you can try "May I be gentle with myself." If you have been able to do this with yourself, it can help to extend these wishes to others, perhaps a relative or friend, visualizing them when you do this. Lastly, you can expand the wishes so that they reach all living beings.

Germer (2009) recommends doing this in a relaxed way and not pushing yourself too hard. What is most important is to try to direct your wishes for well-being toward yourself. If this is really hard to do, it can sometimes help to first visualize some living being (family, friend, dog) to whom it is easier to send the thoughts. Then try to do the same for yourself.

After practicing loving-kindness for as long as feels comfortable and meaningful, return to your breathing for a few moments before ending the exercise.

5

SOURCES OF RESILIENCY

CONSIDERING THE TERRIBLY destructive consequences of disaster, it is perhaps remarkable that so many people recover from catastrophe as well as they do. Large numbers of people exposed to potentially traumatogenic events are still able to have positive emotional experiences and move beyond minor or temporary disruptions in their lives (Bonanno, 2004). Individuals, families, and communities have an impressive capacity for absorbing, processing, and reconstructing meaning after experiencing devastating losses. This is not to minimize the pain, sadness, and often indelible wounds—material, physical, and psychic—inscribed by disasters; they are events fraught with tragedy. Yet not only do most people regroup and reconstitute their lives, but many find special or even transcendent meaning in the ashes of their struggles.

There also seems to be a recursive synergy between the recovery of individuals and the recovery of communities (Landau, 2007; Landau, Mittal, & Wieling, 2008; Miller, 1994, 2001a; Mollica, 2006; Park et al., 2010; Weyerman, 2007). Weyerman argues that there is a "dynamic interplay between the inner life of people and their social and political action" (p. 95) and that an internal sense of power is related to a collective sense of efficacy, which comes from activities and actions taken with others. Miller found that the same is true of families and communities; when communities are thriving, families feel more empowered. Moreover, when families have a sense of efficacy, this contributes to the integrity of communities. Park et al. (2010) discovered through their interviews that Vietnamese American families in Biloxi, Mississippi, rarely separated out their own well-being from that of their community.

Mollica (2006) believes that there is an intricate relationship between connections to the environment and the healing of mind and body; if one can experience beauty or social connection, then neurochemical processes are activated that literally begin to heal psychic wounds. Beauty in the wake of disaster can be experienced through exposure to nature and the arts, while social connectivity comes from family, friends, colleagues, and community groups. Landau et al. (2008) cite research confirming that feeling connected with one's family and culture acts as an inoculation against health threats. Having a vibrant social network is related to positive health outcomes (Wilkinson & Pickett, 2009)—positive emotions and healthy behaviors can be socially contagious (Christakis & Fowler, 2009; Thompson, 2009). Thus, an important aspect of resiliency explored in this chapter is how it involves an integration of bio-psycho-social dimensions. I cover individual, family, and community resiliency in separate sections for the sake of organizational clarity, but in reality, they all interrelate.

Bonanno (2004) defines resilience as the maintenance of relatively healthy and stable life trajectories when confronted with disruptive, even life-threatening, events. What are the sources of resilience? What qualities help a person to withstand chaos, loss, and even trauma? What processes are present in families that help members to stay connected and, as a unit, able to weather the storms that shake their foundations? What attracts and fosters social support from friends and neighbors or encourages people to be there for others? What kinds of social capital and resources make it possible for communities to rebuild and even thrive after disaster? These are some of the core questions that frame this chapter's inquiry.

INDIVIDUAL RESILIENCE

Individual resilience stems from internal resources and social supports, and often an interaction between the two; in a sense, resiliency is more of a process than a set of traits. Internal resources derive from many sources— genetics, personality structure, developmental milestones, prior experiences, coping strategies, cognitive skills, conceptual ability, emotional resources, values, and spiritual beliefs. Although clinical practice and research have led to the identification of some common factors that support resiliency, often the factors are varied and the road to resiliency unpredictable (Bonanno, 2004). A person's developmental stage can influence resiliency in the face of disaster. For example, there may be wisdom later in life that can make an individual more resilient, but also there can be vulnerabilities in older people because of greater dependency or from having less time to rebuild and recover.

Kabat-Zinn (1990) has found three qualities that promote the ability to cope with extremely stressful situations: (1) comprehensibility, (2) manage-ability, and (3) meaningfulness. Comprehensibility means the ability to make sense of what has happened, to be able to create a narrative—a story about what happened to oneself. This narrative needs to include the recognition of what has been lost (Rosenfeld et al., 2005). White and Epston (1990) have described the importance of being able, as part of a process of healing, to rework and rescript narratives so that they are not rigid, fixed, deterministic, and inevitable, which implies not only comprehensibility but flexibility as well, a trait that Walsh (2003) has found enhances resiliency. Another component of comprehensibility is curiosity (Kabat-Zinn, 1990), the desire to understand what has happened and to approach this with an open mind.

Manageability can mean many things. It includes a sense of efficacy, the belief that one can influence one's environment (Bonanno, 2004). Resource-fulness is another component of manageability (Rosenfeld et al., 2005). However, this may be a culturally bound vision of resiliency, as personal efficacy is related to a sense of having control over one's fate and environment, a belief that is not shared by all cultures. Resiliency among some in Eastern cultures, for example, may be fueled by a sense of karma or fate, in which one does not blame oneself for what has occurred or the struggles being faced as one recovers. Park et al. (2010) found evidence of this in their interviews with Vietnamese American survivors of Hurricane Katrina.

Manageability is also linked to access to resources (Walsh, 2003). Park et al. (2010) found that the Vietnamese Americans in Biloxi who had more economic and social resources recovered more quickly from Hurricane Katrina than those with fewer resources. Also, they were less anxious about the future. This is consistent with what other practitioners and researchers have found (Kaniasty & Norris, 1999). It is easier to be resilient when one has assets; socioeconomic privilege enhances manageability.

Meaningfulness accrues from a number of sources. It can come from a spiritual practice or a worldview that seeks significant lessons in misfortune. Positive emotions (see below) encourage optimism for the future, which in turn facilitates meaning-making. The unique traditions and insights learned from one's family and culture give meaning when hardship is encountered.

Finding inspirational meaning has helped people to transcend and survive brutal conditions, such as those in concentration camps (Frankl, 1997; Levi, 1961). Many practitioners and researchers assert that the capacity to make and transform meaning is an essential component of resiliency in the face of disaster and adversity (Bonanno, 2004; Corbin & Miller, 2009; Kabat-Zinn, 1990; Landau, 2007; Landau & Saul, 2004; Miller, 2002; Walsh, 2003).

One of my Chinese colleagues, who was directly involved in managing ongoing social service responses to support survivors of the Wenchuan earthquake, related a story which illustrated her ability to find meaning from tragedy. In managing a relief program, she was feeling severe distress over the suffering that she was witnessing as well as frustrated by the inadequacy of government and NGO responses, leading to a sense of burnout and compassion fatigue (see chapter 12). She had heard from a Buddhist monk that those who were helping people to recover were "little Buddhas" but that those who had perished were "big Buddhas." She was unsure what this meant. Shortly after this, a man in the refugee camp where she was working committed suicide because he was feeling gravely despondent. As a result of this tragedy, NGOs and government resources were poured into the refugee camp. My colleague, who was initially distraught over the suicide, was eventually able to apply what she had heard from the monk and viewed the person who died as a "big Buddha." He had not simply perished: his death had resulted in help for others. She was able to make sense of what had initially appeared to be a cryptic remark and, at the same time, give meaning to a tragic death, relieving some of her anguish.

There is a strong emotional component to resiliency. Feelings such as cynicism, pessimism, disengagement, and hostility trigger neuroendocrine responses that deplete resiliency (Kabat-Zinn, 1990). Over time, toxic residues accrue in the body and weaken both the physical and psychic immune systems. Although there are certainly understandable reasons why people feel this way in response to disasters, particularly when there has been human negligence or aggression, holding on to these feelings increases suffering. Not only do negative feelings drain those holding them, but feeling states, both positive and negative, are infectious and influence almost everyone in the same social network (Christakis & Fowler, 2009; Thompson, 2009).

Christakis and Fowler (2009) have found in their research that social networks have a life of their own and a profound impact on members' physical and emotional well-being. Emotions and social norms are passed through social connections; people are even influenced by individuals with whom they are unacquainted but who are connected to people they know in their social matrix. If a few well-connected individuals in a group are feeling negative or hopeless or are engaged in self-destructive behavior, it increases the possibility that these feelings and behaviors will spread to others in the group. Conversely, positive feelings and behaviors are contagious and flow through a social network through direct and indirect contact; engagement with people who feel hopeful and optimistic, and who are caring for themselves, enhances a sense of being part of a successful and efficacious team. This is why mutual aid and support groups, as part of a psychosocial capacity building strategy, are empowering and foster positive emotions, which in turn enhances resiliency (see chapter 9).

Positive emotions contribute to more optimistic thinking, social connectedness, and a physical sense of well-being (Fredrickson, 2003; Tugade & Fredrickson, 2004; Waugh & Fredrickson, 2006), all of which in turn foster positive feelings, establishing a healthy circuit of resiliency. There is a correlation between positive emotions and having an engaged lifestyle—experiencing a range of positive social relations at work and home—and a more meaningful life (Seligman, Rashid, & Parks, 2006). As Seligman puts it: "Well-being cannot exist just in your head . . . it is a combination of feeling good as well as actually having meaning, good relationships and accomplishment" (Tierney, 2011).

Positive emotions contribute to more creative thinking, resourceful problem solving, emotional regulation, and meaning-making (constructing meaning from stressful events) (Tugade & Fredrickson, 2004). Emotional regulation, meaning-making, problem solving, connecting socially, and sustaining hope are strategies that Hobfoll et al. (2007) found to be essential aspects of recovery from exposure to mass trauma. Another circuit that relates to positive emotions is that happier people are more likely to engage in acts of kindness, which is very helpful after a disaster, and engaging in acts of kindness begets greater happiness (Otake, Shimai, Tanaka-Matsumi, Otsui, & Fredrickson, 2006). This corresponds with Hobfoll and colleagues' (2007) finding that a sense of efficacy, which helping others certainly can contribute to, is an important way that people recover from exposure to mass trauma. A sense of humor also fosters positive feelings and accompanying resiliency (Bonanno, 2004).

Positive emotions expand a person's sense of oneness with others, often referred to as "self-other overlap" (Waugh & Fredrickson, 2006). Feeling a sense of oneness with others decreases feelings of isolation and alienation and enhances a sense of connection and belonging, which generates positive emotions. A connection with others can also come from internalized images of important figures. In psychodynamic literature, this is referred to as object relations or self-objects (Eagle, 1984). Internalized representations of others allow a person to feel in relationship with others even when they are not physically present. Another, more dynamic way of conceptualizing relationships is by focusing on one's ability to form attachments to others, which develops in early childhood and becomes an interactional and bonding style throughout life (Karen, 1998). Thus, an aspect of resiliency in the face of disaster is both the ability to hold internalized images of sustaining and inspiring others (Rosenfeld et al., 2005) as well as having the capacity to form meaningful relationships and attachments with people. However, while traditional psychoanalytic thinking stresses the legacy of childhood experiences as something an adult surviving a disaster can do little to change, positive psychology views relational capacities as much more plastic and fluid (Seligman et al., 2006; Waugh & Fredrickson, 2006). An exciting finding is that loving-kindness meditation can improve a person's ability to "build" interpersonal resources (Fredrickson, Cohn, Coffey, Pek, & Finkel, 2008). Group psychotherapy exercises that include fostering gratitude toward others increase positive emotions (Seligman et al., 2006) and these, in turn, enhance the ability to forge social connections (Waugh & Fredrickson, 2006).

Achieving a sense of "oneness" is easier in societies and regions where there is less social distance between groups—a smaller bandwidth between the wealthiest and the poorest (Wilkinson & Pickett, 2009). This contributes to the greater "self-other overlap" that Waugh and Fredrickson (2006) have found generates positive emotions. Thus, social and economic justice should be added to the circuit of positive emotions, social connections, problem solving, meaning-making, efficacy, and altruism—a theme pursued in subsequent chapters.

FAMILY RESILIENCY

Families and groups are composed of individuals, so the same qualities that foster resiliency in individuals contribute to resiliency in families. However, families are entities in their own right and are greater than the sum of their parts. They are organic and dynamic systems. They have boundaries, roles, and routines, and they foster interactions among members. Families are constantly in flux—with changes in who lives at home, the health and well-being of family members, and the nature of the relationships among family members as well as their relationships with the outside world. Families have developmental cycles, such as a family with young children at home or a retired couple. And as with individuals embedded in social networks, within families there is a dynamic matrix of interactions, communication, bonds, emotional expression, and a shared, co-constructed vision of the world that includes meaning-making. Thus, resiliency with families, as with individuals, is more a process than a set of inherent, static traits (Betancourt & Kahn, 2007; Patterson, 2002). Also, families are entities in which not only are individuals linked to one another but the family itself is connected to social groups and institutions in the community that it is part of (Betancourt & Kahn, 2007; Landau, 2007; Miller, 2001a; Walsh 2007). So when considering families, we need to take into account the family's relationship to its social networks and community.

As I discuss families, I focus, in particular, on families with children living at home, although much of what I describe is applicable to other family structures and configurations.

When thinking of family resiliency in the face of disaster, it may be helpful to consider again the ways that disasters can negatively affect families (see box 5.1). It is the ability to navigate and negotiate these stresses and threats that leads to family resiliency.

BOX 5.1

THE FAMILY AND DISASTERS: CHALLENGES AND STRESSES

- Can cause changes in the family structure
- Can disrupt family routines
- Can lead to role shifts, role reversal, and regression
- Can shatter family consensus about meaning-making
- Can affect trust and intimacy
- Can cause caretakers to become depleted
- Can affect boundaries and privacy
- Can interfere with the family life cycle, impacting critical transitions and developmental challenges
- Can affect the family's ability to provide for itself and remain independent
- Can lead to a loss of social and community supports

Family therapists have been describing for years the qualities of vibrant families—open communication, clear roles and boundaries, the ability to express and respond to feelings and emotions, and collective problem-solving capacities. These qualities are helpful during times of stability and are particularly helpful when confronting a disaster or other crisis (Walsh, 2003). However, they are not fixed or frozen capacities—they are constantly being negotiated and renegotiated. There are times in a family's life course, even in the absence of disaster, when these processes are working more effectively than at other times. No family will be operating at optimum capacity always (Patterson, 2002). What is perhaps more significant than optimal functioning during a disaster is how quickly the family is able to restabilize itself—its capacity to adapt to adversity (Patterson, 2002). Patterson considers family resiliency as the process by which the family responds to the demands of a crisis with its capabilities and in so doing is able to demonstrate adaptability as it reconstructs collective meaning.

In addition to its ability to perform the tasks described above, the family is more resilient when it is able to maintain a connection with ancestors and cultural traditions (Landau, 2007; Landau & Saul, 2004). Landau refers to this as a transitional pathway between the past and present, which serves as a foundation for envisioning a positive future. This can literally mean intergenerational relationships, but it also can be manifested by the continuation of cultural traditions and family narratives (Denham, 2008; Landau, 2007). An example of this is the "protective circle" of oral narratives carried by some Coeur d'Alene Indians of Idaho (Denham, 2008). The narratives describe past traumas and threats and extract survival strategies that can be used to face contemporary crises. Thus, the narrative itself stokes resiliency, but because it is shared, it also functions to spread the circle of resiliency to other family and tribe members, past and present (Denham, 2008), connecting people in the process. Also, the narrative makes resiliency a collective process with shared responsibility in which "webs of relationships are reconstructed through affiliation and trust" (Hernandez, 2002, p. 335). By situating resiliency collectively and culturally, it is available to all families, including adoptive family units and reconstituted and blended families.

Families are part of the social ecology of their community (Betancourt & Kahn, 2007). Family members interact with and rely on a range of institutions, organizations, groups, and associations, both formal and informal (Miller, 2001a). Thus, family resilience is intricately tied up with the family's relationship to its community. The family needs "integrity" from the community, while the community, in turn, benefits from having resilient families (Miller, 2001a). Community integrity includes safety, quality institutions for family members (schools, health care facilities), civic associations, vibrant and informal social networks, and jobs and adequate public transportation to access the jobs. When a disaster challenges the integrity of the community, family resilience is compromised; family resilience is deeply dependent on community integrity.

The resilience of children in the family when there has been a disaster, for example, illustrates this interlocking relationship. Resilient children may have many of the assets described previously in the section on individual resilience—they may be able to easily generate positive emotions and have good social intelligence that enables them to form strong attachments and close relationships. They are part of social networks. But their resilience is also dependent on factors at multiple levels of people and systems in their lives (Betancourt & Kahn, 2007). Clearly, they are dependent on their caretakers, whose physical, psychological, and mental well-being are among the most important factors that help children feel safe and secure and recover from a disaster (Betancourt & Kahn, 2007; Hobfoll et al., 2007; Rosenfeld et al., 2005). But they also rely on the support of their friends, teachers, extended family, neighbors, recreational workers, and other important people and networks in their community (Betancourt & Kahn, 2007). Their resiliency goes well beyond their innate tendencies and is grounded in and dependent on all of these family and community resources.

While this is true in all cultural settings, it is particularly salient in collectivist cultures where the resiliency of the family is inseparable from the resiliency of individual members, and the resiliency of the family is often tied to that of the collectivity. Kayser, Wind, and Shankar (2008) found that survivors of the Asian tsunami in India recovered more quickly when communal interdependence was reestablished and when they were rebuilding family structures and returning to routines, which creates a sense of normalcy. In addition, they discovered that finding benefits (meaning) from the disaster experience was part of the process of resiliency. This is consistent with my experience when I responded to the Haitian earthquake of 2010 in the small village of Fonfrede, which is described in greater detail in chapter 9.

Finding benefits from an experience and positive meaning both contribute to and are generated by positive emotions (Seligman et al., 2006). What Seligman et al. describe as the basis of positive emotions for individuals—

a pleasant, engaged, socially connected, and meaningful life—certainly applies to families. As with most things, this too is culturally bound, as the expectations for what transpires among family members and the role of emotions in the family are culturally contingent. But in at least some cultures, the ability of family members to generate positive emotions together and have fun with one another can be important aspects of family resiliency. Enjoying one another's presence, playing, telling stories together, singing together, pursuing religious and spiritual practices together—whatever the activities that spur connection, bonds, and shared meanings—enhance family resiliency.

COMMUNITY RESILIENCY

Community resiliency makes it possible for some communities to withstand and recover from the consequences of disaster. As has been discussed, resiliency is a process and not a set of traits, and when considering community resilience, it is inextricably and recursively bound with individual and family resilience. Communities are also part of larger entities—counties, states, regions, and countries—and their resilience is tied to the support that they receive from these larger systems that they are part of. An example of this was shared in chapter 3—how Mississippi was able to access and receive post–Hurricane Katrina recovery aid more quickly and effectively than neighboring Louisiana, at least in part because of the political connections between state leaders and the federal administration at the time ("Mississippi's Failure," 2009). This is another example of the social ecology of disaster at work—the interaction of federal policies and politics with state government, local business, insurance companies and insurance regulations, and some, but certainly not all (for example, the Mississippi chapter of the NAACP), community leaders—leading to recovery in some sectors, growth in others, and neglect of many, particularly those lacking resources and political power. The resiliency of individuals and families living in Gulfport and Biloxi, Mississippi, and New Orleans is part of an evolving, dynamic process that rewards some, subjugates others, and involves more than static and inherited traits or dispositions.

Sri Lanka, six months after the tsunami of 2004, which particularly devastated both the eastern and southern coasts, offers another illustration of the relationship between politics and resiliency. Having worked with communities in both regions, I was stunned by the disparities. In the south, dominated by the Singhalese majority and a relatively conflict-free zone, there were luxury hotels already in operation and armies of young Westerners working with local people to build houses and clear away debris. This contrasted with the east, where ethnic Tamils were caught between the government and rebels in a brutal civil war. Although there were many international NGOs, they were engaged mostly in providing shelter and resources for internally displaced persons (IDP) camps. The development that was occurring in the south was not evident in the east, which was cut off from the rest of the country—literally, by damaged roads running through conflict zones and, politically, from the neglect of the Singhalese-dominated government. The collective resiliency of the mostly Singhalese families living in the south offered political and economic handholding unavailable to the Tamil minority in the east. Resiliency, be it individual, family, or collective, is shaped by the social ecology of disaster and is not a politically neutral process.

Another illustration is the difference between what happened in China's Sichuan Province after the earthquake of 2008 and in Haiti after the earthquake of 2011. China had a strong central government as well as a system of local cadres. The country also had a strong economy, army, navy, heavy machinery, and other resources needed to rescue people and help them rebuild their lives. Many more people were pulled alive from the rubble of the Sichuan earthquake than the Haitian earthquake, resulting in a much lower casualty rate. Haiti is a poor and tiny country that is still suffering from a history of colonialism, neocolonial exploitation, economic weakness, and political instability. In China, earthquake survivors were relocated to temporary housing within weeks, and schools and factories were rebuilt. In Haiti, a year after the earthquake, the majority of survivors were still languishing in tent cities, with poor sanitation, diseases such as cholera, and little access to jobs or resources. The collective resiliency of Chinese earthquake survivors has been boosted by many resources unavailable to their Haitian counterparts.

Thus, the resiliency of communities, first and foremost, depends on the availability of resources, some of which are there before disaster, others of which are available after disaster. Wealthier communities have families who are more likely to have home insurance, health insurance, and other resources to withstand or escape catastrophe and rebuild afterward. Wealthier communities are more likely to have political connections and capital that enhance their resiliency to the effects of disaster. And *within* any community, there are sectors better positioned to recover, to exercise their resiliency, than others.

However, as important as they are, wealth and material assets are not the only sources of community resiliency. There are other aspects of the social ecology, such as where the community is located—is it easily accessible or cut off from relief efforts? Another factor is the density of the population—how many people were affected and how many people remain and are in a position to help with recovery? How damaging was the disaster to the community's infrastructure? For example, both the attacks of 9/11 and the Oklahoma City bombing did not destroy the infrastructure of the respective cities in which they occurred, although both caused a lot of damage and created major disruptions. In contrast, Hurricane Katrina and the Asian tsunami destroyed entire communities and devastated their infrastructures for years to come. The epicenter of the Haitian earthquake was in the capital, Port-au-Prince, where a third of the population of the country lived and where most sources of jobs and higher education were located. The postdisaster environment is an important aspect of community resiliency—when it is in a shambles, besieged by armed conflict, or about to be hit by another aftershock or hurricane, individuals and families cannot feel safe, secure, or able to access their own sources of resiliency.

Social capital is another important dimension of the social ecology of disaster. There are at least three types of social capital (Yamagawa & Shaw, 2004): (1) bonding—connections among people with similar demographic profiles or with intimate ties, (2) bridging—ties among people from different neighborhoods or groups but with similar socioeconomic statuses, and (3) linking—ties among disparate groups in the community and important social institutions, like banks and the police. All three stimulate resiliency at the individual, family, and community levels. Bonding can bring people together within a small community or subcommunity, while bridging social capital can connect different sectors of the community. Linking social capital gives communities access to institutional resources. However, it can be difficult to achieve bridging between communities when there are ethnic or religious tensions, and in many instances, linking social capital occurs between elites and elite institutions rather than at the grassroots level. This is less true in more egalitarian societies, where social capital is shared among more groups, which in turn generates more social trust (Wilkinson & Pickett, 2009).

Samson, Morenoff, and Earls (1999) identify five core aspects of social capital that are helpful to the consideration of resiliency: (1) organizations and services (health and mental health, schools, public safety), (2) ties of kinship and friendship, (3) voluntary associations (civic groups and religious organizations and business, consumer, and tenant groups), (4) neighborhood activism, and (5) mutual trust.

In examining this list, we can see that some facets of community social capital are tied to wealth and assets, but there are other factors as well. Organizations and services are connected to the wealth and prosperity of a community, but even when comparing economically similar communities, some have more or better organizations than others. Kinship and friendship ties are related to culture, the history of the community, how homogenous or heterogeneous it is, how egalitarian it is, what the spatial and living arrangements are like, and many other factors. Some communities are laced with voluntary associations, while others are barren in this area. Neighborhood activism and mutual trust are also factors that go beyond economic and social resources. The combination of these features of social capital leads to a sense of "collective efficacy," the collective belief and hope that a community can do things together to achieve cooperative goals (Samson et al., 1997; Samson et al., 1999). Collective efficacy is fostered by social cohesion and in turn contributes to social cohesion. Cohesion, or connectedness, and a sense of efficacy have been identified as important components of resiliency in all of the units of analysis in this chapter—individual, family, and community. If disaster occurs in a community divided by racism or extremes of wealth, ravaged by ethnic conflict, or where families have little relationship to one another and their community, then the rebuilding after a disaster has a shaky foundation to begin with. If a disaster strikes a community and there is already a sense of effectiveness and unity, then it is much more probable that it will be able to respond to the catastrophe with hope and strength. The community is more likely to exhibit what Landau and Saul (2004) have described as signs of community resiliency—publicly mourning and grieving together by sharing stories about the disaster and recovery, reestablishing the routines of everyday life, and standing shoulder to shoulder, facing the future with hope.

WHAT CAN RESPONDERS DO TO FOSTER RESILIENCY?

There is an irony to this question because resiliency implies that individuals, families, and communities have their own assets and capacities for recovering from disasters. Yet I believe there is a role for outsiders, particularly because disasters can temporarily deflate an individual or collective sense of efficacy and take away or disrupt important supports that are part of the process of resiliency. Outsiders can contribute to a web of support, a safety net, a holding environment that, like a temporary shelter after a storm, can give people sufficient breathing space, respite, and a sense of security so that they can access their own sources of resiliency. And yet there is a delicate balance between the offering of support and taking over entirely. I recall a local Red Cross worker in Florida who, after a series of hurricanes brought in Red Cross volunteers from all over the United States, bemoaned, "Once National comes in, we always play second fiddle—they just take over." How can disaster responders do this in a way that provides the scaffolding for recovery without undermining local sources of resiliency?

PARTNERSHIPS

One of the first principles is to work in partnership with local people and to do so cooperatively. While this makes common sense, it is not always as easy to implement as it might sound. Local people are often depleted and feeling temporarily dependent and in need of support—a pattern of benefactor and patron can be established that is difficult to change as affected people become more able to access their sources of resiliency. This is even more pronounced when working cross-culturally or internationally, particularly when responders come from more developed countries than the nation that has been affected by the disaster, which is often the case. I have often encountered very grateful local leaders who have placed me on a pedestal because of my education but also because of my ethnicity and nationality. It is seductive to be offered the chance to play the role of "expert" and be asked to tell people what to do.

Thus, outside responders must enter disaster situations with humility and what Buddhists call a "beginners mind"—we are here to learn as much as to contribute. As Claiborne and Lawson (2005) have conceptualized and Corbin and Miller (2009) have described, collaboration means working out ways to communicate effectively and forming connections between local and outside people. It means cooperation, coordination, and community building. This can be facilitated by developing contracts, formal and informal, between local and outside people about respective roles. It is often helpful to see outsiders as consultants to local leaders rather than as directors or project leaders in their own right. Outside professionals may have much to share with and contribute to, even to teach, local people about ways of recovering from disasters, but the style of sharing whatever expertise the professional brings must be one of collaboration and caution; helping must do no harm.

BELIEVING IN RESILIENCE

A barrier to fostering resilience is the ambivalence many practitioners who respond to disasters feel. Of course, most acknowledge it, but in my work, I have found that many professionals, particularly clinicians, focus more on the negative aspects and consequences of disaster than on the resiliency of affected people and communities. This is not surprising. Many responders have been trained in Western methods of psychiatry, psychology, and social work, in which there is a tendency to make the locus of intervention the individual and the focus of the intervention on psychological problems. Also, responders are there to help. We want to be wanted, needed, and effective at what we do. It is a way of managing our own anxiety about the situation as well as wanting to have a clear role that makes us feel good about our efforts.

All people, families, and communities have the potential to be resilient and have manifested resilience at some point in their histories. Yet even those people and communities that are seen as being resilient have vulnerabilities and times when their strengths are difficult to access. This is not a matter of having or not having resiliency, it is the process of understanding how it operates with whoever is being helped.

Not only must responders believe in resiliency, but a major task is to help those hit by the disaster to believe in it as well. This can be challenging, particularly in the immediate aftermath of a disaster. It is also important to avoid being overly positive or hopeful, particularly when people are in mourning or feeling stunned, shocked, or sad. There is a need for balance—between being present with people wherever they are in their reactions and process, while also holding out hope and confidence in their ability to eventually move forward with their lives. This does not necessarily mean that people will return to what their lives were or ever completely get over the pain of their losses. But responders can help people affected by disaster believe in their ability to eventually recover some of their strength and sources of wisdom. There is a great deal of cultural variance in this area—how optimistic or fatalistic to be in the face of adversity or how much power and control people have over their destinies are two important areas of divergence—but in every culture, there is a wish and desire to not suffer and there are fonts of resiliency that people have drawn on to lesson this burden.

MAKING CONNECTIONS

Positive psychology stresses that connected people make for happier, more resilient people. One of the most helpful things that professionals can do to help people after a disaster is to connect them. There are many ways to do this. A very basic way is reuniting people who have been separated or at least helping people to track down those whom they are concerned about or want to be in touch with. When setting up shelters, it helps to create spaces where families and friends can be together. And when establishing IDP camps, it helps to have people from the same communities relocated together. For example, an initial problem at the Jiannan IDP camp in Sichuan Province after the Wenchuan earthquake was that residents were randomly mixed with people from other communities. This diluted social cohesion.

Finding spaces where people can congregate helps to connect people when public spaces or gathering spots may have been rendered inaccessible. Nurturing self-help and mutual support groups is another way of connecting people. Offering activities that people engage in collectively, such as recreational activities for adolescents and children, brings people together for a common purpose. Moreover, this collective gathering has a tendency to generate positive emotions (see chapter 9). Another way to encourage social connections is by helping to form work or volunteer cooperatives in which altruistic or self-empowerment activities occur. In some instances, it is helpful to bring together people, such as widows or orphans, who have experienced common losses. A training-of-trainers model works well here. Local people with less professional training but greater cultural fluency and local knowledge can be trained to lead and facilitate more specialized types of groups.

Depending on the cultural practices of the groups being supported, it is important to consider how to work with families as units. How can parents be helped to reassume their roles with their children in ways that are compatible with cultural expectations? How can elders be integrated with younger family members? Are there ways to draw on their wisdom? In more collectivist cultures, extended family members have important roles to play in family resiliency and recovery, and responders can encourage their involvement.

Human connection and social support are part of the process of human attachment and there are neurochemical transmitters that are activated by the compassionate presence of others (Charuvastra & Cloitre, 2008; Mollica, 2006). Social support has even been found to be a positive factor for people who have developed PTSD, creating a sense of safety and security that is an important prerequisite for recovery (Charuvastra & Cloitre, 2008). Thus, human connection and social support not only can generate a sense of well-being but are part of the process of healing from trauma and disaster, a form of social resiliency with neurochemical results.

Bringing people together is part of the process of regenerating social networks that were disconnected because of disaster. This seeds social capital. Even in communities where there was a paucity of social networks and associations, the disaster may provide an opening to establish webs of connections that had not been present before the catastrophe. As Yamagawa and Shaw (2004, p. 5) describe in their research on earthquakes in Kobe, Japan, and Gujarat, India: "Post-disaster recovery processes should be considered as opportunities for development, by revitalizing the local economy and upgrading livelihoods and living conditions."

TELLING STORIES

Telling and sharing stories is part of resiliency at many levels (Denham, 2008; Landau & Saul, 2004). There are many ways to do this, and encouraging survivors to articulate and voice their experiences can be an important way responders encourage resiliency. Children can be given the tools to draw at home, in school, or through activity groups. In certain cultures or families, journaling is a method for exploring one's experience and trying to make sense of and attach meaning to it. In other cultures, there is more of an oral tradition, and storytelling can serve as a means for both sharing stories and bringing people together. Photographic exhibits are a visual way to tell stories. And giving people video cameras to record what they see or what they want to share can lead to cinematic storytelling.

Installations are ways of gathering stories and artistic expressions that help to memorialize people and experiences. They can be small, such as the shrine on Cherry Street in Seattle described earlier, or large, such as the many installations that sprouted from the 9/11 tragedy. Installations can exhibit notes, poems, pictures, or symbols (such as ribbons and flowers). They can even be interactive, with places for observers to jot down their reactions or draw pictures. Museums and other memorials, particularly those that are interactive, such as the one in Oklahoma City (described in chapter 11), allow for conversations about a disaster that can span decades.

RECONNECTING WITH TRADITIONAL SOURCES OF STRENGTH

A major tributary of resiliency is a connection with cultural and historical traditions—"transitional pathways" (Landau, 2007). Disasters often lead to temporary blockages of one's traditions. I use the word *temporary* because this can change, even if the conditions last years or even decades. When Native American children were sent to anglicized boarding schools, which were part of a major social disaster, they were often forcibly disconnected from their cultural practices and conditions, which led to depression, despair, and even death (Miller & Garran, 2007). In some instances, tribes abandoned traditional practices, abetted by this forced "socialization," but years later they rediscovered or reconnected with these traditions.

When working in northern Uganda with Acholi survivors of a twenty-year armed conflict that was occurring *among* the Acholi, I partnered with colleagues from the United States and northern Uganda to train young professionals (youth leaders, teachers, social workers) in psychosocial capacity building. The idea was that they would, in turn, train leaders in IDP camps about ways to help people recover—a training-of-trainers model (Corbin & Miller, 2009). At a certain point in the training, we explored cultural traditions. My Ugandan colleague was asked to describe mato oput, a ritual practiced by Acholi when murder has been committed. As he described the ritual, which embodied restorative justice and symbolic healing (described in chapter 10), the group of trainees became transfixed. I saw this process repeated when the trainees, in turn, presented this ritual to residents in the IDP camps. What I learned from talking to participants during this training was how demoralized they had been feeling about themselves as a tribe since the internecine war had commenced. They had lost confidence in themselves and carried a lot of shame, including embarrassment over accepting help from outsiders. When the Ugandan trainer, an elder priest, reconnected them with this powerful ritual, they regained a sense of pride in their ethnicity and confidence that they had mechanisms to respond to the damage wrought by the conflagration.

When disaster strikes communities, some things change and some things are never the same. Although reconstruction is possible, it is not possible to return to exactly the way things were before a disaster. But the severing of pathways to wisdom, traditions, and rituals cuts people off from an important source of resiliency—one that informs identity and group membership. In every culture, there is a playbook for problem solving that is passed along and handed down—hardship is part of the human condition and cultures, societies, communities, and families have created resiliency and survival myths that serve to remind group members of how others before them responded to their own adverse conditions. Reconnecting with the past is a basis of hope for the future.

SELF-CALMING AND TRANSCENDENT MEANING

The ability to regulate one's affect, particularly the capacity to calm oneself, is an important aspect of resiliency. While heightened alertness and experiencing a fight-or-flight state of readiness is functional when people are directly threatened, as we have seen in chapter 4, there are adverse consequences when people continue to remain in this state of siege. Fear, terror, anxiety, agitation, and constant watchfulness do not foster security, or positive emotions, for that matter. Thus, teaching people ways of self-calming and self-soothing helps them to achieve a more secure and focused state, which facilitates resiliency.

One of the most basic ways of dealing with too much cortisol and adrenaline in the system is to flush it out. Vigorous exercise is one of the best ways of achieving this. Critical incident stress management teams (see chapter 7) around the United States are helping firefighters and police officers release the tensions they experience in their work by encouraging them to work out. For people with an existing exercise regime, the task is often to help them reestablish their routines, which may have been disrupted by the disaster, and to figure out ways to implement them under altered circumstances. Exercise is an excellent way to help reduce tension and hypertension and increase a person's physical strength, mental alertness ("The Secret to

Better Health," 2009), sense of well-being, and calmness. It also can improve resistance to illness and make it easier for people to sleep. Clearly, it is important that people who do not normally exercise do so gradually to avoid injury from doing too much too soon.

Another effective way of helping people to self-calm is through mindfulness exercises. I have been sharing very brief examples of these at the end of each chapter of this book. Whether the exercises teach focused concentration, relaxed breathing, heightened self-awareness of one's mental and emotional state, increased self-awareness of one's physical body, or enhanced loving-kindness with respect to self and others, they are all helpful in the process of achieving greater tranquility. I do brief mindfulness exercises with my students at the beginning and end of each class during my course on responding to disasters, and the feedback is consistently positive and enthusiastic. Even in a crowded classroom, people report feeling calmer, more relaxed, less anxious, better able to concentrate, and more connected with one another. Mindfulness exercises can be done under the most adverse of circumstances and they help people manage unfavorable situations, as in overcrowded shelters or refugee camps. While having a regular practice can deepen the effects of mindfulness, practicing for even a few minutes every now and then can have positive effects.

Many mindfulness exercises stem from spiritual practices such as Buddhism, Hinduism, Yoga, and other major religions and spiritual practices. Depending on the people involved and their particular traditions and beliefs, it may be useful to connect mindfulness exercises with spiritual practices. Along with the benefits of mindfulness, spirituality may lead to greater feelings of compassion, connection with others, and even transcendent meaning. Mindfulness as part of spiritual inquiry can be part of the process of meaning-making or even transcendence that is yet another source of resiliency.

WORKING FOR SOCIAL JUSTICE: CREATING SPACE FOR COLLECTIVE RESILIENCY FOR ALL

Western approaches to responding to disaster have emphasized the individual over the collectivity and have focused more on treating psychological reactions than taking social action, with some notable exceptions (Kaniasty & Norris, 1999; Wessells, 1999; Wessells & Monteiro, 2006; Weyerman,

2007). These are not mutually exclusive activities and responders can engage in both, but there is far less written about social action than psychological treatment.

Social action can mean many things and, in this instance, I mean advocating for human rights, inclusivity for those who are marginalized, and social justice for all (see chapter 10). As I have argued throughout this book, the social ecology of disaster must necessarily factor in poverty, racism, armed conflict, and other forms of political and social oppression that interact with the precipitating catastrophic event. These social forces sap and deplete wells of resiliency, as energy is expended on protecting oneself, on survival, and on receiving social respect.

An emphasis on improving social conditions for those affected can be very helpful for individuals, families, and communities recovering from a disaster. It can obtain important resources for people—material resources such as tents and food but also social resources, such as access to planning and decision making during reconstruction. Social action can bring people together for a common purpose in a way that feels empowering, as people take collective action on their own behalf. Social action provides a sense of meaning and purpose and offers efficacious social roles, rather than leaving people feeling dependent and victimized. Social action also creates more social space for more people—contesting social forces that marginalize and render them less visible and valued. And if there is armed conflict, social action can be geared toward reconciliation and restorative justice, which is considered in more detail in chapter 10.

There are also risks when outside responders advocate for social justice. Outsiders have less local credibility and can be seen as meddling in affairs that are not theirs to tamper with. They can alienate one group of people by advocating for another. Power brokers and elites may distance themselves or even respond punitively. This can result in responders being asked to leave a community or having access to important resources or authorizations denied. Social justice needs to be pursued carefully and judiciously.

Disasters offer opportunities as well as losses and challenges. The damage to existing systems and patterns is by and large debilitating for individuals and communities, but it also creates opportunities for social change and reconfiguration; things become unglued, unfrozen, unanchored. Often, there are vested interests taking advantage of disasters to pursue agendas that disempower many local people even further (Klein, 2007; "Mississippi's Failure," 2009). It is not as if the social and political environments after disaster are neutral. This is one of the great obstacles for organizations, such as the American Red Cross, which strive to maintain neutrality while responding to disasters that affect communities in a very unequal way (Park & Miller, 2007). In a sense, a lack of social action leads to de facto collusion with social oppression, which is why engaging in social action, despite the risks, is something that responders can offer to those whose sources of resiliency are blocked by social subjugation.

This chapter has explored individual, family, and community resiliency. Resiliency can be conceptualized as a process rather than as a static set of traits. Considered through a social ecology framework, resiliency is an interaction between physiological, psychological, social, and economic forces; these forces are part of a self-generating circuit. The well-being of the individual is intricately and recursively connected with the well-being of families and communities. Resiliency occurs when people are able to find things comprehensible, manageable, and meaningful and are able to maintain social connections with others. Resiliency has an emotional component, and being able to regulate emotions and self-soothe, as well as achieve and sustain positive emotions, fosters resiliency. All of this leads to better problem-solving skills and fosters altruism and social action, all of which contribute to the process of resiliency.

Family and individual resiliency support processes in which adversity is responded to, sometimes effectively and sometimes not. Resiliency is not something that ensures all challenges and problems will be resolved easily; it is a counterweight to adversity that can tip the balance sheet toward recovery. An important component of individual resiliency is a sense of competency, whereas for families and communities a collective sense of efficacy is vital. Resiliency is sustained by social connections and support and is a component of family and community social capital. Social capital is increased when there are fewer social and economic divisions within a community.

Although resiliency resides within people, families, and communities, it can be helped along by disaster responders. Seven overall strategies are discussed in this chapter: (1) working collaboratively; (2) helping people access their own sources of resiliency; (3) enabling social connections between people and families; (4) helping people tell their stories; (5) helping individuals, families, and communities reconnect with their traditional sources of strength; (6) teaching self-calming techniques that may lead to transcendent meaning; and (7) taking social action on behalf of socially marginalized and oppressed people.

The final section in this chapter has focused on some of the most significant ways that clinicians can be helpful after disaster by supporting resiliency. This is developed further in chapters 7 through 11. However, before considering how psychosocial capacity building is enacted, chapter 6 considers which groups of people are most vulnerable to the negative effects of disaster within a social ecology framework.

MINDFULNESS EXERCISE: GOOD THINGS HAPPEN

Seligman and his colleagues (2006) have described ways that people can generate positive emotions, which are an important source of resiliency. One exercise that they recommend is for people to write down three good things that happened to them every evening and to reflect on why these things happened. I recommend that people try this for at least one week and to think of all of the factors, including luck, that contributed to the good things happening. "Good things" is a subjective notion and can be small or big. If this exercise seems to be helpful, I recommend doing it at least once a week if it is not feasible to do it every night.

6

VULNERABLE POPULATIONS
RISK, RESILIENCY, AND HOW TO HELP

EVERYONE IS AT RISK when there is a disaster, but some are at greater risk than others. This chapter considers five groups that have unique risk factors as a function of their social positioning and the dynamics of oppression. These include women, children, the elderly, the disabled, and those disadvantaged by virtue of race, ethnicity, or social class. Each of these groups is heterogeneous, and it is important to be wary of generalizations. Also at play is intersectionality—the connections between different aspects of identity and forms of social oppression (Miller & Garran, 2007). For example, gender interacts with age, health, race, and class in many complex ways that influence social privilege and experiences (Enarson, Fothergill, & Peek, 2006). It is often difficult to disaggregate one aspect of social identity and to examine its discrete impact on a person's experience. Yet, by being a member of a particular social group, a person has a greater or lesser likelihood of encountering specific types of problems when disaster occurs.

Every group carries a mixture of vulnerabilities and sources of strength and resiliency. For example, although this chapter considers women and ways they are exposed to exploitation and danger in disasters and armed conflict situations, men also have vulnerabilities to contend with. Most combatants in armed conflict are men, and they suffer many direct casualties. However, the focus in this chapter is on groups lacking social privilege before, during, and after disasters. Men, as a group, have more privilege and are subject to less social targeting than women as a group.

Halpern and Tramontin (2007) define vulnerable populations when there is a disaster as those groups having more complex, intense, or specialized needs than others and more difficulty achieving safe and reliable access to necessary resources and services. I use this definition in the chapter. The

five identified groups have been singled out by many researchers and practitioners in the field. One group that is also often mentioned in the context
of helping others is made up of first responders, disaster response volunteers,
and uniformed personnel (police, fire, military, medical). Chapter 12 focuses on self-care for those who care for others.

This chapter emphasizes what is unique about the five groups under consideration. The general principles and trends described in other chapters
also apply to these groups and are not reiterated. For example, the degree
of exposure is always a variable that influences risk and vulnerability in all
groups of people affected by a disaster. Any group already socially targeted
or marginalized, such as by virtue of sexual orientation, is more vulnerable
when there is a disaster, but this chapter limits itself to considering the five
groups mentioned.

WOMEN

Women have unique areas of vulnerability but also sources of strength when
disaster strikes. Two major risk factors for women, which are operant at all
times but even more salient when disaster strikes, are their unequal social
status and the threat of being the target of sexual abuse and exploitation
(McKay, 1998). The mechanisms of social exclusion of women vary from
one society to another. There can be overt exclusion—for example, women
may have less access to certain jobs, an education, or specific legal rights,
including the ability to vote. And there can be covert exclusion—for example, women earn less money for the same positions and are penalized at
work for having children. Many societies have both forms of exclusion. I am
unaware of any society in which, overall, women as a group are doing better than men economically and politically, although there are some where
the gap is less wide. Disasters only exacerbate the inequalities that existed
prior to the disaster process. After a disaster, it is common for women to
have greater difficulty accessing health care, education, and jobs than men
(Hudnall & Lindner, 2006). When relief organizations arrive, they are usually under the leadership of men (McKay, 1998), which often results in less
gender sensitivity when delivering relief services.

Sexual abuse, violence, rape, and exploitation are ongoing risks for wom-
en to varying degrees in different societies, exacerbated by the breakdown
of routines, norms, and social connections when disaster strikes. Armed

conflict is even riskier for women as violence toward and rape of women can be an intentional strategy by combatants to weaken the morale of their enemy (Hudnall & Lindner, 2006). When women are sexually assaulted, there are the immediate physical and health risks from beatings, vaginal injury, and communicable diseases. There are the ensuing psychological and emotional consequences but also the long-lasting social costs (Hudnall & Lindner, 2006; Reis & Vann, 2006). The psychological consequences may include depression, alienation from one's own body, low self-esteem, and addiction, all of which can negatively influence the woman's role as a parent (Swiss Agency for Development and Cooperation [SDC], 2006). Sexually abused women may be viewed as "unworthy" or "undeserving" of social relations or intimacy within their own group or family. There can even be "honor killings" that include the victim of the sexual assault. Not only is there social shame, but rape can result in pregnancy. The children produced from these assaults are often rejected or stigmatized by their extended families or clans (Corbin & Miller, 2009).

Further complicating the situation, aid workers, peace keepers, and family members are all potential perpetrators of violence and sexual abuse of women, contributing to jeopardy in the postdisaster phases of recovery (Reis & Vann, 2006). There are also abductions and women (and girls) being forced into the roles of sexual companions, sex slaves, and sex workers (Corbin & Miller, 2009; Hudnall & Lindner, 2006; Kristof & WuDunn, 2009). The consequences of sexual abuse and exploitation for women are manifold and include social suspicion and alienation from others, as well as personal shame and self-doubt. Sexual abuse of women leads to political alienation, economic decline, impediments to good parenting, and further social inequities (SDC, 2006).

In addition to being structurally disadvantaged before the process of disaster, women are further taxed by the consequences of disaster. They may lose the wage earner in the family or the breadwinner's ability to work. As most women are already burdened by parenting responsibilities, they often have to add economic survival to their task list (Enarson et al., 2006). Both child care and economic responsibilities carry increased risks for women. Children are dependent, so mothers have to look after them as well as themselves. This can slow down their ability to escape danger and widens the circle of those requiring vigilance and protection. Foraging for food and firewood can leave women in exposed and susceptible situations when local routines are altered and social interactions and policing are limited.

Thus, it is not surprising that women and girls report more negative consequences after exposure to disaster and armed conflict than do men (Murphy, 2010; Rosenfeld et al., 2005). Women tend to be more socially connected and expressive of their feelings, but they also seem to suffer more negative consequences when there has been a disaster (Rosenfeld et al., 2005). However, social connection and affective expression are sources of resiliency and can help women themselves recover in addition to creating greater family and social unity. If women have access to education, health care, and economic opportunity, they can be the engines of peace, social cohesion, and overall prosperity (Kristof & WuDunn, 2009). In armed conflict situations, empowered women are more likely to be leaders in promoting health, peacekeeping, and reconciliation (McKay, 1998).

So what can be done to protect, support, and empower women facing disaster? Obviously, greater social equality is a long-term goal that benefits women in a disaster and strengthens their communities and societies overall. Key aspects of this are fostering access to education and health care and supporting economic independence and entrepreneurship through such mechanisms as microcredit programs, the extension of small loans to people in need (Kristof & WuDunn, 2009; SDC, 2006). Social inclusion also means greater political and social power as well as access to basic needs, such as water and food. Additionally, it is important to try to change attitudes through public awareness campaigns (SDC, 2006).

After a disaster, careful planning should include ensuring the safety of women and children in the postdisaster environment, whether this is in an IDP camp, a shelter, or in the community itself. It needs to be assumed that women have been placed at greater risk and require support and attention to prevent further abuse and exploitation. Psychosocial interventions that connect people and discourage social isolation are important for women, as are programs that support families and directly and indirectly work on intergender relations (Hudnall & Lindner, 2006; Reis & Vann, 2006; SDC, 2006). Men need to be part of the equation both through direct interventions, which lessen their predilection for gender-based violence and exploitation, and public awareness campaigns. In developing countries, such campaigns can include radio public service announcements (Staub, 2008). Intervening in this very personal and socially central domain requires cultural knowledge and sensitivity, as well as respect and confidentiality for those involved (Reis & Vann, 2006). There is often a tension between women's rights and traditional cultural practices, and outside disaster responders have to strike a delicate balance between advocating for the rights and protection of women and respecting local cultural norms. This is not an easy equilibrium to achieve, and Okin (1999) has edited a volume whose contributors explore this tension from multiple perspectives. Ultimately, women bear the brunt of the negative consequences from a disaster, both directly and through the suffering of their families. Yet they are the ones who can be counted on to maintain social stability and create the social networks that are so crucial for collective recovery.

CHILDREN

Children are particularly at risk for many reasons when there are disasters. A child's age and developmental level obviously influence how dependent and vulnerable they are and the ways that they comprehend and process the experience of disaster. But overall, children rely on adults as caretakers and are dependent on them to meet many of their needs. Therefore, their well-being is often inextricably connected to the welfare of their caretakers (Gordon, Faberow, & Maida, 1999; Ronan, Finnis, & Johnston, 2006; Rosenfeld et al., 2005). At its most extreme, disaster can cause children to lose their caretakers through death or separation, threatening children's security, safety, and emotional well-being. The long-term psychological consequences of this include threats to a child's ability to form trusting bonds and attachments with others (Gordon et al., 1999; Rosenfeld et al., 2005).

Children are smaller than adults and therefore are at greater risk for serious injury and illness as a consequence of disaster (Boyden, de Berry, Feeny, & Hart, 2006). They are less able to protect and fend for themselves. Children are more easily abducted by adults and, in the chaos of disasters, children have been seized by individuals, armed forces, and even NGOs. Even when not actually threatened, children have the fear of being hurt or taken, which is more likely to occur when there has been a terrifying event, such as large-scale disaster, and their caretakers are not available to offer them a sense of security. These fears are exacerbated when there has been a great deal of destruction and loss of life (Vernberg, 1999).

Disaster creates social disruptions for everyone but particularly for children, who benefit from structure and routine (Boyden et al., 2006). Schools offer these touchstones but are often damaged, shut down, or even destroyed by disasters. In Haiti, after the earthquake of January 12, 2010, more than three thousand schools were destroyed and many may never be rebuilt (Romero, 2010). In disaster, playgrounds and other play spaces are damaged or lost, as are toys (Gordon et al., 1999) and special belongings that may serve as transitional objects. Bedtime routines are also disrupted at a time when children are experiencing great distress and are most in need of calming and settling routines.

Developmental level affects how children comprehend and make sense of the world. Their explanatory systems are less sophisticated than those of adults, making it more difficult to understand what has happened when there has been a disaster. Children's developmental level influences their needs and reactions, as well as how they process the events of a disaster, including their narratives about why the disaster occurred (Zubenko, 2002). They have less life experience to measure the disaster against and to help them understanding its meaning. They are also less able to filter out disturbing, frightening, and overwhelming images. This is one reason why it is so important for adults to try to moderate their exposure to disaster-related information, such as repeated media images of death and destruction (Pynoos, Steinberg, & Brymer, 2007). Children of all ages but particularly younger children often blame themselves for the disaster (Rosenfeld et al., 2005) and can even have magical thinking about something they may have done wrong that led to the catastrophe. This sense of personal responsibility can lead to strong emotional reactions, including anger (Smith, Dyregrov, & Yule, 2002). Like adults, children are dealing with hyperarousal, retriggered trauma, sadness and bereavement, and insecurity—but even more so (Smith et al., 2002). They have less cognitive ability to understand and explain to themselves what they experienced and fewer strategies for coping with their distress. If children have experienced prior trauma (including abuse or neglect), then they are even more vulnerable to the negative effects of disaster (Cohen, Mannarino, Gibson, Cozza, Brymer, & Murray, 2006; Rosenfeld et al., 2005). They are also more susceptible to illness and disease (Boyden et al., 2006).

There is intersectionality between all aspects of social identity. Thus, gender interacts with being a child. Many of the sources of vulnerability for women also apply to children. They are not in positions of leadership or power and can be physically or sexually abused and exploited. In certain cultures, girls are less likely to be given access to school, adequate medical care, or overall support and attention from their families compared to boys (Kristof & WuDunn, 2009). Girls are more likely to express themselves emotionally after a disaster, but they are also more likely to have more severe reactions (Rosenfeld et al., 2005).

I have been summarizing some of the ways that children are vulnerable after a disaster, but children are also extremely resilient. They are adaptable and able to recover from most disasters if they receive adequate social support. If there is stability and a collective and familial trajectory of recovery after the disaster, most children show a partial reduction of symptoms in months and usually full remission within a year and a half (Rosenfeld et al., 2005).

There are a number of ways to be helpful to children after a disaster. It is critically important that they maintain contact, whenever possible, with their parents or guardians (Gordon et al., 1999; Rosenfeld et al., 2005; Vernberg, 1999). Therefore, when there is separation from attachment figures, reunification is a high priority. If the primary caretaker is not physically available, other ways must be sought to maintain contact with the child, such as by telephone or e-mail. It is helpful to reassure children that they will be reunited with their caretakers, but only if this is likely to occur. Transitional objects, such as pictures of caretakers, items of clothing, or for younger children, toys or stuffed animals, can help soothe a child separated from caretakers.

But what if the caretaker has died or is missing? In such instances, it is important to have an adult who can develop an attentive and nurturing relationship with the child. Children can form temporary or substitute attachments that help them feel more secure during times of separation from primary attachment figures. If there are familiar people available—siblings, other relatives, friends, teachers, and the like—then these people can be reassuring to children. Depending on the children's ages and circumstances, it is usually better to first help them feel secure and attached to someone before they have to face the permanent or long-term loss of their parents or caretakers.

Overall, children exposed to disaster need to feel safe and secure, as much as is achievable within a postdisaster context. Reestablishing routines and a general sense of predictability helps children feel more settled and as if things are more "normal" (Gordon et al., 1999; Jagodic & Kontac, 2002; Zubenko, 2002). This is particularly challenging in temporary disaster settings, such as in shelters or IDP camps, yet it is important to strive for.

There is much work that can be done with children's caretakers, be they long-term or temporary caretakers. In many circumstances, they too have experienced the disaster and are working on their own reactions, which can make it more difficult for them to focus on their children. Hence, when caretakers meet their own needs and receive their own sources of support, this can be of indirect benefit to children. Coaching and support for caretakers helps them better understand a child's reactions and be more attuned to the child's needs (Smith et al., 2002). For example, children may misbehave or withdraw because they may view the disaster as punishment for something they did wrong (Rosenfeld et al., 2005). In such instances, they need gentle reassurance and encouragement to not blame themselves. Psychoeducational groups are particularly helpful for parents. They learn how to respond to typical reactions, reestablish routines, and find ways of reassuring children. They also learn what to listen for and the importance of attention and physical comfort (Smith et al., 2002).

Teachers are a critical group for children after a disaster. Many teachers view their roles in primarily, if not strictly, educational terms. But after a disaster, teachers can help children with their emotional expression and to understand and comprehend the disaster. Teachers can also offer more comfort, security, and support than they perhaps usually do (Gordon et al., 1999; Ronan et al., 2006; Smith et al., 2002). Drawing is a particularly helpful activity for children. It allows them to express things that are preverbal or nonverbal about the disaster (Rosenfeld et al., 2005). Drawing, along with storytelling, dance, music, and drama, can all help children not only express their distress but imagine feeling safer, stronger, and more secure (Bryant-Davis, 2005). These activities help children access the nonverbal regions of their brains, where traumatic memories are often stored. After many disasters, such as the Asian tsunami and Haitian earthquake, teachers have been taught the skill of using activities with children to manage stress and trauma and to instill a sense of efficacy and hope. The Children and War Foundation has a manual that responders can use with parents and teachers to help them help children (Smith et al., 2002).

Children get a lot from their peers and group situations. They are used to being in groups and groups have much to offer children. In a group setting, children can work on things together, which is another constructive way of helping them to recover. In groups, children see that other children are having similar reactions. They problem-solve together, play together, offer mutual aid and support, and strengthen relationships and social networks among one another (Jagodic, Kontac, & Zubenko, 2002). There are many different types of groups in which these goals can be achieved—educational and psychoeducational discussions, arts and crafts groups, creative writing and storytelling workshops, drama groups, sports teams, choirs, dance groups, and social circles (Bryant-Davis, 2005; Jagodic et al., 2002; Jagodic & Kontac, 2002).

In the small Haitian village of Fonfrede, teachers in four schools were trained by local NGO CapraCare to help children recover from the 2010 earthquake six weeks after it struck. The teachers reported that many children were easily frightened, hypervigilant, unsure of themselves, and insecure when inside buildings. What emerged during the training, which focused on group activities, was the importance of song and dance in the lives of the children. Trainers and teachers agreed that a rap competition would be a good way to encourage students to express their fears while also helping them to feel strong and connected to others. The teachers engaged in a mock competition with one another and found that the intervention helped *them* to feel empowered, express their fears, and to have fun together. They planned to have schoolwide and possibly community-wide competitions of original rap songs—along the lines of a poetry slam.

The Children and War Foundation manual (Smith et al., 2002) has a variety of activities geared toward children's stress and trauma. The focus is on helping children respond to emotional flooding, reduce hyperarousal, cope with intrusive images and memories, pay attention to their bodies and relax, attain cognitive mastery and achievement, and grieve and mourn. All of these can be done in groups, and the skills to run the groups can be conveyed in a training-of-trainers model. For example, psychologists and social workers can train a group of "master" teachers who can in turn train other teachers. For those children with more severe reactions, focused cognitive-behavioral methods (again often administered in groups) can be helpful with mastery and recovery (Cohen et al., 2006; Ronan et al., 2006).

In summary, children are both resilient and have particular vulnerabilities. They can be helped by strengthening the responses of caretakers and through groups with peers.

THE ELDERLY

Older adults are resilient while also having particular vulnerabilities. Their resiliency comes from their extended life experiences. More often than not, they are familiar with adversity, which may "inoculate" them from some of the negative cognitive and emotional consequences of disasters (Allen & Nelson, 2009; Norris & Murrell, 1988; Tyiska, 2008)—they have been there before or at least somewhere similar. Despite this, the elderly are among those worst affected by disaster, and in natural disasters they have the highest death rate of any cohort (Allen & Nelson, 2009). Thus, it is important to consider the risk factors and sources of strength for elderly survivors of disasters.

Older adults are a diverse group in many ways. Like all age groups, they are socioeconomically diverse and have varying degrees of privilege and resources. There are different age subgroups within the larger category of the elderly. One way to divide them is by the young old (sixty-five to seventy-four), the aged (seventy-five to eighty-four), and the oldest (older than eighty-five) (Halpern & Tramontin, 2007). There are also differences between the well elderly and those with disabilities. As a group, older adults are more likely to experience health problems, immobility, dependency, and social isolation than other age groups (Allen & Nelson, 2009; Halpern & Tramontin, 2007). They are also more likely to have sensory and cognitive limitations, which can hinder their ability to respond to disaster (Halpern & Tramontin, 2007). They may find it difficult to understand and comprehend what is happening, becoming easily confused. This contributes to the elderly feeling spatially disoriented by the dislocations of disaster as they lose familiar people, places, and things (Torgusen & Kosberg, 2006; Tyiska, 2008). When relocated, older adults may experience "transfer trauma" (Allen & Nelson, 2009; Halpern & Tramontin, 2007), as they are necessarily more dependent on social supports than younger adults (Tyiska, 2008) and can feel isolated and abandoned if displaced. They can also feel tired and exhausted by the disaster disruptions and require more rest, which can be difficult to come by in a disaster situation (Allen & Nelson, 2009).

Many elderly people have suffered hardship and tragedy in their lives. The destruction caused by disaster can add to a cumulative burden of loss. There is a particular poignancy to losing much of what has been accumulated over a lifetime, such as assets and mementos, when there is little time left to recoup and replenish. The meaning of one's life is often an object of reflection in later years and a disaster is an unplanned occurrence, often fraught with fear, dislocations, and tragedy, which can disrupt the meaning-making process for seniors. It can be very discouraging to have one's beliefs or assumptions challenged or even shattered late in life (Tyiska, 2008).

Given these vulnerabilities, what contributes to the resiliency of the elderly? As was mentioned earlier, exposure to prior traumatic events can prepare older adults for the effects of disaster. Wisdom, patience, and equanimity are all qualities that can be honed over a lifetime of struggle. I am wary of idealizing seniors, as they are a mixed group and have their sources of anxiety, insecurity, and worry as does any age cohort, but there are usually lessons that have been learned over the life course that can be useful when confronting a disaster. What these lessons are will vary, but it is important for responders to honor and value the acumen of older adults and to work to elicit it. The sharing of wisdom is empowering for seniors and offers valuable lessons for others. To facilitate this process, disaster responders can try to slow things down, whenever possible, to allow storytelling and narratives to emerge.

As with children, routines and predictability are important for the elderly (Halpern & Tramontin, 2007). Reassurance is helpful, as is regaining possessions and reconstructing social support networks (Allen & Nelson, 2009; Halpern & Tramontin, 2007). Pets can be significant companions for older adults (Torgusen & Kosberg, 2006).

For those elderly who are more frail or disabled, long-term care may be necessary, including nursing services (Gatty, 2009). This necessitates creating a modicum of stability in an environment where there is a sense of crisis and volatility. It is also important, however, to give seniors time to recover. They may well regain some of their prior skills and abilities that were temporarily dislodged during the chaos of disaster. It often takes time to medically stabilize an elderly person after a disaster. Whenever possible, they should be the authors of their own planning and, if they experience cognitive challenges, their family and legal guardians should be consulted before plans are made.

PEOPLE LIVING WITH DISABILITIES

People living with disabilities are also a diverse group with tremendous variation in the type of disability and the impact and limitations imposed by their disabilities. Disabilities affect mobility, sensory capacities, cognitive and mental abilities, and levels of autonomy and dependency. Some disabilities are chronic while others are acute. Some are visible and obvious while others are hidden. With so many variations, how can we generalize about how people living with disabilities fare in disaster?

Essentially, anything that impedes a person's ability to receive information and communicate with others, restricts mobility, or constrains autonomy puts a person at greater risk during a disaster. People with disabilities might not have easy access to warnings and important information about safety, disaster response plans, and important services and resources. Difficulty communicating with others hampers a person's ability to articulate and share her questions, needs, and problems. Challenges with mobility increase vulnerability during a disaster, hindering the ability to evacuate. Disasters often involve relocation, and many temporary sites are not handicapped accessible. Living in tents or IDP camps poses severe challenges for people with impaired mobility. Often, gaining access to simple but basic resources—such as water, food, and sanitary facilities—is a major undertaking. A cognitive challenge, such as mental illness or a developmental delay, is an impediment to grasping what has occurred and being able to respond in an efficacious fashion. Routines and structure help people stay oriented and focused but are often disrupted by disasters.

Thus, people with a range of disabilities are vulnerable to isolation, marginalization, and exploitation when a disaster strikes (Halpern & Tramontin, 2007). This, as well as prior experiences of discrimination and bias, can make people with disabilities wary of shelters and service centers (Spence, Lachlan, Burke, & Seeger, 2007). Therefore, outreach and sensitivity to the needs and concerns of those living with disabilities is called for by disaster responders. It is important to strike a balance between respecting a person's autonomy and offering special accommodations that allow people living with disabilities to fully participate in postdisaster community life and to thrive and recover. It is also helpful to consider how information can be presented so that it is accessible and to think of creative ways in which the media can be used to help people with disabilities communicate and connect with others (Spence et al., 2007).

RACE, ETHNICITY, AND CLASS

Historical and contemporary patterns of discrimination against groups of people, by virtue of race, ethnicity, or class (as well as religion), put these groups at even greater risk when disaster strikes. There are many examples of this. In the United States, the cost of being African American or Vietnamese in Hurricane Katrina–affected areas is well documented (Davis, 2005; Dreier, 2006; Frymer et al., 2005; Green et al., 2007; Kates et al.,

2006; Park & Miller, 2006, 2007). In Sri Lanka, being a Tamil or Muslim living in the east when the tsunami struck meant living in a more isolated, war-torn area where there were fewer government services and a pattern of discrimination combined with social and political isolation. There are many reasons people are at risk because of their ethnicity, race, caste, or class—historical patterns, neocolonial legacies, institutional and political barriers, cultural exclusions, discrimination, prejudice and bias, intergroup conflict, and internalized racism.

The 2010 earthquake in Haiti offers a poignant example. Historically, Haiti has suffered for centuries because former slaves had the audacity to successfully revolt against a Western power—France. This led to attacks by major Western governments, crippling debt repayments, enforced embargos, the exploiting and pillaging of Haitian resources, and internal meddling, notably by France, the United States, and Great Britain. This fostered resource depletion, international isolation, political corruption, instability and repression, and extreme poverty (Fraser, 2010). Nearly half of Haiti's population is made up of children. All of this interacted with the ecology, including higher population density and less rainfall than the neighboring Dominican Republic (Diamond, 2010). Also, Haiti, by virtue of being a Creole-speaking nation unique in the world, is linguistically and culturally isolated; thus, there are fewer resources (such as books in Creole) and fewer connections with other countries in the region. Haiti was a poor and isolated country *before* the earthquake struck.

As mentioned in chapter 5, before the quake, many people, one-third of Haiti's population, lived in dense conditions on a mountain slope in Port-au-Prince. Their houses were poorly constructed and located on an earthquake fault line. When the earthquake struck, many people died instantly in the collapse of buildings. But many also died because this poor, underresourced country could not rescue them in time or provide adequate medical assistance. Since the earthquake, tens of thousands of people live in unsanitary, dense, poorly sheltered tent cities. They have no access to jobs or the hope of rebuilding their lives. The prospect of resettling them in even temporary housing appears dim. Yet there are discourses in the West blaming the Haitian people for their misfortunes—that they are backward, corrupt, inept, and religious heathens (Fraser, 2010). This is an extreme example of the interaction of racism and disaster—the catastrophic conditions that led to such a high loss of life and social disruptions, both during and after the earthquake, were part of a global historical legacy of racism and colonialism. Still, the Haitian people are blamed by some for their own misfortune.

Blaming the victims of discrimination has a long history and is a common trope used by people unaware of their racial and ethnic privilege (Miller & Garran, 2007). It serves to justify extreme discrepancies in wealth and privilege and alleviates any sense of responsibility or shame on the part of those who have benefited (often with limited awareness) from the exploitation. This, in turn, affects the reactions of responders from privileged classes, which are often patronizing and punitive. Moreover, it lowers the trust level of those in need of services and resources from the outside. Scapegoating and blaming the victim are products of intergroup conflict and competition, which is explored in detail in chapter 10.

Discrimination based on race, ethnicity, or social class interacts with disaster in a number of ways. People within marginalized groups are more likely to be living in substandard housing, which is less able to withstand the impact of a disaster. Their homes tend to be located in vulnerable or hazardous locations (Bolin, 2006). In New Orleans, poor African Americans were more likely to be living in low-lying, flood-prone areas (Brookings Institution Metropolitan Policy Program [BIMPP], 2005) and in areas close to chemical storage sites (Miller & Garran, 2007), both of which placed them at greater risk for bodily harm and property destruction when Hurricane Katrina struck. Those who are most socially disadvantaged in a community consistently incur the greatest losses from disasters (Kaniasty & Norris, 1999).

In the immediate aftermath of a disaster, socially disadvantaged people have fewer resources with which to protect themselves. They are less likely to have cars and more likely to live in areas where the infrastructure for transportation is inadequate (BIMPP, 2005). When they try to move to safe areas, they are less likely to be helped and more likely to be discriminated against by authorities, which again was in evidence when African Americans tried to escape from New Orleans. They were at times blocked by police from entering neighboring, predominantly white communities (Park & Miller, 2006). Once survivors are relocated, they are more likely to be treated in a hostile or culturally insensitive fashion (Park & Miller, 2006, 2007). What many white responders (and other people with social privilege) are unaware of is that there is a "web of institutional racism" (Miller & Garran, 2007) faced by people of color before, during, and after disaster. This web includes discrimination in housing and mortgage lending—and less access to education and health care as well as to safe neighborhoods, lack of fair treatment in the criminal justice system, and much more. The web of institutional racism impedes access to resources, increases the experience of discrimination, and deepens the stress caused by a disaster. And, ironically, most people with racial privilege who benefit from this web are unaware of its existence, as they carry passports of privilege protecting them from its effects.

Poor and socially marginalized groups of people are less likely to have property insurance and, more generally, economic, social, and political resources to enlist in their recovery. Also, they are more likely to find that the toll of displacement and relocation creates more roadblocks to finding new jobs and homes. Linguistic and cultural minorities are particularly fractured and destabilized by disasters. The Vietnamese community in Biloxi, Mississippi, which faced hurdles in accessing federal and NGO resources because of language barriers, were reluctant to enter Red Cross shelters owing to cultural insensitivity. They faced the long-term dissolution of their ethnic enclave, which had provided support, social networks, security, and jobs (Park & Miller, 2007; Park et al., 2010). Many residents were displaced, property values soared as casinos bid for land where Vietnamese residents had once lived, and the fishing industries that had previously provided extensive employment never regained their predisaster levels of functioning. The storm not only affected individual lives but splintered a vibrant ethnic enclave that had served as a social and economic incubator for immigrants, protecting them from white American discrimination and hostility, which they had experienced in other parts of the country.

Given the historic and contemporary patterns of discrimination and prejudice, people of color are less likely to trust those who offer help, particularly if the helpers come from the groups or classes that have exploited and subjugated them (Miller & Garran, 2007; Norris & Alegria, 2006). This can include government officials, the police, medical practitioners, psychologists, and social workers. Disasters have too often been used, in the experience of the oppressed, as openings to further exploit and subjugate (Davis, 2005; Klein, 2007). In addition, the helping professions are less likely to be culturally responsive to the needs of their clients, with a mismatch of white professionals treating poor people of color, which can lead to poor communication and misdiagnosis, earning the mistrust of those being served (Miller & Garran, 2007).

People who are used to adversity are also resilient and have crafted strategies for coping and survival. They have skills and sources of strength to help them to withstand the double dose of disaster and discrimination. It is important to recognize, validate, and build on these strengths when work-ing with socially disadvantaged people after a disaster. This entails seeking out local leadership and working collaboratively and in partnership, being sensitive to the dynamics of privilege and oppression, and avoiding the re-creation, albeit unintentional, of patronizing or neocolonial patterns of in-teraction. There is a great risk for this after a disaster, a time when local people are feeling shocked, numb, and overwhelmed. Outside responders are eager to offer immediate help and may "take charge" in a way that rein-forces their authority and status.

Whenever possible, the approach should be to develop the capacity of local people to help their own communities to respond. This is a principle for all communities in all disasters, but it is particularly salient when low-income and/or ethnic- and racial-minority communities are involved. Out-siders can be more effective, more respectful, and leave a deeper and longer legacy if they focus on developing the capacity of indigenous people to help themselves and others, as opposed to offering direct counseling services. Chapter 8 describes how local capacity can be enhanced through a training-of-trainers model.

It is therefore especially important for responders, particularly if from ra-cially and economically advantaged groups, to do a privileges-and-prejudices self-inventory. Stereotypes, which fuel prejudices, are carried by all people. However, when these are mirrored by culture and social structures, they are often invisible to the people holding them. As well as this, there are often assumptions about health and well-being that are culturally bound; many responders come from individualist cultures (where one-on-one counseling is the norm), whereas the communities being served may be more collec-tivist (Norris & Alegria, 2006). In these collectivist communities, greater emphasis is placed on social connection and mutual aid and support. Thus, the maxim "know thyself" is an important one for responders working across class, race, and nationality; a nondefensive, humble, and inquisitive stance can help with this process.

All people are vulnerable after a disaster, and all people carry reservoirs of strength and resiliency. In this chapter, I have explored sources of risk and resiliency in populations that face unique and complex challenges in a di-saster, focusing on women, children, the elderly, the disabled, and socially and economically disadvantaged groups. It is prudent to be wary of general-izations; people in some social-identity categories have multiple challenges when faced with disaster, but members of these groups also have sources of resiliency. It is important to assess the specific needs and strengths of the individual while also conducting an inventory of the assets of the community at large. Individuals have membership in a variety of social groups, while multiple social groups constitute a community. Therefore, consideration of the challenges faced and assets carried by particular social groups is an important part of the assessment process for disaster responders.

MINDFULNESS EXERCISE: MEDITATION ON STEREOTYPES

As with all mindfulness exercises, sit comfortably and maintain an upright posture. Begin this meditation with focusing on breathing for a few minutes. Then, try and access a negative feeling that you have about members of a social group other than your own—it might be based on discrimination with respect to race, ethnicity, social class, gender, age, sexual orientation, or disability. Focus on just one negative feeling at a time. Explore where the feeling is located in your body. It is important that you not be afraid of this feeling but rather that you investigate it without judgment. After situating it in your body, try to deconstruct the feeling: What values fuel it? Where did you learn those values? What experiences have you had that reinforce that feeling?

There are two more steps in this meditation. The first is to apply the negative feeling to yourself—have others ever felt this way about you? Try to embrace the discomfort of being the target of this feeling. Then, shine compassion and light on yourself. Lastly, think of someone who contradicts the feeling or stereotype—perhaps someone you know or else a public or historical figure. Visualize this person and breathe in their strength and wisdom. After doing this for a few moments, return to focusing on your breathing for a minute before ending the meditation.

7

DISCOURSES OF DISASTER RESPONSE AND RECOVERY

THE CAPACITY OF PEOPLE and communities to rebound from the adversity of disaster is remarkable. Nevertheless, there is a role for professionals and volunteers from both inside and outside of the community to aid in recovery when there has been a disaster. Throughout human history, there are people who foster healing or who help people find meaning in destructive events: shamans, spiritualists, faith healers, herbalists, elders, priests, and alchemists, right up to the present-day array of medical, psychological, social work, and religious and spiritual personnel who respond to disasters. An aspect of collective resiliency is the availability of specialized people to assist with recovering, grieving, and healing. What is challenging, however, is the fine line between supporting and supplanting, between giving a boost and taking over; responders need to find ways to nurture resiliency and not inadvertently undermine it.

I have used the word *discourse* to describe the narratives of response and recovery that are part of the dialogues and debates about disaster. There is no consensus about how best to respond to people suffering from the distress of disaster, and every voice is informed by cultural assumptions; professional training and experiences (which are always limited); differing criteria about psychosocial well-being, health, and pathology; and what to hope for and expect after a disaster. There is no objective place to stand in this disaster salon; even those who strive to be dispassionate researchers are constrained by the criteria they seek to test and measure and how they go about measuring them. Indeed, even a simple notion, such as positive versus negative outcomes, bespeaks a dualism common to some cultures but alien to others, creating a dichotomy that is meaningful to some and baffling to others. I believe that it is helpful to think of the approaches, guidelines, procedures, protocols, and mandates that inform the work of helping professionals responding to disaster as discourses that reflect a particular stance, often informed by good practice or research, but that are always an incomplete story without absolute certainty or claim to universal truth. Discourses can be analyzed and deconstructed so that the embedded cultural and epistemological assumptions can be articulated, scrutinized, and critiqued.

The parable of how, to a hammer, everything looks like a nail has some relevance to this discussion. Western-trained psychiatrists often look for, see, and find trauma in the human response to disaster, as they have been taught to anticipate its occurrence in such situations and have developed an analytic lens that sharpens their ability to see it. Western-trained psychologists versed in cognitive behavioral techniques know how to help people recover from trauma, whether chronic or acute, and want to share their expertise to relieve human suffering. People trained as community psychologists or social workers are more likely to integrate the social with the psychological and conceptualize conducting their work on many social levels. Family therapists gravitate toward working with the family unit, while clergy look for the spiritual losses and sources of hope that are present with disaster. People trained in critical incident stress management, whether professionals or peers, look for opportunities to use their interventions when a disaster has occurred. Western-trained quantitative researchers seek correlations, using randomly controlled trials, to confirm relationships and the impact of interventions. None of these are bad—they all have some validity and have helped many people—but they are all incomplete and are never the final word on what should or should not be done. Moreover, universal practices, to be used with all people from all cultures and parts of the world in all disaster situations, cannot be inferred from them.

One of the largest sticking points in the discourse surrounding response and recovery is determining which is most important—outcomes or the process of recovery. These are not mutually exclusive, and certainly practitioners can pay attention to the process of recovery as well as goal setting and benchmarks to measure and evaluate outcomes, but often people line up in one camp or the other. And Westerners often line up with those who favor outcomes. As I have argued, disaster involves a process and not an event, and the same is true of recovery. Outcomes are important because they set goals, offer baselines, and serve as points of comparison; they can indicate how a person is doing according to certain criteria two years as compared with two weeks after a disaster. But the measurement itself freezes the complexity of reality into a static value that punctuates a dynamic process, and in some ways, this process never ends. When is recovery from anything really complete? If a person has a bad dream about a disaster two years later, does this represent ongoing suffering from the effects of the disaster? Does this mean the individual has not recovered? Does recovery really mean that a person regains a former level of functioning? Even people who are not exposed to disaster, are they operating at the same level of functioning as they were two years ago? Is this a unidirectional phenomenon? If an interviewer asks me to complete a survey about my state of functioning when I am having a period of insomnia or have had some setbacks at work, I might report a fairly bleak picture. But if this is placed in the context of, say, a ten-year period of my life, this might be just a dark time, coloring my interpretation of the past and future but not representing my overall, long-term outlook and functioning.

Westerners often conceptualize recovery from disaster as a linear process, while Easterners tend to view recovery in more cyclical terms. The Wheel of Recovery (figure 1.3) from chapter 1 illustrates the integration of both these notions. There are past and future parts of the circle with disaster poised between them. But the outside of the circle portrays resources and entities that support recovery. These are present some of the time and can rotate in and out of a person's life. And the wheel itself can turn so that the past, present, and future merge. The band that depicts the disaster is folded into old and new experiences, including future challenges and losses. Thus, I am arguing that recovery from disaster is an ongoing, perhaps never-ending, process, as the disaster experience (along with other experiences) is continually being reworked, reexamined, and reintegrated into the warp and weft of a person's life. The disaster experience is never on its own, and there is no final resting place known as "recovery." At certain times in a person's life, the disaster experience may be less salient, although this wheel can turn as well. An example of this involves Jewish survivors of German death camps during World War II. Many went on to lead meaningful, even happy, lives. For some, the experience was relegated to a nightmare of a distant past, while for others it signified an experience that they continually revisited and used to understand world events. As well, the disaster served as an indelible marker of their own psychological and emotional terrain (Levi, 1988; Wiesel, 1960).

One of the most profound areas affected by disaster is the destabilizing and deconstruction of meaning, and in the long term, recovery from disaster involves the reconstruction of meaning. Given the centrality of meaning, it is important to give priority to the voices of those who were affected by disaster when considering the process of recovery. Discourses of recovery need the voices of those directly and indirectly affected by disaster. A major criticism of psychological debriefings—a structured single-session group process that is considered later in this chapter—is that post-traumatic stress disorder (PTSD) levels remain the same for both those exposed to debriefings and those who do not receive them (Bisson et al., 2000; Deahl, 2000; McNally et al., 2003; Miller, 2003). But most critiques also acknowledge that the majority of people who participate in debriefings report that they find the experience to be positive. This is not to dismiss legitimate criticisms of debriefings, including their inability to prevent certain forms of psychological pathology. And there are certainly valid concerns. For example, there is the issue of emotional contagion, in which some participants become emotionally contaminated by the experiences of others or find that their distress is retriggered by undergoing a debriefing. However, the vast majority of those who participate in debriefings say they are glad they did so. This is one reason debriefings are still so popular with firefighting departments across the United States. This speaks to the importance of seeing recovery as a process, not just an outcome, and listening to those who receive certain interventions. It is an incomplete result when researchers decide on a clinical standard by which to measure and evaluate while dismissing the voices of those who experience an intervention (Kos, 2008).

It is also important to include the voices of practitioners alongside those of researchers and those who are the targets of interventions. Although it is true that practitioners, in their desire to help, may bring a positive bias to their evaluations, there is also a type of knowledge, if not wisdom, that comes from being on the inside of a process and not merely evaluating it from the outside. Kos (2008) has raised some concerns about relying exclusively on the judgments of external evaluators: measurable outcomes are not necessarily an accurate picture of what is important in the process of recovery because the views of those receiving interventions are often discounted or minimized. External researchers can pull rank over fieldworkers in articulating what is important. While it is important to agree on certain values—such as supporting and not undermining sources of resiliency, doing no harm, and respecting and responding to cultural differences— there is room for different perspectives and approaches to helping people recover from disaster. When determining the efficacy of interventions, it is important to honor multivocality and encourage listening among different speakers in this forum. Ultimately, understanding what helps individuals, families, and communities recover from disaster is based on many sources and ways of knowing.

Another issue is one of timing; some interventions are more useful in the earlier stages of disaster recovery, such as psychological first aid, while others seem more suited to mid- or long-term work with disaster survivors, such as an ongoing grief group or psychotherapy for PTSD. Chapter 2 summarizes some models of phases that people and communities pass through after a disaster. As with the phases of grief and mourning I discuss in chapter 4, these are not rigid or exact templates that map out what every individual and community will go through. Different people will not necessarily follow the same progression and adhere to the same timelines. For the purposes of this chapter, I consider mostly immediate and short-term interventions with some reference to midterm interventions, with the understanding that each individual, family, and community has a unique trajectory of recovery and blend of needs that emerges at different points in time after a disaster. Many of these interventions fall under the umbrella of disaster mental health. In the next chapter and subsequent chapters, I describe interventions that form the basis of psychosocial capacity building.

WHAT IS PSYCHOSOCIAL HEALING AND RECOVERY?

In all cultures, there is a desire to recover from catastrophe and disaster, although the expectations of what can be hoped for and achieved vary. Recovery from processes that cause overwhelming reactions, loss, and death involves healing and repair. What are some of the core ingredients of this process, and are there universal generalizations that can be made?

Recognizing the lack of a global consensus and inadequate research evidence to cover the range of disaster reactions and responses, a panel of experts was convened to agree on principles of intervention supported by empirical research (Hobfoll et al., 2007). They acknowledged a range of reactions to disasters and a need to have flexibility when responding. The panel found five intervention principles that are evidence supported and constitute good practice when responding to disasters. The five principles are presented in chapter 1 as part of eight essential elements when responding to mass trauma (see box 1.4), and I have touched on them in other chapters. The principles promote a sense of safety, calm, self- and collective efficacy, connectedness, and hope. They are a helpful starting point when thinking about disaster response and recovery, although much of the authors' evidence is research rather than practice or consumer generated, with a decidedly Western tilt to their concepts and criteria for evaluation. Although the authors assume the need for trained mental health professionals to respond, they acknowledge that to reach the numbers of people affected by disaster, local, nonclinical personnel need to develop the skills to promote the five principles of care and recovery. This is an important concession by Western professionals because in many non-Western cultures and underdeveloped countries, the infrastructure and social expectations for implementing Western-style psychotherapy, using evidence-informed techniques, are lacking (Jones, Greenberg, & Wessley, 2007). Progress in the five areas that the authors of this study have outlined may also be accomplished in some communities through social and economic interventions, attending to structural inequities and boosting a sense of community efficacy and competence rather than through psychotherapeutic methods (Jones et al., 2007; Norris & Stevens, 2007). Although researchers are more likely to advocate evidence-based practices that can be observed and measured, practitioners tend to stress empathy and the formation of relationships, attachments, and connections (which certainly fit with the five areas), which are less easy to empirically verify (Raphael, 2007). Actual interventions after disasters require flexibility (Jones et al., 2007) as well as an ability to tolerate ambiguity and respond spontaneously (Raphael, 2007)—manuals and protocols are helpful, but if practitioners do not consider these less quantifiable human factors, the protocols can only go so far. However, overall, the article offers an excellent framework to use as a guide for what will help people of all ages and from a variety of cultures to recover from a disaster.

When teaching my students in China about this framework, they frequently challenged me to say which of the five principles is the most important. My response was that in the short term, safety is the most important objective—that all else stems from the foundation that a relative sense of safety provides. But as I continued to think about the five principles, I realized that they are all recursively interconnected. Safety can enhance the ability to self-calm, but in turn, being able to reduce anxiety and agitation can help people to *feel* more safe, even if conditions on the ground remain unchanged. The same multidirectional relationship exists among all five principles. I try to sketch this in figure 7.1, which includes three additional

Assessment and triage

Psychoeducation

Crisis intervention

Psychological first aid

Debriefing

Clinical groups

Individual counseling
and therapy

Family support
and counseling

Mindfulness

Grieving and mourning

Critical incident stress management

Restoring social networks

Mutual-aid and support groups

Empowering activities

Training-of-trainers

Community organizing

Resource and capacity
development

Human rights and
social justice

Peace and reconciliation

Collaborative memorializing

Responder Activities

FIGURE 7.1 The Web of Psychosocial Recovery

elements and also portrays the relationship among individual, family, and community and the types of activities that responders can engage in to support resiliency and the five dimensions of recovery.

Ultimately, psychosocial recovery involves achieving the five principles at the individual, family, group, and community levels in a manner consistent with local cultural norms and practices. And achieving these principles must be subjectively experienced by affected people and their communities as progress. Recovery is always contextual, and the ultimate authors of a recovery narrative should be the affected people and communities; they should not be expected to fit into universal models of recovery. There is no final end point to progress, and even substantial progress (or recovery) does not mean that there will be a return to the functioning and social realities of the predisaster situation; things are always changing even without the disruptions caused by disasters. War and disaster unfreeze rigid systems and add velocity to the rate of social change. They create social upheaval that is accompanied by great pain and suffering.

This is not meant to sound fatalistic or deterministic—the direction that people and communities move in after a disaster is not predetermined and can be exploited and subverted by vested interests or informed by humanistic values and ideals. Outside responders to disasters can work to alleviate suffering, support the human rights of affected people, and use the principles of equity and social justice as guidance. The types of responses described in the remainder of this chapter are neither neutral nor apolitical, and thus a clear articulation of the values and goals of responders provides an important framework and map to guide response efforts and makes the aims of responders transparent to those being helped.

As I propose initially in chapter 1, there are three other categories of interventions that I believe should be added to the list of five, based on my own experience. One dimension of recovery not articulated by Hobfoll et al. (2007), which I have found to be an essential aspect of disaster recovery and which has been emphasized by Landau (2007) and Landau and Saul (2004), is reestablishing severed links, albeit reconfigured relations, with the past. Whether this is the larger historical and cultural past or the more quotidian past of routines and social practices, disasters often disrupt or disconnect people, individually and collectively, from this important source of meaning. In many ways, it takes a connection with the past to be able to make sense of the present and to envision the future. So I have added it as a sixth spoke to figure 7.1 as another way of helping individuals, families, and communities in the process to recover from disaster.

A seventh dimension is what Prewitt Diaz and Dayal (2008) call "a sense of place." Large-scale disasters destroy communities, neighborhoods, dwellings, businesses, shops, and public spaces, and they sever the social ties that bind people together. Such places have symbolic meaning to a person's sense of self and identity and represent much of an individual's history and sense of belonging to a community (Csikszentmihalyi & Rochberg-Halton, 1981; Prewitt Diaz & Dayal, 2008). An example of this is the woman whom I previously described encountering when I was walking the streets of D'Iberville, Mississippi, after Hurricane Katrina. She bemoaned the loss of her grandmother's house, crying that she felt as if she had lost her childhood. Reestablishing a sense of place is essential for survivors of disaster and contributes to the foundation of feeling safe, secure, socially connected, and living a meaningful life.

The eighth dimension of the web of psychosocial recovery is grieving and mourning. There are many ways to do this, but when there have been large-scale and/or devastating losses, people need the space and opportunity to grieve and mourn, as individuals, families, and communities in their own culturally specific and meaningful fashion.

All eight sections of the web represent both processes and outcomes. There is the process of increasing a person's safety and of the resultant feeling of being safe. Self-calming is part of a process of stabilization and healing, but it can lead to a sense of equanimity and efficacy. This is true of all the dimensions—thus, they are dynamic and usually in flux rather than goalposts in an end zone. Ultimately, psychosocial healing and recovery are phenomenological. Healing and recovery provide the meaning people derive, based on their experiences of the disaster, that they can then integrate with their sense of the past and hope for the future. Of course, there are measurable indicators that point toward progress and revitalization—having steady employment, experiencing significantly fewer nightmares—but only those affected by the disaster can put all these factors together and make judgments about their overall sense of well-being.

TYPES OF INTERVENTIONS

PSYCHOLOGICAL FIRST AID

Psychological first aid (PFA) fits well with the five essential elements (Flynn, 2007) and offers a philosophy and methodology of intervention that is compatible with supporting resiliency. Moreover, it can be offered by nonclinical personnel who have received training. Therefore, it is a realistic, effective, multidimensional intervention that can be implemented in a variety of countries, communities, and cultural settings, including those without the infrastructure to offer widespread clinical services. It is more empowerment based than traditional psychotherapy and seemingly offers support without risk for harm.

Many have written about PFA and its goals (Everly et al., 2006; Halpern & Tramontin, 2007; National Child Traumatic Stress Network and National Center for PTSD [NCTSN], 2006; Raphael, 2006; Reyes & Elhai, 2004). Box 7.1 lists the goals of PFA. It "is designed to reduce the initial distress caused by traumatic events and to foster short- and long-term adaptive functioning and coping" (NCTSN, 2006, p. 1). There is a recognition that meeting basic needs is paramount in the immediate aftermath of a disaster, so psychological stabilization and creating a sense of safety are primary goals in PFA, as is helping meet the physical needs of survivors. Other goals include

---

BOX 7.1

GOALS OF PSYCHOLOGICAL FIRST AID

- Establishing a sense of safety and meeting physical needs
- Providing information /education
- Offering comfort and support /relieving suffering
- Accelerating recovery
- Promoting mental health /improving short-term functioning
- Helping access strengths and sources of resiliency
- Fostering social connection
- Providing links to critical resources
- Assisting with traumatic grief

FROM EVERLY ET AL., 2006; HALPERN & TRAMONTIN, 2007; NCTSN, 2006; RAPHAEL, 2006.

---

offering comfort and support, alleviating suffering, promoting better short-term functioning, providing information and education, and connecting people with others and critical resources. Also, Raphael identifies helping people work through their traumatic grief and stresses the importance of trying to reconnect people with friends and loved ones.

Psychological first aid skills can be taught to nonclinical responders and are similar in essence and spirit to crisis intervention. There is a big emphasis on quickly establishing a trusting relationship using basic interpersonal skills, such as asking open questions, engaging in active listening, and conveying empathy, compassion, and concern. Other core skills are remaining calm, being genuine, and establishing and maintaining professional boundaries. There is a roll-up-your-sleeves ethic that accompanies PFA. For example, if finding material resources is needed, then this is part of the job. If a person is thirsty, you offer a bottle of water or cup of tea. Normalizing reactions to disasters is a central discourse within PFA, and psychoeducation about typical reactions and the importance of self-care are part of the intervention repertoire. As PFA often involves nonclinical personnel in acute situations, triage skills and the ability to assess risk and know when to refer people for more specialized help are an important aspect of the work.

As an example, a few days after Hurricane Katrina, I walked through an African American neighborhood in Gulfport, Mississippi, for the American Red Cross. Because of the debris, people were not able to get around easily; therefore, many had not yet talked with outside responders. A number of residents came out of their homes and described to me their experiences and immediate needs. A lot of what I did was offer comfort, encouragement, and a way for people to find the necessary resources. After talking outside a house with a cluster of people, mostly extended family, a man in his thirties asked to speak with me alone. He described his terror during the night when the hurricane hit. He then conveyed a deep sense of shame because, during that night, he had thought only of how he could save himself rather than having concern for his family. He talked about how this moment of dread was at odds with his view of himself as a strong provider. After some validation and probing, it emerged that he was having some suicidal ideation. At that moment and under those circumstances, I was unable to offer even crisis intervention counseling, so I immediately referred him to a psychiatric outpatient facility, which had resumed operation, for an evaluation. He was immediately seen and assessed as being at risk for self-harm and admitted to an inpatient psychiatric unit.

Although there is a surface simplicity to PFA, it draws on many theoretical streams—crisis intervention, stress and trauma theories, grief and bereavement counseling, cognitive-behavioral theory, mutual-aid and empowerment traditions, and narrative approaches to healing. There are even many psychodynamic concepts embedded in PFA—the importance of ventilation, accessing ego strength, providing a holding environment, mirroring and validation, and responding to metaphor and content that is below the surface. It is also relationally based, even if the relationships are brief and transitory. As Raphael (2006) has identified, this is all done through talking, emotionally connecting, and devoting sufficient time to a person in need. As PFA employs nonclinical disaster response workers as well as clinicians, it is important that there be adequate training, good supervision, and an organizational structure that ensure high standards of practice in very unstable conditions.

CRISIS INTERVENTION

While PFA is an appropriate first-line response immediately after a disaster, a more in-depth model of responding during the early disaster period is crisis intervention (CI). While PFA begins immediately after a disaster, CI is more often delivered in the first week to month after a catastrophic event. Although similar to PFA with an emphasis on immediacy, problem solving, containment, and short-term but meaningful relationship development, CI usually relies on trained clinicians (Reyes & Elhai, 2004) and assumes a longer period of available time in working with someone. Crisis intervention responds to psychological problems, such as confronting cognitive distortions, in more depth than PFA (Halpern & Tramontin, 2007). Over the years, it has been particularly useful in identifying potential self-harming behaviors and in developing short-term plans that help prevent lethal outcomes. The overall goal of CI is to restore a person's psychological homeostasis, which was disrupted by a precipitating event (Roberts, 2005; Roberts & Ottens, 2005). Although CI is a short-term treatment modality, it makes connections between current problems and past sources of psychological conflict (James & Gilliland, 2001; Roberts, 2005).

Roberts and Ottens (2005) have mapped out seven stages of crisis intervention: (1) planning and conducting a biophysical assessment that includes screening for self-harming behaviors, (2) making contact and establishing a relationship, (3) identifying major problems and their antecedents and precipitants, (4) encouraging the exploration of emotions and feelings, (5) exploring alternatives to the problem and new coping strategies, (6) generating a plan of action, and (7) working out a plan for follow-up and "booster" sessions. Since CI often goes deeper than PFA, Halpern & Tramontin (2007) offer some cautions. They warn of piercing the *trauma membrane* that might be helping a person hold it together while he is in an unstable situation. Citing Lindy, they urge practitioners to delve into problems in small doses so as not to overwhelm defenses that are productive in the short term.

Although traditional crisis intervention models focus on restoring psychological stability, the steps outlined in Roberts and Ottens's (2005) model can be expanded to fit with the social interventions of psychosocial capacity building (see chapter 8). All the above activities can be conducted with families, groups, and communities as well as with individuals.

CRITICAL INCIDENT STRESS MANAGEMENT

Critical incident stress management (CISM) encompasses a number of interventions and is intended to be a wraparound strategy after a disaster, comprehensively meeting a range of needs. A central aspect of CISM has been the use of debriefings, sometimes called critical incident stress debriefings (CISD).

DEBRIEFINGS   A debriefing is a single-session structured group process for people who have experienced either primary or secondary traumatic stress in response to a disaster, tragedy, or other overwhelming event (sometimes referred to as a "critical incident") (Everly & Mitchell, 2000; Miller, 2000, 2003, 2006a; Mitchell, 1983; Mitchell & Bray, 1990; Mitchell & Everly, 2001). The American Red Cross defines debriefings as structured discussions to bring closure to experiences such as exposure to a disaster or the stress of disaster response work (Armstrong, O'Callahan, & Marmar, 1991).

For the past several years, the topic of critical incident stress management has generated a great deal of discussion and controversy in the field of disaster mental health (Bisson et al., 2000; Chemtob et al., 1997; Deahl, 2000; Dyregrov, 2000; Everly & Mitchell, 2000; Flynn, 2007; Friedman et al., 2006; Gist & Woodhall, 2000; Halpern & Tramontin, 2007; Hobfoll et al., 2007; Macy, Behar, Paulson, Delman, Schmid, & Smith, 2004; McNally et al., 2003; Miller, 2003, 2006a; Raphael, 2006, 2007; Raphael et al., 1995). Many practitioners and trained peer responders still use debriefings after disasters and many researchers and practitioners caution or actively argue against their use. This section sketches some of the disagreements and describes how debriefings fit within the larger framework of critical incident stress management. Appendix 7.1 describes the process of conducting a debriefing and appendix 7.2 presents the questions in the process. Appendix 7.3 offers suggestions for lead facilitators, and appendix 7.4 reproduces a typical handout used by a debriefing team.

Many debriefings, particularly those used for uniformed personnel, rely on trained "peers" to facilitate the process. The goal is twofold: to lessen the impact of the overwhelming event and to accelerate recovery (Everly & Mitchell, 2000; Mitchell & Bray, 1990; Mitchell & Everly, 2001). In addition to these two broad goals, there are more proximate goals for debriefings. One is to establish a climate where trust is developed and fostered among participants as well as between the participants and the group facilitators (Dyregrov, 1997, 2003). Debriefings help individuals construct a narrative about what happened to them during and after exposure to a stressful situation, but it also creates a group narrative of the event and its aftermath, which fosters group cohesion while diminishing isolation and personal blame. This reduces the stigma associated with having strong or debilitating reactions. Debriefings follow a wave pattern, where the initial questions are quite factual, moving to questions about feelings and powerful reactions midway through the process. Helping participants become self-aware of their cognitive, emotional, physical, and social reactions can be cathartic. It allows them to reflect on themselves, illustrating how people share a range of reactions. At this point, participants may be in an emotionally open state, so debriefings move to focusing on the fact that many reactions are normal responses to abnormal events. The focus then becomes self-care strategies, which provide a sense of efficacy. And this allows for a more positive ending to the process as a whole. In my experience facilitating debriefings, many participants comment that the normalizing and self-care process makes them feel more hopeful and gives them a greater sense of agency, and by talking about this as a group, they learn from the experiences and resourcefulness of others, as well as feel closer to their colleagues.

Group work emphasizes the resonance and social support that group processes bring, compared to individual processing. Debriefings are informed by a range of clinical theories (Bisson et al., 2000; Miller, 2003, 2006a). The value of ventilating and processing difficult experiences comes from trauma and stress theory, as well as from psychodynamic approaches. The short-term single-session nature of debriefings has its roots in crisis intervention theory. There are elements of other theoretical traditions as well: having a group process disturbing material together is a collective form of desensitization, and when there has been death or serious injury, the group discussion is part of a process of mourning and memorializing. The emphasis on normalizing and self-care is consistent with empowerment-oriented theories of recovery. Also, sharing personal stories and weaving them together to form a collective narrative has elements of narrative traditions of therapy and recovery.

Debriefings were initially used in the United States to help uniformed providers (emergency medical technicians [EMTs], firefighters, police) deal with particularly distressing events (critical incidents) that impaired their ability to continue with their jobs. The intervention was designed to help responders with what is now known as "compassion fatigue" (Figley, 1995) or "secondary" (Yassen, 1995) or "vicarious" traumatization (Pearlman & Saakvitne, 1995). Mitchell (1983) wrote a seminal article about the benefits of debriefings to uniformed personnel who experienced a critical incident. The article argued that debriefings could help participants process persistent negative feelings by sharing their experiences with fellow responders, learning what constituted normal reactions to abnormal events, and focusing on self-care strategies. At this time, debriefings were seen as possibly mitigating against PTSD.

Mitchell (1983), working with his colleagues, eventually established the International Critical Incident Stress Foundation (ICISF), which offers training in debriefings, particularly for teams responding to fellow uniformed workers, using a peer approach. The peer approach was critical in the early manifestations of debriefings and to this day. The model emphasizes the importance and benefits of training a firefighter, for example, to debrief other firefighters after a critical incident. The peer, being a nonclinician, is viewed as having more credibility. Essentially, the process was constructed as non-therapy for normal reactions to critical incidents, which carries less stigma. Peers help to normalize reactions and are able to encourage their fellow workers to trust the debriefing process, share thoughts and feelings that are often not discussed by uniformed personnel, and build a sense of group solidarity and social cohesion in response to the critical incident.

While debriefings caught on with emergency medical services (EMS) teams, there was a movement to make them more "psychological" and to use them with a wider range of people, including civilian populations (Armstrong et al., 1991; Dyregrov, 1997, 2003; Raphael, 1986; Young, 1997). This added complexity to the intervention because now it was being used with groups that were not natural work groups and a greater emphasis was being placed on the psychological components of the process. Dyregrov (2000) observed that there were risks as well as benefits from using debriefings. The debriefings approach got a major boost when the American Red Cross used it with disaster responders (Armstrong et al., 1991; Armstrong et al., 1998), eventually expanding this to people directly affected by the disaster. Debriefings were used in schools after tragedies and disasters. They were used extensively in Littleton, Colorado, after the Columbine massacre. Debriefings were also widely used after the Oklahoma City bombing. This reached its apotheosis with the American Red Cross after 9/11 in New York City, where they, and every other organization responding to the disaster, used debriefings for workers who escaped from the World Trade Center and for other residents of the city, as well as for disaster responders and uniformed workers (Miller, 2002). By 9/11, not only were debriefings being offered to great numbers of people, but there was often pressure for people to participate. When I responded to 9/11, working with employees of a firm that had escaped from the World Trade Center, supervisors were telling their workers that they needed to attend debriefing sessions. I heard from colleagues that this was happening in many places.

Researchers identified negative consequences of debriefings, particularly concerns about emotional contagion and flooding and retriggering of overwhelming affect, as well as skepticism whether debriefings could prevent PTSD (McNally et al., 2003). Also, when there is insufficient time to complete a debriefing (as happened after 9/11) or the debriefing is not effectively facilitated to ensure that all steps in the process are covered, it can leave people in a very emotionally open and vulnerable state, which was troubling to practitioners and researchers. These are important concerns. I have witnessed emotional contagion from more distressed to less distressed participants in my own work. Debriefings can retrigger people by evoking intense, if not intrusive, images of the disaster or earlier traumatic events. And the research is clear that there is no evidence that debriefings prevent PTSD—claims to this effect were overstretching the value of debriefings.

And yet debriefings are very popular, particularly among firefighters, EMTs, and other uniformed personnel. They are a relatively low-key way for responders to help participants construct a collective narrative of response to an event, which is helpful for individuals and aids in strengthening the cohesion of groups. Debriefings normalize reactions that people are having, helping them focus on coping strategies and self-care, which are very important when people have been exposed to disasters and other critical incidents. Like clinical interventions, debriefings provide mutual aid and support, which is one of this approach's most significant strengths.

I have conducted many debriefings with uniformed personnel and with people directly affected by disasters. With uniformed personnel, there is no doubt that debriefings are well received and viewed by participants as helpful, cohesive group exercises. When they are peer led with a clinical or religious support person, they are most effective. With nonresponders, I have also found debriefings to be helpful, but they work better when there is an interrelated group, such as a work group (bank employees at a branch that has been robbed) or social group (friends grieving the shooting death of someone they were close to). I agree that debriefings do not prevent PTSD, but most people exposed to disaster do not develop PTSD. Debriefings do help with acute stress disorder (ASD) because they normalize reactions, anticipate a diminution of responses, and remind people of their own coping mechanisms, which can foster calming, hope, and efficacy. Debriefings are like aspirin—they do not cure anything but they can go a long way toward relieving short-term pain. It would be helpful to shift the focus of debriefing research to the sense of group cohesion that can result from debriefings rather than evaluating the abatement of psychological symptoms.

No one should ever be pressured to participate in a debriefing—participation should always be voluntary. People should always be informed beforehand what a debriefing entails and the potential risks and benefits—this is ethical practice. If someone finds that she is being triggered in a debriefing, or that the group affect is making her feel worse, and she would like to leave, she should be encouraged to do so without any pressure, overt or subtle, to remain. With due respect to the ICISF, which has done some wonderful work in developing debriefings and other aspects of critical incident stress management, there needs to be more flexibility when delivering debriefings, and clinicians and peers who are trained to facilitate debriefings should not be taught to follow the script formulaically, like a recipe. Structure is important but so is flexibility, and the rigidity of some debriefings detracts from their potential helpfulness. It is true that this makes it more difficult for researchers to evaluate their effectiveness or harm, but as a practitioner, I would opt for trusting the wisdom of those leading the debriefing. After all, they are the ones picking up cues and responses from the group as they proceed. Also, flexibility should be demonstrated with respect to the number of sessions involved in any given debriefing group. There is nothing magical about the single-session culture that has been spawned within the debriefing industry, and in fact, there are situations in which follow-up is helpful. This could take the form of continuing to examine how people are doing with their reactions and revisiting self-care plans. Or groups could move to either more of an action orientation (self-care or altruistic, group-building activities) or more of a clinical focus (teaching more CBT techniques for managing stress or more mindfulness approaches for achieving calm).

Another reason for flexibility is that debriefings were designed by Westerners, and the format and ways in which questions are asked are not necessarily appropriate for participants from non-Western cultures. How one helps a person process cognitive responses and emotional reactions to disasters and other critical incidents varies considerably across cultures. Therefore, norms and expectations about how to develop a process that is helpful to people within their own cultural traditions must be carefully thought through and reworked from the original model. Proponents of debriefings have too often taken a "one size fits all" approach. Much work needs to be done to translate the goals and norms of debriefings into a range of cultural patterns if they are to be effectively employed internationally.

OTHER INTERVENTIONS In critical incident stress management (CISM), debriefings are but one part of a raft of interconnected responses immediately after a disaster or critical incident (Everly & Mitchell, 2000). This management strategy is conceptualized as a comprehensive set of services and responses that ranges from individual to small- and large-group interventions and addresses crisis on many levels: micro, mezzo, and macro.

Psychological first aid, described earlier, is now a major plank in the CISM repertoire (Everly et al., 2006). Defusing is another small-group intervention that is part of CISM. It is a modified version of debriefing and is used within the first forty-eight hours after an incident or disaster (Mitchell & Everly, 2001). Defusing is particularly geared for use with responders after they have worked on a disaster or critical incident. A defusing is like an abbreviated debriefing; it takes less time and does not probe as deeply. It usually has three phases—the introductory phase, a general exploration phase of various types of responder reactions, and then an information phase that normalizes reactions and educates about stress and stress management.

A defusing that lasted about an hour was used when a school bus accidentally ran over and killed a young child in a small community. The firefighters and paramedics (many of them seasoned veterans) who responded to the event were understandably disturbed and distraught by the accident scene. A defusing was held at the fire station shortly after many people had finished their shifts. The participants were asked to describe their roles and to briefly summarize overall how they were doing. Most said that they were not doing very well, which was reflected in their somber tone and deflated body postures. As the defusing was held within twenty-four hours of the event, unlike a debriefing, there was not a focus on specific reactions, such as thoughts, feelings, and crises of meaning—it was too soon for many people to articulate answers to these questions. Normal reactions and typical self-care strategies were shared by the facilitators in a more didactic fashion than at a debriefing. Rather than articulating a full-blown self-care plan for each participant, there was general assent to the notion of the importance of self-care and agreement by group participants that they would seek to implement self-care strategies. Group participants were particularly responsive to suggestions that they get exercise. A defusing such as this may or may not be followed up with a full-scale debriefing; it depends on how the participants are doing a week or two later.

Another effective intervention, which can reach larger groups of people, is crisis management briefing (CMB) (Everly & Mitchell, 2000). This has essentially two goals—to provide information to response teams or the public about what has occurred and to anticipate and normalize common reactions to the event. For the first goal, it helps to have public officials (a mayor, fire chief, or police chief) describe what has happened, what is being done, what is known, what is still unknown, how information about the crisis will be disseminated, and what future plans and actions are envisioned. This is reassuring to people, conveying leadership and, it is hoped, an honest appraisal of the situation. The second goal is often offered up by a clinician, who is able to predict and anticipate common reactions to a disaster and to recommend what people can do to care for themselves and others. Although this does not offer the opportunity for people to share their own experiences and reactions, it does help to normalize responses. The clinician can help move reactions from the realm of individual weakness to collective coping, offering encouragement for self-care and social support as well as providing information about resources for further help. A CMB affords an opportunity for social service and mental health professionals to work with community leaders and offer consultation to them about how they can best reassure the public and respond effectively to their needs. Although CMBs were initially conceived of as being offered to large, in vivo groups of responders, with improvements in mass communication, it is now possible to enact the principles of a CMB and to reach millions of people.

The meltdown of the Fukushima nuclear reactor in Japan is an example of what can happen when leadership that builds community confidence through proactive and transparent communication about the consequences of a disaster is not forthcoming. The earthquake and subsequent tsunami led to the meltdown of reactors in the Fukushima nuclear power plant and the release of radioactive gases. Parents living near the reactor were concerned about the risks to their children's health because they did not trust the information given to them by the owners of the power plant or the government (Tabuchi, 2011, May 25). This further undermines a sense of safety and inhibits recovery.

One particular CMB was held in a rural community in the evening, a few days after a woman was murdered at a gas station. About fifteen people attended. The chief of police opened up the meeting with a summary of the events and reassurances about the investigation, although he was unable to offer details. When the discussion was opened up to questions, a lot of fear and anxiety was expressed by participants. The chief offered a few suggestions about how people might be able to feel safer (by keeping in touch with one another), while also reassuring people that others in the community were not at risk. Then a clinician normalized the fear and anxiety and suggested other typical reactions to such situations. She then described typical self-care strategies and encouraged people to do what worked for them. The floor was then opened to more questions.

CLINICAL INTERVENTIONS FOR MID- AND LONG-TERM TREATMENT

Clinical interventions, such as counseling and therapy, are often helpful to survivors of disaster in the weeks and months following the catastrophic event, particularly in Western cultures. Although many unresolved issues remain about when to offer interventions, what combinations of interventions are most effective, and how long services should be provided, sufficient evidence supports the use of certain interventions (McNally et al., 2003). The most promising types of interventions fall within the overall category of cognitive behavioral therapies (CBTs), both individual and group, many of which were derived from work with sexual assault survivors who had developed PTSD and other trauma syndromes (Australian Centre for Post-traumatic Mental Health [ACPMH], 2007; Halpern & Tramontin, 2007; McNally et al., 2003). Treatment is particularly targeted toward people with PTSD, ASD, and those who have developed lingering anxiety disorders. Cognitive behavioral therapies are a familiar part of the response repertoire in Western nations, where most of the research for their effectiveness has been tested, but are not necessarily appropriate for use in non-Western societies. In these cultures, psychological interventions are less familiar, if not alien, and strengthening social supports and social networks may be more effective and culturally consonant (McNally et al., 2003).

Behaviorally oriented strategies include systematic desensitization and exposure therapies (Halpern & Tramontin, 2007). With systematic desensitization, patients are taught muscle relaxation techniques and then gradually and systematically exposed to imagined distressing stimuli in increasing doses. Exposure therapy also involves imagining anxiety-inducing scenes but tends to introduce the aversive stimuli in a more full-tilt fashion. The goal is to help patients tolerate and manage overwhelmingly distressing images or frightening situations that they are avoiding. Another type of exposure therapy is eye movement desensitization and reprocessing (EMDR). This involves moving a finger back and forth in front of patients' eyes or having them tap themselves on the shoulder, each shoulder in turn, as they imagine the dreaded events. It is still not clear why this is helpful (Halpern & Tramontin, 2007). If the exposure proves to be overwhelming, patients are taught to imagine a "safe space" that they can retreat to in their minds where the feelings of dread and anxiety should subside. Bryant and Harvey (cited in Halpern & Tramontin, 2007) caution against using exposure therapies if patients have some of the following symptoms: extreme anxiety, panic attacks, disassociation, borderline personality disorder, psychosis, anger as a primary stress response, severe depression, risk for suicide, substance abuse, or other complicating factors or ongoing stressors. As mentioned in chapter 4, somatic experiencing is being used to help people with trauma symptoms process and resolve their reactions. Somatic experiencing seeks to "unlock" traumatic symptoms encoded in the body by resetting the nervous system through "working with small gradations of somatic activation alternated with the use of somatic resources" (Leitch et al., 2009, p. 11). Attention is paid to posture, skin tone, breath, and other ways that trauma is stored in the body (Leitch et al., 2009).

Another way of approaching trauma and anxiety is through cognitive processing, as in cognitive processing therapy (CPT). CPT also evolved from work with survivors of sexual assault but is now used in the treatment of disaster-induced trauma (ACPMH, 2007). The focus on CPT is to revise and rework the cognitive messages that accompany the traumatic reactions. These messages include distorting reality, catastrophizing possible outcomes, drawing erroneous conclusions, overgeneralizing about the traumatic event, and personalizing one's role as a victim (Halpern & Tramontin, 2007). The goals of CPT are to help the person feel a greater sense of safety, increase the capacity for trust, and give the individual a sense of efficacy, personal power, and control (ACPMH, 2007).

Other CBT-based approaches include stress inoculation training (SIT), which focuses on developing the skills to manage affective reactions, increasing self-acceptance, and taking advantage of social support (Halpern & Tramontin, 2007). Another CBT program, acceptance and commitment therapy (ACT), has been used with veterans suffering from PTSD and places a strong emphasis on noticing, observing, and learning to accept without reacting to what gets stirred up emotionally (Dewane, 2008). This resembles Buddhist approaches to mindfulness. Acceptance and commitment therapy is part of a proliferation of newer contextual-based behavior therapies (Dewane, 2008), many of which have the potential to help people who are suffering from ASD, PTSD, and anxiety disorders as a consequence of disaster. However, they rely on trained clinicians, and the goals of therapy have embedded Western notions of self and efficacy, so their use in many non-Western social and cultural settings should be approached with caution and some skepticism.

Psychodynamic approaches have not been as empirically validated as CBTs when helping disaster survivors (McNally et al., 2003), but they are useful in some situations (ACPMH, 2007; Halpern & Tramontin, 2007). Psychodynamic approaches are particularly helpful when the client's current psychological distress has its roots in earlier intrapsychic or developmental issues. For some people suffering from adverse consequences after a disaster, there is a relationship between their current trauma and their psychological and interpersonal patterns of coping, so placing their struggles in a deeper developmental context can lead to greater integration of the disaster experience with earlier experiences in their lives. Brief psychodynamic treatment places an emphasis on the relationship with the therapist and the transference and countertransference that may occur (ACPMH, 2007), which can help people to focus on and moderate their relational and attachment style with others. Psychodynamic approaches also focus on discourses and narratives that clients use to explain their lives and make meaning and sense of their current predicament; so telling one's disaster story in the context of one's life story can be helpful. An offshoot of this narrative process is narrative exposure therapy (NET) (ACPMH, 2007). This therapy type encourages clients to construct a whole-life narrative, focusing on traumatic events in greater detail, along with associated thoughts and emotions. This narrative process serves to desensitize a person to traumatic reactions through exposure to the events, while placing traumatic incidents in the context of a much larger, holistic autobiography.

Since disasters affect families and social groups, therapeutic family and group interventions are also helpful, particularly in societies and cultures where there is a collectivist orientation or a strong emphasis on the family and interdependence among individuals and groups is valued. Family therapy helps when there are challenges to roles and boundaries and obstacles to communication (Halpern & Tramontin, 2007). The debriefing format can be adapted to work with families as well as groups of friends as a starting point, but when utilizing this approach, it is important to encourage continuing actions and activities and to be able to schedule follow-up sessions (Miller, 2003, 2006a).

THE TENSION BETWEEN GRIEVING AND COPING

Much of the disaster response literature about immediate and midterm interventions focuses on coping and managing, resolving lingering anxiety and trauma, and moving forward with one's life. Yet, given the loss of life, pets, property, and cherished material possessions after a disaster, grieving and mourning are an essential aspect of disaster recovery. As discussed in chapter 4, disaster often makes these processes more complicated. The magnitude of the loss, the sudden onset of the disaster and often unexpected consequences, the major social dislocations, the need for relocation, and the ongoing or renewed threats to one's survival all make bereavement more complex than under normal circumstances. However, I have also found that if individuals, families, and communities neglect grieving and mourning, it is difficult for them to move on. Recognizing the tension between grieving and coping is important when working to help people recover from disaster. So how can workers help survivors manage this tension?

In my experience, what is most helpful is creating space for affected people to grieve and mourn in their own way and at their own pace. This means respecting the fullness and complexity of people who are affected by but not totally defined by their losses. Even in the early phases of bereavement, many people will also pay attention to other parts of their lives and even play and have fun at certain moments. The door to mourning should be left unlocked for people to enter when they wish, but it need not be held ajar so that it cannot close. Most people will open that door when they need to and will also allow it to close when they prefer to focus on other tasks and challenges.

These processes are mediated by culture; within larger cultural frames, individuals and families have their own ways of negotiating the process of adjusting to the loss of loved ones and of reconfiguring their relationships to those who have died. In some cultures, people will express a great deal of affect, while in others, the bereaved will exhibit stoicism. Some families find comfort in grieving with other families. Then there are families who prefer to grieve alone. Responders should come to understand the family's style and be present and supportive of this process. As relationships deepen and develop, stories emerge, and what is probably most important is for responders to listen to them. Ultimately, an attentive, attuned, empathic presence—someone who can tolerate deep and direct expressions of grief but not focus only on this—is most helpful to individuals and families.

Recovery from disaster is a process and not a static end point that is finally achieved. Recovery is ultimately a subjective process that is best understood through the subjective experiences of those who were affected by disaster. Integrating the disaster experience with the past, present, and future is an ongoing project for affected people and involves reworking experiences, meanings, and one's sense of self.

This chapter describes how responders can intervene in ways that are supportive and mindful of both the vulnerabilities and strengths that disaster survivors carry. The emphasis has been on interventions that are targeted to individuals, families, and small groups. The types of interventions include psychological first aid, crisis intervention, critical-incident stress management and critical-incident stress debriefings, cognitive behavioral approaches, other clinical modalities, and ways to support grieving and mourning. These interventions broadly fall within the field of disaster mental health. Many of these interventions rely on trained practitioners who intercede directly. The next chapter describes psychosocial capacity building, which expands the role of outside responders to that of consultant and supporter, while more actively involving the participation and leadership of locally affected people. Psychosocial capacity building can incorporate these interventions, but it also integrates them with social support and self-help, building on resiliency and intervening on multiple levels as it links individuals, families, and groups—and promotes community healing.

MINDFULNESS EXERCISE: BREATHING IN THE PAIN

When offering direct interventions to help people who are recovering from disaster, we hear many sad and painful stories. However, it is so important for us to empathically listen and to witness what people have experienced. This means absorbing a lot of sorrow, which may leave us feeling depleted or even overwhelmed. I have had times in my career when this led to my own compassion fatigue. I have since found the following exercise to be helpful. It is adapted from Pema Chodron's (2001, 2002) descriptions of Tonglen, a Buddhist-style meditation that directly involves being present for the suffering of others. Although its emphasis on breathing in the suffering of others can appear to be counterintuitive, I have found that it leads to greater compassion and a sense of well-being.

1. Sit in a comfortable position and focus on your breathing. This can be done with your eyes either closed or open, whichever you find most helpful. Do this for about five to ten minutes, until you feel a sense of focus.
2. Imagine someone you have been working with who has been suffering. Visualize their suffering as an image (smoke or color). On each in-breath, visualize breathing in their suffering.
3. On each out-breath, breathe out an image of healing and compassion (light, warmth). Do this for at least three breaths (or more if desired).
4. Repeat this with other people you have been working with who have also been suffering. It is helpful to form an image of the person and to breathe in the individual's suffering.
5. Continue to breathe out healing and compassion to all whom you have visualized.
6. Expand your compassion to all who may be suffering, as have the people whom you have been envisioning, until you are breathing in sorrow and breathing out healing to many people. Continue this for a few minutes.
7. Focus on your own pain. Breathe in your own suffering and send healing and compassion to yourself. You can end the mindfulness session here.
8. For some, it helps to end by verbalizing, a few times, phrases similar to those used in chapter 4: may I be safe; may I be happy; may I be healthy; may I be at ease. Visualize yourself as if you were watching another person (Germer, 2009).

Appendix 7.1

CONDUCTING A DEBRIEFING

PERSONNEL

There are often three roles for people facilitating debriefings:

1. *Lead facilitator*: This person leads the debriefing and is responsible for facilitating most of the process. He or she opens the debriefing, explaining what a debriefing is; ensures that participants are there voluntarily and know what they are getting into; develops ground rules; answers questions; and guides the group process through asking questions and validating responses.
2. *Assist facilitator*: This individual takes responsibility for the teaching phase of the debriefing.
3. *Support facilitator*: This person is available to spend time with anyone who wants or requires one-on-one support. Often it is made clear that if anyone leaves the room during a debriefing, the support facilitator will accompany them to check and see how they are doing. The support facilitator often takes responsibility for distributing self-care and normal-reaction handouts after the debriefing.

When conducting debriefings for uniformed personnel (police, fire, EMT), it is usually helpful to have a trained peer as the lead facilitator and a clinically trained person as the assist facilitator. The support person is often a nonclinical trained peer. However, roles can be flexible as long as the facilitators have a plan of action and a rationale for conducting the debriefing in a certain way.

SPACE AND MATERIALS

It is helpful to conduct the debriefing in a room that offers privacy and to seat people in a circle, with or without a table in the middle. A flip chart or whiteboard is recommended for the assist facilitator to use during the teaching phase. Coffee and snacks can help people feel at ease as long as they are not allowed to become a distraction. It can be helpful to have tissues available. Some teams make up note cards for facilitators to use that have the phases of the debriefing and appropriate questions written out to help facilitators stay on track in a coordinated fashion.

GROUND RULES

Ground rules are shared at the beginning of the debriefing. The lead facilitator usually suggests some while also asking the group to consider any other rules that would be helpful for its process. Examples of typical ground rules:

- Confidentiality: Personal information shared during the debriefing will not be shared outside of the room.
- No writing: This is to support confidentiality and to help participants to focus on one another and the process in the moment.
- No cell phones, pagers, or radios: Electronic devices are not permitted in the group sessions.
- No media: This supports confidentiality and protects participants from violations of privacy and from exploitation.
- Speaking for oneself: Participants are encouraged to talk about their own experiences and refrain from speculation about what happened to others and from intellectualizing about the event.
- Right to pass: If a question is asked that participants would rather not answer, they should be permitted to do so without explanation.
- Sharing the airspace: It is important to encourage participation while cautioning everyone to refrain from taking up too much group space at the expense of others. It is much easier to monitor this as a facilitator if it has been agreed upon as a ground rule before the debriefing begins.
- The debriefing is not an operational critique: Participants need to know at the outset that what they say during the debriefing will not be criticized, that this is a safe place in which to talk.

ASKING QUESTIONS

It helps to begin a debriefing by asking questions that go in a circle, choosing the person on the lead facilitator's left to start the process. This may be the best way to proceed for the first two or three questions. This process has the effect of including everyone and ensuring all voices are heard. Once people are participating, it is helpful to loosen the facilitation reins and to let them respond to questions spontaneously ("popcorn style"). If this leads to monopolizing by a few participants, the facilitator can always return to going around the circle in a more structured fashion. (See examples of questions listed in appendix 7.2.)

GROUP SIZE AND TIME REQUIRED

A debriefing usually takes between one and two and a half hours, depending on the number of participants, the cohesion and culture of the group, and the nature of the critical incident being debriefed. Sufficient time should be allocated so that there is not a feeling of being rushed or pressured. Conversely, some debriefings accomplish their goals in a relatively short period of time and there is nothing to be gained by keeping them going for longer than is necessary. Also, it is important to ensure that a debriefing ends with a focus on self-care and empowerment. The "wave pattern" of a debriefing is the route through which questions lead to deeper revelations and explorations. When participants have delved deeply in this process, it is important they resurface again, that they not be left in emotionally open or vulnerable states.

I have conducted debriefings for as few as three people and as many as twenty. I do not believe that there is an optimal size for a debriefing. What is most important is the natural work-group configuration and to try and support this because it makes it more likely that the social support and mutual aid generated in the group will continue after the debriefing. If the group is small, it can make sense to cut down the number of facilitators from three to two. With large groups of more than twenty, breaking into smaller groups to have debriefings is often best, which will necessitate more facilitators. When doing this, it is important to be mindful of mapping out natural work-group configurations.

WHO SHOULD PARTICIPATE

Participation should always be voluntary. There is sometimes a fine line between "encouraging" people without "pressuring" them to join a debriefing.

In my debriefings with uniformed responders, the participants have found the process to be so helpful that they enthusiastically encourage others to engage in a debriefing when the need arises. This is helpful for many people, but it can also create a social climate that makes it difficult for people to decline to participate.

A usual way of thinking about who should take part is to include those who participated directly in a disaster or critical incident. This often includes those who responded to an event or incident and those who may have stayed behind but were gathering or relaying information. For example, police dispatchers are often included in a debriefing when they took the initial call for help or sent out a response team.

For some groups, there are people not directly involved in the incident who wish to participate and those directly involved who want them to participate. For example, in a small fire department, an individual may have had the day off but wishes to be part of the debriefing to offer social support. Decisions about this should be made by the participants, those who requested the debriefing, and those facilitating the debriefing. It is important to remind participants that they may feel worse than they did before the debriefing by talking about what happened. Those who were not present at the incident may feel stirred up by listening to accounts of the disaster.

Another thing to consider is the hierarchy and rank of participants. I have done debriefings at schools where principals did not participate because they did not want to inhibit teachers and guidance counselors from being open. The same has been true for police and fire chiefs. The rule of thumb is to have people participate who are at the same rank or level of authority. However, with small schools, work groups, or departments, the importance of team solidarity outweighs concerns about inhibiting discussion. Flexibility about this and engaging in a process of mutually collaborative assessment before deciding who will and will not attend a debriefing is more responsive to the needs of a particular group than having a rigid rule about who should and should not attend.

Appendix 7.2

THE PROCESS OF A DEBRIEFING

This model was developed by the Community Crisis Response Team of Western Massachusetts.

PHASE 1: INTRODUCTION AND GROUND RULES

- Speak only for yourself.
- Maintain confidentiality.
- Try to listen.
- Use the pass rule if necessary.
- Share the airspace.
- Try to stay in the room.

PHASE 2: FACTUAL NARRATIVE

- What is your name and where were you when you realized what was happening?
- If not at the scene, where were you when you heard what was happening?

PHASE 3: THOUGHT NARRATIVE

- What was the first thought that entered your mind when you heard what was happening?

PHASE 4: REACTION NARRATIVE

- If at the scene, what did you hear, see, smell, taste, or touch?
- How has this event affected you?
- What kind of reactions have you noticed?
- What has been the hardest part of all this?

PHASE 5: MIND/BODY NARRATIVE

- What physical reactions, responses, and signals have you experienced?
- Is there anything not going away?

PHASE 6: NORMALIZATION AND TEACHING

- Review what came up in phase 5.
- Normalize: Convey that these are normal reactions to abnormal events.
- Discuss neurochemical reactions.

PHASE 7: COPING STRATEGIES

- What have you found to be helpful?
- What has helped you in the past?

PHASE 8: RESOURCE UTILIZATION AND SELF-CARE

- Now that we have talked about specific coping strategies, what specifically will you do?
- Are there any actions that you would like to take as a community group in response to this event?

PHASE 9: IMMEDIATE PLANS AND WRAP-UP

- **Assist:** Asks participants whether they will be able to accomplish safety and coping plans in the next few days.
- **Support:** Thanks participants, reminds them about confidentiality, and distributes handouts.
- **Lead:** Asks facilitators for final comments, thanks participants, and lets people know facilitators will hang around.

PHASE 10: AFTER THE DEBRIEFING

- Team members debrief one another.
- With particularly stressful debriefings, outside debriefers may be needed for the team.

DEBRIEFING FACILITATION

- **Lead:** Conducts as well as opens and closes session.
- **Assist:** Carries out normalization and teaching, offers coping strategies, and directs resource utilization and self-care.
- **Support:** Performs individual crisis intervention, offers support, and takes responsibility for handouts.

Appendix 7.3

FACILITATION OF DEBRIEFINGS

I. Things to think about before the debriefing
    A. Group culture and norms (profession, ethnicity, gender): use of language, comfort with affective expression, and so on
    B. Group homogeneity or heterogencity: its composition
    C. Group longevity: its history and future
    D. Nature of critical incident or disaster and its valence for the group: context, history, meaning
    E. Political, social, cultural factors: these may affect what is shared and how things are shared
II. Forming relationships with group members
    A. Use the debriefing to form relationships with group members as this is key to the success of the process.
    B. Use opening phases Dyregrov stresses to establish trust, set boundaries, articulate norms, foster motivation, relieve anxiety, encourage group cohesiveness, and prepare people for what is to come.
    C. Use wide vision and balance to permit tracking and working with the entire group.
    D. Listen to members and convey genuine empathy.
    E. Use nonverbal cues to convey empathy nonverbally. It is important to sustain and share eye contact, maintain an attentive posture, and use an empathic voice.
    F. Mirror and validate as well as normalize what people say.
    G. Respect where group members are and trust the group process.
III. Facilitation
    A. As Dyregrov says, establish trust, outline goals, motivate the group, build relationships, be a good role model, clarify important issues, help build cohesion and support, guard against destructive group processes, assess strengths and vulnerabilities of members, and stimulate and fine-tune a positive group process.

B. Be relevant and real: avoid clichés or stock phrases.

C. Affirm everyone: create space for everyone to have his own unique reactions.

D. Be cognizant of timing and pace: know when to talk and when to listen, stay with a theme or phase or move on, keep track of the time, and ensure that debriefing does not end with people being left emotionally wide open.

E. Balance the needs of individuals and the group.

F. Balance between being structured and directive and being flexible and responsive to the group process.

G. Cofacilitate to convey a respectful, cooperative relationship.

H. Stay in the role of facilitator:

    1. Balance between facilitating and presenting.

    2. Foster interaction between members.

    3. Do not use this as an opportunity to debrief yourself.

I. Explain and clarify without explaining too much.

J. Summarize and highlight.

IV. Using and knowing oneself in the group

A. Track and manage your own affect.

B. Be aware of triggers and blind spots that need to be navigated.

C. Manage difficult emotions.

V. Special circumstances

A. Handling extreme anger and emotional reactions: allow strong emotion if directed outside the group, assume control and set limits if it is directed inside the group, reflect (is anger because of a sense of helplessness?), do not let old issues get played out in the group, reframe anger as caring.

B. Handling conflict: set limits, reframe conflict as caring, do not let conflict derail the process, encourage follow-up after the debriefing,

C. Handling monopolizers: prevent monopolizing in the first place, watch for cues, do not postpone intervention, intervene in a polite and supportive way, consistently set limits, use nonverbal signals, ask what others think about a given question.

Note: Much of this outline was inspired by Dyregrov (1997, 2003) and reworked based on my own experiences with facilitating debriefings.

Appendix 7.4

WESTERN MASSACHUSETTS EMERGENCY MEDICAL
SERVICES STRESS MANAGEMENT PROGRAM

CRITICAL INCIDENT STRESS INFORMATION SHEET

As an emergency services responder, you have experienced a traumatic event or critical incident (any incident that causes unusually strong emotional reactions with the potential to affect your ability to function either at the scene or later). Although the event is over, you may now be experiencing or may later experience some strong emotional or physical reactions. It is very common and in fact quite normal for people to experience emotional aftershocks from a horrible event.

Sometimes the emotional aftershocks (or stress reactions) appear immediately after the traumatic event. Sometimes they appear a few hours or a few days later. In some cases, weeks or months can pass before the stress reactions appear.

The signs and symptoms of a stress reaction may last a few days, weeks, months, or occasionally even longer, depending on the severity of the traumatic event. When you have the understanding and support of loved ones, your stress reactions can pass more quickly. At times, the traumatic event is so painful that professional assistance from a counselor may be necessary. This does not imply you are crazy or weak. It simply indicates that the particular event was just too powerful for you to manage on your own.

Here are some common signs of a stress reaction:

PHYSICAL	COGNITIVE	EMOTIONAL	BEHAVIORAL
■ fatigue	■ blaming	■ anxiety	■ change in activity
■ nausea	■ confusion	■ guilt	■ change in speech patterns
■ muscle tremors	■ poor attention	■ grief	■ withdrawal
■ twitches	■ poor decisions	■ denial	■ emotional outbursts
■ chest pain*	■ heightened or lowered alertness	■ severe panic (rare)	■ suspiciousness
■ difficulty breathing*	■ poor concentration	■ emotional shock	■ change in usual manner of relating
■ elevated BP	■ memory problems	■ fear	■ loss or increase of appetite
■ rapid heart rate	■ hypervigilance	■ uncertainty	■ alcohol consumption
■ thirst	■ difficulty identifying familiar objects or people	■ loss of emotional control	■ inability to relax
■ headaches	■ increased or decreased awareness of surroundings	■ depression	■ antisocial acts
■ visual difficulties	■ poor problem solving	■ inappropriate emotional responses	■ nonspecific bodily complaints
■ vomiting	■ poor abstract thinking; loss of time, place, or person	■ apprehension	■ hyperalert to environment
■ grinding of teeth	■ disturbed thinking	■ feeling overwhelmed	■ startle reflex intensified
■ weakness	■ nightmares	■ intense anger	■ pacing
■ dizziness	■ intrusive images	■ irritability	■ erratic movement
■ profuse sweating		■ agitation	■ change in sexual functioning
■ chills			
■ shock symptoms*			
■ fainting			

*Indication of the need for medical evaluation.

WAYS TO ALLEVIATE YOUR SYMPTOMS

- *Within the first twenty-four to forty-eight hours*, try strenuous physical exercise—this will alleviate some of the physical reactions.
- Structure your time—keep busy.
- You are normal and having normal reactions—do not label yourself crazy.
- Talk with people—talk is the most healing medicine.
- Be aware of numbing the pain with overuse of drugs or alcohol—you do not need to complicate the situation with a substance abuse problem.
- Reach out—people *do* care.
- Maintain as normal a schedule as possible.
- Spend time with others.

- Help your coworkers as much as possible by sharing feelings and checking how they are doing.
- Give yourself permission to feel rotten and share your feelings with others.
- Keep a journal—write your way through those sleepless hours.
- Do things that feel good to you.
- Realize those around you are under stress.
- Do not make any big life changes.
- Make as many daily decisions as possible that will give you a feeling of control over your life—if someone asks you what you want to eat, answer them even if you are not sure.
- Get plenty of rest.
- Recurring thoughts, dreams, or flashbacks are normal—do not fight them. They will decrease over time and become less painful.
- Eat well-balanced and regular *meals* (even when you do not feel like it).

WAYS FAMILY MEMBERS AND FRIENDS CAN HELP

- Listen carefully.
- Spend time with your upset loved one or friend.
- Offer your assistance and a listening ear even if you have not been asked for help.
- Provide reassurance of his or her safety.
- Help with everyday tasks, like cleaning, cooking, caring for the family, and minding the children.
- Allow space for private time.
- Do not take anger or other feelings personally.
- Do not say that he or she is lucky it was not worse—traumatized people are not consoled by such statements. Instead, express that you are sorry the event occurred and offer understanding and assistance.

For further information, contact:
Western Mass EMS
168 Industrial Park Drive
Northampton, MA 01060
413-586-6065

8

PSYCHOSOCIAL CAPACITY BUILDING

THIS CHAPTER DESCRIBES psychosocial capacity building (PCB) and provides two case examples of it in action: one involving construction workers assigned to Ground Zero in New York City after 9/11 and the other involving the Acholi, who experienced twenty years of armed conflict in northern Uganda. The groundwork for this chapter is laid in chapter 5, which focuses on resiliency. Respecting and fostering resiliency is a cornerstone of PCB. Psychosocial capacity building encompasses the types of disaster responses described in chapter 7 but goes beyond individual and small-group interventions in the immediate and short-term aftermath, involving organizational, systemic, and community-level initiatives as well.

Interventions for psychosocial recovery at the individual, family, and group levels are described in the Web of Psychosocial Recovery (figure 7.1). The eight sections of the web help guide the multisystemic, multilevel, interconnected actions and responses that are aspects of psychosocial capacity building. But chapter 7 considers only a small part of PCB. One way to situate these interventions in a PCB framework is through an intervention pyramid of responses, as illustrated in figure 1.2, from the Inter-Agency Standing Committee (IASC). The top of the pyramid identifies the population who would benefit from intervention, which is targeted toward those in distress and usually delivered by a trained clinician or specially trained peer. Some interventions focus on groups—such as responders to a disaster. Groups may benefit from targeted services that are not "therapy" per se but involve small-group processing and support. Intervention for groups falls at the second level in the pyramid: focused, nonspecialized supports. But there are many other possible small-group interventions geared toward those directly affected by a disaster, such as support groups for widows, job-training programs, and social activities for the elderly. The pyramid's third level—services and programs for individuals, families, and social groups—targets those who have experienced significant disruptions and is of benefit if connected with key family and community supports. Examples of this support include family reunification, collective grieving and healing ceremonies, psychoeducation about self-care and coping, activities that strengthen livelihood, recreational activities, and ways to improve social networks. The bottom and largest layer of the pyramid—basic services and security—considers fundamental human needs and rights: shelter, food, security, access to health care, water, civil rights, and so on. These are essential for all members of an affected community. This chapter considers all levels of the pyramid, with particular attention to the lower three.

WHAT IS PSYCHOSOCIAL CAPACITY BUILDING?

The IASC defines mental health and psychosocial support together as "local or outside support that aims to promote or protect psychosocial well-being and/or prevent or treat mental disorder" (2007, 16). Psychosocial capacity building, as I define it, is *intervention, provided by professional and nonprofessional people, both local and from the outside, that constitutes a multisystemic, culturally grounded, empowerment- and resiliency-oriented approach designed to help individuals, families, social groups, and communities recover from a disaster. Psychosocial capacity building seeks to be sustainable over time and builds on the foundation of local capacities and resources.* President Bill Clinton (2006) submitted a report to the United Nations after responding to the Asian tsunami. His first principle reads as follows: "Governments, donors, and aid agencies must recognize that families and communities drive their own recovery." Cox and Pawar (2006) note that psychosocial capacity building needs to be people centered, participatory, and sustainable. Thus, psychosocial capacity building engages local people in all phases of disaster response—planning, implementation, and evaluation (Corbin & Miller, 2009; Mollica, Lopes Cardozo, Osofsky, Raphael, Ager, & Salama, 2004; Prewitt Diaz & Dayal, 2008; Wessells, 2009). The emphasis on sustainability means that there is an effort to find long-term solutions to the short-term crisis posed by a disaster (Prewitt Diaz & Dayal, 2008).

GOALS OF PSYCHOSOCIAL CAPACITY BUILDING

It is helpful to break psychosocial capacity building into more specific goals. A foundational one is that it seeks to reduce and alleviate the suffering caused by a disaster. Related to this, PCB interventions are geared toward helping people cope in the aftermath of disaster by supporting their sources of resiliency. Although initially this may require outside intervention and erecting the scaffolding of a support network, over time it is the goal that affected people and communities will have autonomy and agency and become less reliant on specific, often temporary, disaster-related initiatives. Although self-sufficiency is the aim of PCB, this is not intended to discourage interdependence and connectedness—to the contrary, interconnection and social imbrication are signs of resilience and robustness, whether this occurs inside or outside families or within or among communities. There is also a role for ongoing social support that is part of government and nongovernmental safety nets. Self-sufficiency indicates the desire of most people to avoid dependency on the ongoing charity of others, to be more economically and socially independent, and to be able to enter into equitable and reciprocal relationships.

Disaster involves major and significant losses, and PCB permits space for processing, grieving, and mourning. As I often urge, there is no one way to do this, and it is important to respect cultural traditions and practices as well as individual and family preferences. The infrastructures for managing death—funeral parlors and burial grounds, for example—may be lost or destroyed. Part of the goal of PCB is to help affected residents reconstitute the social systems and networks they find helpful and necessary after disaster. Because disaster disrupts cultural traditions, working with individuals and families to creatively reconfigure and reconstitute such practices is part of how PCB can help people grieve and mourn.

Meaning-making is an important aspect of grieving and of overall recovery from disaster. Responders working from a PCB perspective cannot create or impose meaning for others, and there are times when the meaning people take away is the event's unmitigated tragedy, fraught with losses (Summerfield, 2004). But the search for meaning is complex, ongoing, and a primary human endeavor. Whether meaning is attained through individual reflection, spiritual work, storytelling, or talking and sharing with others, it is an important part of the healing process and of reconciling the past, present, and future. Psychosocial capacity building involves listening to individuals and family members as they strive to make sense of what happened. It also involves facilitating the coming together of informal or formal groups in a community for discussions or activities in which the meaning-making process is collectively constructed. After a disaster, meaning-making is often imposed on the affected people by outsiders, and the narratives they construct can become a kind of discursive straitjacket that impedes and constrains creative meaning-making. Examples of this are media and government discourses about the meaning of a disaster that quickly circulate in the disaster's aftermath and risk becoming reified and overly simplified visions of what occurred.

A noteworthy objective of a PCB approach, which is much less evident in a disaster mental health orientation, is an emphasis on economic security, social networks, social capital, and collective recovery, all of which are inextricably linked to psychological recovery. Thus, one of the main goals of PCB is to repair a torn social fabric and restore social connections, associations, and trust in the wake of disaster (Pyles & Cross, 2008). If PCB can help to reconstruct a social web, then the paths of resiliency are reestablished.

All these objectives are aimed at rebuilding a viable community. If there is a collective sense of efficacy and of social and economic well-being, then this will contribute to individual and family psychosocial healing and recovery. To summarize, PCB is based on strength and resiliency, informed by culture, focused on natural social groupings (families, informal social networks), and built on the resources and assets of local people. Moreover, PCB promotes sustainability, repairs and rebuilds social networks, and links collective economic and social recovery with individual recovery. It fosters coping, creates space for grieving, and recognizes the significance of reconstructing meaning. All these aims are intended to reduce suffering, stimulate efficacy, reconstruct local interdependence, and lead to individual and collective autonomy over time. While working to achieve these objectives, practitioners should rely on ethical standards that guide this approach.

ETHICAL STANDARDS

The IASC (2007) has articulated ethical standards for delivering psychosocial assistance after a disaster. This is a good starting point for developing a code of ethics specifically geared toward the responder in psychosocial capacity building. The code serves to respect human rights and equity, provide for full participation, do no harm, build on available resources and capacities, and offer multilayered supports. I have added two more: cultural responsiveness and organizational receptiveness. By following these guidelines, practitioners can do the most good and the least harm.

RESPECT HUMAN RIGHTS AND EQUITY As I have argued, disaster often accentuates and exacerbates social divisions and marginalizes vulnerable populations even more than before the disaster. It is more difficult and takes longer for poor people to recover than those with economic and social assets and resources (Kaniasty & Norris, 1999). When there are racial, ethnic, and other social divisions in a community, any targeted and oppressed groups are even more vulnerable after a disaster, as was often in evidence after Hurricane Katrina (Dreier, 2006; Frymer et al., 2005; Green et al., 2007; Henkel et al., 2006; Kates et al., 2006; Park & Miller, 2006, 2007). And as I discuss in chapter 6, women suffer disproportionately when there is disaster, war, and conflict, particularly when such events occur in societies that are patriarchal in structure (Kristof & WuDunn, 2009). Thus, it is important for responders using a PCB approach to consider the historical, economic, social, and political aspects of the social ecology of a given disaster when planning interventions and assessing the differential impact of the catastrophe. A guiding principle is to respect and advocate for human rights and equity for all.

What makes this particularly challenging for outsiders responding to disasters is that they often serve at the pleasure of a national, regional, or local government authority, and such entities are often implicated in the oppression of certain social groups. Thus, strong advocacy can result in an early exit for responders and can at times lead to a backlash against the very groups that are being discriminated against. What I recommend is for responders to hold the principle of human rights and equity as paramount but to evaluate and negotiate the tactics and strategies that will best achieve these objectives. Diplomacy, compromise, mediation, and facilitation are important skills to have in the PCB toolkit. Also, there are times when advocacy and pressure are necessary and called for, but the positive consequences of such stances need to be weighed against a possible backlash.

PROVIDE FOR FULL PARTICIPATION Full participation means that local people, particularly those directly affected by a disaster, are strongly encouraged to completely participate in the planning, implementation, and evaluation of efforts to help them recover. This relates to human rights and equity, as it is important to ensure that there are seats at the table for all affected groups. I have been at many disaster sites and have seen firsthand how easy it is for responders to take charge and map out their responses with very little input from the people affected. When outside experts intervene, there is a sense that they know best about what will be helpful. This dynamic is amplified by the numbing, confusion, and social disorganization that are often evident as immediate consequences of a disaster—affected people can often appear to be passive or even welcome outsider decisiveness and control. If the interventions are occurring in a poor or underdeveloped community, particularly if the responders represent a group that has more historical and social privilege (white British workers responding to a disaster in a former colony), then deference and consent by affected people should be critically evaluated. Having an ethical imperative to seek full participation helps to mitigate against this tendency.

Wessells (2009) raises the issue of informed consent when planning and implementing interventions. This is an important subset of full participation. Often, affected people are exposed to interventions with very little preparation or sense of what they are getting into. Particularly, they have little sense of what risks might be involved or other alternatives they can access. A local NGO may gather its volunteers to attend a workshop by a "distinguished" professional from another country without the participants knowing what they are signing up for. Thus, full participation should include informed participation, and responders should consider authentic and meaningful ways to ensure that there is informed consent for all participants.

DO NO HARM   Helping professionals and volunteers tend to focus on the benefits of their interventions and less attention is paid to risks and negative consequences. Every well-intentioned response can have an unintended or negative effect. Aid efforts can lead to dependency and a lowering of self-esteem for those receiving relief. Offering Western-style individual counseling in cultures that are more collectively oriented or where the expression of feelings is taboo (Wessells, 2009) can lead to people feeling confused, vulnerable, or even as if they are harming themselves or others (Wikan, 1989). Wessells gives the example of a counseling tent set up for women who were raped in Albania. The women who participated in the program risked opening themselves up to social ostracism. This fueled a cycle of revenge and violence involving enraged family members. The values and meanings that guided the responder differed sharply from the social context of the client, which the responder was probably unaware of.

There are other negative consequences to be mindful of. Encouraging people to participate in a debriefing can lead to emotional contagion or flooding of overwhelming affect (McNally et al., 2003; Miller, 2003). When a person affected by disaster forms a relationship with someone offering psychological first aid, there can be detrimental effects, particularly if the person becomes very attached to a responder who then leaves after a few days. This risk is heightened for children. A rule of thumb for all responders should be that any intervention may have a negative consequence and there should be a careful assessment of this potential before wading in with helpful intentions.

BUILD ON AVAILABLE RESOURCES AND CAPACITIES As discussed in chapter 5, individuals, families, and communities are resilient, capable, and have many strengths and assets. Disaster can be overwhelming and lead to transitory disempowerment and dependency. Upon entering the situation, responders may initially offer the support and resources needed that are normally unavailable to affected persons or at least difficult for them to access. However, it is all too easy for responders to neglect to work with local people to identify available resources and individual and social capital for the sake of expediency. Sustainability, one of the core goals of PCB, is best enacted by working with available local resources from the beginning of an intervention and to increasingly endeavor to uncover, augment, and develop these assets so that they are there when outside helpers withdraw.

OFFER MULTILAYERED SUPPORTS In the West, psychologists and other clinicians who offer counseling and therapy usually work out of an office and provide therapy without directly working within their client's social sphere. There is a split between case managers, who engage in systemic work, and therapists, who focus on intrapsychic, behavioral, or cognitive changes. This dichotomy is not useful when responding to disasters. It is even more problematic when responding to disasters in non-Western societies, where there is less of a division between the psychological and sociological.

Multilayered supports means conceptualizing the interlocking of needs and responses in a way similar to what Weyerman (2007) has described as "linking economics with emotions." Every system is affected by a large-scale disaster. There are those systems outside of the individual, such as the economic, political, and social environments, and those within an individual, such as cognitive, emotional, and psychological systems. As has been described, family systems are challenged and often altered. All of these systems interact with one another. Thus, a comprehensive response to the psychosocial needs of survivors after a disaster should be multisystemic and multilayered with the coordination of all of these different levels of intervention. It is not just that needs on multiple levels should be addressed, but when affected people are feeling more connected and empowered socially, this helps them recover psychologically. Park and Miller (2007) recommend that when offering multisystemic services, these should be located together so that there is synergy and coordination among the different levels of operations rather than housing discrete services in silos, where there are organizational boundaries and separate administrative systems, which can lead to separation and/or competition between services

STRESS CULTURAL RESPONSIVENESS   Although cultural responsiveness is not listed as a separate ethical standard by the IASC (2007), it is one that is mentioned by many other practitioners (Corbin & Miller, 2009; Keane et al., 1996; Kirmayer, 1996; Miller, 2006b; Park & Miller, 2007; Prewitt Diaz & Dayal, 2008; Summerfield, 1995, 2000, 2004; Wessells, 2009). Every practitioner carries cultural biases and assumptions, often unconscious, particularly when working within his or her own culture. When there are cultural mirrors reflecting back one's professional values and assumptions, they appear to be normal and there is a sense of working from a standpoint of empirically and rationally validated objective truths. When carrying such certainty into different cultural settings, it is common to hold on to these assumptions even more tightly while viewing the cultural practices of the "other" as "odd" or even "dysfunctional." Wickramage (2006) complains that Sri Lanka became a virtual psychosocial "playground" in the aftermath of the tsunami, with many outside responders offering interventions with confidence about universal applicability. Although well-intentioned, such a stance may lead to a great deal of miscommunication and even damage, violating the "do no harm" ethical imperative (Summerfield, 1995, 2000, 2004; Wessells, 2009; Wickramage, 2006).

Thus, at a very minimum, it is ethical practice for responders to reflect on their own biases and assumptions and also to try to learn about and respect the cultural practices of the people they are attempting to help. This usually works best when there is intercultural dialogue, rather than having this conversation solely within one's own cultural group. Multicultural planning and intervention teams can then help to identify and uncover cultural misconceptions and mismatches. An illustration of this is given in the second case example in this chapter.

Wessells (2009) warns against romanticizing or idealizing local cultural practices, which can be oppressive and subjugate social groups such as women or ethnic minorities. While it is important to not replicate or support cultural oppression, which violates the ethical premise of human rights and equity, it is also critical that outsiders not take upon themselves the task of trying to uproot, transform, or modify a culture in the wake of a disaster. A responder can appreciate and respect the culture of those being helped, recognizing its importance in sustaining people and giving meaning to their experiences without overtly colluding with oppressive practices. This balancing act is part of the complexity of responding to disasters and working cross-culturally.

MAINTAIN ORGANIZATIONAL RESPONSIVENESS ORGANIZATIONS There is an organizational level to disaster response that reflects, embodies, and encodes cultural values and practices (Park & Miller, 2006). Major disaster response organizations, such as the International Red Cross, Save the Children, Doctors Without Borders, and others often bring people from host or donor countries (the United Kingdom or United States, for example) to both provide and administer direct services. Even when local people are hired or recruited as volunteers, the leadership positions are usually staffed by outsiders. I have witnessed tensions between the world views of outside NGO administrators and lower-level indigenous employees with the resolution, more often than not, favoring outsiders, who have more power and privilege within the organization.

Thus, part of the ethical imperative for disaster responders using a PCB framework is to interrogate the cultural assumptions and cultural practices that organizations bring to a disaster. This includes examining what the operant value systems are, how the organization does business, and who the organization hires to implement its services. Organizations, as with individuals, need to be acceptable to the authorities of the host countries or communities where they are operating. This involves compromise and negotiations but should not lead to either neglecting or excluding certain social groups or colluding with authorities, whether intentionally or not, against those who are targeted or subjugated by the government. An example of this was the active participation and complicity of social workers with the internment of Japanese American citizens during World War II (Park, 2008). This violated the ethical standards of the profession and there can be no justification for colluding with such blatant abuses of human rights.

Park and Miller (2006, 2007) have also argued against organizations taking an excessively neutral stance in the face of blatant social inequities, criticizing the nonaligned stance of the American Red Cross when responding to the rampant racism in communities affected by Hurricane Katrina. There are situations when certain social groups—women, ethnic or religious minorities—require special outreach or accommodation, recognizing that the playing field is anything but level. Again, there is a balance to be struck between fealty to the principle of human rights and equity and negotiating with the governments of host communities and countries that feel threatened by such a stance. Work must proceed in a way that benefits survivors without threatening an organization's ability to continue to provide services.

PSYCHOSOCIAL CAPACITY BUILDING ACTIVITIES

Having considered the definition, goals, and ethical standards of PCB, it is important to discuss what workers actually do when operating within a PCB framework. All the interventions discussed in chapter 7 can be part of a broad PCB response to a disaster-affected community. But these interventions, which fall more within the tradition of disaster mental health (DMH), do not constitute a comprehensive PCB initiative and fall short of the goals and ethical standards already discussed. Thus, in this section, I describe activities and programs that do not fit within a traditional DMH framework and involve more mezzo- and macro-level activities.

One factor determining the choice of a particular approach or strategy is to consider which activities are most appropriate at different phases of recovery from disaster. Rao (2006) uses a classic four-phase model:

1. Rescue ("heroic"): first two weeks after a disaster
2. Relief ("honeymoon"): two to six months
3. Rehabilitation ("disillusionment"): one to two years
4. Rebuilding ("reconstruction"): many years, to suggest intervention priorities

During the rescue phase, Rao proposes psychological first aid (PFA). The relief phase is marked by crisis intervention and group approaches. During the rehabilitation phase, specialized psychological care is indicated. And the rebuilding phase focuses on social rehabilitation and community reconstruction. There is a good point here—that some types of intervention are more appropriate at certain times. Psychological first aid is not as appropriate in later phases as in the immediate aftermath, while long-term planning and rebuilding is not something that affected people can engage in immediately after a disaster. However, I am wary of phases that seem to fit a formula or consistent pattern. There are elements of different phases that overlap, and it is artificial to try to fit them into discrete, linear categories. Communities affected by disaster do not always react the same way or recover according to some prescriptive paradigm; if responders expect certain linear phases of recovery, they are more likely to fulfill these preexisting expectations. It is important that many different types and levels of activities occur simultaneously, when appropriate, and that responders not hold back based on models of phases of recovery. These activities should include collaborative planning and assessment, community organizing and mobilizing, economic recovery and psychosocial healing, social network restoration, teaching and psychosocial education, consultation and supervision, and an exit strategy for outside responders.

COLLABORATIVE PLANNING AND ASSESSMENT   Collaboration is where psychosocial capacity building begins. Before entering a community or implementing programs and responses, an organization or individual should identify local partners—be they officials, organizations, or residents—to assess the impact of the disaster, identify vulnerable groups, and prioritize the most urgent needs of individuals, families, and communities. The planning should be multileveled and multisystemic, considering targeted interventions for those most in need and a broad range of capacity building initiatives for the population at large. Affected people should be part of the assessment and planning process from the beginning. The following are examples of capacity building initiatives that can emerge from such a planning process:

- Forming representative councils or committees in the community to advise, plan, and implement activities
- Developing ways for people to communicate with one another and the community at large—forums, broadsheets, Web sites, community radio

- Forming and facilitating groups to work on particular issues—economic well-being, collective bereavement and memorializing, social activities
- Linking different groups to provide social connection, support, and mutual aid—a link between isolated seniors and children needing adult oversight
- Providing recreational activities for youth and adults
- Initiating community service projects that involve people working together to help the community to rebuild
- Promoting cultural activities—dance, drama, storytelling—that engage people and are connected to the disaster and rebuilding
- Offering artistic activities and presentations, including writing, photography, and other methods of postdisaster expression and collective memorialization

As part of the planning for PCB programs, it is helpful to take an inventory of the community and to map community assets and resources, as well as liabilities and areas needing attention (Kretzman & McKnight, 1993; Landau, 2007; Landau & Saul, 2004; McKnight, 1997; Prewitt Diaz & Dayal, 2008). Inventories can range from corporate or government resources to individuals with particular skills or talents (Kretzman & McKnight, 1993; McKnight, 1997; Prewitt Diaz & Dayal, 2008). It is helpful to actually draw this, and the available research offers useful templates (Kretzman & McKnight, 1993; Landau, 2007; Landau & Saul, 2004; McKnight, 1997). Mapping can also include representing the physical setting before the disaster, the current landscape, or goals for the future (Prewitt Diaz & Dayal, 2008).

Other areas to include in the mapping process are demographic information and residential patterns, political systems and personnel, transportation systems, and information about civic organizations, religious institutions, and other formal and informal NGOs (Miller & Garran, 2007). Mapping, when done collectively with adequate community representation, results in important information about the impact of a disaster on a community and the assets and resources available to rebuild. It also creates a process that brings community members together to envision community recovery and rebuilding, which socially connects people in an empowering fashion.

COMMUNITY ORGANIZING AND MOBILIZING Assessment, mapping, and planning are initial strategies of an overall community-organizing framework. Community organizing is an approach that involves actions fostering democratic, participatory activities to improve the well-being of a community and its residents. There is an emphasis on local involvement, responsibility, and decision making. Community organizers recognize that there are disparate interests and unequal levels of social and economic power and capital in any community but, despite this, it is possible to bring people and groups together to work toward their shared interests and the common good through coalitions, meetings, task forces, study and focus groups, and other ways of sharing ideas, needs, plans, and responsibility. By emphasizing participation, community organizing shifts people from the role of victims to activists with the capacities and abilities to influence their own recoveries and futures. Working together on behalf of the community creates a social synergy that generates hope.

The specific parameters of community organizing are shaped by the social ecology of the disaster. For example, in large, rural, thinly populated swaths of country, with a relatively homogenous population, the emphasis may be on communication, transportation, and mutual aid and support. In a densely populated, ethnically diverse urban area, the focus might be on mobilizing religious and cultural organizations to strengthen microcommunities, while also forming representative bodies or councils to coordinate the efforts of different subgroups within the larger community. Cultural traditions, patterns, beliefs, and meaning-making systems are important parameters of the social ecology that shape how community organizing should be conceptualized and implemented in a given area. Community organizing needs to take into account the parameters of what is and is not possible within a given political system. For example, in some situations, organizing displaced, injured, or bereft stakeholders is an important strategy, which may result in greater public awareness and a more compassionate government response. Yet in others, the same actions might lead to official denunciations, crackdowns, and repression. Economic resources are also critical to any community-organizing approach with a realistic appraisal of funding possibilities, regulations and codes, and other factors that determine what is and is not possible. Community organizing relies on a clear vision of the social ecology of a disaster and constant reevaluation of the significance of this for the recovery of the community.

Pyles (2007) has discussed the relevance of a community-organizing approach in response to disaster. She stresses the importance of linking social action with social development as this is critical for the long-term recovery of an affected community. Social justice is valued in all community organizing and is particularly salient in the aftermath of disaster. The social upheaval caused by disaster can result in further social divisions and increase social inequality and the neglect and oppression of vulnerable social groups. However, social disorder also presents an opportunity to work toward greater inclusivity and equity within a community while it rebuilds, disrupting and dislodging old patterns and structures. As with any crisis, there is opportunity as well as disarray. When aiding in recovery from a disaster, it is important to work on behalf of people—a concept that often is reflected in the formal and informal policies that enhance or constrain their lives. Some of these are short term and directly in response to the disaster, while others are longer term and will influence the fortunes of communities and their members into the future.

In all community organizing, but particularly after a disaster, the role of the worker/responder is one of catalyst, connector, supporter, and facilitator—rather than leader and decision maker. It is important to be mindful of this because disaster-affected people are initially vulnerable, which makes them open to the influence of outsiders (Pyles, 2007). This influence is best used to foster collaboration, local efficacy, and empowerment, rather than to exert privilege.

ECONOMIC RECOVERY AND PSYCHOSOCIAL HEALING   A psychosocial capacity building framework encourages workers to initiate and support activities that connect macro and micro realities and the social with intrapsychic functioning. Groups are good vehicles for forging such connections. A microcredit group can, for example, bring women in a disaster-affected area together to develop entrepreneurial skills and pool economic resources, which can be loaned to group members to encourage start-up businesses (Kristof & WuDunn, 2009). Such a group can connect women who might want to share their feelings about losing their homes, sources of livelihood, and even family members, which is somewhat similar to what takes place in a psychotherapy group—accessing feelings, ventilating, creating narratives, listening empathically. Such a venue can also serve as a mutual-aid group, offering both economic and social support. Moreover, it is a place where information can be shared about resources and how to access them. Thus, groups can be established with the goal of having multiple functions, ranging from supporting economic self-sufficiency (empowerment) to describing significant losses (grieving). Such groups may also be more culturally familiar, as opposed to "therapy" groups offered to people who do not usually seek therapy.

SOCIAL NETWORK RESTORATION The group framework is but one example of how frayed social networks can be reestablished in the wake of a disaster. There are many ways to bring affected people together—recreationally, socially, psychologically, politically, locally, artistically—so that much of PCB is a combination of community organizing and social group work. This can result in a network of formal groups or informal gatherings. In some communities, Web-based networks supplement face-to-face meetings. In a small New England town where there were a series of arson-based fires resulting in death and property loss, a Web site was immediately established to share information, offer connections, and mobilize and organize the distribution of resources. This occurred in tandem with formal community meetings held in churches, community briefings by public officials, and informal support groups and buddy systems that sprung up to help people feel more connected and safe. Often after a disaster, people are more open to communicating or interacting with one another than before the disaster—such as was experienced after 9/11 in New York City. But this opening can also close if there are not efforts to build and nurture social networks.

TEACHING AND PSYCHOSOCIAL EDUCATION Teaching, educating, and training are important components of psychosocial capacity building. This instruction should be targeted toward those directly affected by a disaster or geared toward strengthening the capacity of local workers, helpers, and residents to help others, such as in the training-of-trainers model. Ideally, these activities involve collaboration between outsiders with special knowledge, skills, and expertise in helping people recover with locals who have insider understanding of the community and culture. Education encompasses many areas, ranging from helping people understand their psychosocial reactions to offering instruction in the writing of grants to enable accessing resources for rebuilding. An empowerment-oriented strategy includes deepening the skills and capacities of affected people so that they have more resources to make decisions and take actions on their own behalf. In this partial list of areas targeted for education and training, a local responder can learn how to:

- Recognize the typical psychosocial reactions to disaster
- Use self-help and self-care strategies

- Recognize adverse reactions, such as excessive drinking, drug use, and PTSD, and help people experiencing them
- Conduct community needs assessments
- Facilitate focus groups
- Form support groups
- Engage in economic development (how to start a small business, how to access microcredit)
- Access resources and capital (loans, grants from government and NGO sources, foundation funding for projects)
- Rebuild, repair, and renovate buildings
- Use tools (fishing equipment, computers, sewing machines)
- Provide healing recreational activities for children and youth
- Tap into cultural traditions and rituals that are activated when there is sadness and loss
- Run workshops helping people to write, take pictures, create art
- Implement media and communication projects
- Integrate and teach the concepts of peace, reconciliation, and psychosocial healing in conflict and war-affected areas

These are but a few examples of the many types of skills, activities, and areas of knowledge that can be taught to people, groups, and organizations to facilitate recovery. There are many ways to conduct educational activities. They can be done in a classroom or workshop style. Groups, whether ongoing or one-time only, are places where skills can be taught or problems solved. A useful resource is the media—radio shows, public service announcements, video clips, blogs, Web pages—depending on what is available and accessible to local people.

Interactive teaching is preferable to a banking model of education, in which knowledge is deposited by teachers into students. It is more empowering to interact and engage with the learner, rather than simply providing information or lecturing. Interactive teaching stimulates social interaction and collaboration. Interactive thinking kindles creative and critical thinking and problem solving. Interactive teaching conveys respect and leads to better thinking and ideas through the collaboration of many minds. Interactive teaching ensures that general ideas and principles are interrogated and modified to fit local cultures and societies.

One of the most effective methods of teaching is a training-of-trainers (TOT) model (Corbin & Miller, 2009; Cox & Pawar, 2006). This usually involves a collaboration between local and outside people so that the training is conceptualized and implemented by a diverse group that has disaster recovery skills and local knowledge and wisdom (see the second example at the end of this chapter). The planners for such an initiative might be some outside "experts" in PCB, or some aspects of PCB, who work with local leaders (clergy, educators, local NGO officials, government officials, local social workers or psychologists) to assess need and plan a tiered system of psychoeducational programs. The plan should include some of the following:

- Analysis of the social ecology of the disaster, with particular attention to sociopolitical, cultural, and psychosocial factors
- Assessment of the differential needs of various subgroups in the community
- Articulation of the short- and long-term goals of the intervention
- Evaluation of potential barriers to success and negative unintended consequences from the intervention
- Creation of a curriculum to achieve the goals and objectives of the intervention
- Identification and formation of the master training team
- Identification of the first tier of trainees (youth workers, clergy, recreational personnel, and union shop stewards), who have some psychosocial, organizational, and training skills with the capacity to serve as links with other people and to train less-skilled community workers and leaders
- Identification of the second tier of trainees (people living and/or working in the affected community with important roles and/or skills), who as the primary workers on the ground, are trained in strategies, techniques, and approaches to mobilize and organize people as well as to offer direct intervention
- Identification and implementation of the logistics of the training (space, materials, equipment, transportation, meals)
- Identification and organization of the people who will serve as ongoing supervisors and consultants overseeing the implementation of the PCB project. These may be drawn from the master trainers and/or the first tier of trainees. They should have the skills, time, access, and motivation to remain in ongoing contact with the second tier of trainees as they work to implement the PCB programs. Attention to this supports sustainability.
- Collaboration around the design and implementation, by all levels of trainers, trainees, and workers, of an action-oriented, participatory evaluation of the project

This model builds the capacity of local people to respond to their own needs and problems through a series of psychoeducational programs that equips these individuals with the skills, experience, and connections to offer training, supervision, consultation, and leadership to other local people on the ground (see figure 8.1). This leads to local leadership and ownership of the program and expands the number of people who are implementing the PCB project in the community, which in turn contributes to longevity and sustainability. It also is a way to titrate professional skills and expertise

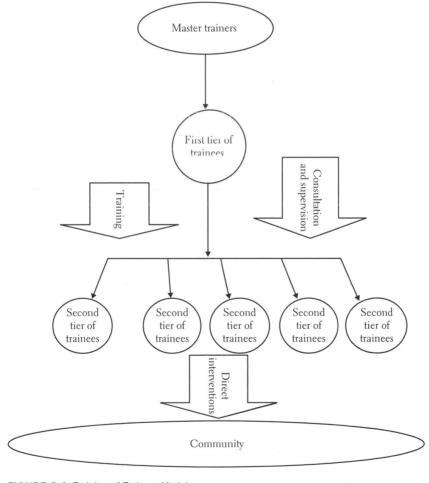

FIGURE 8.1 Training-of-Trainers Model

from the outside with local knowledge, customs, and practices so that any interventions are consistent with local cultural norms and values.

The example of the Acholi in northern Uganda, described at the end of this chapter, illustrates how this multiplier effect works (Corbin & Miller, 2009). A group of five planners (two foreign and three indigenous) developed a curriculum and identified twenty-one first-tier trainees. The planners served as master trainers. After the first group was trained, it was then divided into five teams (of four people each), with one member of the planning group serving as the consultant. Each team implemented a series of psychosocial trainings for leaders and workers in five separate internally displaced persons (IDP) camps. Thus, the initiative resulted in the skill and capacity building of 120 indigenous people in five IDP camps. The success of the program relied on cooperation, collaboration, communication, and community building (Claiborne & Lawson, 2005). The effort was people centered, participatory, and sustainable (Cox & Pawar, 2006). As well, it integrated outsider PCB expertise with local knowledge through mutual respect and articulated shared goals (Corbin & Miller, 2009).

CONSULTATION AND SUPERVISION   For many professionals using a PCB model, serving as consultants, supervisors, and trainers, rather than directly intervening, is the most effective way to help. This represents a shift for some practitioners who are used to offering counseling and therapy to clients and patients. As is discussed with the use of a training-of-trainers model, by working with others and deepening *their* capacity to be helpful, responders multiply their impact, reaching far more people. Working in collaboration with others increases the likelihood that interventions will be culturally responsive. By developing the capacity of local people, there is greater potential for sustainability. And empowering local people to be the leaders and implementers of projects fosters efficacy, empowerment, and social connections.

When working as consultants and supervisors, it is helpful if practitioners begin by asking questions: What are people on the ground seeing? What is causing them concern? What questions do they find particularly difficult to answer? What problems seem to be especially challenging to their usual ways of responding to people's needs? What do they most want to help people with? Consultants can also focus on what will be the best ways to address problems (individual counseling, mutual aid groups, recreational activities) and how to implement PCB programs. Outside consultants should strike a balance between being knowledgeable, as this engenders confidence, while also being humble, avoiding being placed in the role of all-knowing expert. Without such a balance, consultants may find that they are given too much deference and authority.

Thus, outside consultants are most effective if partnered and teamed with local consultants. Improved technology has made it easier for outside consultants to keep in touch with colleagues via e-mail, Skype, teleconferencing, and cell phone. Even in impoverished or underdeveloped areas, cell phone use is a common and viable way of remaining in contact. This also means that outside consultants need to realistically assess how much time and effort they can devote to a project and they need to be transparent about this with local colleagues. Setting realistic boundaries and limits about availability is helpful as it does not raise false or unrealistic expectations. Another issue is the ongoing funding of projects, which outside consultants can support by working with local colleagues and NGOs to write proposals and position papers and to publish articles that support and buttress the rationale for continuing the PCB programs.

Supervision is another activity that outsiders can effectively engage in with local partners. Supervision implies more direct responsibility for on-the-ground activities and detailed oversight of interventions and programs. With supervision, in addition to clarifying roles, responsibilities, and expectations, issues of liability should be considered and attended to by use of written agreements and contracts. With both supervision and consultation, the goal of building ongoing local capacity should always be kept in focus.

EXIT STRATEGY FOR OUTSIDE RESPONDERS   It is useful for outside responders to have an exit strategy as part of PCB interventions (Wessells, 1999). The intention of PCB is to help a community and its members develop their own capacities to respond to and recover from a disaster and for this to be long term and sustainable. Although there are times when outside professionals form and maintain ongoing working relationships after a disaster, it is far more common for them to intervene and then return to their regular day jobs or move on to another area where there has been a new crisis or catastrophe.

Having an exit strategy is helpful in a number of ways. Whenever anyone or any group enters a community during a vulnerable time and offers support, it has an impact on the local community, both positively and negatively. The positive aspects of outside intervention should be evident at this point. Common negative consequences of an intervention are the undermining of local efficacy, providing culturally inappropriate programs, and creating dependency on people or entities that cannot be relied on indefinitely. In well-executed psychosocial capacity building, it clear that outsiders have a focused time-limited role, which respects local agency and autonomy. It lets everyone know where they stand and sets limits and boundaries around interventions that are clear to all. And having a finite time frame helps focus activities and provides an impetus for the work that needs to be done.

EXAMPLES OF PSYCHOSOCIAL CAPACITY BUILDING PROJECTS

Having described PCB, I now offer two concrete examples of PCB projects, one involving construction workers in New York City working at Ground Zero after 9/11 and the other a training-of-trainers program to help Acholis in northern Uganda recover from a brutal twenty-year armed conflict.

COLLABORATIVE PSYCHOSOCIAL CAPACITY BUILDING AFTER 9/11

After the attacks of 9/11 on the World Trade Center in New York City, many people were evacuated from the area around Ground Zero in lower Manhattan. Construction workers then arrived en masse to work to remove debris under dangerous and stressful conditions. Many worked long shifts and saw this as a contribution to their country after a terrorist attack. They encountered human remains, body parts, and personal belongings and were exposed to hazardous and unhealthy work conditions. A significant number of the workers were cleaning up the rubble of buildings that they had helped to construct. The work continued, for weeks and months and extended for years after the attacks.

The vast majority of the workers at the site were unionized, and the many trade unions who served their members were concerned about their physical and mental health. The incidence of respiratory problems among the workers and volunteers was high, and almost 60 percent of those tested by a medical-screening program were found to have elevated levels of trauma-like emotional stress. Traditionally, construction workers, who are predominantly male and working class, are not predisposed to seeking therapy or counseling when they encounter stress, as this is viewed as a sign of weakness and carries a social stigma. There is more of a tradition of lateral mutual aid and support for one's "brothers" and "sisters." Additionally, there was the complication of language. Many of the construction workers were Hispanic and Polish and were more comfortable speaking Spanish or Polish than English.

New York City already had a number of entities that represented construction workers and their employers, organizations that had in place an infrastructure for offering social support. There was the Building and Construction Trade Council representing unionized workers, the Building Trades Employer Association, and the Construction Industry Partnership, an umbrella organization of workers and employers. All three entities had a close relationship with Cornell University's School of Industrial and Labor Relations (ILR). Thus, there were already effective organizational structures for key actors, a history of collaboration and cooperation, a culture of mutual aid and support, and an educational entity closely tied to workers and employers—assets that could be mobilized for a psychosocial capacity building project.

Building on these assets, a Building Trades Support Network was established with the support of the above organizations and managed by a social worker at ILR. Labor organizers and psychologists were part of the core project team that mapped out a PCB strategy to support construction workers. An advisory group was established from the participating organizations, which included clinicians with experience in working with labor unions, trauma, and disasters. Rather than refer union members out to counseling services, a PCB project was designed with the following characteristics:

- A range of supportive services offered to construction workers with an emphasis on psychoeducation and mutual support
- Psychological and emotional services that could be accepted and assimilated by workers and acted on if necessary
- Outreach and the establishment of credibility for the program to ensure its effective use by members
- Multiple modalities of interventions, taking into account different adult learning styles and incorporating different cultural traditions and languages

The project consisted of three major strategies to assist workers:

1. Peer support and outreach
2. On-site psychoeducational workshops
3. Educational outreach

The first strategy involved training volunteers from a pool of union members who could serve as "peers." Peers attended workshops to learn about the psychological and emotional effects of working at Ground Zero and about self-help and mutual aid activities to counter the stresses of the work situation. Ways of identifying more severe problems and how to seek and access help were also included. Peers then assisted with psychoeducational workshops for rank-and-file members. In addition, they served as outreach personnel, encouraging construction workers to participate in the psychoeducational workshops. As Ground Zero workers themselves, these peers had credibility.

Psychoeducational workshops were offered for Ground Zero workers at a number of accessible sites, available in English, Spanish, and Polish. The workshops lasted for two and one-half to three hours and were facilitated by a clinician with assistance from union peers and a member of the clergy. They covered the following topics:

- Emotional health issues after traumatic experiences: normal responses to an abnormal situation
- Common cognitive, emotional, behavioral, and physical reactions to traumatic stress
- Emotional health issues for young children of construction workers
- Self-help tips: behavioral, physical, emotional, and spiritual care
- Relaxation and meditation exercises

Although these were workshops and covered similar territory as debriefings, there was much emotional sharing and disclosure, which was why it was so important to have clinicians and clergy present. Workshop participants were given booklets summarizing the key points in the workshop and were also offered referrals for individual and group clinical services if needed. From October 2002 to December 2003, the project offered 144 workshops to 1,523 union members working at Ground Zero, reaching about 1 percent of approximately 15,000 workers.

Educational outreach involved three strategies in addition to the use of the peer outreach workers. Construction workers were provided with:

1. A hard-hat decal advertising a hotline established to publicize the outreach program and to offer information about resources for workers
2. A brochure focused on engaging workers that included personal testimonies and mental and physical health referrals, as well as the hotline number
3. A popular-culture adult cartoon booklet called *Rebuilding Our City*, using visual vignettes and designed for three audiences (rank-and-file workers, adult family members, and children), which served as both an outreach and a psychoeducational intervention

The booklets linked Vietnam-era PTSD with some reactions experienced by the construction workers, as many of them were Vietnam War veterans. They described normal reactions to abnormal situations, including the impact of worker reactions on their families. The booklets stressed resiliency while also offering readers descriptions and telephone numbers of resources for further help. More than twenty thousand brochures were distributed.

Approximately 25 percent of participants completed questionnaires at the end of the workshops, and the vast majority reported that they found the workshops to be very helpful. There were also qualitative interviews with the leaders from the participating unions. They reported very favorable responses from their membership. However, there was no long-term follow-up with participants or randomly controlled trials comparing them with nonparticipants. Conceptually, the project combined aspects of a disaster mental health approach, focusing on normal psychological and emotional reactions to a disaster, employing a PCB emphasis on resiliency, self-help, and mutual support. Project designers regretted that they were not able to offer workshops directly to family members. This would have been difficult to implement within a union structure but would have probably increased the effectiveness of the interventions. But overall, thousands of construction workers and their families received either booklets or workshops, which helped them to understand their reactions, connected them with social supports, and pointed the way for more specialized clinical help. The project offers a model for future PCB projects with similar populations, although more rigorous research is needed to evaluate the effectiveness of such endeavors and to fine-tune them and adapt how they are implemented.

(Much of the information for this section comes from Miller, Grabelsky, & Wagner, 2010.)

COLLABORATIVE PSYCHOSOCIAL CAPACITY BUILDING IN NORTHERN UGANDA

Northern Uganda was the site of a brutal twenty-year armed conflict instigated by the Lord's Resistance Army (LRA), resulting in the deaths of thousands of Acholi, the recruitment of child soldiers, and the displacement of the vast majority of the population in the region into IDP camps. The history of the conflict is too complex to do it justice in this brief vignette, but the main perpetrator of violence was the Lord's Resistance Army, composed of rebels primarily from the Acholi tribe, who attacked, maimed, killed, and terrorized Acholi living in northern Uganda. There were also atrocities committed against the civilian population by government soldiers ostensibly sent to protect them. Tens of thousands of children were abducted during the conflict. Some were killed while others were forced to become soldiers. Abducted girls were raped, with some becoming consorts to the rebels. Children were forced to attack their own families, sometimes killing family members. When children did escape and return, it was difficult to reunite them with their families and reintegrate them into their communities because of mistrust, hostility, guilt, and many other complex dynamics accruing from the forced parricide and fratricide. Girls returning with their own children, fathered by rebel soldiers, found that their offspring were not always welcome or eligible to receive the social and economic benefits of clan membership. Also, the war had completely disrupted the ability of villagers in this agrarian society to farm for themselves. Crops and livestock were seized and destroyed, and it was unsafe for civilians to go on with their daily chores of farming and gathering. Access to potable water was limited. Family members sometimes spent hours, if not most of a day, acquiring water. All this led to citizens having less independence and being more reliant on government and NGO aid.

The epicenter of the Acholi region in northern Uganda is the town of Gulu. An American social work professor, Joanne Corbin, after having visited this area for a number of years, designed a psychosocial capacity building project with two of her Ugandan colleagues, a Catholic priest, who is a venerated member of the community, and an Acholi social worker attached to a large international NGO. Together they planned a training-of-trainers model of intervention to respond to the psychosocial needs of war-affected villages in the greater Gulu area. After mapping out the contours of the training, the team was expanded to five with the addition of another U.S. professor of social work (the author) and a Gulu public social service administrator.

The goal of the project was to deepen and expand the capacity of local social service providers to respond to the psychosocial needs of the war-affected people in IDP camps. The five project leaders functioned as master trainers, organizing a three-day training program for twenty-one social service, youth, and education workers. The training focused on the psychological and social consequences of armed conflict for individuals, families, and the community; ways of supporting coping and well-being; case management; and topics such as how to foster psychosocial healing and linking this to peace and reconciliation. There was consideration of other subjects, such as child development, the effects of alcohol abuse, and domestic tensions and conflicts within families as a consequence of the armed conflict. Western notions of trauma were compared with Acholi traditions of managing stress. The topic areas were identified by the master trainers, but each training session involved negotiating with participants about priorities, interests, and needs. Training was conducted in an interactive, as opposed to didactic, fashion, ensuring full participation and mutual exploration of issues. Although problems were raised, there were always attempts to consider sources of resiliency, strength, and available assets. Participants commented how important it was that they and their people not be viewed as victims needing to be rescued by outsiders. There was also a strong emphasis on cultural traditions, and when psychosocial problems were presented, the first line of discussion was to explore how Acholi customs and rituals had addressed these problems in the past and what barriers were interfering with their operating effectively in the current environment.

After the initial training sessions, the first tier of trainees switched hats and prepared to offer training to others about the psychosocial impact of the armed conflict and strategies for local empowerment and recovery. They were divided into five teams with one master trainer assigned to each team. Each team was assigned to one IDP camp. The teams met to prepare and rehearse their training curriculum before entering the camps.

Camp leaders had been approached by the original project leaders and, in each of the five designated camps, had identified about twenty people who would receive the second tier of training. The trainees were chosen for their ability to be high-impact people within the camp—teachers, religious leaders, nurses and other health professionals, business leaders, elders, and youth leaders. Some of the participants were people who had been abducted by the LRA as children and had since returned to the IDP camps. While the initial training had been conducted in English, which was spoken by all participants, the second tier of training was conducted in Luo, the language spoken by everyone in the camps. The content for this training was similar to the original topics, but the focus was more on down-to-earth practical applications of offering psychosocial support. There was much role playing to explore issues and ways of responding to problems. There was also an emphasis on daily activities and social and recreational groups that could be used to bring the affected people together, reconnect them with cultural traditions, and help them feel safe, hopeful, and efficacious. Some of the training in the IDP camps involved dancing and drama. Trainers ate in the camps with the trainees. The food was prepared by camp residents.

After the second tier of training, the IDP camp trainers met individually with the master trainer in their team to receive feedback about their effectiveness as trainers and to look at how to build on their strengths for future training sessions. There was also consideration by the larger group about ways to support the work of the project. The group decided to have first-tier trainees serve as consultants to second-tier trainees on an ongoing basis as a way to support sustainability. Monthly meetings between the first-tier trainees and the local master trainers were scheduled to focus on how to best support the work of the second-tier trainees in the IDP camps.

Joanne Corbin, the project leader, is continuing to evaluate the effectiveness of the training and has monitored the continued psychosocial capacity building efforts by all levels of participants. The trainings were conducted in 2007. In the ensuing years, many people have left the IDP camps to return to their villages. As yet, it is too early to tell what the long-term impact of the project will be. The initial evaluations of both levels of trainees were very positive, particularly regarding the use of cultural rituals and practices to address psychosocial needs. There was also a very positive response to linking psychosocial healing with peace and reconciliation. Because of the lack of a technological infrastructure, precluding the use of video and computer conferencing, much of the ongoing work falls on the shoulders of the local people who participated in the project at all three levels, which illustrates why it is so essential to build local capacity. (Much of the discussion in this section is based on Corbin and Miller, 2009.)

Psychosocial capacity building is multilevel and multisystemic. It is a culturally grounded, empowerment-based, and resiliency-oriented approach that helps individuals, families, social groups, and communities recover from a disaster. It addresses all levels of the IASC intervention pyramid for psychosocial support after a disaster. Although PCB incorporates the short-term individual and small-group support described in chapter 7, it also includes interventions directed toward social groups, organizations, and communities, which are intended to have long-term effects. Thus, it is important to seek sustainability, which involves developing the capacity of local people to help their own communities recover. As Bill Clinton stated, "Families and communities drive their own recovery" (Clinton, 2006), and the well-being of individuals, families, and communities are intricately related.

A PCB approach seeks to alleviate suffering, support grieving, and facilitate meaning-making. There is recognition of the importance of economic security, social networks, and social capital as key components of the recovery process. In summary, psychosocial capacity building follows these ethical precepts (IASC, 2007):

- Respect human rights and equity
- Provide for full participation
- Do no harm
- Build on available resources and capacities
- Offer multilayered supports
- Stress cultural responsiveness
- Maintain organizational responsiveness

The core PCB activities are summarized as follows:

- Collaborative planning and assessment
- Community organizing and mobilizing
- Economic recovery and psychosocial healing
- Social network restoration
- Teaching and psychosocial education
- Consultation and supervision
- Exit strategy for outside responders (Wessells, 1999, 2009)

The two instances of PCB outreach described in this chapter appear to have been helpful to the many people affected by disasters in New York and northern Uganda. Although they illustrate two types of PCB projects, neither project is perfect or complete. And though there were efforts to conduct evaluations of the projects' effectiveness, randomly controlled trials were not done, and there has not been research into their long-term effectiveness. Yet despite working in the shadow of incomplete knowledge and limited resources, it is important for responders to intervene in the absence of absolute certainty. The respectful, participatory, ethically grounded nature of PCB maximizes its potential to help communities recover from disaster while minimizing the potential negative consequences of intervention.

MINDFULNESS EXERCISE: MEDITATION ON ASSETS

This meditation involves the use of guided imagery, focusing first on the individual meditator and then expanding out to the community.

- Begin by sitting comfortably with your eyes closed or open, depending on your preference.
- Focus on your breathing for a minute or two.
- Think of one personal asset that you have at your disposal when the going gets rough. It may be something like having a sense of humor or leadership skills—or knowing when to engage in self-care. You may come up with more than one asset but, at this point, focus on just one.
- Picture yourself using the asset that you have identified. Visualize a time when it came into play. As you breathe in, feel the strength of this asset and, as you breathe out, direct it toward others.
- Now think of an asset that someone else has that gives you strength. For example, it might be your friend's sense of calmness and transparency or a family member's unconditional love. Breathe in their strength and breathe out your gratitude.
- After doing this for a few breaths, imagine your community. Think of one thing it gives you that supports your well-being. For example, it could be a park where there is natural beauty; your church, synagogue, or mosque; or a group you are a member of or an educational facility where you take

classes. Picture this community asset. Reflect on what makes it important to you. Eventually, breathe in and out your sense of connection to this asset.

- Return to your breathing for a few breaths before ending the meditation. If you wish, you can write down the assets that you identified in yourself, others, and the community for future use in your disaster response work.

9

THE USE OF GROUPS AND ACTIVITIES

WHEN DISASTER STRIKES in developed Western nations, trained counselors and therapists generally are available. They tend to work for disaster response organizations or serve as volunteers with nonprofits or professional crisis response networks. In the immediate aftermath of the disaster, they usually provide services such as psychological first aid, crisis intervention, critical incident stress management, and short-term counseling. During the postdisaster phases, ongoing therapy and counseling (either individual or group) may be provided. Many practitioners use cognitive behavioral techniques (CBT), while others prefer more psychodynamically oriented approaches. There are also services for those who are grieving and mourning. Such services were offered in the United States after Oklahoma City and 9/11.

In other parts of the world, therapy is neither normative nor available. There is an absence, or shortage, of trained therapists. People do not usually think of therapy as a preferred means of solving problems. They may be more likely, in a time of need, to turn to their family, church, or other members of their community. As mentioned previously, the articulation of inner feelings and sharing them with others runs counter to many cultural traditions and practices. This is what I encountered in Sri Lanka, northern Uganda, Sichuan Province in China, and Haiti after major disasters.

Even Western countries have many subpopulations that do not use therapy to solve their problems. This can be a function of cultural orientation as well as religious and social-class differences. Sometimes it is a question of a lack of available resources and the structure and restrictions of the private health insurance industry, but it is also a reflection of different styles of help-seeking behavior.

Therefore, should the occasion of a catastrophic event be the time to encourage people who do not normally use counseling and therapy to engage in it? As has been mentioned, one of the goals of disaster intervention is to help people to return to "normal," to reestablish routines and practices and to draw on traditional sources of strength and resilience. Disaster causes profound disruptions. Is offering counseling and therapy another form of cultural displacement?

People who experience more serious reactions to disaster—such as acute stress disorder, extreme anxiety, depression, traumatic grief, or in the long-term, PTSD—are likely to benefit from clinical services. In such instances, many, including those from non-Western cultural groups, find it helpful to express and ventilate their feelings, to learn about normal reactions to disaster, and to receive counseling about how to deal with intrusive memories, hyperarousal, and avoidance. Trained clinicians can help assess the level of psychological impairment or trauma as well as the risk of self-harm or suicide. But even when therapy may be helpful, if clinicians descend on a site where therapy is not normative and offer direct psychological services after a disaster, chances are they will be there for a limited time and will reach only a limited number of people.

Disaster mental health stems from the larger field of mental health, which is essentially a Western project. It has its roots in middle-class European and U.S. communities, although it has spread, particularly through the use of community mental health clinics, to a wider population. The project involves the cost of training and credentialing, a process that often excludes rather than includes, as well as the cost of services. It assumes that forming a relationship with a professional and talking about problems is helpful. The project has tended to emphasize universalism—that people are people with similar reactions everywhere, needing similar services—and until recently has de-emphasized culture (Roland, 1996). It has enshrined Western Enlightenment values about the relationship of individuals to one another and their polity, as well as what is considered a healthy, normative process of development—leading to individuation and a "me self," as opposed to a "we self." In fact, the project reflects a circumscribed and delimited worldview.

Yet this culturally limited worldview is often applied to disasters in non-Western parts of the world. I make this critique as a licensed, trained therapist. I work in many settings around the world and use many techniques taken from my clinical toolbox. But I have increasingly come to view the use of therapy in postdisaster settings, particularly with non-Western populations, as having its limitations and even the potential to inadvertently undermine traditional cultural practices and other routes to collective healing and recovery. And I have learned through experience that even when local people in the community specifically request Western clinical approaches, these should be applied with caution. After a disaster, people and communities feel overwhelmed and disempowered, so they are vulnerable and susceptible to the influence of outside "experts." This is reinforced by neocolonial patterns of privilege and respect for authority, as the outside "experts" often seem to know what they are doing and come from more developed nations. There is also a cultural imperialism that emanates from the West, as anyone who has traveled through non-Western countries will observe: billboards advertise beauty products and clothing with white models, imposing a form of international cultural hegemony, reinforcing status inequities. And although some members of local communities who have been trained in Western schools or professional programs as clinicians may welcome such interventions, they do not represent the community at large. The first rule of disaster intervention is do no harm, and by advancing the Western approach to mental health, clinicians from outside can inadvertently cause people to feel de-skilled, disempowered, and disconnected from their cultural traditions.

This chapter explores alternatives to the emphasis on talk therapy and counseling by considering how groups and the use of activities employed in a culturally grounded fashion can help people recover from disaster. I have found that even when using a training-of-trainers model, action is often more effective than talking. Again I reference the Web of Psychosocial Recovery (figure 7.1), which illustrates processes that help people recover from disaster—feeling safe and secure, expressing painful feelings, being able to calm oneself, feeling connected with others, having a sense of efficacy, regaining a sense of hope, linking to past cultural practices, and recapturing a sense of place. All these can be achieved through activities, particularly in groups. Disaster involves collective losses, while groups and activities bring people together and help them collectively recover. This chapter considers how to do this.

GROUPS

Whenever possible, after a disaster, I prefer to work in groups for a number of reasons. Groups create a situation in which mutual understanding, healing, mutual aid, and support can occur. This means that people with common experiences are learning from one another and forming links and relationships, rather than relying on an "expert" to help them recover. There is reciprocity and equity, talking with a friend or fellow group member is egalitarian and mutual, and there is not the dichotomy of a person being helped and a helper. Groups bring in multiple perspectives and create a support system, which is more likely to endure, as opposed to a supportive outside person who is likely to leave. One of the valuable aspects of groups after a disaster is that they can create a group narrative of what has occurred, amplifying individual experiences and bringing people closer to one another through their bond of common experience. Group members feel validated when they learn that they and others have had similar reactions—they feel less alone. And hearing about differences in experiences, particularly the strategies employed by people to draw on their strengths and foster resiliency, expands the possibilities.

Groups can often accomplish more than can two people in a counseling relationship. When a group of individuals pool their assets and resources, they can achieve much more and share the burden of responsibility. Groups create their own energy and synergy, connecting people and creating a circuit of power that strengthens and is contagious. People of all ages can participate in groups. Some groups have homogenous populations—like five- and six-year-olds—while others can bring together children to entertain senior citizens, or conversely, elderly community members can supervise activities for children.

In societies with more of a collective orientation, many activities are done in groups—socializing, working, praying, and so on. These societies have a different sense of privacy and more of an emphasis on public and communal life. So while groups can be helpful in all cultures and societies, groups are a particularly good fit with collectivist societies, where congregating and working in groups is normative. Using groups after a disaster builds on practices that are already in place.

There are many different types of groups, and later I consider four—psychoeducational, support, task, and activity—that are particularly effective in postdisaster work. But first I discuss some fundamentals that are important to the effective functioning of any group but particularly groups formed in response to disasters. These include ground rules, boundaries, facilitation and participation, a contract, review of the group's work and purpose, tasks and responsibilities, and time and duration.

GROUND RULES

Every group works best if norms are articulated and agreed upon by its members. These serve as guidelines and codes of conduct for the participants. They help give the group direction and coherence and ensure that all members are working from the same game plan. Every group develops norms for how to perform—some explicit, others implicit. Given the intensity of reactions to a disaster and often the brief or time-limited nature of the group, it helps to make guidelines for conduct as clear and unambiguous as possible. It is always best when the group generates its own norms—this is empowering and creates a consensus by which members can collectively abide. This is preferable to group facilitators imposing norms, although any important rules that are left out by group members can be introduced by those leading the group.

Norms can be revisited by group members and facilitators and, when necessary, revised or amended. Norms create standards of conduct and operation that everyone can monitor and uphold. For example, a good norm urges members to remain mindful of how much they talk, making sure others get to join the discussion as well. If the norm is established and a group member "takes up too much space," it is much easier to enforce the norm with a friendly reminder than attempt damage control after the fact. When I was working in Haiti after the earthquake of 2010, I neglected to introduce this ground rule before leading a psychoeducational group. One participant spoke first every time I asked a question and went on for much longer than other people in the group. I could see other group members spacing out and losing interest when this person talked. Yet because I had not established the norm, it was difficult for me to address this without directly confronting the person, risking feelings of humiliation, bewilderment, and even disrespect.

BOUNDARIES

Because all groups have boundaries, it is helpful to have members articulate and agree on what these will be. Norms and ground rules help establish boundaries. Another important aspect of group boundaries is deciding whether the group should be open or closed. Expectations about this vary considerably among different cultures. Closed groups maintain the same membership over the course of meetings (and during a given meeting). They make it clear who is in the group and who is not. Psychoeducational groups are often closed, which facilitates trust and hence encourages dis-closure. However, in my experience in some cultural settings, the notion of a closed group runs counter to familiar patterns of collective engagement. Also, the exigencies of daily living may make it difficult if not impossible to honor commitments to attend all groups. Thus, open groups may work better and create greater comfort for group members who may feel less pres-sure if they have more agency surrounding attendance. In addition, open groups are more inclusive and can bring in people who initially did not know about the group or were not sure whether they wanted to participate. What can be challenging about open groups is not being able to anticipate how many people will show up at a given meeting and that a changing membership makes it difficult to gain traction and move forward with cer-tain themes and issues, as the group often has to reiterate themes or cover ground that has already been explored to bring new attendees up to date.

An important aspect in establishing boundaries is to determine what is confidential and what is not. A good rule of thumb is to encourage people to talk about the themes that come up in group with people not in the group, as this can mean that more people are reached and are part of the conversa-tion. At the same time, it should be made clear to members that personal and identifying information not be conveyed outside of the group, as when a member discloses something very private. Again, the cultural context in which the group takes place shapes expectations and comfort around issues of confidentiality, and it is important to adapt notions of confidentiality to the cultural and social realities of group members.

FACILITATION AND PARTICIPATION

Group facilitation is a complex task with many aspects: building trust with group members, keeping the group process on track and moving forward, articulating goals, clarifying issues, resolving conflict, and creating group cohesion so that the group performs effectively (Dyregrov, 1997, 2003). All these aspects are important when facilitating any kind of group after a disas-ter. Facilitation involves leadership without dictatorship, being active with-out dominating, setting an example while encouraging others to participate and step forward, and listening and observing as well as talking. For most groups, facilitation most critically means to maximize group participation and to ensure that people stay as focused as possible on the reason they have come together. It involves maintaining a wide vision, focusing on the entire group and not becoming sidetracked with one or two group members. It requires a constant level of awareness and alertness to what is happening in the group, paying attention to nonverbal as well as verbal cues and signals.

While full participation is the goal, how people participate will vary. Some will be more active than others, particularly in a large group setting. There are many cultural differences in group interaction. Many of my students, a significant number of them Asian and Asian American, have told me, for them, courteous behavior in a group is listening respectfully and deferring to others who seem eager to speak. There are many Asians and Asian Americans who do not behave this way in group, but I have seen this pattern for some, particularly when teaching in China. Other families and ethnic groups may have a more assertive and active style of conversation. Growing up in my Jewish American family, if we did not interject when there was a millisecond of an opening, or even interrupt, then we did not get a chance to speak. Bringing together diverse cultural traditions in a group setting means that facilitators should use a variety of methods and techniques to create space for different people to participate in ways that they feel comfortable—breaking people into pairs or small groups, for example. Otherwise, the large group dynamic may be one that is dominated exclusively by a few people or by people from a certain cultural background.

CONTRACTING

When a group forms after a disaster, a contract stating the purpose of the group can serve as a frame of reference (Schwartz, 1971). The contract need not be a written, legalistic document; it should, however, be an explicit articulation of why people are meeting and what they hope to do together. Attendees and facilitators should be able to come to some basic agreement as to what they hope to get out of the group.

REVIEWING

All groups work better if the facilitators periodically review why people are gathering, summarize what has been accomplished up to that point, and help the group focus on the task at hand. Reviewing also involves looking ahead to future meetings, agendas, and work that the group will engage in. Concise, periodic summaries by facilitators help group members stay focused on where they have come from and where they hope to go, furthering the work of the group.

TASKS AND RESPONSIBILITIES

After a disaster, when people join a group, they often have a lot of homework between group sessions. This depends on the nature of the group, which I discuss shortly. However, for most groups, it is helpful to spend some of the group time focusing on what group members will do outside of group. For example, for a psychoeducational group, it might be a self-care regime. Or a task group's duties may lead to other responsibilities—planning, interviewing, assessing, and intervening. Clarity about the roles and responsibilities of group members helps not only when the group is in session but also outside of group meetings by laying out what needs to be done and who is accountable for doing it.

TIME AND DURATION

People work most effectively in groups when they know how long they will be there. This applies to defining the length of a given session (that is, knowing when it will begin and end) as well as the total number of group meetings (how long the group plans to remain in existence). Some groups, such as support groups, are open-ended, but many groups will meet for a specified period of time—weekly for ten weeks, for example. What is important is to be clear on the commitment that people are making. Are they expected to attend every meeting? Is the protocol to be present for an entire session or can people drop in and move on?

If a group is time limited, it helps to have a clear ending and to use this as an opportunity to review the progress that has been made by the group and the outstanding issues that group members will continue to work on even after the group has formally ended.

EFFECTIVE GROUPS IN DISASTER WORK

PSYCHOEDUCATIONAL GROUPS

In the West, psychoeducational groups are among the most frequently used in response to disaster; debriefings and psychological first aid are examples of this type of group. There are two distinguishing aspects of such groups: they create space for people to process their cognitive and affective reactions and they provide a platform for validation and normalization, teaching "normal" versus unusual reactions to a disaster. Sometimes psychoeducational groups are one-time affairs, whereas others meet regularly for a specified period of time. These groups can be adapted for use in many cultures and maintain a balance between a directed group process, in which the facilitator serves as the authority, and a collaborative group process, in which members share and learn from and help one another.

The psychological part of a postdisaster psychoeducational group allows for people to share their experiences and reactions during and after a catastrophe. Unlike long-term therapy groups, the focus is not on deepseated issues or long-term sources of daily stress. These issues might be touched on and connections made to current dilemmas a person is grappling with, but the emphasis is on the disaster and its consequences. Most postdisaster psychoeducational groups consider what happened, how people are doing, and what can be done to help people help themselves heal and recover. By doing this in a group setting, participants learn how they are similar to and different from other group members, and they may experience resonance with other people's experiences. The process of sharing often leads to ties with others and diminishes feelings of being isolated and alone. However, as has been mentioned, in some cultures, particularly non-Western ones, it is not easy or helpful to discuss feelings, particularly negative feelings, with nonfamily members in a group. Psychoeducational groups should factor in cultural norms and expectations, and in some cultural contexts, this type of group may not be the best one to use under the circumstances.

The educational part of psychoeducational groups involves reviewing and normalizing typical reactions to disasters, in addition to explaining, when possible, why these reactions occur. I have found that it is helpful to keep this simple and down to earth, depending on the communication style, education, and cultural norms of a given group. For example, after the earthquake in Haiti, many people were afraid to step into buildings and exhibited symptoms of hypervigilance and extreme anxiety when entering rooms. A helpful metaphor was that their brains were trying to keep them safe—that subconsciously they had recorded what the conditions were when the earthquake struck and were reminding their bodies to be aware and afraid when entering buildings. This seemed to resonate with group participants and helped them think of strategies that would enable them to manage these reactions and eventually reduce their severity—what in the West might be called desensitization and calming approaches. It also helped to provide a cognitive frame for the reactions that people were experiencing, which made it possible for them to think about how they could help themselves.

I want to distinguish a postdisaster psychoeducation group from a therapy group. In a therapy group, there might be cognitive behavioral protocols about how to help people who are exhibiting trauma reactions to an event like an earthquake. This could include desensitization, cognitive processing, or calming techniques. In some groups, there may be deeper exploration of the psychodynamic reasons people are experiencing certain reactions. While these techniques can be helpful, they rely on an expert—the group leader—and a cultural expectation that the use of psychotherapeutic techniques is efficacious to a person's recovery. A psychoeducational group elicits more active participation of group members, encouraging them to think of strategies they have used in the past or might employ in the present to respond to their symptoms. This lends itself more easily to a range of cultural styles and traditions. In Haiti, a decision to hold meetings outside might be one response to the hypervigilance experienced after the quake. This might not directly respond to the symptoms, but in this geographical and cultural environment, it may put people at ease and be a viable way to alleviate anxiety. This was particularly salient when there were repeated aftershocks and very rational reasons for people to hesitate to enter buildings.

This example illustrates another component of psychoeducational groups, that of engaging group members in planning for their own self-care. While group facilitators may suggest certain self-care activities—such as vigorous exercise—group members are more empowered when encouraged to ask questions and offer ideas. In so doing, individuals can generate ideas about how to care for themselves or how members can care for others.

SUPPORT GROUPS

Support groups may have elements of psychoeducation, but their primary purpose is to bring people together around a common theme to offer mutual aid and support for one another. The form of support may be emotional, social, practical, economic, or a combination of different types of encouragement, collaboration, care, aid, and assistance. Support groups foster connection and collective efficacy.

This was recently illustrated in a small town in Haiti by a group of community members who had been injured during the earthquake; they were brought together by a local NGO. Most injuries were severe, with people having lost fingers and sustained broken bones. Initially, people in the group were wary about sharing their experiences during and after the earthquake; they wanted to know the purpose this would serve. After some discussion about their experiences, the conversation turned to their concerns about the future. Would they be able to work again? How would they be able to make a living and care for their families? What was the prognosis for their recovery? Would they be permanently disabled?

What emerged was a sense of common experience and solidarity from the group participants. They found it helpful to talk with one another and to share their concerns and hopes. This led to a desire to meet on a regular basis and to bring other people to the meetings who were also injured. It was possible that the group would eventually move to identifying tasks or collective actions, but at that particular point, they met mainly to support and encourage one another's recovery. Group members even decided to find some physical therapy exercises that they could all use to accelerate their recovery.

TASK GROUPS

Task groups bring people together to accomplish certain goals. The work often takes place outside of the group—for example, trying to accomplish something in the community. Task groups engage in planning, implementation, assessment, and evaluation, and they often try to involve other people in the community in activities after a disaster. For example, a group might try to inform the post-Katrina Vietnamese residents of Biloxi about resources and services available to them by translating information into

Vietnamese. Another group might organize patrols in a disaster-devastated neighborhood so that residents can check up on one another's needs and well-being or to help people to feel safer. Such groups assist people in regaining a sense of control in their lives as well as bring people together for a common purpose. They also achieve concrete objectives that respond to collective needs, encouraging a sense of efficacy and engendering hope.

Another example can be found in a task group in a small village in Haiti after the earthquake. Local volunteers met to consider how to help people grieve and mourn. So many people had died in this tiny country that nearly everyone was touched by loss. Many bodies were never recovered. Because of the scale and nature of the disaster casualties, the many traditional Haitian ways of grieving and mourning were not being followed—such as personal visits to families who lost people, neighbors offering support to bereaved relatives by bringing gifts, engaging in a ceremonial service with the family, playing music before burial, visits to cemeteries the day after burial, and creating memorials with pictures. This meant that many people were not only carrying the weight of many intimate losses but were unable to grieve in traditional ways as part of a process of bereavement and recovery.

The volunteers decided to organize a task group in response. They identified ways that the community could collectively grieve, mourn, and memorialize those who had died during the earthquake, including organizing visits to raise money for families who lost loved ones. They made plans to establish a public memorial in the village, including an informational presentation about the earthquake and its consequences. Also, social and recreational activities were organized. The task group invited interested people in the community to participate in the planning and implementation of the strategies.

ACTIVITY GROUPS

Activity groups bring people together after disaster for socializing, sports, dancing, singing, writing, storytelling, game playing, arts and crafts, and other recreational pursuits. The activities themselves help with the expression of feelings and reactions. They also help people experience a sense of efficacy and empowerment. Such groups bring people together to do things that are engaging, meaningful, therapeutic, and at the very least, fun and distracting. Additionally, they provide structure and can give people a sense of purpose. The activities are familiar and draw on cultural rituals and traditions that offer people hope and strength.

Another example from Haiti illustrates the use of an activity group through a training-of-trainers model. After the earthquake, children throughout Haiti were feeling frightened and unsettled. They had lost their structure and sense of routine after schools were closed for six weeks. Some, living in Port-au-Prince, had lost their caretakers and were subsequently sent to live with other family members in new communities. Once some schools reopened (many, unfortunately, did not), children were fearful about entering buildings and were distracted and anxious. These fears were echoed by parents, some of whom kept their children home.

Teachers had their own psychosocial reactions to the earthquake. Although many had not been paid in months, they were dedicated to helping children return to school. Some teachers realized that the earthquake needed to be addressed in some way—children would not be able to simply return to their classes and resume their lessons. Yet these teachers were not therapists or counselors; therefore, they were mandated to resume teaching the class material required by the state.

After consulting with administrators and teachers, training sessions were set up by a local NGO to encourage teachers to think of activities that could be used both inside and outside the classroom to help children resettle in school and process the earthquake experiences and reactions. The three goals of the activities were to help children describe their experiences and reactions during the earthquake, share how the earthquake had affected their lives, and draw on Haitian history, culture, and traditions that would allow them to access sources of strength and hope for the future.

In Haiti, many people engage in song and dance, and among teenagers and children, there is a tradition of rapping, which combines music, movement, and narrative. While many activities were identified that could address the three goals, rapping was viewed as one that would actively engage children of all ages. A plan evolved to have each class divide into small groups with each group assigned to develop a rap song that addressed the three areas. The groups would then perform the songs for the class and compete to be named the best act. The winning acts would enter a schoolwide, and possibly a community-wide, performance and competition.

To prepare for this activity, teachers themselves broke into small groups and prepared rap songs, which they presented. Singing a cappella, all the teacher groups came up with rap songs that covered the three areas. Some had enactments of the earthquake that included people throwing themselves on the ground and shouting and yelling. All finished with a rousing finale about the strength of the Haitian people. Some acts were so compelling that members of other teams jumped up and joined the performers in singing their songs. Some involved "slamming," in which, on a rotating basis, individuals ad-libbed their rap, building on what previous performers had done. One act finished with a traditional Haitian folk song that had the entire group up dancing, singing, and arranging their hands in a circle of solidarity.

This illustrates how an activity group can encourage people of all ages to express their reactions to disaster collectively and explore their sources of strength, reconnecting with sustaining cultural traditions. Other types of activities are explored in upcoming sections.

GROUP SUMMARY

Four effective types of groups employed in postdisaster work are described in this chapter—psychoeducational, support, task, and activity. The typology is not rigid and there is overlap between kinds of groups. Psychoeducational groups often offer mutual support, and support groups will sometimes identify goals and tasks that are planned for outside of the group. And activities can be part of any type of group experience. It helps to have a clear idea of the central purpose of the group. All four categories of groups respond to the filaments of the Web of Psychosocial Recovery (figure 7.1). They offer a place where people can form relationships, connect, and interact. This enhances feelings of safety, reinforced by actual activities that also foster a sense of efficacy. Specific topics help with healing, such as learning ways of self-calming or recasting ways of grieving and mourning within traditional cultural parameters. All the types of groups can reconnect people with their histories and cultural sources of strength, and all the groups can foster and reconstruct a collective sense of hope.

ACTIVITIES

The vignette describing the rap competition illustrates activities using narrative, song, and movement and fostering small- and large-group interactions. There are many other activities that can be used to help people understand their reactions and map out their recoveries—arts and crafts, drama, journaling, dance, nature walks or hiking, sports, games, spiritual practices, discussions, role playing, and exercises and simulations. The list is long, and in every culture, some activities will be more salient than others. Activities do not require leaders who have master's and doctoral degrees to be effective and successful. They can also be done in many settings, indoors and outdoors, and can involve little or no equipment. Creativity makes anything possible. For example, rural areas in poor countries such as Uganda and Haiti have few balls available. Yet local people are adept at fashioning balls from masking tape wrapped around a hard object or using a hard fruit.

Activities can distract people from the heavy burden disasters pose by encouraging fun, amusement, and interactions. These are in themselves important. But activities can also be more intentional and cover much of the ground that Western-style talk-therapy modalities do. Thema Bryant-Davis's (2005) book *Thriving in the Wake of Trauma* and the Children and War Foundation's manual for helping children recover from natural disaster (Smith et al., 2002) are two resources that suggest activities with very specific therapeutic goals.

Some core clinical goals can be achieved through activities that help people (1) describe their experiences and express their reactions; (2) feel safe; (3) achieve relaxation, distraction, and a sense of calm—and even have some fun; (4) find connection to and engagement with other people; (5) feel empowered and efficacious; (6) reconstruct hope; (7) reconnect with cultural sources of strength; and (8) establish routines and create structure. Other, more clinically specific goals, such as reducing intrusive memories and arousal and helping people confront avoidance (Smith et al., 2002), require more specialized training of group leaders, although this can be done with teachers and other community volunteers. Goals, such as helping people redevelop trust, reduce shame and self-blame, mourn losses, and manage anger, can also be realized through activities (Bryant-Davis, 2005). I briefly illustrate the various activities and provide specific examples but recommend reading the previously mentioned resources for greater detail.

NARRATIVES AND EMOTIONAL EXPRESSION

All therapeutic approaches emphasize some form of expression and ventilation of powerful reactions. However, caution should be exercised. It is important not to be too direct or forceful with people experiencing severe trauma reactions. It is helpful for most people to articulate a narrative that describes their experiences and to be able to air and communicate the range of their reactions, but not if this will emotionally flood or overwhelm them.

It can be tempting to have activities that take people to a happier and more optimistic place without sufficiently going through the phase of identifying and expressing reactions to the disaster. However, the more empowering activities have greater resonance if there is some narration and emotional discharge of frightening and distressing experiences. Activities that get at this material must be voluntary and people must never be pressured to participate or disclose more than they want. Having a pass rule or opt-out clause will allow people to withdraw if they need to do this to feel safe or to protect themselves from affective flooding. It is also important an activity group not end on this note. Rather, it should close with activities that are more optimistic and empowering.

An easy activity to do with children is to have them draw what was happening when the disaster struck. They can depict earthquakes, tsunamis, terrorism, floods, chemical spills—any type of disaster. I have seen this used with children in Sri Lanka after the tsunami and in China and Haiti after the earthquakes. Children of all ages tell stories as fluently through drawings as they would with words, if not more so. It can be useful to have children explain their drawings to adults or to groups of children—to tell the stories their drawings depict. These drawings can be preceded by drawings of the children's communities before the disaster struck. They can then make drawings of their communities after the disaster, followed by drawings of something empowering—such as a place they find to be safe, beautiful, or where they would want to live.

This activity can be used with adults as well as children. I have asked adults to draw a powerful experience (Rosenfeld et al., 2005). Initially, there is often hesitation—what is powerful? Why should I draw it rather than talk about it? But I have found that drawing seems to elicit feelings or experiences that talking may not uncover. It sparks an earlier mode of expression that all adults used at some time. And the ambiguity of the word *powerful* can elicit both positive and negative associations, leading to a discussion of how both misfortune and opportunity can be attached to disaster.

SAFETY

People cannot recover from a disaster if they do not experience a minimum level of safety and security. Thus, activities that foster feelings of security are essential. Bryant-Davis (2005) describes activities involving journaling, movement, arts and crafts, music, drama, spirituality, social support, nature, and activism that all foster a sense of safety. For example, using journaling, people are asked to write a short story or poem about times when they felt safe. These are compared to current conditions that are associated with a lack of safety. Then people are asked to describe what would need to change or improve to make them feel safer. This type of activity can be done by individuals in a group, or in pairs or small groups, to increase collaboration and connectedness. Even if some of the things needed to achieve greater safety are unattainable in the present, the goals can be broken down into smaller pieces so that a process of achieving safety is initiated. Sharing the cumulative results of this exercise identifies what can be done collectively for the group (and community) to attain a position of greater security.

Bryant-Davis (2005) also uses a movement exercise to help people feel safer. People are asked to hold a position that represents feeling unsafe. Then they are asked to hold a position that demonstrates feeling safe. With both positions, she suggests breathing deeply a number of times. This exercise helps people get in touch with their physical, nonverbal ways of holding and expressing fear or security, increasing their self-awareness of what their bodies are conveying and enhancing their ability to actively adopt different physical positions, which in turn helps them feel stronger.

Another activity that helps people feel safer is borrowed from eye movement desensitization and reprocessing (EMDR) and other cognitive behavioral approaches and recommended by the Children and War Foundation (Smith et al., 2002). It involves asking people to imagine a place where they feel very safe—a safe space. This can be home, a place in nature, the beach, a space with a special person. The person is asked to imagine the details of this place—the light, sounds, ands so on. It can help to ask participants to draw their safe spaces or to describe them to others, which makes it easier for some to visualize. Then participants are encouraged to imagine their places when they are feeling frightened, insecure, or agitated. It helps to practice this in the group—having people imagine things that make them feel anxious (but not overwhelmed) and then having them move in their minds to their safe places.

RELAXATION, DISTRACTION, CALM

Helping people learn to relax, calm themselves, or simply distract themselves momentarily from their disaster reactions aids them in responding to anxiety, agitation, and hypervigilance (which is covered shortly). Also, it is reassuring when people find that they have some agency and ability to modulate their affect on their own or with the help of others. Here are some activities that can achieve these results.

Mindfulness activities, similar to the ones shared in this book, have the potential to profoundly reduce anxiety reactions. They can range from focusing on breathing and awareness of sounds to connecting with the natural environment and guided imagery. Mindfulness helps with calming but can also assist people with accepting and tolerating negative feelings and affect—they are taught to just notice them without clinging or having an aversive reaction.

Activities that create a literal rhythm also seem to help people feel calmer. This can be achieved by group activities in which one person establishes a beat and rhythm by tapping on a desk or table. The chosen rhythm then goes around a circle as each successive person tries to replicate it and then add something new. A variation is to have one individual in the group establish a rhythm and to then have the entire group play it at the same time, with participants adding their own embellishments (such as a call and response, backbeat, or echo). Another activity that works well with younger children is a variation on an EMDR technique. Children cross their arms and then tap their shoulders, alternating the action. The group leader can start with a steady rhythm that the children follow. The leader can then vary the rhythm by going fast and then slow, tapping hard then gently, and then return to the original steady rhythm. This has the added benefit of demonstrating how children have some control over their rhythms and can slow things down or speed things up. With any type of rhythmic activity, participants can also engage in larger physical action, such as body movement, dance, or hand clapping.

CONNECTION AND ENGAGEMENT WITH OTHERS

The rhythmic activities described thus far are collaborative and can be joyous so that participants have fun together and feel connected to one another. It is in the nature of group activities that people work and play together. Activities encourage partnership and emphasize how the group as a whole can achieve a desired result. This can be done through games in which each person has a piece of information or a tool that will be needed to piece together a puzzle, solve a riddle, or construct something. Singing is another activity that fosters a feeling of group engagement.

Competition also fosters group engagement by creating bonds among people who are on the same team. Sport is an obvious example of this, although it can exclude people who do not feel athletic. The rap competition is an instance in which storytelling and musical ability are helpful. When using competitive activities to engage people, it helps to do activities in different domains so that people with different abilities and talents have a chance to shine. It is also important to have rituals that bring different teams together at the end to create a sense of larger group solidarity.

Collaborative and competitive activities should be in keeping with cultural norms in a given community. All activities should draw on cultural norms and practices, reconnecting participants with important and familiar parts of their heritage. These are some of the steps people can take in returning to "normal."

EMPOWERMENT AND EFFICACY

Competency is the key theme in activities that kindle feelings of empowerment and efficacy. Activities should be varied so that all participants can find one that makes them feel comfortable and capable. Such activities remind people of times when they felt strong and capable and highlight ways they can feel competent in the moment or imagine what it will take to regain a sense of proficiency, step by step.

There are many ways to have people reflect on what they are good at and to then illustrate this within the group. Comfort levels about sharing positive attributes vary across cultures, so this should be taken into account. If participants know one another, one person can stand and other members can call out their strengths and attributes. This can be done with people standing in a circle and throwing a ball from one person to another, calling out their strengths as the ball is thrown. A more reflective method is to have people list (or draw) their strengths and assets. They can then discuss them with a partner; their partner can then introduce them to the group and vice versa. The group leader can map out the assets of group members and, at the end, illustrate how they complement one another and collectively are more comprehensive and powerful than are individual assets.

Another variation is to have people demonstrate one thing they are good at. They can be given the option to draw, sing, read a poem or story, perform, dance, play music, or juggle as a way to demonstrate this. The activity can be done individually, in pairs, or in small groups. Assigning "homework" encourages participants to engage in the activities in which they have confidence between group sessions.

RECONSTRUCTING HOPE

Bryant-Davis (2005) suggests a powerful activity for reestablishing hope after a disaster. She asks participants to imagine they are historical figures encountering the disaster and then to think about what the figures might say to others to inspire them and instill them with hope. She encourages people to think about details such as posture (How erect would the person stand?) and voice (How forcefully would they speak?).

This activity can be enacted in many ways. Individuals can think of the historical figures and then discuss their choices in pairs. Or each person can dramatize his or her character for the group. Yet another approach is to break into smaller groups and each group can do a skit involving the historical figure responding to the disaster. Another variation involves not limiting the exercise to historical figures but including sources of inspiration or living heroes—such as a parent or friend.

This type of activity reminds people of other periods when there were tragedies and challenges, and it draws on mythic figures or significant people in a person's life who provided leadership, inspiration, strength, and hope. It connects participants with their history and culture, offering a platform for facing the future.

RECONNECTING WITH CULTURAL SOURCES OF STRENGTH

The previous activity also illustrates ways of reconnecting with cultural sources of strength. All cultures have traditional forms of music, song, dance, rituals, myths, and literature. When using a training-of-trainers model with indigenous people abroad, I have noticed how enlivened, engaged, and empowered participants appear when the topic draws on traditional cultural practices or when people actually participate in singing and dancing. It fills people with pride and reminds them of familiar and nourishing stories and practices.

In chapter 5, I present the energetic reaction of Acholi participants in a training-of-trainers session. A respected priest describes the indigenous ritual of mata oput in response to murder in the community. There was consternation that the International Criminal Tribunal was planning to indict rebel leaders (who had murdered many people in the community where the training was occurring), because this involved outsiders imposing their system of retributive justice on the local community. But the discussion about mata oput gave participants a sense of self-respect and pride.

As an outside responder, the task is not so much knowing the answers as it is asking questions about cultural practices, particularly situations involving hard times or loss of life, encouraging participants to recollect and reconnect with their cultural wellsprings.

REESTABLISHING ROUTINE AND STRUCTURE

All cultures and communities have routines that offer security and a sense of structure. Children, in particular, seem to appreciate having routines, norms, and boundaries. All of these are disrupted after a disaster, particularly if schools are closed and people are relocated to IDP camps. Engaging in any of the activities described thus far can offer a sense of routine if it is structured, predictable, and practiced regularly. Activities should be structured so that they offer both consistency and variety. Consistency leads to predictability—group members expect a warm-up activity or quiet time before closing, for example—and variety maintains interest and encourages creativity. Involving group members, particularly adolescents and adults, in planning the ways that routines are structured deepens ownership and commitment.

RESPONDING TO TRAUMALIKE SYMPTOMS

Intrusion, arousal, and avoidance are three clusters of symptoms commonly found in postdisaster stress responses, such as acute stress disorder and post-traumatic stress disorder. The Children and War Foundation (CAW) (Smith et al., 2002) recommends group activities as a way to respond to these, all of which can be used by trained staff and nonclinical volunteers. However, the CAW feels strongly that facilitators should be adequately trained by clinicians who are familiar with the methods used in the manual and that evaluation is always built into any project that uses the manual's curriculum as the basis for intervention.

With intrusion, a person is besieged by memories of the disaster that can feel invasive and overwhelming. If there are activities that help the person learn strategies that give him more control over his thoughts, then invasive images are less frightening, and the affected person may feel a greater sense of agency and control. Thus, imagining the safe space described previously can give people a place to go to in their minds as a refuge from intrusive images. Once this is established, a person can "play" with intrusive images by breaking them down into smaller parts and doing so in an intentional way (Smith et al., 2002). To this end, the CAW manual recommends that children play with dimensions of the images—such as brightness, movement, focus, level of detail (and many more)—and try to modulate these dimensions and even get to the point of being able to switch them off. There are exercises—such as imagining that the images are being watched on television, placing a picture frame around them, or locking them away somewhere—that help create greater distance (and control). Positive exercises, which conjure up positive images, safe places, and helpful people, give the person alternative metaphors that can increasingly be substituted for disturbing ones. The CAW manual also has exercises for using other senses and working with dreams.

Hyperarousal is a common symptom after experiencing a major disaster. I found, when working in Haiti after the earthquake, that many people, children and adults, suffered from this if they had directly experienced the earthquake. It would be easily triggered if people were expected to enter buildings, particularly if there was not a short and easy escape route. Children were anxious about entering school buildings, as were their parents. As with intrusion, regaining a sense of control is important. A good baseline activity is one that helps people describe their reactions in detail when they are aroused in a very specific and bodily way (Smith et al., 2002). Normalizing these reactions is helpful but being able to play with them and eventually modulate them begins to give a person a sense of greater agency. Other helpful activities include muscle relaxation (Smith et al., 2002), body scans (Kabat Zinn, 1990), and mindfulness and breathing techniques. The CAW manual (Smith et al., 2002) also has guided imagery exercises and activities that encourage coping self-statements as antidotes to catastrophizing thoughts. Children as well as adults should establish bedtime rituals and routines so that they are less aroused and more likely to be able to sleep (Smith et al., 2002).

For avoidance, CBT approaches, such as gradual, segmental exposure to what a person is avoiding, can be helpful. I strongly urge practitioners to avoid flooding or deep-exposure techniques for people who have just experienced a disaster, particularly if they are in the early stages of recovery. The CAW manual (Smith et al., 2002) has a number of activities that help children use their imaginations to increase their "graded" exposure to aversive stimuli. With children, it is helpful to enlist the support of adults, both through actual relationships and activities as well as by encouraging children to imagine helpful adults. The use of coping self-statements also helps with avoidance as it does with arousal. Bryant-Davis (2005) recommends listening to soothing songs at the beginning of each day to foster coping.

REESTABLISHING TRUST

Trust is often a casualty of disaster, particularly if the disaster was caused by human error or intention. Because human connection and social support are so essential to disaster recovery, lack of trust is an impediment and it is important to use activities to help to reestablish trust. In general, activities that require group members to rely on one another help to foster trust. In developed nations, there are outdoor activities that require people to work together—ropes courses, rock climbing, camping—but these require time and equipment as well as instructors with specialized skills. Games involving teamwork to complete a task or solve a puzzle require less skill and gear.

Meditation can be helpful for people who are feeling mistrustful. Pema Chodron (2001, 2002) encourages people to use guided imagery to empathically engage with those whom they feel oppressed by or alienated from. The exercises involve owning one's fears and projections. Bryant-Davis (2005, p. 57) suggests a meditative activity that involves imagining the "strength and courage" needed to heal the wounds caused by the breach of trust. Also, she recommends creating lists of people who have been helpful in addition to lists of those who have caused harm. It can often be helpful to do these exercises *before* seeking to be empathic to those whom one feels mistrustful of.

Bryant-Davis (2005) suggests an activity that helps people express their fear and anger over lack of trust by having them write letters to government officials that promote policies that will protect them in the future. This activity helps people to "raise their voices," which is empowering, and to express their fear and anger, emotions often associated with lack of trust.

REDUCING SHAME AND SELF-BLAME

These are very common feelings after experiencing a disaster. They are even more poignant when people have lost someone close to them. In China and Haiti after the earthquakes, where there were high death tolls that included many children, these feelings were prevalent.

Activities that foster cleansing and self-love can be helpful at times such as these. Bryant-Davis (2005) suggests an activity in which a person sits by a body of water (or even by a bowl of water) and reflects on the water, thinking about how it sounds, feels, smells, and tastes. Then she suggests visualizing water as a cleansing force, having it wash over you and carry away the shame and self-blame. Another activity that she suggests is sitting in a room alone and wrapping your arms around yourself and humming or singing a song (or making up a song)—a form of self-caring. My only reservation about this activity is that it has people working on their own, which can be isolating for some. In my experience, having direct discussions in groups about blame and shame can be helpful because participants will often confront these feelings in other people in a supportive way. Also, it helps to hear that other people are feeling similarly as this normalizes the reaction. Moreover, it is easier to forgive other people and to alleviate their sense of responsibility than for people to be gentle with themselves—so a group process can be liberating for everyone. Singing comforting songs is a nice way to end such discussions.

BEREAVEMENT

Grief and mourning are universal but every culture has its own unique practices and rituals. Disaster often disrupts the ability of people to engage in these practices—bodies are not recovered, the scale of losses depletes the ranks of mourners and supporters, families suffer untimely and sometimes multiple deaths. After the Wenchuan earthquake in China, it was initially difficult for some families to engage in the customary practices that maintained their bonds with the deceased. The situation improved when they were able to reestablish traditional grieving and mourning practices (Wang Xiao Lu, personal communication, April 3, 2010).

In the section on task groups, I describe a project to facilitate grieving and mourning in Haiti after the 2010 earthquake by reconstituting traditional practices within the parameters set by the disaster. Whatever activities a group engages in, they should be grounded in the mourning traditions of the culture. Although individuals and families undergo their private experiences of grieving, the particular rituals reflect a collective consensus. Every family may creatively adapt their bereavement practices to the new realities, but given the shared nature of disaster, it is helpful to recast mourning customs through a group process of creative problem solving.

MANAGING ANGER

Anger is a common yet complicated response to disaster. Anger is uniquely human (Young-Eisendrath, 2010). As with mistrust, anger is more common with human-caused disasters as there are suitable targets for the anger. However, even with "natural" disasters, anger over losses occurs, but it can be less clear where to direct the anger, so it is often displaced, sublimated, or directed toward oneself. Another complication is that responders find it easier to comfort people who are sad or overwhelmed than those who are irate. It is important to help people manage their anger. Not only can anger be alienating and lead to destructive or self-destructive actions but it can eat away at the soul, doing harm to the person who carries it.

Writing about anger can be helpful. Bryant-Davis (2005) suggests encouraging people to write poems about their anger, describing both their intense emotions and the people who make them angry. Because many people do not write poems, she also recommends that people draw a picture that represents their anger. Whether people draw a picture or engage in movement or drama to express their anger, the key is to represent the emotion artistically; this puts it someplace, taking a raw emotion and transmuting it into something beautiful. Meditation is also helpful with managing anger. I have found loving-kindness meditations (Germer, 2009) are effective for people who are hurt, angry, or alienated. The goal is to try and direct compassion to oneself either visually or through repeating mantras, such as "May I be safe, happy, healthy, and at ease." Meditations that help a person get in touch with nature, with the bad and the beautiful, and with the tranquil and destructive place anger in a larger natural or cosmological order. Describing one's anger to other people, such as in pairs (but not to the person with whom you are angry), helps to ventilate and release some of the strong affect. Also, such discussions may generate ideas about ways to productively manage the anger.

There are positive aspects to anger. Anger sets boundaries, which can be protective and can also fuel protests and actions against injustice (Young-Eisendrath, 2010). Engaging in collective social action stemming from anger can connect people, help memorialize losses, and lead to lasting social change and improvements.

This chapter describes the use of groups and activities to help people recover from disaster. It emphasizes the power of relationships and collective activities and actions as well as the advantages of drawing on familiar cultural sources of strength and capability. The use of activities and social support is not meant to minimize the challenges posed by a disaster or the time that it takes to heal. When hundreds of thousands of people are sleeping outside in inadequate shelters in the rain, as was the case in the aftermath of the Haitian earthquake, activities may seem like minor, if not inconsequential, responses. When people have suffered terrible losses, they may withdraw and even recoil from engaging in many activities. Disaster responders engaged in psychosocial capacity building should do what is within their power to help people find adequate shelter and engage in groups and activities.

And yet even in the direst of circumstances, there is a place for groups of people working, and even playing, together. Most healing occurs in small doses through minute measures and the passage of time. Sharing with others and drawing on the collective resources found in groups can accelerate this process—or at the very least, make it more palatable. Even when the forces of oppression try to extinguish them, human connections can be found and are an essential ingredient for survival (Levi, 1961, 1988).

In their most basic formulation, activities help people recover from disasters if they (1) encourage them to process their experiences; (2) get them in touch with and allow them to express their reactions; (3) encourage them to create narratives, both verbal and nonverbal, about what happened; (4) get them to draw on cultural sources of strength and resiliency; and (5) allow them to rekindle hope for the future. Actions and activities have the potential to transform victims into survivors.

MINDFULNESS EXERCISE: MEDITATING ON JOY

This exercise is adapted from an "awakening joy" meditation by James Baraz (2010). Sit in a comfortable posture and focus on your breathing for a few minutes. Then direct your attention to the part of your body where you feel your heart. On inhalations, imagine drawing in "benevolent energy," and on exhalations, breathe out any negative feelings, such as those described in this chapter. After doing this for a while, reflect on a person who or situation that gives you a sense of gratitude. Say the phrase "I'm grateful for" or "I'm grateful to" and complete it. Notice how this sense of gratitude feels in your body. Send a thought of appreciation to this person or situation. If you would like, repeat this with other people and situations you feel gratitude toward. Complete the meditation by thinking of any commitments you would like to make to directly express the gratitude you are feeling when you are done meditating. Notice any feelings of well-being in your body as you conclude.

10

RESPONDING TO DISASTERS CAUSED BY INTERGROUP CONFLICT

In many ways, the most complex disasters to respond to are those involving intergroup conflict, which in their extreme form are manifested as armed clashes, wars, ethnic cleansing, apartheid, genocide, forced migrations, or terrorism. These terms carry embedded meanings when viewed through the prism of group positioning ("we and they," "us and them," "internal and external," "good and evil") and are always contested by conflicting groups — reflecting the dynamics of the conflict as one group seeks to legitimize acts of violence toward another. Intergroup conflict:

- Is fueled by cultural myths, stereotypes, and historical legacies
- Influences how people construct social identities for themselves and others
- Poisons intergroup relations
- Has cultural, social, economic, and political dimensions
- Affects how people think and feel — about themselves and others
- Shapes how people make sense of the world, the stories and narratives that are shared with children, what is taught in school
- Is amplified by public discourses that define what is good, real, and legitimate
- Leads to social catastrophe — endemic racism, institutional discrimination, apartheid
- Undergirds acute catastrophe — wars, forced migrations, intentional acts of violence (such as terrorism)

As we consider in previous chapters, helping individuals, families, and communities after a disaster is multifaceted and demanding, but intergroup conflict makes this task even more daunting. Many who have been taught to assist people after natural disasters have not been trained in areas such as mediation, conflict resolution, intergroup reconciliation, peace building, or restorative justice, all of which are critical for resolving intergroup conflict. However, an understanding of the dynamics of intergroup conflict is helpful for all disaster workers and volunteers, even if directly confronting the roots of the conflict are beyond the purview of those who respond.

This chapter considers what is known about the causes and dynamics of intergroup conflict on the micro, mezzo, and macro levels. This includes a brief consideration of international human rights and how intergroup conflict can lead to cultural and collective trauma. Also, the chapter explores how such conflicts affect the people who are directly caught up in them and what disaster responders can do to be helpful and avoid exacerbating the situation. Critical processes—conflict resolution, conflict transformation, peace building, and restorative justice and truth commissions—are considered. Even when disaster responders do not directly engage in these activities, their work can support such courses of action.

As this book is about responding to disasters, I focus on more acute rather than endemic or intractable intergroup conflicts, although many of the dynamics of intergroup conflict operate in both types of situations. Also, there is no clear-cut distinction between them—endemic racism or ethnocentrism is often an undercurrent in a flashpoint of armed conflict and ethnic cleansing. Thus, it is important to gain an understanding of how intergroup conflict contributes to enduring and prevalent social inequalities, and I provide this understanding in *Racism in the United States* (Miller & Garran, 2007) but do not cover the subject here. Moreover, I am guided by a postcolonial perspective (Young, 2003), which interrogates and critiques historical and contemporary power relations, emphasizing the rights of subjugated groups and people and the importance of empowering the poor, dispossessed, and disadvantaged. Without social justice, there can be no peace and reconciliation; without peace, there can be only partial psychosocial healing and recovery; and without psychosocial healing, it is difficult to achieve intergroup respect and reconciliation, which has the potential for greater social justice (Corbin & Miller, 2009; Deutsch, 2008). If progress is made toward intergroup reconciliation, then a society has the potential to respect human rights, achieve intergroup equality, expand economic prosperity, and improve social cohesion (see figure 10.1).

FIGURE 10.1 Recovering from Intergroup Conflict

HUMAN RIGHTS

Human rights (and the abrogation of those rights) are central to a consideration of intergroup conflict. Although human rights are formally enshrined in constitutions and laws, they are subject to informal and extralegal practices. Nations and societies grant such rights to individual citizens and residents and to social groups (a child's right to education, for example). And international laws and treaties grant rights to nation-states.

In 1948, in the aftermath of World War II, the United Nations passed the Universal Declaration of Human Rights, which articulated three levels (or "generations") of rights (Reichert, 2006). The first set of rights is considered to be negative—what cannot be abrogated. These include due process; freedom of speech, assembly, and religion; and freedom from slavery, subjugation, and torture. The second set of rights is considered to be positive—those that citizens are entitled to, such as access to food, shelter, an adequate standard of living, medical care, and at least primary levels of education for children. The third set of rights are those granted to the conclave of nations—for example, a social and economic world order that supports both negative and positive rights, and discourages economic and environmental practices by one state that may harm other nations.

While all countries have signed the Universal Declaration of Human Rights, it is not legally binding in any country (Reichert, 2006). Thus, it has not been enforceable and, in the years following the ratification of the declaration, there have been many violations between nations as well as by nations toward their citizens. Ethnic, racial, and religious minorities (and other groups targeted by virtue of their social identities) have been denied the same rights as majority groups (full citizenship, religious freedom) in their countries and have suffered from discrimination, persecution, violence, forced migration because of conflict, ethnic cleansing, and even genocide.

Certain social groups are particularly vulnerable to human rights transgressions that emanate from other social groups or directly from the state. Those groups at risk include women, children, the aged and disabled, and ethnic, religious, and racial minorities—the groups that are considered in chapter 6. Thus, those groups most vulnerable to a disaster's negative effects are also those groups that often suffer from human rights violations before the disaster. Other vulnerable groups include those who are economically disadvantaged as well as lesbian, gay, bisexual, transgender, and transsexual people. Therefore, group social identity often determines who faces rights violations.

One of the thorniest issues surrounding human rights is the balance between universalism and respect for local cultures. Although all countries of the world endorse the Universal Declaration of Human Rights, power imbalances and a postcolonial legacy have meant that the ideals and economic and political systems of Western nations have been viewed as more "universal" than those of non-Western states. Okin (1999) has explored the tension between the universal rights of women and the actual cultural practices in certain societies. Women are not always granted full citizenship and, in some instances, are physically and emotionally abused and mistreated. Some contributors emphasize the universal position, while others, including women in some of the countries where discriminatory practices occur, deny that they are exploited or unhappy and dispute the contention that they have little or no agency.

Reichert (2006) has suggested questions that can be asked about both positions. For universalists, she suggests interrogating colonial legacies and infrastructures, which may be embedded in theories and values about human rights. Are one group's practices being elevated over another's? For cultural relativists, she asks who defines culture, whose voices are being heard, and whose voices are silenced. She points out that culture is not static and that often cultural relativists present a frozen, traditional slice of culture as a national template. She recommends balance between the two positions.

For disaster responders, balance is also called for. As I have argued, responders must be respectful of local cultural practices and not impose outside standards of health and sickness, help seeking, emotional expression, and trajectories of normalcy in healing and recovery. When there is intergroup conflict, responders should recognize where they are positioned in the conflict and whose narratives they have access to and whose are unavailable to them. If responders find themselves in a position to mediate conflicts, it is essential that they be empathic to multiple perspectives.

However, it is also vital for responders to respect human rights and adhere to the ethical codes of the professions they represent. For example, we can never condone torture or discrimination, which has become an issue in the intergroup conflict between the United States and the group it has defined as "other"—terrorists. As mentioned previously, when Japanese American citizens were interned in the United States during World War II—a gross violation of human rights—social workers aided and abetted this process (Park, 2008). But there are gray areas where it is less clear how a professional should react. For example, responding to a disaster in a country where people are imprisoned without due process is a fuzzy area. Should a responder from a country with Western codes of ethics leave that country in protest? Most would argue no, and yet it is a slippery slope—how much should professionals compromise and when does this lead to collusion with human rights violations? There are no simple answers to these dilemmas. Struggling with them and processing them with others is part of intercultural disaster work.

THE DYNAMICS OF INTERGROUP CONFLICT

Threats to a group's identity are central to intergroup conflict (Alexander, 2004; Lederach, 1997; Maynard, 1999; Smelser, 2004). In Northern Ireland, it was whether one was Catholic or Protestant, loyal to Ireland or to the British crown. There were certainly structural and institutional issues — Catholics being shut out of jobs, law enforcement, and political and civil service positions. Viewing such conflict as a political squabble or competition for material resources captures important surface reasons for the dispute, but such a formulation ignores deep-rooted threats to a group's identity. If these are not resolved, they can emerge as sources of further friction for generations. In the same conflict, Protestant Loyalists had a complex identity, neither Irish nor English or Scottish, with the roots of that identity going back hundreds of years, when Scottish workers were brought over to work on plantations in Northern Ireland. They felt like a minority on the island of Ireland and within the United Kingdom, and yet they were the privileged and powerful group in Northern Ireland. It is, therefore, important to consider both the "realistic" material causes of intergroup conflicts while also seeking to understand the underlying concerns over threats to collective identity.

Identity is not a fixed, stable, endogenous trait; rather, it is unstable, contested, primed by context, and always adapting and evolving (Miller & Garran, 2007). Identity has both individual and social aspects, including an internal sense and a personal story. As well, it has external customs, behaviors, cultural practices, and rituals (Kwan & Sodowsky, 1997). Identity is not only self-authored but is socially constructed by others and society at large. An African American man may want to focus on his male identity but may be stopped by the police while driving through a predominantly white neighborhood because of profiling based on the social construction of his racial identity.

Thus, identity links the personal with the political (Pederson, 2002). The social/collective dimension of identity aligns individuals within certain groups, which gives meaning to who they are in relation to other people. Collective identities, and perceived threats to them, are part of colonial occupations, nationalist movements, social inequalities, and ethnic/racial/religious conflicts. Boundaries between who is in and who is out, who is good and who is bad, and who is superior and who is inferior are essential to social conflicts (Volkan, 1988) and to sustaining their durability (Miller & Garran, 2007). Severe intergroup conflict, such as war, is a fixation with group boundaries (Volkan, 1988) and collective identity.

It is always difficult to determine when a particular intergroup conflict begins because each party has its own narrative about who was the instigator and what precipitated the conflagration. Often there are perceived threats to the group's safety, viability, and stability. Deutsch (2008) has identified five factors involved in most instances of intergroup conflict. One is that communication breaks down, which refers not only to the groups' failure to communicate with one another but also to the filtering of communication through the distorted and truncated prisms of their group narratives (Bar-Tal, 2007). A second factor is that there are perceived threats: another group plans to attack, or seize water supplies, or control shipping lanes. These are often referred to as "realistic" threats—material and observable threats to a group's well-being, although even realistic threats are subject to collective interpretation. A third factor is the belief that one's group is being treated unfairly or unjustly by another group. This sense of oppression is not limited to minority groups. For example, in the United States, many white people feel resentful because they perceive that people of color have inside access to jobs and services, despite overwhelming evidence that whites enjoy privileges unavailable and denied to people of color (Miller & Garran, 2007). This relates to a fourth factor—competition between groups for limited resources, which is a competition often framed in zero-sum terms. If one group succeeds, the other group must fail. This is another aspect of "realistic" threats; but again, it is subject to the filters of collective cognitive frames and distorted group narratives. The fifth dimension identified by Deutsch is internalized stereotypes and attitudes toward the other group, which of course shape how the motivations, intentions, and behaviors of "out-group" members are perceived.

As these factors coalesce, major social consequences ensue: forced mass migrations, violent conflicts, disrupted economies, loss of agricultural and industrial production, and fractured social cohesion (Pederson, 2002). Also, external factors lead groups to feel squeezed and besieged: population growth; climate change; environmental degradation; pandemics; the international arms trade; and competition for water, land, oil, minerals, and other resources (Winter & Cava, 2006). When conflict erupts over such concerns, resources are often captured and controlled by one group, dislocating populations and further exacerbating intergroup suspicion and tensions. It becomes difficult to discern when an action is actually offensive or defensive, depending on who is defining it.

Maynard (1999) points out that because conflicts involve identity, everyone within the sphere of influence of the conflict is implicated; it is not possible to remain aloof or neutral. Families may be torn apart by identity conflicts when there is intergroup conflict, as illustrated in the example of Rwanda, which I discuss shortly. Because conflicts involve issues of identity, all social institutions in a conflict zone become caught up in the disaster; they are trusted by some yet feared and mistrusted by others. In all major disasters, social systems collapse and social networks are ruptured. With natural disasters, they are often reconstituted in informal ways as people band together to form temporary communities (Solnit, 2009). However, disasters caused by intergroup conflict pose continuous threats to safety, making it much more challenging to form stable temporary communities.

Winter and Cava (2006) argue that when people categorize themselves as members of a group, they seek to boost their self-esteem, which is manifested through in-group preferences and out-group denigration. Categorizing members of another group in negative terms often serves to bolster the positive identities of in-group members (Crocker & Luhtanen, 1990; Triandafyllidou, 1998; Volkan, 1988). It also leads to misattributing the motives of the members of the other group—such as seeing malevolent intent behind benign actions—which in turn serves to justify hostile action (Brewer, 2001). For the group to feel good about itself, it goes through a process of externalizing and projecting bad and negative qualities, behaviors, values, and motives onto those who are viewed as being part of the "outgroup," the proverbial "other" (Miller & Schamess, 2000; Volkan, 1988).

When there have been egregious human rights violations as a result of intergroup conflict, there are collective wounds that damage cultural self-esteem. Events such as genocide or ethnic cleansing leave an indelible mark on the consciousness of ethnic and cultural groups, stamping memories and causing collective psychic scars (Alexander, 2004). Tarnished group identity and the loss of a positive sense of self instills fear, insecurity, and concern about the future, particularly involving the group's ability to protect itself and thrive. This may lead to a crisis of confidence in the group's culture (Smelser, 2004), which no longer offers sufficient meaning and stability, and conversely, this cultural crisis creates a collective crisis (Alexander, 2004). Collective identity is critical to this process: culture both shapes and is shaped by the collective identity of a group. Threats to identity are threats to group integrity—whereas responding to a perceived external enemy strengthens in-group cohesion (Bar-Tal, 2007). The psychic and social scars of collective victimhood and diminished self-worth can be assuaged by the group's becoming perpetrators, contributing to an ongoing cycle of victimhood and aggression (Staub & Bar-Tal, 2003). Vengeance begets violence, which leads to more violence (Minow, 2002).

Intergroup conflict leads to material losses. In addition to the damaged self-esteem that comes with victimization on both sides, victims suffer from humiliation, and perpetrators carry feelings of guilt and fear of retribution. Many generations can carry a sense of victimhood, justifying aggressive action toward others to protect the group from further victimization, aided by the creation of a historical-cultural narrative justifying and legitimizing current and future acts of aggression (Bar-Tal, 2007). Past wounds and experienced threats and injustices become foundational to the group's collective identity (Elcheroth, 2006). Therefore, cultural and collective trauma, when unaddressed, perpetuates cycles of violence and conflict. A mutual process of dehumanizing the other ensues. Dichotomous narratives of good and bad are then used to demonize those who are "evil," justifying retaliatory violence (Volkan, 1988).

People have a need to both affiliate with and differentiate from others (Brewer, 2001). But the flattened, reductionist discourse of good versus evil results in a heightened awareness of group boundaries, highlighting the differentiation of identities between in-group and out-group members. This results in a lack of identity differentiation between in-group members (Volkan, 1988). This in-group homogeneity fosters a form of group-think in which public discourses become rigid, formulaic, and at times fanatical. Bar-Tal (2007) describes how a sociopolitical apparatus develops to support this process, demanding the loyalty and patriotism of in-group members while countering the perceived threats of an out-group. Internal debate is curtailed and dissension stifled. A consensual "ethos" develops—a worldview with shared values that becomes the prism through which group members see, hear, understand, and discuss their reality. There is a tendency toward "catastrophic thinking"—suspecting and fearing the worst from others (Elcheroth, 2006). Leaders often exploit the enabling narratives and resulting fears to obtain political advantage. The distortions of both collective memory and the social ethos legitimize the group's aggression toward another group, usually framed as a preoccupation with safety that leads to defending in-group members from external aggression. To maintain this ethos, there is a prevailing collective emotion of fear, in which survival is of the essence, and of hatred, in which demolishing one's enemy becomes a fixation. Both the sociopolitical apparatus and the enabling narrative becomes entrenched, unyielding, and impervious to interrogation and change.

Intergroup conflict hastens social change. These sudden shifts further destabilize a group's cultural connections and sense of positive group identity (Sztompka, 2004). This can lead to a shared stance of mistrust, feelings of powerlessness, and a glorification and idealization of the past. The contentious history is elevated to mythic status, which freezes culture so that it is no longer vibrant and adaptable. Pessimism about the future takes hold. All this contributes to a communal sense of victimhood, setting the stage for escalating, often violent and intractable, conflicts that portend future collective trauma.

RESOLVING INTERGROUP CONFLICT

Given the complexity of the dynamics described in the previous section and the depth of the individual and collective wounds, it is no wonder that resolving intergroup conflict is a daunting challenge. Many conflicts become unremitting, lasting for generations, and even those that appear to have been resolved can be rekindled by the spark of a misunderstanding or misapprehension of motives, leading to a renewed conflagration. This raises the question of whether clinicians, trained in disaster response, can be effective in the process of conflict reconciliation. Yet if we do not respond to the psychological and social wounds and losses that come from intergroup conflict, people lose hope, even their capacity to love, and the more likely it is that trauma will be transmitted across generations (Minow, 2002).

Helping parties in conflict to achieve transformation, or even resolution, is both a science and an art (Lederach, 2005). It involves training, knowledge, and skills but also creativity and imagination. Clinically trained workers responding to disasters will have varying degrees of skill and expertise with intergroup mediation and conflict resolution. But is helpful for all workers responding to a conflict to understand what helps and what hinders reconciliation, integrating this knowledge into an overall psychosocial capacity building approach. Either directly or indirectly, the work of trying to help people and communities to heal and recover from disaster intersects with the process of peace and reconciliation. I outline some of the ways that conflicts are resolved in this section, describe different forms of justice in the following section, and then move to a consideration of how disaster responders can contribute to this work.

This kind of work uses many different terms—conflict settlement, conflict resolution, conflict transformation, reconciliation, peace building—which should be clarified. According to Kelman (2008), conflict settlement refers to the cessation of hostilities but without resolving the deeper issues that affect relationships and identity. Conflict resolution refers to improving the relationship between the conflicted parties. On the other hand, conflict transformation means that there are shifts in interdependent group identities: the affirmation of one group's identity no longer depends on the negation of another. Although conflict transformation is the most difficult to achieve, it has the most far-reaching consequences.

So how can intergroup reconciliation be achieved? Kelman (2008) identifies five conditions. The first is that there needs to be a mutual acknowledgment of the humanity of both groups. This is difficult to achieve given the process of dehumanization that fuels intergroup conflict, but it is essential to work toward. The second condition is that there needs to be a common basis for peace, grounded in moral principles that both sides can respect. The third condition is that the history of the conflict must be confronted. Lederach (1997, p. 31) frames this as "an open expression of the painful past on the one hand, and the search for the articulation of a long-term independent future on the other hand." Part of this process involves collective bereavement over what has been lost (Maynard, 1999). This leads to the fourth condition: an acknowledgment of responsibility by the warring parties. The sense of vulnerability that comes with taking responsibility and apologizing must be met with forgiveness if there is to be intergroup reconciliation. Those who have been victimized need to feel empowered, while those who have offended require moral rehabilitation (Maynard, 1999; Nadler & Shnabel, 2008). Taking responsibility for destructive actions and offering forgiveness in response is an ideal that is important to work toward but difficult to achieve, as both sides often feel they are the victims. And in some intergroup conflicts, one side really is the victim—such as the Jewish holocaust of World War II and the earlier Armenian holocaust at the hands of Turkey. The fifth condition is to establish institutional and social scaffolding that supports an enduring peace and reconciliation between both parties (Kelman, 2008; Lederach, 1997).

Returning to the challenge of attaining the first condition—acknowledging the humanity of the other—what are strategies that help to expedite this process? For one group to dehumanize another, there need to be socially constructed categories of identity that differentiate members of one group from another. This could be the social construction of race, ethnicity, culture, religion, nationality—any socially constructed category that allows for an us-them dichotomy. With interventions that soften these distinctions, it is less easy to demonize the other. Social psychologists have developed a range of strategies to psychologically alter the social construction of group identity. One is to deconstruct the categories and then to reconstruct new categories (Miron & Branscombe, 2008). For example, if African Americans and Korean Americans are engaged in intergroup conflict in Los Angeles, the identity "people of color" can be used as a way to dissolve the categories that divide them and to reconstruct a common, superordinate category that unites them. This gives both groups a common identity, one that transcends their conflictual identities and reconfigures their relationship as being part of a meta-category, in which they are both united in their positive identification and in many of the forms of oppression they encounter. Even if the original categories are not dissolved, there are "cross-cutting," multiple identities that can be called on by encouraging the use of the new meta-category, which highlights the similar rather than dissimilar (Miron & Branscombe, 2008).

Another way to think about this is that because identity unites the personal with the political, there need to be strategies that respond to both levels (Stephan, 2008). Strategies aimed at societal attitudes and beliefs as well as those of individuals have greater synergy and force than single-level approaches, whether the goal is to reduce racist attitudes among whites in the United States or anti-Arab sentiment in Israel. Stephan describes barriers at both the individual and societal level and then offers suggestions about how to surmount them. At the individual level, there are feelings of fear, helplessness, shame, anger, and outrage over injustices, in addition to consternation over the cognitive distortions of the other, which Bar-Tal (2007) also describes. On the societal level, there are symbols, discourses, institutions, and social structures that are geared toward conflict and denigration of the other (Bar-Tal, 2007; Miller & Garran, 2007; Miller & Schamess, 2000; Stephan, 2008). It is important not to minimize these barriers; resolving entrenched intergroup conflict is time consuming and fraught with obstacles and failed initiatives. Peace building is a process, not an outcome. With many conflict situations around the world, there have been moments of success and, all too often, flashes of failure. Over time, peace building can be successful, as in Northern Ireland and South Africa. In both instances, critics will rightly note all of the unresolved issues, inequities, and potential for future conflict. But hostilities in Northern Ireland have ceased dramatically, and racial apartheid has ended in South Africa even though entrenched racial disparities persist.

A comprehensive strategy to ameliorate barriers involves change at all levels of society, which includes interventions at the community, regional, and national levels; organizational changes; the reconfiguration of cultural symbols and discourses; and activities at the intergroup level. Legal protections, reparations, and truth commissions are other examples of important societal-level activities. At the individual level, suffering needs to be alleviated, a sense of security needs to be bolstered, psychological needs have to be met, identities must be respected, stereotypes need to be reduced, acceptance of the other should be fostered, and negative emotions need to be diminished (Stephan, 2008). For people to feel safe, there need to be mechanisms that ensure mutual security (Deutsch, 2008; Maynard, 1999). Stephan breaks down the psychological processes that need to be addressed into three domains: cognitive, affective, and behavioral. Cognitive activities include taking the perspective of the other, getting more accurate information that counteracts cognitive distortions and using the strategies previously described that recategorize identity. Affective strategies focus on reducing fear and anxiety, strengthening empathy, highlighting discrepancies between stereotypes and consciously held values, and with perpetrators, helping them to experience regret, remorse, and guilt. Behavioral actions include increased opportunities for contact and fostering changes that lead to greater social equality.

Stephan (2008) suggests four kinds of programs that work to achieve intergroup reconciliation: enlightenment, contact, skills, and healing and problem solving. Enlightenment refers to exchanging information and education about the other that goes beyond the usual demonizing discourses. Understanding the origins of the conflict from multiple perspectives is an important component of enlightenment (Staub, 2008). Contact allows for greater interpersonal access between groups and more opportunities for shared work and problem solving. Regular contact also mitigates against stereotypes. Intergroup dialogue is a structured form of contact. People do not automatically have problem solving skills, particularly when it comes to negotiation, compromise, and mediation. Training that offers such skills can be helpful as there are ways of talking about issues that can either escalate tensions and mistrust or lower the emotional temperature. For instance, language is important. If one side refers to the other as devils or heathens, this does not promote trust, while talking about "the other side" or even referring to people as adversaries is less toxic. Effective problem solving is more likely to occur when participants have the skills to productively engage in this process, provided there has been sufficient contact and education to lower mistrust and cognitive distortions. For lasting reconciliation to occur, there needs to be not only a cessation of hostilities but the experiencing of healing and a sense of justice, taking of responsibility, and showing of forgiveness (Lederach, 1997; Staub, 2008).

All in all, these processes are geared toward humanizing the other (Deutsch, 2008), which, in a sense, is a reverse of the process of dehumanization already described. Humanizing comes from contact and from developing understanding and empathy. It also involves putting into place social and political structures that foster trust and security. Leaders have an important role in this process but so do midlevel managers and informal leaders, who are often those who have excellent connections and local influence (Lederach, 1997). Outsiders can help broker the conditions that create greater security. Mutually agreed upon rules and procedures institutionalize the process of mutual dependence and trust (Deutsch, 2008), which also leads to greater interdependence. Changes in what is taught in schools, the content and form of media discourses, and other public texts and symbols are also important interventions (Deutsch, 2008; Stephan, 2008). Staub (2008) and his colleagues have used radio public service vignettes to do this kind of work in Rwanda following genocidal conflict.

Many of the ideas in this section focus on what activities should occur to resolve conflict. However, in nearly all situations in which they are applied, they fall short of achieving the ideal of peace and reconciliation. They are nonetheless worth attempting, and as imperfect as peace building is, there are usually benefits from the process. Taken in their entirety, all the mechanisms described in this section contribute to healing—on the individual, group, and societal levels—which is why there is such a close relationship between psychosocial capacity building and intergroup reconciliation. As we have seen, trauma occurs on individual and collective levels and is often intergenerational (Yoder, 2005). Olga Botcharova has conceived of a model called "From Aggression to Reconciliation" that illustrates how intergroup reconciliation and psychosocial healing can lead groups out of an unending victim-perpetrator cycle (see figure 10.2). Yoder (2005) has developed a Star Model of a healthy society that involves five interacting points: trauma

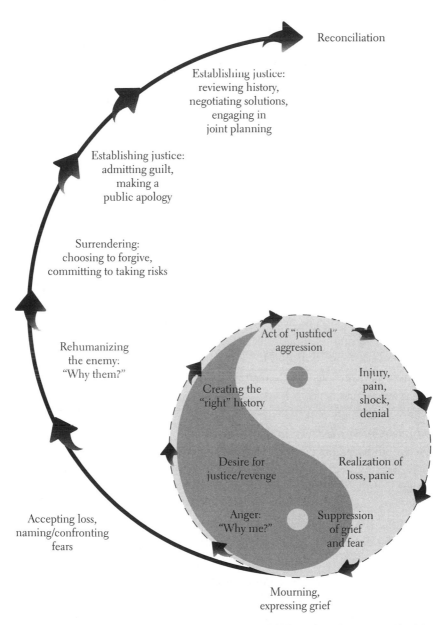

FIGURE 10.2 From Aggression to Reconciliation. © 1998 by Olga Botcharova. Used by permission.

healing, peace building, human security, justice, and spirituality—all of which have been considered in this chapter and elsewhere in this book. Before considering how disaster responders can directly engage in this process, I briefly consider the processes of restorative justice and truth and reconciliation commissions and their impact on conflict resolution and intergroup reconciliation.

RESTORATIVE JUSTICE AND TRUTH AND RECONCILIATION COMMISSIONS

There are many levels and degrees of intergroup conflict. When it reaches the level of genocide, apartheid, and ethnic cleansing, competing concerns arise that ensure international standards of justice are upheld while also fostering intergroup reconciliation—which one-sided trials can upend. Goldstein-Bolocan (2004) describes retributive justice as looking backward—holding people accountable—and restorative justice as looking forward, fostering rehumanization, social reintegration, and reconciliation. There needs to be a truthful and comprehensive ventilation of massive human rights abuses and crimes, while pursuing peace and the repair of intergroup relationships. In the process, standards of law must be upheld while civil society and the rights of citizens are strengthened. This section considers how restorative justice and truth commissions can work to bridge these competing priorities and examines in more detail the Gacaca process in response to genocide in Rwanda, which combines elements of retributive and restorative justice.

RESTORATIVE JUSTICE

Despite the Universal Declaration of Human Rights and global justice entities such as the International Criminal Court, many people at the local level of a conflict, including those who have been victimized, are wary of international tribunals. In my experience working in northern Uganda with Acholi in response to the armed conflict involving the Lord's Resistance Army (LRA), I encountered many people who were against the involvement of international commissions or courts to punish the leaders and key instigators of the LRA. They preferred that local Acholi rituals be used to achieve justice, restoration, reparations, and collective healing. They believed that a retributive model of justice, imposed by outsiders, would only contribute to an enduring cycle of violence and conflict. They also sought to have agency in their process of justice and healing and were wary of proceedings imposed by people not native to the area.

Criminal justice practices in Western nations are predominantly retributive and punitive. The state steps in when there has been a crime, levels charges, and adjudicates penalties for offenders. Convicted offenders are fined or imprisoned—they are, in essence, punished for their crimes. This usually involves a trial or a court-brokered settlement, which is adversarial in nature. Adversarial processes involve winners and losers, and their discourses are not geared toward empathy and understanding but rather toward assigning blame and meting out punishment. Openness and disclosure are discouraged. Western criminal practices condone secrecy, dissembling, blame, and even demonization and dehumanization. Convicted criminals are viewed as deviant and are socially shamed and spurned. Responsibility is unidirectional and consideration of social and historical influences is discouraged, often viewed as being irrelevant or self-serving.

Such a model has its strengths—for example, it validates the human rights of victims (Zehr, 2002) and is geared toward discouraging antisocial and violent behavior. On the international level, this style of justice punishes war criminals where there are clear examples of major human rights abuses. Perhaps the most visible example of this is the Nuremberg trials, which punished Nazi war criminals for their role in fomenting genocide and disregarding international human rights agreements, such as the Geneva conventions. But overall, retributive justice, while punishing egregious offenders, is not the best forum for resolving most intergroup conflicts. Emphasizing punishment and blame means less space for mutual recognition and responsibility taking. The existence of asymmetrical power relations between conflicting parties means that punishment of the powerful is less likely to occur. Rehabilitation is diminished in favor of retribution. Responsibility for the process rests with higher authorities and is not grounded in the community. Those held accountable often find the process unfair, particularly when there are intractable conflicts that have deep historical roots and when there are dueling narratives of victimhood and differing interpretations of whether actions are aggressive or defensive in nature. It is not that the Western tradition of retributive justice is wrong or ineffectual;

the emphasis on impartiality and the rights of victims has been an important bulwark in the evolution of liberal democracies. But this form of justice does not actively engage a range of stakeholders nor does it foster healing and the social rehabilitation of offenders, all of which are crucial to the resolution of intergroup conflict.

While retributive justice focuses on crimes committed against the state, restorative justice focuses on conflicts between individuals and the harm done to a community (Goldstein-Bolocan, 2004). Zehr (2002, p. 37) defines restorative justice as "a process to involve, to the extent possible, those who have a stake in a specific offense and to collectively identify and address harms, needs, and obligations, in order to heal and put things as right as possible." The "three pillars" of this approach are a focus on undoing harm, committing to obligations, and promoting engagement and participation (Zehr, 2002, pp. 22–24). Roche (2006, p. 218) describes the "golden threads" of restorative justice as an inclusive and informal deliberative process rather than a formal judicial one, in which an attempt is made to achieve outcomes that not only minimize harm but also strengthen relationships. An emphasis on punishment and retribution is replaced with "the healing of breaches, the redressing of imbalances, the restoration of broken relationships" (Roche, 2006, p. 229). People need to be reassured about the trustworthiness of the process (Goldstein-Bolocan, 2004). Thus, the focus is not only on who has been hurt and who has offended but on how justice can be served in such a way that healing occurs. To achieve healing, the needs of victims, offenders, and other affected people are taken into account. The notion of "stakeholders" broadens the umbrella of participants in the process and can include family members of both victims and offenders as well as other community members who have a investment in the outcome. Goals of restorative justice include restitution to victims and the obligations of wrongdoers but also the rehabilitation and social integration of offenders. Such a model envisions justice as a participatory process, grounded in the community where the offenses occurred. This has the potential to empower the local community (Goldstein-Bolocan, 2004). This contrasts with more formal models of justice, in which trained lawyers or barristers argue cases in front of a judge who is often not from the local community—and where objective distance and dispassion is a virtue.

Restorative justice has been practiced in Western and non-Western countries at the local level and at the level of the nation as well as between states in conflict (Roche, 2006). It is better conceptualized as a circle with

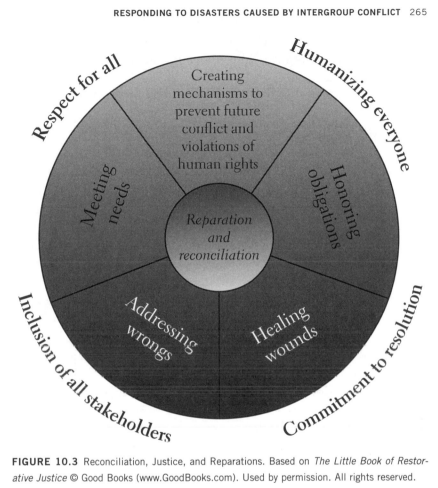

FIGURE 10.3 Reconciliation, Justice, and Reparations. Based on *The Little Book of Restorative Justice* © Good Books (www.GoodBooks.com). Used by permission. All rights reserved.

relationships than as a linear process of right and wrong. Building on Zehr (2002, p. 33), I have diagrammed this circle with four preconditions for success—respect for all, humanizing everyone, inclusion of all stakeholders, and a commitment to resolution—as the outer layer. The core of the circle is what is being sought—reparation and reconciliation. Sandwiched between the goals and the preconditions are the five activities that lead to reparation and reconciliation—meeting needs, addressing wrongs, healing wounds, honoring obligations, and establishing mechanisms to prevent future conflicts. (See figure 10.3.) Zehr (2002, p. 38) asks questions such as: Who has been hurt? What are their needs? Whose obligation are these needs? Who has a stake in the process? What process will engage stakeholders and "put things right"? Putting things right is a goal of restorative justice, which includes intergroup reconciliation rather than merely the punishment of the offenders.

TRUTH AND RECONCILIATION COMMISSIONS

Truth commissions (TCs) were first used in Latin America in the 1970s in response to the systemic and massive human rights abuses perpetrated by states (Argentina, Chile, Guatemala) against their citizens (Roche, 2006). Governments killed, abducted, tortured, and incarcerated people without due process in the name of fighting communism or defending capitalism. The TCs were usually established years after the atrocities and often granted at least partial immunity to perpetrators. Truth commissions have gained greater world recognition as they have been used in other parts of the world (particularly in Africa), including South Africa after the ending of apartheid, Rwanda following the genocide of the Tutsi by the Hutu, and Sierra Leone after a murderous civil war, as well as East Timor, where genocide was perpetrated by Indonesia (Roche, 2006).

Truth commissions emphasize the participation of victims and perpetrators in public hearings in order to acknowledge what happened in the past, particularly the pain caused to victims and (usually, although not in all instances) acknowledgment of responsibility by perpetrators, but without leading to formal prosecutions (Roche, 2006). They present "an appealing middle ground between retribution and amnesia," as they investigate human rights abuses and allow an accounting of past misdeeds while also providing a platform for victims to tell their stories, which offers some sense of conclusion (Goldstein-Bolocan, 2004, p. 6).

The Truth and Reconciliation Commission (TRC) of post-apartheid South Africa had three goals: (1) to offer a complete picture of what had occurred during apartheid, (2) to provide a platform for victims to describe their suffering, and (3) to give perpetrators an opportunity to disclose what they did (Gobodo-Madikizela, 2008). All in all, 24,000 victims offered their testimony, which was not only cathartic for them but contributed to a "social truth" that would stand the test of time (Goldstein-Bolocan, 2004, p. 7). Unfortunately for many victims (and perpetrators), perpetrators did not have to formally apologize for what they had done, and there was no process for mediation or reparations (Roche, 2006). In a political compromise (made between the African National Congress and the apartheid regime), the TRC attempted to document human rights abuses, establish a process of amnesty for those perpetrators who testified, and offer recommendations to the government about reparations and rehabilitation. The TRC did not address the economic and social disparities in South Africa based on race, which are a profound legacy of the apartheid years. As one colleague put it to me, "With the TRC, black Africans got the crown while white Africans kept the jewels" (N. Walaza, personal communication, August 2004).

Another significant African experience with truth and reconciliation was the Rwandan Gacaca process, which also had elements of restorative and retributive justice. The complexity of this situation warrants further analysis.

GACACA

In 1994, Rwanda experienced catastrophic intergroup conflict that resulted in genocide. More than eight hundred thousand Tutsi and sympathetic Hutu were slaughtered by rampaging Hutu during a three-month period (Borland, 2003; Broneus, 2008; Goldstein-Bolocan, 2004; Schabas, 2005; Uvin & Mironka, 2003; Wierzynska, 2004; Zorbus, 2004). Eleven percent of the population was killed in less than one hundred days (Wierzynska, 2004). Seven million out of a population of ten million were either killed, fled the country, or displaced (Goldstein-Bolocan, 2004). "Neighbors murdered neighbors, family members murdered family members," and "sexual violence was systematically used" (Broneus, 2008, p. 55). "Killings came to be referred to as umaganda (communal work), chopping up men as 'bush clearing,' and slaughtering women and children as 'pulling out the roots of the bad weeds'" (Mandami, as quoted by Broneus, 2008, p. 56). Extremist Hutu murdered moderate Hutu along with the targeted Tutsi, and radio broadcasts exhorted everyone to participate in the killing. There were perhaps one million perpetrators (Schabas, 2005).

Like all disasters, there was a social ecology for this genocide, which is too complex to adequately cover in this brief summary, although certain factors relevant to the discussion are highlighted. As with most instances of intergroup conflict, there are competing narratives that attempt to explain and justify why certain events happened. Rwanda had a colonial history with Germany and Belgium and with the typical ethnic division of groups by the colonizers—a characteristic of European colonial rule in Africa and other parts of the world, privileging one group over others. Rwanda is also a poor country. While the precipitating spark for this tragedy was the death of Rwanda's Hutu ruler in an airplane crash, there was already the tinder of intractable, long-term intergroup suspicion and mistrust. However, it is also important to note that many Tutsi and Hutu had intermarried, creating families with mixed ethnic identities. And although it is generally agreed that extremist Hutu committed genocide against Tutsi and moderate Hutu, many believe that the Tutsi-dominated Rwandan Patriotic Army (RPA), which put an end to the genocide when it took control of the country, committed war crimes before, during, and after the genocide (Corey & Joireman, 2004; Zorbus, 2004).

There were three different legal responses to the genocide. The first, called the International Criminal Tribunal for Rwanda (ITCR), was convened by the United Nations and held in a nearby African country (Borland, 2003; Uvin & Mironka, 2003; Zorbus, 2004). This employed a retributive justice model, somewhat like the Nuremberg trials, and was viewed by Rwandans as a system of justice imposed from the outside. It was even viewed by some as a symbolic response by European nations to assuage their guilt over their terrible inaction during the genocide (Uvin & Mironka, 2003). It took control away from Rwandans and was disempowering; over a ten-year period, it resulted in only ten convictions (Zorbus, 2004). Therefore, this response was inadequate and, even if well intentioned, mistrusted by many Rwandans.

A second response was to use the Rwandan criminal justice system. But this was problematic as well. The genocide had resulted in the loss of 80 percent of the personnel (judges, lawyers) of the criminal justice system (Goldstein-Bolocan, 2004). The criminal justice system was viewed as being entirely in the hands of the victorious RPA and thus biased against the Hutu. There were only one thousand verdicts a year and, given the number of possible perpetrators and the paucity of criminal justice resources, it might have taken a century to clear the backlog (Uvin & Mironka, 2003).

In response to the inadequacies of the ITCR and the local criminal justice system, the Rwandan government drew on a traditional, locally based restorative justice program known as Gacaca. The origins of Gacaca date back to precolonial times and have continued to the present in local communities (Goldstein-Bolocan, 2004). It is a process used to resolve local disputes, such as land use, cattle rights, inheritances, property disputes, marital issues, and minor physical altercations. Local mediators seek to engage all parties involved in the conflict as well as other interested parties in order to craft a mutually agreed upon resolution that will restore social cohesion and reintegrate offenders into the fabric of community life. As Goldstein-Bolocan points out, the process, which engages so many stakeholders, is as important as the outcome. It depends on the cooperation of all parties. Everyone must engage in the process of public shaming, apology and recognition of the harm done by offenders, and restitution and reintegration into the community.

The version of Gacaca instituted by the Rwandan government in response to the genocide builds on this tradition but also incorporates elements of restorative justice, retributive justice, and truth and reconciliation commissions. Gacaca tribunals involve local people specially trained in this process as judges, known as *inyangamugayo*, which translates as people with integrity who do not blame (Uvin & Mironka, 2003). They are empowered to try all cases involving genocide perpetrators that do not carry the death penalty. The restorative justice aspect of the tribunals involves reliance on voluntary participation, involving the presence of stakeholders, confessions, taking responsibility, and asking for forgiveness. The fact that the *inynagamugayo* can impose sentences adds a retributive justice component to the process (Wierzynska, 2004). However, sentences are usually reduced if the accused perpetrator cooperates, confesses, and names others who were implicated in the targeted crimes (Schabas, 2005; Zorbus, 2004). Many accused perpetrators have agreed to participate in the process because of the expedited hearings and reduced sentences. The truth and reconciliation aspect of Gacaca is that they are public hearings that document the extent and details of the genocide, which will forever be part of the public record.

Gacaca has its supporters, who stress how it is empowering, is locally based, builds on a traditional Rwandan practice of restorative justice, and is speedy and simple procedurally (Goldstein-Bolocan, 2004). It was developed by Rwandans and not the international community, which makes it responsive to the concerns of the local community (Wierzynska, 2004). Wierzynska argues that although Gacaca was established by the government, in operation it fosters local civic participation which encourages people to openly voice concerns and dilutes absolute government hegemony in the post-genocide justice process. If this can contribute to a culture of civic engagement, then it may prevent future intergroup violence.

But there are also many criticisms of Gacaca. First and foremost is that it focuses only on genocide and not war crimes, which include those of the RPA. This makes it appear to be one-sided and validating of the victimhood of one group but not the other (Borland, 2003; Corey & Joireman, 2004; Wierzynska, 2004; Zorbus, 2004). A related criticism targets Gacaca's individually oriented approach, in which the hearings focus on individual misdeeds and do not get at the roots or dynamics of the severe, long-standing intergroup conflict (Goldstein-Bolocan, 2004). Moreover, there has been concern about the poor training of the judges and lack of separation in their roles as prosecutors, as well as the absence of due process—for example, the accused have no right to lawyers and sentences have been inconsistent. This has opened the process to charges of corruption and bowing to social pressure (Uvin & Mironka, 2003). There have been fears of retaliation expressed by victims and perpetrators alike (Borland, 2003), and women in particular have described being threatened as well as feeling traumatized by reliving their experiences through having to testify (Broneus, 2008). Safety is a prerequisite for healing in communities where there has been intergroup conflict (Maynard, 1999). When people do not feel safe, it is difficult to participate in a process that depends on trust and the willingness to accuse, confess, and reconcile. This could be the reason so many people, perhaps half of the population, do not trust the Gacaca process (Goldstein-Bolocan, 2004).

Kanyangara, Rimé, Philippot, and Yzerbyt (2007) surveyed fifty survivors and fifty prisoners accused of participating in the genocide who took part in the Gacaca process. The surveying was conducted forty-five days before and after their involvement with the Gacaca courts. Initially, Kanyangara and colleagues found there was an increase in negative emotions for both victim and perpetrator, contributing to an overall negative climate. But they also suggest that, in Rwanda, emotional expression is "traditionally intolerable," so having a contained process within a traditional social ritual may have helped people to process their emotions in a constructive fashion (p. 401). As evidence of this, the researchers point to reductions of negative stereotypes held by members of one group toward members of the other group and less of a tendency to see the other as one homogenous mass.

Journalist Philip Gourevitch (2009), who wrote about the genocide at the time, returned to Rwanda in 2009 to interview survivors and perpetrators about Gacaca. He described ambivalent responses to the process, particularly among Tutsi survivors. They articulated how difficult it was to forget atrocities, even when someone confesses their wrongdoing and asks for forgiveness. And in their view, many perpetrators were not being truthful about the extent of their role in the massacres. One woman, who lost many family members, stated, "Every time I come to Gacaca with an open mind, I just get more upset" (Gourevitch, 2009, p. 42). But she and other survivors concluded that they could not think of a better solution—even if true reconciliation did not occur, the Tutsi and Hutu needed to coexist and Gacaca probably made that more possible.

Goldstein-Bolocan (2004) suggests that the Gacaca process should be augmented by a truth commission. This would be a body, independent of the government, made up of members of both ethnic groups. Such a commission would allow for a wider range of perspectives and more likely result in greater fairness. Its mandate would extend beyond the genocide and include war crimes, which, over time, could allow for a broader sense of responsibility and improve the prospects for intergroup reconciliation. Goldstein-Bolocan also recommends that the local Gacaca leaders be given greater flexibility in how they implement the process and over what sentences they impose, with more of an emphasis on the restorative rather than retributive aspects of the process.

These critiques point out the dilemmas in trying to respond to the most egregious forms of intergroup conflict. How will justice be served without inflicting further collective wounds and inflaming future conflict? How can justice look backward and hold people accountable while also looking forward and bringing groups together (Goldstein-Bolocan, 2004)? How can individuals be brought to justice when crimes against humanity were committed at the group level? What is the role of the international community in ensuring adherence to universal rights and standards of fairness when there are trials? What about the fact that the international community contributed to the structural conditions that fueled the conflict and is culpable for not having made a sufficient effort to prevent or end the ensuing slaughter? How can these standards of justice be balanced with the need for local direction, local traditions and customs, and local concerns? How can local parties come together when the state apparatus is controlled by only one faction of the aggrieved parties? These are but a few of the many questions raised by Gacaca and other efforts to respond to heinous crimes and severe and excessive intergroup conflict. And it is in a context of such complexity and ambiguity that disaster responders find themselves when reacting to situations involving intergroup conflict. The next section considers how to work effectively in such circumstances despite the swirling mélange of needs, narratives, and priorities.

PSYCHOSOCIAL CAPACITY BUILDING AND INTERGROUP CONFLICT

Intergroup conflict challenges even the most skilled and seasoned of professionals, requiring a multiplicity of skills in group intercession, including negotiation, mediation, brokering, and peace building. Responders to "natural" disasters in places where intergroup conflict is ongoing may or may not directly engage in intergroup conflict resolution. However, it is important for disaster responders to at least understand the context of intergroup conflict as it affects their work. The intercession of a "natural" disaster can have a positive or negative effect on intergroup conflict—it at least temporarily interrupted active armed conflict in both Banda Aceh, Indonesia, and Sri Lanka, while exacerbating the dynamics of racism in New Orleans. As I have argued, psychosocial healing is essential to intergroup reconciliation, and intergroup reconciliation furthers psychosocial healing. This section explores what responders can do to contribute to this cyclical process, even while not directly addressing the sources of the armed conflict. These are careful positioning, contributing to an overarching framework for reconciliation, creating opportunities for people to interact and form relationships, fostering positive social roles and social reintegration, offering opportunities for healing for all affected people, engaging in collective grieving and mourning, and fostering leadership committed to reconciliation.

POSITIONING

Whether or not one becomes directly involved in intergroup reconciliation, it is important to understand the social ecology of the conflict as a context for disaster-related work and to open as much relational space as possible to work with a wide range of people. Of particular relevance are the contested historical narratives that give meaning to the conflict and the identities of participants. Thus, disaster responders should not work under the illusion that there is a master narrative that explains everything; there are usually a number of competing narratives, each with its own passionate adherents. Recognizing this helps when trying to maintain a stance of neutrality so as to be available to help anyone, whatever their social positioning in relation to the conflict. This is very difficult to achieve and many political and structural factors work against it. Helping one group may lead to alienation of another. One of my former students was working with Somali refugees in a predominantly white state in the United States. She did not understand the clan structure that Somali families adhere to and the dynamics of conflict between clans that were transplanted to the United States. She found herself on one side of an interclan dispute and was unable to regain a neutral position, eventually losing her job.

Therefore, it is helpful to be able to map out the dynamics of a conflict, including who affiliates with whom, the core issues of social identity and culture that influence how people see the world, and the metaphors people use (or that will trigger them) to communicate and make meaning. Part of this mapping process involves understanding the social identities of the people being worked with (Miller & Garran, 2007). It also entails knowing what parts of their social identities (race, ethnicity, religion, gender) are most salient for them and under what circumstances they are activated. Understanding this helps to decipher the parameters and constraints of people's cognitions and behaviors. Throughout the book, I have been stressing the importance of understanding cultural values and idioms, but this goes beyond that; it involves comprehending how people construct meaning and their sense of self in relation to other people with whom they are in conflict. For example, if I am working in Sri Lanka with Tamils and my collaborator is Sinhalese, I must consider how this will influence issues of trust and what people will and will not share.

When responding to a disaster, each of us is affiliated with an organization or government agency that legitimates our work and provides access to clients, offers resources, and frames (and constrains) what we are trying to do. We have to be cognizant of how our social and structural positioning via our organizational affiliations situates us in relation to different sectors of society or townships. Realistically, this means that we have access and credibility with some groups more than others. Some responders are able to work with one side of a conflict and other responders will be better positioned to work with the other. An awareness of this helps us to have realistic expectations about who we can help and how we can best help them.

One of the thorniest issues is the tension between neutral positioning and advocacy. In intergroup conflict between two opposing sides of more or less equal strength, advocating for one will disqualify a responder from helping the other. This should be avoided unless one is only intending to operate within a discrete sphere of influence and with only one group. For example, it may not be possible to offer services to both Pakistanis and Indians when there has been an acute outbreak of hostility in Kashmir. But when there are asymmetries in power, advocating for those who are marginalized, oppressed, subjugated, targeted, and discriminated against may be the most effective way of trying to obtain rights and resources for that group. However, when a responder engages in ways that alienate those in the more powerful group, this in the long run jeopardizes the responder's ability to help anyone at all.

In each situation, disaster responders should evaluate the unique dynamics of the conflict, including the trigger issues for each group, and as carefully and intentionally as possible position themselves to help the most people in the most effective and sustaining way possible.

A FRAMEWORK OF OVERARCHING GOALS

One of the reasons the Asian tsunami led to at least a temporary cessation of hostilities in areas of armed conflict is that in the immediate aftermath, everyone in the area was experiencing the same threats, struggling with the same issues, and sharing the same needs. Some of this was because of the sudden, catastrophic stripping away of the social and political edifice and artifice, leaving what was most basic and essential, which of course was not planned or foreshadowed. But it offered an opportunity that guided the provision of aid and services at a time when needs were at their greatest. In eastern Sri Lanka after the tsunami, many countries and aid organizations offering services insisted on a policy of nondiscrimination and equal access to all communities in need in the affected areas. For a significant period—more than six months—the Sri Lankan government was willing to suspend its formal policy of Tamil harassment and informal policy of Tamil isolation and neglect. Even the hard-line Tamil Tigers did not initially target aid workers who were helping Tamil, Sinhalese, and Muslim communities. Sadly, this did not last and eventually many aid workers and responders had to withdraw because of threats from both sides of the conflict.

Relief organizations can attempt to establish a framework of neutrality through the articulation of shared and overlapping goals between the conflicted parties, advocating for at least a temporary cessation of hostilities. The fact that the relief organizations are focused on something other than the dynamics of the conflict can actually help to create an overarching framework—responding to a natural disaster—with buy-in from a range of stakeholders. At the ground level, practitioners should both understand the dynamics of the conflict and direct their work toward goals that transcend the details of the conflict.

When the disaster unveils and exacerbates long-standing intergroup conflict and social injustice, as it did with Hurricane Katrina, advocating for the human rights of all affected people is important, as is encouraging relief organizations to consider unique needs and cultural patterns for oppressed, targeted, and minority groups.

OPPORTUNITIES FOR INTERACTING AND FORMING RELATIONSHIPS

Intergroup conflict often leads to isolation between groups and limited opportunities for meaningful interaction. Disasters can force people out of their usual routines and into reconfigured social interactions that cut through accepted group boundaries and distinctions (Solnit, 2009). As I describe in the previous chapter, the use of groups is ideal for helping people recover and reconstitute their relationships with others after a disaster and engage in meaningful work together. When possible, the groups should include members of both parties in a conflict and have overarching tasks and goals that members work on together. In such situations, groups should also be structured by facilitators who are viewed by different stakeholders as being unaligned with either side or who represent both factions and can model working together. If one group is a minority in relation to the other group, it is important that its members be granted some measure of equitable standing (such as equal numbers of participants) or else the dynamics of majority-minority status are likely to be enacted in the group (Miller & Garran, 2007). When groups consist of members of blocs that have been in conflict, then it helps to create space for each group to share its narrative of the struggle and to have ground rules and mechanisms that foster listening, such as structured questions and responses. Otherwise, these conflicting narratives are likely to emerge in the form of mistrust, alienation, or even open conflict. Often, members of different factions have never been exposed to alternative narratives that give meaning to the other group's actions and behaviors and that present them in a human, rather than demonic, light. This is a form of what Stephan (2008) terms "enlightenment." Such groups can focus on tasks and activities or directly on interpersonal relationships among group members. Tasks and activities help people work together, which can enhance trust and reduce suspicion. Focusing directly on the interpersonal relationships of group members can lead to increased understanding and empathy.

Focusing on both the symbolic and realistic impediments to intergroup reconciliation is important (Kelman, 2001). Symbols—both historical and contemporary—contain powerful meanings for constitutive group narratives (Miller & Garran, 2007). These symbols, such as the parade of Protestant Orangemen through predominantly Catholic neighborhoods in Belfast, bolster some while humiliating or excluding others. It helps to consider alternative symbols and rituals. These can be constructed to express in-group pride without fostering out-group shame and denigration. Social divisions, such as racism or ethnic exclusion from jobs, property ownership, or government positions, also form realistic impediments to intergroup reconciliation. As long as these remain, they are sources for intergroup mistrust and social divisions. Those most affected by these social obstructions may feel that it is a waste of time to be in groups that talk about issues without taking action to ameliorate these conditions (Miller & Donner, 2000). Disaster responders may have little direct ability to influence these conditions, but at the same time, they cannot be ignored. Economic assistance is often more valuable than therapy when helping people to recover from armed conflict (Wessels & Monteiro, 2006). Responders can at least help people creatively think of strategies for responding to these conditions in ways that are empowering but do not foment further violence or do harm to others.

It is also important to note that bringing together people who have been in conflict and harbor mistrust involves some risk; intractable arguments can be rekindled and alienation can worsen, particularly if participants regress into rigid social scripts or are provocative to other participants. Thus, responders should not attempt to bring opposing sides together without adequate preparation, support, and structure. If the potential for exacerbating tensions outweighs the potential for thoughtful listening, then it is better to err on the side of caution and to work with people in homogenous groups.

POSITIVE SOCIAL ROLES AND SOCIAL INTEGRATION

Wessells and Monteiro (2006), in their consideration of working with youth involved in a civil war in Angola, stress the importance of social integration and of having positive social roles. Wars create social *dis*integration, fracturing families, splitting communities, and alienating neighbors from one another. Social integration means reconstructing the bonds and networks that bind people. Helping communities form neighborhood associations, task groups, mutual-aid and support groups, and other mechanisms that foster social integration, works toward this goal. Responders can also work with families and clans to reintegrate those who have been separated, alienated, or have caused harm to their own families.

Participants in social conflicts have often lost their positive social roles and have become victims, perpetrators, or bystanders (Staub, 2001). Conflicts cut down on social space and there are fewer choices; roles are more rigidly circumscribed and social positioning less complex and nuanced. Either-or thinking ensues—one is either for or against, good or bad, patriotic or unpatriotic. Ambivalence over such dichotomies usually leads to sitting on the sidelines, while those challenging orthodox discourses are marginalized, targeted, and scapegoated. When hostilities cease or reconciliation is being pursued, it is important to help people regain a positive social role in their families and communities and move beyond rigid social roles that were defined by the conflict. This involves a redefining of one's sense of self in relation to others, but as Wessells and Monteiro (2006, p. 127) point out, there also need to be "positive life options"—social opportunities—to achieve social roles that are affirming and socially constructive.

CREATING OPPORTUNITIES FOR EVERYONE TO HEAL

There is no process that offers absolute healing from and resolution to intergroup conflict. Many wounds and sorrows are deep and can never be completely repaired. What can at least be attempted are opportunities for people to tell their stories, listen to the stories of others, validate the suffering of others, and take responsibility for actions that have been harmful to people. Restorative justice and truth and reconciliation processes attempt to encompass these activities. But disaster responders can create space for these processes independently of more formal procedures. This can be done through individual conversations, family meetings, small-group ses-sions, and in larger, more public venues, such as open community meet-ings. While it is ideal to have members of opposing sides involved in these activities, healing can at least partially occur in more homogenous groups where these discussions can still occur. In fact, sometimes it is more fruitful to talk about these subjects in homogenous groups before bringing people in conflict directly together; they can process strong feelings and reactions and think about how to share these with the other group in a way that they are likely to be heard.

There is no one way that all people will respond to interventions de-signed to foster healing and recovery—although many interventions are on the group and collective levels, this is a very individual process. Therefore, disaster responders need to open up different spaces and create different mechanisms for the range of ways people respond to conflict and loss. Ask-ing those being assisted to articulate what will help *them* to recover is a good starting point, and then programs and interventions can be designed accordingly. The advantage of collective endeavors is that social cohesion is enhanced by public events and activities that encourage social sharing (Paez, Basabe, Ubillos, & Gonzalez-Castro, 2007), but there is also a need for individual tailoring within these group processes.

Eventually, it is important, if possible, to engage in a process in which individuals and groups take responsibility for actions that have harmed others. This includes recognizing the humanity of the other group, taking responsibility for one's part in past wrongs, reconstructing fractured rela-tionships, and working toward healing and making reparations (Yamamoto, 1999). These are complex and often long-term projects in which disaster responders will have limited ability (and availability) to engage. However, it is helpful to imagine the trajectory of a process of healing in which every responder can play a small role or make a slight contribution. Even small interventions that help people feel more secure in themselves and outward-ly empathic can "prime" them to be more receptive to others, which con-tributes to an emotional climate that fosters trust and feelings of compassion rather than suspicion and fear (de Rivera & Paez, 2007).

COLLECTIVE GRIEVING AND MOURNING

One of the biggest complications when there is any disaster, but particularly when there has been entrenched and violent intergroup conflict, is how to engage in traditional ways of grieving and mourning. Every culture has its own customs and rituals of bereavement, but often they cannot be enacted during armed conflict. Safety and security are important when grieving, and they are hard to come by in dangerous circumstances. Recovery of bodies and the ability to engage in traditional burial and cremation activities may also be abrogated by the realities of armed conflict. Communal processes that honor the deceased and support the family also depend on a modicum of safety and stability to enact. Yet, whatever the circumstances, helping people to grieve and mourn is an essential task. Collective grieving and mourning are such critical activities in response to disaster that they are exclusively the subject of chapter 11.

LEADERSHIP THAT FOSTERS RECONCILIATION

On occasion, disaster responders will have the opportunity to consult with local community leaders about how they can be helpful to the process of recovery and reconciliation. If responders have access to leaders, they can be encouraged to give voice to hope and reconciliation and not to inflame fears and stereotypes. Leaders are often caught up in the narratives of the groups with whom they identify, so it can be useful for them to consult with people who are outside of the circle of conflict and who can offer perspective. Leaders can be coached to pay attention to language, symbols, metaphors, and tone, and they can be encouraged to speak to people from multiple audiences. Leaders can also be encouraged to acknowledge past divisions and losses while also offering hope by responding to challenges in a way that envisions future unity.

This chapter has considered the unique dynamics of intergroup conflict that can lead to disasters such as armed conflict, war, ethnic cleansing, apartheid, and genocide. Although disaster responders may not work directly to resolve such conflict, the dynamics can be a significant part of the social ecology when there are coexisting natural disasters, such as hurricanes and earthquakes. Although direct interventions to resolve entrenched intergroup conflict require specific skills, disaster responders should understand the dynamics of intergroup conflict and what helps to ameliorate it. There is a recursive relationship between psychosocial healing and peace and between reconciliation and social justice. Thus, the activities of disaster responders can enhance the prospects of intergroup reconciliation, which are in turn aided by efforts to resolve intergroup conflict. Even when practitioners are not engaged in direct conflict resolution, they can offer supports and services that foster healing and lower the intensity of antagonisms. Without psychosocial healing, everyone feels like a victim. The social role and emotional state of victimhood does not foster empathy, magnanimity, compassion, or curiosity about, respect for, or the ability to see the other in a complex and discriminating fashion. And it does not encourage compromise or the taking of responsibility. Moreover, it is disempowering.

This chapter has considered the importance of identity, particularly social identity, as central to the dynamics of intergroup conflict; perceived threats to a group's socially constructed identity unite the personal with the political and meld the concrete situation on the ground with resonant symbols and narratives. Entrenched intergroup conflict can lead to a sense of collective and cultural trauma, which can be passed down for many generations and fuel an endless cycle of dehumanizing one's enemies in the name of anticipatory or retaliatory violence.

The chapter summarizes much of what is known about what helps to resolve intergroup conflict. It has explored the tension between acknowledging universal human rights and respecting the norms and mores of local cultures. Strategies respond on multiple levels: national, societal, legal, communal, organizational, and cultural (particularly symbols and discourses), while alleviating suffering, increasing safety, and meeting the social and psychological needs of those affected by the conflict. This is a tall order and it is no wonder that so many intergroup conflicts are intractable and difficult to resolve. Yet there have been reconciliation efforts that, for all of their flaws, have led to social changes and reductions in overt intergroup tensions. The ending of apartheid in South Africa and the peace agreement in Northern Ireland are but two examples. This chapter has considered some of the major mechanisms used to respond to intergroup conflict—retributive justice, restorative justice, and truth and reconciliation commissions. As described, the process of Gacaca illustrates how some of these mechanisms work and the problems and difficulties that are part of any attempts to achieve peace and justice after extreme intergroup conflict.

The chapter has concluded by considering how psychosocial capacity building can augment and support direct conflict resolution interventions. It suggests seven overall strategies:

1. Positioning that allows access to as many stakeholders as possible
2. Opening up space by providing the scaffolding of overarching goals

3. Creating opportunities for people to interact and form relationships
4. Offering positive social roles and social reintegration for those who were part of the conflict
5. Creating opportunities for healing
6. Engaging in collective grieving and mourning
7. Fostering leadership that facilitates reconciliation

Intergroup conflict is a disaster in its own right and accentuates the impact of coexisting disasters. Using a psychosocial capacity building approach entails understanding the social ecology of the conflict and integrating psychosocial approaches with intergroup reconciliation and peace building.

MINDFULNESS EXERCISE: COMPASSION FOR A DIFFICULT PERSON

Some of this exercise is inspired by Pema Chodron (2001, 2002) and Christopher Germer (2009). It is best to begin this kind of work by trying to develop compassion for someone about whom you feel ambivalent or negatively but who has not hurt you in a major way.

Sit comfortably and focus on your breathing for a number of breaths until you feel centered. Imagine a person you experience positively, perhaps a mentor or benefactor. Fix the person's image in your mind as you breathe. Breathe in the individual's good energy. Breathe out loving-kindness to the person—may he or she be safe, happy, healthy, and at ease. Relax into that space.

Now bring to mind someone who causes you discomfort, frustration, or pain—or about whom you feel negatively. Acknowledge the pain that the individual has caused you. Feel where it resides in your body. Breathe into it. Shine some loving-kindness on yourself as you breathe—may you be safe, happy, healthy, and at ease.

After doing this for a while, imagine the difficult person again. Try to breathe some loving-kindness toward him or her. This might be difficult and you may experience negative feelings—such as aversion, anger, guilt, shame, sadness—or this may feel like a hollow exercise, that you are incapable of directing loving-kindness toward the person. If this happens, go back to giving yourself some loving-kindness. Perhaps you can try again to visualize the difficult individual and give him or her loving-kindness.

If this does not seem to be working, visualize the person who gives you good energy. Imagine him or her facing the person you find difficult and breathing loving-kindness toward that individual. If you are able, imagine joining a circle with both people and breathe loving-kindness to all in the circle. If you do not want to visualize forming a circle with both individuals, you can opt to imagine directing loving-kindness toward your mentor/benefactor as he or she faces the difficult person.

Try to end the meditation with this thought: "May I and all beings be safe, happy, healthy, and at ease." Refocus on your breath for a few moments before leaving the meditative space.

11

COLLECTIVE MEMORIALIZING

DEATH IS DIFFICULT to accept and process even when it announces its arrival, as with long-term fatal illnesses. However, disasters involve sudden and multiple deaths, which is all the more challenging. In chapter 4, in a consideration of postdisaster bereavement, I compare different conceptual models of grief and mourning and emphasize the centrality of culture in making sense of death while providing guidelines and signposts for mourners. This chapter further pursues that discussion by reflecting on the process of collective memorializing, looking at public expressions, and understanding symbols of grieving and remembrance.

All cultures have a private aspect of grief and loss (what an individual feels or how a family copes with the loss of a member) and a public, collective component, including obituaries, funerals, wakes, memorial services, sitting shivah, and many other culturally determined rituals. The balance between what is private and what is public varies depending on social norms, cultural expectations, and the unique wishes and needs of survivors after the death of a loved one. Disaster by its very nature is a collective event, replete with private sorrows. Chapter 10 describes the ways intergroup conflict can damage a society's collective identity and lead to a crisis of confidence in the ability of a culture to explain and meaningfully render profound losses (Smelser, 2004). Such crises of identity and culture also occur with other forms of major disaster. A collective crisis calls for collective measures to reconnect people with their culture and past and to reconstruct a sense of social relatedness and belonging. Informal communities and networks emerge after a disaster, reconfiguring collective engagement and community life in a postdisaster environment (Solnit, 2009), which can include spontaneous attempts at memorializing. There are times, however, when intentional planning and organizing is needed to help prepare the conditions that will foster collective memorializing.

Collective memorializing after a disaster refers to public processes of grieving and remembrance, marking a profound social event, acknowledging and honoring losses, and seeking comfort, hope, and even transcendent meaning. This chapter considers how collective memorializing helps people and communities heal, what is involved in the process, what the specific issues are, and how disaster response workers can contribute to the process. Before discussing these issues, I briefly review the unique challenges to grieving and mourning posed by disaster.

BEREAVEMENT AFTER DISASTER

As Halpern & Tramontin (2007) point out, many factors complicate grieving and mourning after a disaster: the suddenness and scale of losses, concern about the suffering of the dying, the disfigurement of bodies and even the loss of bodies, loss of homes and property, and the interaction of stress and trauma with the grieving process. The challenges posed by everyday survival after a disaster often make it difficult to even think about grieving and mourning. Moreover, it is common for survivors to experience feelings of self-blame or guilt. Such feelings can arise even when an elderly relative dies of natural causes. These emotions can elicit questions such as: Was I attentive enough? Did I do all I could to reduce their suffering? Did they know that I loved them? Did I say goodbye? Such questions are further magnified if death was caused by a disaster and new questions are raised, such as: Why did this have to happen? Did authorities do all they could to prevent this? What is the meaning of this death? What should be done in response? Deaths from disasters may leave survivors tinged with ambivalence. Boss's (2006) term "ambiguous loss" is particularly resonant for those grieving the loss of disaster victims, especially when there is uncertainty about a person's fate (unrecovered bodies lost in rubble, for example) or a person is no longer who he once was, as in cases of head injury that lead to serious brain damage.

Unlike a timely death in the family, disasters leave people feeling a sense of collective as well as personal loss. On a more positive note, a feeling of "group survivorship" (Zinner, 1999) may develop among those who have suffered losses as well as among those in a wounded community, with this shared experience drawing people closer together.

The meaning of death and the ways that people respond are deeply rooted in culture. When disaster occurs, cultural practices are disrupted and it is difficult for people to engage in accustomed mourning rituals. In Haiti after the 2010 earthquake, many traditional procedures and rites broke down—visits from community members to grieving families, visits to graves after burial, the giving of small gifts to survivors—because people were living in temporary camps, often separated from those they knew, and were overwhelmed by the scale of the losses.

Outsiders providing aid after a disaster can complicate mourning. Outsiders are often unfamiliar with cultural bereavement styles and customs. Often with good intentions, they inadvertently impose their own. An example of this was when an airplane crashed in New York City carrying many Dominicans and Dominican Americans shortly after 9/11. Non-Dominican mental health responders attempted to "calm people down," even by medicating them, because they were unprepared for the expressive outpouring of sorrow and anguish that was customary for grieving survivors in this cultural context.

GOALS OF COLLECTIVE MEMORIALIZING

Collective memorializing is a process that is part of a universal human desire to acknowledge and remember the dead and to help the survivors grieve and recover. The ways in which this is operationalized and ritualized vary considerably across cultures. Understanding certain explicit and implicit goals for collective memorializing is helpful for disaster responders who may be called on to help people with this process.

ACKNOWLEDGING AND REMEMBERING LOSSES

An essential purpose of collective memorializing after a disaster is commemoration. Tributes and memorials honor those who have died, but they go well beyond that. They also remember and mark a significant social occurrence. Many communities devastated by disaster have memorials of remembrance that inform them of some of the details and often attempt to transform the tragedy of the disaster into beautiful art, a place for reflection, or an exhortation to prevent future catastrophes and tragedies. The notion of community is not necessarily geographically based—the Nazi attack on European Jews, memorialized in the Holocaust Memorial Museum in Washington, DC, refers to a pan-national ethnic community. While the Holocaust Memorial Museum, the Vietnam Veterans Memorial in Washington, and memorial statues and installations in cities all over the world are formal, sometimes government-sponsored memorials, there are also smaller-scale, informal memorials that arise after disasters—such as the pictures, ribbons, notes, art, and candles found on street corners in New York City after 9/11 or the crosses with flowers that mark stretches of highway where fatal accidents occur.

TELLING THE STORY OF THE DISASTER

Collective memorializing creates spaces and opportunities for narratives of the disaster to emerge. There are many ways to recount this story—in words, poems, images, pictures, symbols. What is most important is that narratives of the disaster are told and shared—and that many voices are part of this process. The story of the disaster is part of a larger social and collective narrative, one that began before the disaster and continues beyond it. Efficacious collective storytelling reopens "transitional pathways" connecting people to their histories and cultural traditions, while shining a beacon toward the future (Landau, 2007; Landau & Saul, 2004).

BRINGING PEOPLE TOGETHER

Collective memorializing acknowledges the shared public impact of a disaster. It is a reminder that what happened affects an entire community or subcommunity. It helps create a sense of connectivity by bringing people together through rituals, ceremonies, events, and fixed and interactive installations. Although there are collective losses, there can also be group unity in a community of survivors. Collective memorializing has symbolic as well as literal significance; the choice of metaphor and symbol establishes a narrative frame for understanding the event and helps people (and cultures) reconstruct meaning. This is why the planning process for collective memorials that commemorate large-scale disasters is so important; different people and groups of people in the community have their own ideas about what is important and how the story of the disaster should be told. If a collective memorial is to unify a community rather than lead to dissension and splintering, then an inclusive planning process, involving a range of stakeholders, is critical for its success.

INVITING REFLECTION AND EXPRESSION

Collective memorializing is an invitation to pause and reflect on a profound occurrence that stands outside of the patterns and rhythms of daily life. In some cultural contexts, this leads to emotional expression and perhaps release. In other cultural contexts, reflection focuses more on lessons learned from the disaster—a form of cognitive expression—or on the importance of family, community, or spiritual beliefs. Effective collective memorializing creates spaces and processes for a range of people in the community to reflect, honor, and remember in their own way, but in concert with others, those who have been lost.

SEEKING RESOLUTION

Closure is an unrealistic goal for people affected by a disaster. Some argue that complete healing can never be achieved given the scale of losses in a major disaster (Summerfield, 1995, 2000, 2004). Perhaps "resolution" is a more realistic term, meaning sufficient integration of losses so that people, communities, and societies can move forward in their lives—not forgetting the past or letting go of profound losses—but being able to live in the present while looking to the future. Resolution also implies integrating the catastrophic events with what existed before the disaster (historically, socially, culturally) so that there is a link between the past, present, and future, with the disaster being a significant part of that narrative without its becoming the sole prism through which everything else is experienced. What resolution means in practice will vary considerably across societies and cultures and among families and individuals. Outsiders should not stand in judgment of how those directly affected by the disaster negotiate this process. It is up to those who have been directly involved to manage their own way of grieving. Thus, one criterion for evaluating collective memorials is how well survivors find they have been helped in their process of bereavement.

INVITING CREATIVE ANARCHY

Disaster has the potential for liberation and transformation. Solnit (2009) has compared it to the revolution that uproots an ancient regime. There certainly is the potential for disaster to open society from closed and restrictive customs and practices, although there is also the possibility for the elite and powerful actors to use the disaster as an opportunity to consolidate power and exploit victims (Klein, 2007). The process of collective memorializing has the potential to heal and offer hope or to be used as an empty, repressive vessel of domination. The process itself is not inherently beneficent. Much depends on who is driving the process, who participates in it, and what the goals and intentions are. This is why effective collective memorializing involves a creative anarchic process. There is no entity that can claim to represent everyone, no memorial that will have transcendent and transformative meaning for all. Collective memorializing involves what Lederach (2005) has referred to as the "moral imagination," a process that embodies ethics and creativity. Ethics refer to the quest for healing and peace and justice, while creativity invites imaginative, new, and artistic ideas—an aesthetic of transformation. Anarchy implies a plethora of responses by a range of social actors who embrace chaos and complexity. The roadside accident and street-corner assault memorials are examples of this, as are murals painted on the sides of buildings—some commissioned by the government, others sprouting spontaneously or informally.

After the fatal shooting of a federal judge and five other people, as well as the critical wounding of Arizona congresswoman Gabrielle Giffords, who was the target of the attack, many forms of collective memorializing sprung up in Tucson, Arizona, where the attack took place (Lacey, 2011). At the hospital where Giffords was recovering, there were "stuffed animals of all different species and notes written by children in crayon. There were inspiring bible verses, photographs of the departed and candles summoning a plethora of Saints" (Lacey, 2011). There were also mementos left at Safeway, a chain grocery, where the shooting took place, and at the school of a nine-year-old victim. According to Karen Mlawsky, the chief executive of the hospital, "It's 100 percent unorganized . . . spontaneous and changes every day" (Lacey, 2011). In addition, there were plans to name university buildings, baseball fields, scholarships, and food drives after victims. The father of the nine-year-old announced that his daughter's corneas had been donated to two other children, who could see as a result. All these spontane-ous activities have helped the community of Tucson not only to grieve but also to come together, remember the lives of those who died, and—within weeks of the tragedy—plant seeds of hope in other people's lives.

TRANSFORMING LOSSES

Two ways to transform devastating losses are reconnecting with beauty and engaging in social activism. If art and beauty can arise from the ashes of destruction, then hope can flower. If loss and devastation can lead to collec-tive action that prevents future losses, aids people affected by a disaster, and advocates for new laws, policies, and practices, then people feel empowered and able to transcend the role of "victim."

Another way that losses can be transformed by collective memorializing is by the reconstruction of meaning. Meaning can be rational, scientific, social, or spiritual—there are many ways people engage in the construction of meaning, and there are different lessons and truths people will draw from a disaster. Collective memorials can have a profound transformative impact when they stimulate the meaning-making process, engaging participants to do this in their own way as well as with others. They ideally offer sites, pro-cesses, and metaphors in which imagination and creativity lead to a sense of the profound and even sacred.

WAYS OF COLLECTIVE MEMORIALIZING

There are many forms of collective memorializing. Sometimes it leads to something fixed—such as an installation, exhibit, or museum. But it can also be a process—a series of skits, a concert, or a dance performance. Both products and processes can achieve the goals described in the previ-ous section. Ideally, collective memorializing engages individuals, fami-lies, organizations, groups, and the community at large in a process that leads to unique and meaningful ways of remembering the disaster and honoring its victims and survivors. There are no prescriptions for collec-tive memorializing, and models should not be imposed from the outside. Although spontaneous installations with pictures, notes, flowers, ribbons, and candles sprung up in Tucson after the shooting discussed previously and in New York City within days of 9/11, memorials were not created along the Mississippi coast in the immediate aftermath of Hurricane Katrina. At one point, some Red Cross workers tried to engage people in constructing memorials, based on the workers' experiences responding to 9/11, but local people found this to be bewildering and somewhat artificial, and the memorials failed to gain traction. The process, which had emerged spontaneously in one community in response to a given disaster, was neither indigenous nor meaningful in another community responding to a very different disaster.

With this note of caution, I describe some types of collective memorializing that may be meaningful for communities in response to disaster so that responders have ideas about how the process can work.

COLLECTIVE NARRATIVES

There are many individual stories about a disaster that, when combined, can form a collective narrative. Although the process of creating collective narratives may occur spontaneously, it does not always emerge on its own. Informal and formal groups and organizations can create platforms for collective storytelling to emerge.

Books, journals, and oral histories are one way of collecting stories. Written narratives can be collected and kept in archives or published in edited journals. For people who are unlikely to write their stories, accounts can be taped or recorded on video. Sometimes it is helpful to bring people together in groups to talk about their experiences. These discussions can be recorded or used as preparation for people to write or speak their accounts individually. As with all collections of narratives, it is important for people to be aware of how their stories will be used—who will see them and to what purpose—and to always have the right to redact or retract their contributions.

Another type of collective narrative is the visual exhibit. After Hurricane Katrina, there were installations that showed videos recorded by people trapped in their homes as the waves came ashore. Photographs taken before, during, and after a disaster can be exhibited in the locale or region where the disaster occurred or in other parts of the world. The renowned Brazilian photographer Sebastião Salgado has mounted around the globe many of his moving portraits of people affected by war, natural disaster, famine, and displacement, sharing the stories of masses of disaster-affected people. This serves as a witness to what has happened as well as alerts people to the human dimensions of disaster—in the hope of stimulating compassion, empathy, and even relief and support. The United Nations agency UNICEF thought highly enough of Salgado's work to name him as a special representative, charged with raising the world's awareness of the rights of young people worldwide.

A memorial to victims of the Khmer Rouge in Cambodia is a simple yet deeply moving example of how pictures can honor victims and stimulate reflection. At one of the killing centers during the country's period of genocide, known as S-21, photographs had been taken of the prisoners before they were executed. The prisoners had been tortured and forced to "confess" to a range of "crimes." It is thought that fourteen thousand people perished at this location. Years later, a group of photojournalists found the pictures and catalogued them, using them as the basis for establishing the Tuol Sleng Museum of Genocide at the site of the former camp. The pictures are of men, women, children, and the elderly. Some victims look terrified; others stare courageously and defiantly at the camera. They serve as an immediate and personal memorial to the victims while having a profound, if not indelible, impact on observers; one cannot look at the exhibit without being forever changed. Some of the photographs have been exhibited in galleries and museums around the world. They are available online as a cyber collective memorial (http://www.tuolsleng.com).

STANDING MEMORIALS

Most people are familiar with standing memorials commemorating great people and special and significant events. The Lincoln Memorial in Washington, DC, not only honors Abraham Lincoln but also serves as a reminder of the U.S. Civil War and the formal abolition of slavery. Every country has memorials like this. Many small towns in the United States have memorials with the names of those who served in major wars and those who died in active service. Washington, DC, has a great number of major war memorials, including the Vietnam Veterans War Memorial, a large, black granite slab listing the names of all U.S. soldiers who died in that conflagration. Its size and color are as striking as is the length of the list.

There are also less formal memorials, such as the clock in Hanwang, described earlier in the book, that stopped at the moment the Wenchuan earthquake struck in 2008. The tower and the remains of the empty town serve as reminders and memorials of the devastating earthquake. Another example is a memorial in response to the 1977 dormitory fire at Providence College in Rhode Island that killed seven women. The college chapel now has a small alcove to remember the victims with seven candles burning in their memory.

Museums are another type of standing memorial—such as the Tuol Sleng Museum of Genocide in Cambodia and the Holocaust Memorial Museum in Washington, DC, commemorating the Jewish Holocaust, both mentioned earlier. Museums are memorials that can serve as educational platforms—telling stories and remembering victims but also drawing conclusions and inviting participants to reflect on the meaning of what occurred and even engage in social action.

Another form of standing memorial is an installation, which is often interactive and uses multiple forms of media, such as pictures, essays, art, computers with which people can interact, and notepads that people can write comments on. Such memorials can arise spontaneously at a grassroots level or be presented by an organization or government entity.

In Oklahoma City, the Alfred P. Murrah Federal Building was bombed and destroyed in 1995, killing 168 people, many of them federal employees and children who attended the day care center there. The site is now the Oklahoma City National Memorial & Museum, a standing memorial that incorporates a number of elements discussed here. Twin gates, known as the *Gates of Time*, mark the moment when the bomb went off and serve as an entrance to the park, which is part of the museum. The park provides a peaceful place for contemplation and mourning. It has a reflecting pool with the calming sounds of flowing water and 168 chairs in the *Field of Chairs*, 1 for every person who perished, including 19 small chairs for the children who died. An elm, known as the *Survivor Tree*, which withstood the blast, has been left as a symbol of resilience and life. The *Rescuers Orchard* is dedicated to those who responded and helped. The *Children's Area* has tiles sent by children from around the world and chalkboards that children visiting the memorial can write on. Lastly, a fence surrounding the park has preserved some of the mementos left by mourners after the tragedy, and part of the original fence is available for visitors to leave their own tokens of remembrance. The museum and memorial are a very moving, beautiful, and thoughtful example of an interactive installation commemorating a disaster. (For more information, visit the Web site at http://www.oklahoma citynationalmemorial.org/index.php.)

MEMORIALIZING PROJECTS

Another way to help others after a disaster remember and commemorate losses is through projects that strive to transform the destruction of a disaster into actions, policies, and practices geared to mitigate against future disasters and to relieve the suffering of those affected by the current disaster. For example, in Fonfrede, Haiti, after the 2010 earthquake, university students who survived the quake and whose universities were destroyed volunteered to help their community by reaching out and offering social support and material assistance to those who had lost people. They established a group to plan a memorial in the village commemorating those from the community who had perished.

There are many other examples. In China, after the Wenchuan earthquake of 2008, parents who had lost children got together to publicize how poorly constructed Chinese schools were and to lobby for higher safety standards in school construction. In the United States, after a spate of publicity about children who were sexually assaulted and physically attacked by previously convicted sex offenders, parents and other concerned citizens campaigned for legal reforms. The result was Megan's Law, named for a New Jersey child who was raped and murdered, which requires that sex offenders register with the police. There are now laws in all fifty states requiring the registration of convicted sex offenders. After 9/11, many people across the country set up funds and foundations to aid victims of terrorism and to prevent intergroup conflict, with names such as the September 11th Fund, September 11 Memorial Fund, World Trade Center Fund, and 9/11 Scholarship Fund. A group called the Oklahoma City National Memorial Institute for the Prevention of Terrorism published a pamphlet to help other communities that experience terrorism. Information in the pamphlet is geared toward a range of groups, including the medical community, clergy, schools, counselors, and the media.

RITUALS, PERFORMANCES, CEREMONIES

Artistic performances, cultural rituals, and remembrance ceremonies are all ways of engaging people as performers and spectators in acts of collective memorializing. Rituals and ceremonies spurred by a disaster have been enacted to re-create events, exorcise spirits, ask for forgiveness, facilitate healing, foster peace, and many other purposes. Disasters have inspired ballets, plays, concerts, dances, films, television shows, and other types of performances. Ritual and performance sometimes directly address the disaster while at other times use themes and metaphors to explore subjects raised by the disaster.

ART

While performances are a form of art, other kinds of collective memorializing include paintings, photographs, sculptures, statues, and computer and electronic art. Even light displays, such as the beacons in the shape of the destroyed Twin Towers created in New York City immediately after 9/11, can be used as a form of artistic expression and remembrance. Children in eastern Sri Lanka were encouraged to draw pictures of the tsunami, which were then collected and exhibited. One of the most famous artistic renditions of a disaster is Pablo Picasso's painting *Guernica*, which depicts the Italian and German bombing of the Basque city of that name at the behest of Spanish fascists. Sebastião Salgado's photographs transform massive human suffering into art. Art not only transforms debris and destruction into beauty but also promotes public awareness and offers a lasting monument with emotional resonance for those who endure calamity.

ANNIVERSARIES AND SPECIAL OBSERVANCES

Anniversaries have special meaning for people who have survived a disaster. While annual dates are often significant anniversaries, in some cultures other intervals, such as the passing of three or six months, hold special meaning. Anniversaries often bring back pain and can retrigger reactions experienced immediately after a disaster. Any of the previously mentioned types of memorializing can occur on anniversaries. Reunions are often held on anniversaries. Anniversaries are a good time both for looking back at what was lost and for appreciating and assessing how people and the community have moved forward.

CONSIDERATIONS FOR DISASTER RESPONDERS

Collective memorializing works best when it evolves organically and embodies indigenous social and cultural practices. It cannot be imposed by outsiders; nor can it be forced from within if people are not yet ready or prepared. Yet there are ways that disaster responders can be helpful and supportive of this process. In essence, the approach is to ask questions and help articulate goals, establish mechanisms to implement ideas, and engage as many people as possible in the process. This section covers areas where questions commonly arise and responders can help local people think through what they would like to do.

HELPFUL QUESTIONS

I have found three questions about grieving and mourning to be useful in most disaster situations:

1. How have people traditionally mourned the deaths of people in your community?
2. How has the disaster made it difficult to engage in these traditional practices?
3. Given the realities of the disaster and its aftermath, what are some ways in which you and others can grieve and mourn that will have meaning within your culture and traditions?

These questions usually lead to creative problem solving and the generating of ideas about how the community can resume grieving and mourning in a culturally meaningful way.

WHEN?

There is no right time for memorializing—any time can be helpful and any time can be challenging. Even in the earliest phases of bereavement, when people still seem stunned and shocked, I have seen spontaneous memorials appear that carry great emotional weight and help people express themselves, acting as receptacles for their anguish. I have also found that talking with people about memorializing, and sharing ideas gained from other communities, can help them start thinking about what *they* would find to be helpful and meaningful. An important part of this conversation is to consider what dates and anniversaries are significant from cultural, religious, and social perspectives. There are often many dates and many time frames for different types of memorializing—it is not as if there is only one memorial and then it is over.

WHAT?

The previous section described some general types of collective memorializing. In my experience, affected people and local helpers are very interested in hearing about what has been done in other countries and communities to memorialize disasters. Often, when people are in a state of grief and trying to cope with recovery, it is difficult for them to think about how they can engage in their traditional bereavement practices, let alone figure out how to manage mourning in the disaster's aftermath. Hearing about different types of memorializing can help local people generate ideas about what would be most helpful and appropriate for them under the circumstances of a particular disaster. It is also important to share ideas from the outside to expand the universe of possibilities, while encouraging affected people to creatively generate their own ideas.

HOW?

This is an area where disaster responders can be particularly helpful. There are usually many ideas and many subgroups within a community that may have differing notions of what should be done and how to go about it. Responders can encourage inclusivity and grassroots participation in the planning and implementation of any memorializing projects. They can encourage groups to think through who is included and excluded (whether intentionally or inadvertently) by their plans and to consider who a given type of memorializing will be most and least meaningful for. It is important to pay attention to hidden assumptions and cultural or religious symbols that may not speak to everyone. This is particularly germane when there has been intergroup conflict.

There are also basic issues to consider. Who will sponsor the process? How will leadership be determined? What significant roles will need to be filled and how will people be recruited into them? What kind of a planning process will be established to ensure maximum participation? Will there be some kind of review by key stakeholders after plans have been drawn up? If there is disagreement or conflict during the process, what mechanisms will be in place to help people resolve it?

It can be helpful to distinguish between big projects, such as an official, community-wide memorial, which usually involves some form of government entity—as was true for the Oklahoma City memorial, for example—and smaller or more localized projects, which a segment of the community or a particular group want to enact. Multiple projects create more space for different groups of people and allow for variation in both style and substance. But unified projects have greater potential for bringing more people together to collectively share in a memorial process.

This chapter has considered collective memorializing, a process of shared grieving and mourning after a disaster. Collective memorializing brings people together, creating a sense of shared survivorship to mark a profound social event by grieving losses, remembering victims, and making sense of and constructing meaning from what happened. Disaster disrupts the ability of individuals, families, and communities to grieve and mourn in culturally familiar and traditional ways. Moreover, disaster is a profoundly social event that calls for shared forms of bereavement. Collective memorializing is most effective when there is an inclusive, participatory planning process that engages many stakeholders and segments of a community, reflecting the range of local cultural, social, religious, and spiritual practices and traditions.

Collective memorializing seeks to achieve a number of goals:

- Commemorating and memorializing people and events
- Creating a platform for a polyvocal telling of the story of the disaster
- Bringing people together to grieve, mourn, remember, and create meaning
- Helping people to reflect on what happened and to express their thoughts and feelings

- Helping people to achieve a relative sense of resolution about the disaster
- Fomenting creative anarchy so that there are spaces for many people and groups of people to memorialize in ways that are meaningful to them
- Transforming losses by reigniting hope and regaining a sense of empowerment

The chapter has discussed different types of collective memorializing while stressing the importance of having a local creative-planning process so that memorializing comes from the ground up and is not imposed from above or the outside. Collective memorializing can take the form of a fixed memorial, such as a museum, or a process, such as a performance. Six ways of collective memorializing have been considered:

1. Collective narratives—stories told in words or pictures
2. Standing memorials—museums, exhibits, statues, monuments, installations
3. Memorializing projects—public and communal bereavement practices
4. Rituals, performances, and ceremonies that artistically respond to the disaster
5. Works of art that respond to the disaster
6. Anniversaries and special observances to mark the disaster

The chapter has concluded with a discussion of three questions for disaster responders to consider: when to memorialize, what the product or process should look like, and how to engage people in the planning and implementation of memorializing.

There is power in collective actions that have the capacity to validate individual losses and, at the same time, unite people in their process of grieving, healing, and facing the future. Collective memorializing is an essential part of that process.

MINDFULNESS: SOURCES OF STRENGTH

Begin this mindfulness exercise as with the others by assuming a comfortable position and focusing on your breathing.

Think of a loss in your family—for example, it could be the death of a person or pet, or it could be someone who moved away or someone you yourself left behind. (I recommend that you not focus on an incident of trauma or abuse in this exercise.) This might raise some sad or painful feelings. Whatever feelings this brings up for you, notice where you are holding them in your body and breathe into them.

Think of one thing that you, a person in your family, or someone you knew did to respond to the loss that had a positive effect. It can be a small thing, like maintaining a sense of humor, just being present with someone, or asking others in the family for help. Did your family draw on any cultural or social supports? What made you feel less able to cope and what helped you feel better? Do you carry any lessons from this with you today? If so, how do you use them in your life? Finish this segment of the mindfulness exercise by remembering one source of strength that you carry from this experience and hold it in your awareness for a few breaths.

Finish the mindfulness session by first returning to your breathing and, after a few breaths, noticing where your body is supported by the ground, mat, cushion, or chair where you are sitting. If you feel like it, after ending the exercise, share the strength that you hold with one other person, and ask her what strength she carries with her.

12

DISASTER DISTRESS AND SELF-CARE

ALL DISASTERS, whether large or small, have the potential to unsettle and even wound those who take action to help others. Those responding to a major disaster are transported outside of the parameters of their usual experience—whether the responder is a professional or a volunteer, a veteran or a rookie. One's senses are aroused, familiar supports and landmarks disappear, and the environment is frequently chaotic if not dangerous. Responders are witness to severe destruction and great suffering. Social systems have broken down, social networks may be in tatters, and the usual rules governing social behavior are suspended. This has the potential to be stressful and overwhelming but can also feel enlivening and inspirational. Disasters are the worst of times yet can bring out the best in people (Solnit, 2009).

There is intensity and immediacy, even a sense of exhilaration, that goes with responding to disaster, and life seldom feels pointless. Precisely because survivors and responders alike have been thrown out of their comfort zones and stripped of their usual protections and social armor, profound and memorable interactions occur. Disaster responders report similar sensations of clarity and meaning described by hospice workers when working with clients who are dying; artifice is removed as the sacred displaces the quotidian. Under these conditions, relationships form quickly, without the usual social dances, and the inner, private, guarded places of the psyche may suddenly be exposed. However, unlike the conditions hospice workers experience, disaster workers usually operate far from home without their usual supports, and they are thrust into situations where along with intimacy comes vulnerability.

The intensity of the disaster situation and the fact that so many familiar guideposts and rule books are missing can quickly lead to a sense of closeness among survivors, amid responders, and between survivor and responder. This can deepen empathic connections, which has the potential to help survivors with their recovery but also can increase the risk of vicarious or secondary suffering in responders. Responders often experience heightened levels of adrenaline and cortisol, which sustains them through long shifts and harrowing landscapes. However, over time, this heightened alertness can be depleting and make it difficult to physiologically tone things down or switch off enough to sleep, eat, and relax. In certain disaster situations, responders find themselves facing hardship—sleeping on floors, eating too little, not being able to shower—which can increase stress.

It is often difficult for responders to communicate with family and friends and to rely on traditional sources of social and emotional support. Many disaster responders find that even when they return home—whether from a shift or from a three-week tour of duty through a disaster site—they feel distanced or alienated from loved ones. It can seem daunting to try to articulate what the disaster experience was like for those who were not there, and there may be a desire to protect others from harrowing stories. Friends and family, although loving and supportive, may not be interested in hearing about all of the details of a disaster experience, which the responder may have been storing up to talk about.

This chapter considers the personal and psychological challenges disaster workers encounter and the potential adverse reactions they experience in response, including severe consequences such as compassion fatigue, vicarious traumatization, and secondary traumatic stress. The concept of disaster distress is introduced. As with all of the concepts and phenomena considered in this book, culture and social practices strongly influence the nature and meaning of reactions. The syndromes described in this chapter were conceived of by Westerners and usually refer to Western disaster workers, so it is important to flexibly and creatively adapt them to other social and cultural contexts. The chapter focuses on ways workers can exercise self-care to prevent serious psychological outcomes and ways to help workers when they have been emotionally wounded or impaired. It concludes with an examination of the responsibilities of supervisors and managers to support, protect, and care for disaster responders.

RISKS AND VULNERABILITIES

Most disaster responders will experience some adverse effects in their work, often mild stress reactions (Cronin, Ryan, & Brier, 2007), which resolve with self-care and social supports. Responders may have symptoms in all of the domains described in earlier chapters—physical, mental, emotional, behavioral, social, and in the realm of spirituality and meaning-making (Yassen, 1995). Musa and Hamid (2008) found in their review of the literature regarding psychological reactions in relief workers that there are often health problems, psychosomatic reactions, increased drinking and risk-taking behavior, intrusive thoughts, and anxiety about the future. Much of this comes from an empathic engagement with disaster survivors and a desire to help alleviate their suffering. It is compounded when the disaster is particularly vivid and overwhelming and responders are working long shifts under arduous conditions.

More research has been done on the long-term effects for clinicians of ongoing work with trauma survivors, but the concepts that have emerged from this work can shed light on the reactions of disaster workers. The terms to describe these reactions are often used interchangeably; however, researchers and practitioners believe that there are subtle but important distinctions between them (Adams, Boscarino, & Figley, 2006; Canfield, 2005; Deighton, Gurris, & Traue, 2007; Tosone, 2007; Tosone & Bialkin, 2003; White, 2006). Here are some of the major categories.

BURNOUT

Burnout comes from the strain of working with people with psychological and social wounds over a long period of time, often under demanding and isolated conditions (Tosone, 2007). It can undermine a responder's sense of optimism and lead to pessimism, emotional distancing, exhaustion, and other physical symptoms—and it can affect interpersonal relationships (Tosone & Bialkin, 2003). Burnout occurs in many nondisaster situations and can be the cumulative toll of working in stressful conditions with challenging clients and lack of adequate support. For example, workers in state child welfare agencies who deal with child maltreatment on a daily basis often suffer from burnout. They have heavy caseloads, low salaries, excessive bureaucratic responsibilities, and are subject to intense public scrutiny. Disaster workers, particularly when in the field for a long time, can also be subject to burnout. Workers are more vulnerable to burnout when they feel professionally isolated, emotionally drained, and the markers of success are ambiguous or difficult to achieve (Rosenfeld et al., 2005).

COMPASSION FATIGUE

Compassion fatigue (CF), a term coined by researcher Charles Figley, was initially equated with secondary traumatic stress (STS) and vicarious tramatization (VT) but is seen as less pathologizing and stigmatizing to professionals (Figley, 1995). Although having similarities to burnout, CF emphasizes a reduced capacity for empathic engagement with clients while at the same time bearing their burdens (Adams et al., 2006). Figley, appearing in a video (Within Foundation, 1998), emotionally describes his own bout of CF when counseling Vietnam War veterans. He found he was feeling unsettled and irritable. Moreover, he was overreacting and snapping at colleagues. When he tracked the source of his malaise, he realized that it was fueled by his knowledge that, as a veteran, he too was vulnerable to all of the maladies suffered by the people he was counseling. This example illustrates the duality of taking on the pain of clients while having a reduced capacity for empathy that comes with CF (Tosone & Bialkin, 2003).

Compassion fatigue goes beyond burnout to include emotional contagion and even secondary victimization (Tosone, 2007). Figley (1995, p. 1) describes this as the "cost to caring." Canfield (2005) notes that CF is situational and may recede if a person is removed from the conditions that spawned it.

VICARIOUS TRAUMATIZATION

Although CF and vicarious traumatization have some similarities, Pearlman and Saakvitne (1995) contend that VT transforms the person's construction of the self. Like CF, VT stems from empathic engagement with people who have suffered trauma. But VT leads to cognitive and emotional transformations that impact the full spectrum of a person's life (Pearlman & Saakvitne, 1995; Tosone, 2007). Distorted cognitions can lead to professionals' negatively appraising their competency and self-worth, which can also occlude their interpersonal relationships (Way, VanDeusen, & Cottrell, 2007). These are internal shifts that are not just situational and can have lifelong impact (Canfield, 2005). This is not necessarily a bad thing—vicarious traumatization can lead to people reevaluating what is important in life and how they wish to conduct themselves. However, it can also be overwhelming and destabilizing, resulting in flashbacks, dreams, hyperalertness, and sensitivity to trauma and violence (Tosone & Bialkin, 2003). It can leave people feeling threatened by their environment and pessimistic about the world as a good and safe place.

SECONDARY TRAUMATIC STRESS

Secondary traumatic stress, or secondary traumatic stress disorder (STSD), also results from empathic engagement with clients who have experienced trauma, but it can cause symptoms nearly as severe as those of people suffering from PTSD (Figley, 1995). This can include the familiar triad of reexperiencing symptoms, attempting to avoid triggering stimuli, and being in a state of hyperarousal (Adams et al., 2006). The onset of these symptoms may occur suddenly, and they are dependent on the worker's empathic connection with the client rather than on overall working conditions (Tosone, 2007). Canfield (2005) distinguishes between STS, which lasts less than six months, and STSD, which lasts more than six months.

CRITICAL INCIDENT

Another way to think about reactions of responders is in terms of having a specific experience—a critical incident (CI) (Mitchell, 1983). In a CI, a person is exposed to events that pierce defenses and that, at least momentarily, are disturbing, upsetting, and overwhelming. The concept of CI came to the forefront in considering the stresses and risks for uniformed responders (police, firefighters, paramedics), who often regularly encounter what would be very stressful circumstances for civilians. But CIs are perceived and processed as qualitatively different from ordinary job stresses; they have the potential to cause any of the above syndromes or reactions and can affect the domains (physical, behavioral, cognitive, emotional, social, spiritual) discussed throughout the book. The spectrum of responses to a CI range from merely registering that a big event occurred to developing full-blown STSD. By locating the abnormal in the incident rather than the person, CI, as a term, is viewed by some as being less pathologizing of the worker.

DISASTER DISTRESS

I have developed the term *disaster distress* (DD) to describe the types of negative reactions that can occur specifically when responding to disasters. While it incorporates many of the foregoing patterns, DD is specific to disaster response. Responders, of course, have ample opportunity to be exposed to trauma, which can be a spark for VT or STS. Also, they experience conditions in their work that can be overwhelming and alienating, which contributes to CF. Given the chaotic nature of disaster response, workers receive less supervisory and organizational support than when working in nondisaster conditions. Exposure to death and physical and social destruction can be very destabilizing. What is unique to the concept of disaster distress is that the stress response is not only to a critical incident or specific client or a function of an ongoing stressful work situation—but it is a reaction to the totality of a disaster, an event that is greater than the sum of its parts and that often causes workers to feel overwhelmed and powerless.

Thus, with DD a responder may be triggered or overwhelmed by the scale of destruction, the depth of suffering, and/or the lack of hope for the future. Having responded to many large-scale disasters, I have found that while I have extraordinary energy in the field, there is almost always a difficult transition when I return home. It is hard to settle down; the concerns of family and friends can sound petty compared to the life-and-death struggles of people in the disaster zone; and I often have dreams, if not nightmares, about the disaster. I am often more irritable, fragile, and emotionally labile. And when returning from a disaster, such as the Haitian earthquake, where I left hundreds of thousands of people still living in inadequate tent cities as the rainy season was about to commence, I feel guilty and pessimistic about the future, despite having engaged in meaningful psychosocial capacity building while I was there. I not only carry with me the faces and feelings of people with whom I worked, but I am haunted by a vision of the disaster.

Although DD affects different people in a variety of ways, it implies that their reactions from the accrued experience of responding to disaster continues well after the most recent round of disaster work has been completed.

At times, DD is situational and transitional, while at others it can lead to deep-seated cognitive and emotional changes, as well as shifts in one's sense of self, much like VT. Disaster distress includes a spectrum of reactions, large and small, some of which resolve on their own and others that require special effort and perhaps help from others. Some reactions may connect with a person's past and unresolved issues and schemas, while some may be new and grounded in the disaster experience. Disaster distress is a meta-category—it can encompass CF, VT, and other syndromes, but it also includes the various other ways that workers and volunteers have been negatively affected by the overall experience of responding to disaster.

RISK FACTORS

All workers and volunteers carry their own risk factors (as well as strengths and sources of resiliency) when responding to disaster. These factors are based on who they are and their experiences. Some situations seem to have an impact on most people who respond to them—a fire where children have died, for example. Social and organizational factors can increase support or heighten vulnerability. Although the previous discussion of stress disorders highlighted some of their differences, there are many similarities in their risk factors.

A consistent risk factor comes from empathic engagement with clients who have experienced trauma or severe suffering. In fact, those who are most empathic and most invested in their clients have the highest risk of experiencing STS (Tehrani, 2007). Thus, the combination of empathic attunement and high investment in clients can increase the risk of a secondary stress reaction. Empathic attunement is often a highly successful resiliency strategy, but the key here is the added dimension of intensive investment on the part of the responder. This is not to suggest that responders should not be invested in their clients—on the contrary, this is part of ethical practice and also a source of meaning and satisfaction for responders; it is more that the responder should understand the degree of investment and the importance of boundary setting and self-care. I do not like to use the term *realistic expectations* as it implies that too much hope is unrealistic and suggests an objective measure of what is a very subjective notion. But within the context of a given situation and the parameters of what a responder can do, it is helpful to strike a balance between wanting clients' situations to improve and having perspective about what is likely or unlikely to be accomplished. The point for DD is that if the worker's expectations are much higher than what is feasible and possible in a given situation, then the worker is prone to disappointment, frustration, and through his empathic identification with clients, despair and hopelessness.

One way to think about risk is seeing it as the interaction among the nature of the client's suffering (or of the disaster), the vulnerabilities of the responder, and the availability of organizational supports. Some sources of susceptibility to stress for the worker are a prior history of trauma (Deighton et al., 2007; Pearlman & Saakvitne, 1995; Radey & Figley, 2007), professional isolation (Rosenfeld et al., 2005), and social isolation. When considering DD, prior exposure to disasters can serve as a source of resiliency ("been there, done that") or of vulnerability from having reached the saturation point of exposure to human suffering. Personality plays a role, and those with very high expectations and lower thresholds for frustration and failure are more at risk. The construction of meaning and social construction of professional identity are factors as well (Pearlman & Saakvitne, 1995). If one's identity is shaken by lack of success or prolonged suffering of clients, this can in turn deepen feelings of self-doubt and incompetence. Ambiguous markers of success can be very difficult for high achievers (Rosenfeld et al., 2005). Being young and inexperienced is yet another risk factor.

Another dimension of susceptibility to stress responses is the availability of supports for the responder: professional, social, and personal. The inability to control work stressors and lack of professional support are important factors in the etiology of CF and other stress responses (Radey & Figley, 2007). Thus, lack of supervision and exposure to particularly challenging or overwhelming clients contributes to DD. Being on an extended tour of duty can push a person past her limits of caring as well. Although some organizations have a collaborative orientation, interpersonally engaged staff, and procedures for protecting employees from burnout and other forms of stress, many others are much more atomized and productivity driven and leave individual clinicians fending for themselves.

Having access to friends and family and the ability to engage in self-care activities helps mitigate against DD, but this is often difficult to achieve in the field. Responding to disasters takes people away from their support systems, and the intensity, chaos, and lack of safety in disaster zones can make self-care and relaxation strategies difficult to implement.

SPECIAL ISSUES FOR FIRST AND UNIFORMED RESPONDERS

Responders encompass a large and diverse group of people. Responders in uniform—police, firefighters, paramedics, first responders, the National Guard, and other military and law enforcement officials—have unique professional cultures and needs. These are often the first responders at a disaster site, and they experience the raw destruction and the immediate tragic consequences of the event. Some, such as police, firefighters, and military veterans, have had repeated exposure to critical incidents, while others, such as newly recruited National Guard men and women, may be encountering disaster for the first time.

Recurring exposure is a double-edged sword. On the one hand, it can help responders develop a tougher skin and manage chaotic situations—which would be overwhelming for many people—with cool and aplomb. On the other hand, constant exposure to stressful situations can take a collective toll, leading to CF and depleting a person psychologically and emotionally. This may account for why firefighters and paramedics have high rates of drinking during their leisure time (Canfield, 2005). I have also found in my work that even the most experienced and hardened uniformed responders are vulnerable to certain types of critical situations. A common one is the loss of life of a child or teenager. Many police and firefighters have broken into tears when recounting responding to a scene where a child died. When the responders have children of their own, the empathic identification with the victims and their families can be powerful.

Other major stressors for uniformed responders are threatening situations and the death or injury of one of their own. These were a major source of anguish for police and firefighters responding to 9/11 in New York City. The video *When Helping Hurts* (Within Foundation, 1998) has a segment featuring a firefighter who lost one comrade while responding to a fire and witnessed another suffer severe injuries that permanently impaired her vision. The featured firefighter was injured himself and had to take time off from work. He felt trepidation about returning to the front lines and seemed to be experiencing some form of trauma reaction. A theme that he articulates in the video is a sense of responsibility for the misfortunes of his coworkers and what can be termed "survivor guilt," which is common among uniformed responders when a colleague has been killed or injured.

Regehr and Bober (2005) confirm in their research that the death of a child, personal threat of injury, and the loss of a colleague are difficult situations for uniformed responders. In addition, their research indicates that scenes of extreme violence, multiple casualties, and death are also sources of stress and trauma in the line of duty. Even those who respond to disasters on a regular basis may experience situations that still pierce the protective membranes that have thickened over time.

To do their jobs, uniformed responders need a certain degree of hardiness, and signs of weakness or vulnerability can make it more difficult for them to carry out their responsibilities. Managing their empathy and protecting against demonstrative expression of feelings helps them respond to very emotionally charged situations. I have often encountered suspicion and skepticism from uniformed responders toward mental health workers and mental health jargon. Although their reactions are understandable and even well founded at times, this might, at least partially, be their way of keeping vulnerability at bay. It reveals an attitude held by some uniformed responders. They see most mental health workers as not having to deal with the same realities and responsibilities that uniformed responders do; therefore, in their minds, the clinicians lack credibility.

On the positive side, a strong in-group bond often develops between uniformed responders, supporting and helping to sustain them through difficult situations. New York City firefighters describe their job as "a way of life" (Greene, Kane, Christ, Lynch, & Corrigan, 2006, p. 35). This is one reason that debriefings are so popular among this population, as these are a group-building type of intervention. The use of teasing and humor also helps team members to discharge difficult feelings. But the humor can also mask the pain and suffering that uniformed responders may be feeling. And while there is solidarity among team members, the transition to family life can be difficult. Many uniformed workers with whom I have worked have indicated that they are reluctant to share their experiences with family members. This can be to spare them the stress of vicariously experiencing the traumatic events or because there is a sense that people outside of the work team will be unable to understand what the experience was like. Family members have reported to me that under such circumstances, they feel alienated and distant from their partners. Thus, family interventions can be useful in addition to directly working with the team of uniformed responders (Greene et al., 2006; Regehr & Bober, 2005).

PREVENTION AND AMELIORATION

Many approaches to mitigate against secondary stress disorders can be taken *before* people respond to disasters, *during* their actual response time, and *after* they have completed their interventions. A good place to start in this discussion is to consider what it means to experience "compassion satisfaction" (Radey & Figley, 2007).

COMPASSION SATISFACTION

Radey and Figley (2007) have reversed the lens by asking what conditions lead to compassion satisfaction (CS). This approach lends itself to the perspective taken in this book, which seeks to understand what fosters resiliency and satisfaction. The authors found that "flourishing" occurs when offering services to others "connotes goodness, flexibility, learning, growth and resilience" (p. 208). They argue that there is a three-way relationship among resources (physical, intellectual, social), affect, and self-care. All have the potential to positively influence one another—self-care can enhance positive affect while positive affect can lead to having and accessing more resources. The authors have devised a "positivity ratio" (p. 210), which establishes the relative amount of positive affect to negative, and have found that flourishing usually occurs when this ratio is at least 3 to 1 on the positive side of the ledger. As Ruysschaert (2009, p. 163) puts it: "Compassion Satisfaction mitigates Compassion Fatigue." Thus, preventing DD involves both reducing the exposure to and impact from overwhelming events and profound suffering and also increasing compassion satisfaction.

SELF-AUDITS

One way to try to prevent DD or to respond to it when it occurs is for disaster responders to engage in the practice of administering self-audits. These can be done before, during, and after disaster response. This is a simple, low-tech way that practitioners can track their own responses and know when self-care is called for. A good starting place is to self-administer the Personal Quality of Life Scale (Stamm, 1999; www.proqol.org/ProQol_Test.html). If completed before disaster response, the test can establish a personal baseline, and if done during or after disaster response, it can help highlight and identify symptoms of both CF and CS, which may indicate the need for remedial action.

The audit presented here (table 12.1) focuses on a range of actions that workers can take to enhance their well-being and guard against DD. It is an

TABLE 12.1 Self-Audit to Prevent Disaster Distress

AREA	ACTIVITIES
1. Investment	Identify goals (professional and personal) *before* responding Uncover personal needs that may be tied up in goals Monitor while in the field and afterward Avoid critical judgment
2. Empathic engagement and identification with clients	Seek empathy with boundaries Track sources of strong, negative feelings Be mindful of postural mimicking and somatic mirroring Identify personal triggers and schemas
3. Supervision and support	Buddy system Regular supervision Regular team meetings Groups Postdisaster transition supports
4. The basics	Ensure adequate food and water intake Get rest and sleep
5. Physical activity	Develop routines *before* responding to disaster Identify time to do physical activity while in the field Continue after disaster response
6. Recreational activities	Identify activities before disaster that are portable Bring materials (pen, paper) to the field Ensure some engagement with activities, however brief
7. Mindfulness and meaning	Engage in journaling, conversations, meetings Develop mindfulness practices before responding Practice mindfulness exercises in the field Maintain broad perspective Integrate beauty and suffering Seek to create meaning Work to generate positive emotions Imagine metaphors of strength and resilience
8. Connection with others	Identify important people Work out methods of communication in advance Track frequency of social contacts, monitor possible isolation
9. Help when wounded	Professional resources—colleagues, supervisors Personal supports Clinical resources Self-help and mutual support with other wounded workers

opportunity for responders to ask questions of themselves and to map out self-protective strategies. The following are key areas of inquiry that can be included in the audit.

INVESTMENT   Workers can ask themselves before responding to a disaster what they hope to accomplish and what is manageable versus overreaching. Sometimes it is better to set lower goals rather than goals that are too high, as it is important to feel as if there has been some progress and success. One can always exceed goals, but it is disappointing when they are set very high and not achieved. Part of the audit should involve checking one's personal investment and what personal needs and issues might be part of one's hopes and goals. This should be done gently—not in a judgmental way but rather as an act of checking in and behaving as one's own consultant. It is helpful to use this exercise as a baseline and reminder while actually responding to the disaster and when reflecting on and assessing how the interventions went after the direct work is completed.

EMPATHIC ENGAGEMENT AND IDENTIFICATION WITH CLIENTS   Disaster responders engaged in psychosocial capacity building rely on the use of relationship, whether that is with individuals, families, or groups. This involves empathic engagement with clients, many of whom have experienced severe stress, possible trauma, and tragic losses. Empathy involves the activation of mirror neurons, so the responder's body may literally feel many of the same reactions as the disaster survivor (Rothschild, 2006; Ruysschaert, 2009). Often, somatic mirroring occurs unconsciously; it is part of an interactive dance people engage in to communicate with one another. One dimension of this is postural mimicking, in which the worker assumes the client's body position (Rothschild, 2006). When doing this, workers may not notice that they have also assumed many of the survivor's feelings—anger, sadness, fear. Thus, the empathy needed to be helpful to others can also lead to the ingesting of negative feelings—a form of emotional contagion in which responders may be feeling distressed without an awareness of what engendered these feelings (Rothschild, 2006).

Responders carry unresolved issues when they engage with clients, and these can be inadvertently activated. Before responding to a disaster, it is helpful to go over trigger points and schemas that may be activated when in the field—for instance, a schema that makes a person feel valuable if others acknowledge the individual's effort or makes the person feel the need to perform at heroic levels to have a sense of professional value and self-worth. While in the field, it is always helpful to track strong emotional and affective reactions to clients and situations as well as to monitor relationships in which there are passionate feelings of attachment and investment. This too should be done from an inquisitive and nonjudgmental stance. Inevitably, workers will become very attached to and engaged with clients, sometimes in deep emotional ways, but there is a better chance of not getting caught up in an emotional vortex or riptide if there is consistent monitoring and awareness of these reactions.

It is also important to maintain clear boundaries and set limits (Harrison & Westwood, 2009), which can be achieved with attention to emotional investment. At the same time, Harrison and Westwood, who interviewed experienced trauma therapists, found that empathy is an important source of meaning and satisfaction—it is part of why people do trauma and disaster work. As long as this deep empathy is experienced in a relationship with clear boundaries, then it is more likely to engender positive emotions and less likely to lead to VT or DD. Boundary setting also involves mindfulness about the limits of our ability to help others (Rand, 2004). While we can empathically witness other people's suffering, we do not have the power to relieve them of their burden.

SUPERVISION, CONSULTATION, AND PEER SUPPORT   It should be evident by now that it is essential to have teammates who help disaster workers maintain perspective and buffer and protect them from the excesses that are latent in any disaster situation. Supervision is an important part of this process and should be provided whenever possible. It involves offering guidance, feedback, limit setting, and critical evaluations, all of which are helpful in the process of self-care. Consultation from other team members is also valuable. It can help to have a buddy system, pairing team members to look out for one another. Regular team meetings, including daily debriefings when in the field, offer a place to ventilate and process reactions as well as to receive feedback and support.

Groups, both informal and formal, are a good mechanism for fostering solidarity and team support. Ulman (2008) notes that groups foster a sense of community and that talking about DD issues can normalize reactions and reduce feelings of shame. Clemans (2004) recommends single-group sessions that educate about the nature of VT and help group members increase their self-awareness and articulate self-care strategies that reinforce the balance between work and home.

One of the more challenging aspects of responding to a disaster is the aftermath—managing the transition back to a noncrisis way of life. Many of the foregoing are significant interventions after returning from a disaster, although workers often are resistant to using them, and organizations often do not make them available.

THE BASICS By "the basics," I mean that responders must make sure they get adequate sleep, food, and water. Although it is easy for responders to assume they have got the basics covered, at least for workers living in communities where sufficient food and potable water are available, they can be forgotten in the turmoil of a disaster. The physical, psychological, and emotional exertion needed in disaster response requires fuel. It also requires rest and at least some sleep, even if it is less than usual. Consciously auditing food and water intake can help responders make sure the basics are not dropped while they are in the line of duty.

PHYSICAL ACTIVITY Physical activity and exercise are important for anyone engaged in stressful work, and it can be useful to develop regular routines and exercise habits before responding to a disaster. Activities that are portable are particularly helpful—such as running, walking, yoga, or calisthenics. During disaster response, it is often challenging to find time to engage in physical activity or to find a place where this can occur. But as part of the self-care audit, at least some modified activity schedule can be maintained. Much of this requires accepting the importance of physical activity and trying to find a time (usually early in the morning or late in the day) to do it. It is helpful to maintain an exercise schedule after the disaster work. Physical activity decreases harmful internal toxins, reduces stress, and contributes to positive emotions and a strong sense of self.

RECREATIONAL ACTIVITIES Part of the audit can be focused on what kinds of enjoyable activities can be engaged in while in the field. Reading, writing, listening to music on an iPod or MP3 player, singing, and playing music are a few examples of relatively portable activities that many people find relaxing, distracting, and enjoyable. They are good transition activities, especially at the end of the day, and help with letting go of some of the recurrent images that are endemic to disaster response work. Keeping track of this on a daily basis can make it more likely that responders will include these important activities in their daily schedules.

MINDFULNESS AND MEANING It helps responders to be able to make sense of what they are encountering and to be able to construct meaning. There are many ways to do this. Simply journaling at the end of each day helps to reconstruct experiences and to both record them and to let them go. Having a daily meeting or chat with a colleague to process the day is another way to make meaning of events. Mindfulness practices are extremely useful, whether they are focused on breathing, beauty, Vipassana, loving-kindness, Tonglen, guided imagery, Zen meditation, body awareness, yoga movement, transcendence, self-hypnosis, prayer, chanting, or simply being present. It is, of course, helpful to develop a practice or set of practice skills prior to engaging with a disaster so that the practice feels comfortable and familiar. Practicing in a disaster zone presents its challenges—finding time and privacy, dealing with distractions and uncomfortable conditions—but it is possible to practice some sort of mindfulness in any situation, if only for a few minutes.

Harrison and Westwood (2009) found that clinicians kept their frames of reference broad and expanded the perspectives of their consciousness and awareness through use of imagery and metaphors. This practice helped them embrace ambiguity and hold and tolerate cognitive complexity, including the simultaneous awareness of both suffering and beauty. They found that "ultimately, this expanded perspective encompassed openness to the unknown, and a belief or tacit sense that meaning and purpose transcend the limits of individual identity, language and quantifiable knowledge" (p. 210). Also, mindfulness is a way to focus on positive emotions and achieve "active optimism" (p. 211). Specifically, it can help to imagine metaphors of resilience (Ruysschaert, 2009), such as wearing protective armor.

After returning from disaster work, another layer of meaning-making can occur when one looks back from a place less embedded in the disaster. Perspective can be gained with some time and distance. It can help to reflect on the overall experience and to see how the various parts of the self-audit worked, or did not work, and to make mental notes and suggestions for future adjustments and adaptations. For some people, talking with others after disaster response is a helpful way to make sense of what happened, while for other people, writing formal and informal essays on the experience or giving presentations can help articulate a narrative that gives meaning to the work.

CONNECTION WITH OTHERS Social isolation is a risk factor and contributor to DD. People vary in how much they like to be in the company of others and what they feel comfortable sharing. With the possible exception of solitary monks, it is important for all disaster responders to maintain some social connections. These can be in person, through letters, or by telephone or text, Twitter, e-mail, Skype, and other forms of electronic communication. What is important is to engage with people whom you are not trying to help and where there is sharing, mutuality, and emotional connection. Family, friends, and colleagues all can play important, helpful roles, depending on the needs and style of the responder. Using an audit to keep track of social contacts can help responders see how often they are in connection with others, who is particularly helpful, and which social connections are most (or least) sought after. This can serve to alert people to times when they are withdrawing and as a reminder that more outreach may be called for.

HELP WHEN WOUNDED All the previous strategies should minimize the risks of disaster distress and should be helpful if DD sets in. The techniques work as long as responders are able to recognize their own reactions and have the capacity to counter them with self-care strategies. Danieli (cited in Rosenfeld et al., 2005) encourages people to take the time to heal and recover when wounded from disaster work. Part of this is accepting that the experience of responding to the disaster is transformative and that one may not feel the same way about the world and one's place in it as before. But Danieli reminds responders that the emotional reactions (such as sadness, grief, rage) that are precipitated by empathic engagement with disaster survivors can tap into old wounds and schemas that have not yet been resolved.

Thus, disaster responders sometimes need help outside of their own resources. Supervisors, as well as other colleagues and friends, may give feedback or make suggestions that are hard to accept and even provoke resistance. Our professional and social networks are not always on target when they give us advice, but as they care about and know us, they often provide important feedback that is worth listening to. When wounded, we can lose our ability to self-audit and reflect and can be enveloped by sadness, melancholy, and a sense of ineffectiveness. Sometimes we need others to draw attention to our wounds and to help us to figure out pathways out of our dark moods. This may include seeking counseling or therapy or spiritual guidance. Mutual-aid and support groups with other people who have suffered wounds is also helpful. Establishing a network of people who can help us when we are wounded is important to do *before* we are psychically injured, as once that happens we may lose sight of what we need to do for ourselves.

I know this from firsthand experience. When I was twenty-five and living and working abroad, one of my clients was murdered by her husband in front of her children (Miller, 2001b). I developed many symptoms of secondary traumatic stress—intrusive and recurring images, hyperalertness, avoidance of triggering stimuli, and an overriding sense of guilt and responsibility. I had few friends and was overloaded at work. The sense of responsibility coupled with being young and alone meant that I could work many hours with the survivors of the family. Although this seemed to be helpful for them, and certainly gave me professional and personal meaning, it was also debilitating and impossible to sustain. When my supervisor offered a consultation with a psychiatrist because she was concerned about me, I was guarded, resistant, and wary of showing signs of weakness. It took me years to recover from and process this event. Yet, on the positive side, it is a source of motivation for my current work with disaster responders.

ORGANIZATIONAL ISSUES

Disaster distress is not just the responsibility of the worker. Organizations need to help to protect workers from DD and create conditions in which they can achieve compassion satisfaction. Organizations have an ethical responsibility to care for their workers and this in turn benefits the organization. When workers are experiencing DD and related disorders, they are often less effective on the job. They have higher rates of absenteeism, more sickness, lower morale, and poorer quality of care and services (White, 2006).

Organizations can take many steps to support and assist workers. Ensuring adequate supervision is critical. It is also important to make sure workers have balanced work assignments so that they are not always dealing with the most stressful and disturbing situations. In addition, organizations can create schedules that encourage workers to have breaks and time to recoup, recover, and relax. Offering training and educational opportunities for workers helps them to understand the risks of the work and the symptoms of DD and to develop strategies for individual and team self-care. Pearlman and Saakvitne (1995) stress the importance of pleasant work spaces, adequate resources, and a culture of respect. What is most important is an overall work situation that fosters human connection, compassion toward employees, and a willingness to protect and care for workers. While work spaces and resources are not always optimal in disaster situations, organizations can try their best under the circumstances: respect for the worker is part of an organizational culture that can be adapted to many different work environments.

Disaster distress refers to a range of negative reactions that workers and volunteers may experience while responding to a disaster. This can happen to anyone, although some disaster situations are more likely to cause DD than others. Empathic engagement with disaster survivors is a source of meaning for responders, but it also can be a door through which there is emotional contagion. Having unrealistic goals, being professionally and socially isolated, and having vulnerabilities, such as a history of trauma, are other factors that can contribute to DD.

Responders should develop self-care plans that help lead to greater compassion satisfaction and reduce the risk of DD. A useful tool is the self-audit, which responders can use to plan, implement, and monitor self-care activities. Responders should seek help when wounded and organizations should aid in this process. Agencies and programs need to proactively plan and assess how workers and volunteers placed in triggering situations will be given the resources, protections, and supports they need and are entitled to.

MINDFULNESS EXERCISE: MIRRORING AND UNMIRRORING

This exercise is adapted from Rothschild (2006). Based on her research into how people develop somatic empathy through mirroring and mimicking, she has created "unmirroring" exercises. These involve consciously breaking an empathic connection when it is leaving us with negative emotions. Rothschild's exercises are done in pairs. This adaptation is for work on your own.

Assume a straight posture and focus on your breathing. Notice how your body feels sitting up straight and then concentrate on your breath. After about five minutes, imagine someone you know or have worked with who is or was feeling distressed. (It is better for the purposes of this exercise not to recall someone who in any way abused you or a situation in which someone was out of control.) If you have trouble doing this, it might be easier to recall a scene from a film in which someone is fearful, sad, or angry, or you might try to visualize yourself when you were a child and upset about something. Whomever you visualize, notice facial expressions and posture. Perhaps the person hunches over or crosses his or her arms. Maybe the individual fur-rows his or her brow or frowns frequently. Try to mimic both the individual's facial expression and posture.

After doing this, notice what you may be experiencing. What are some of your thoughts and feelings? Where do you experience sensations in your body? Notice your breathing—is it the same, faster, or shallower? Are there any narratives that accompany your images?

After conducting this inventory, shift your posture—perhaps sit up and recross your legs—adjust your face, and try to frame your mouth in a smile. Focus on your breathing for a few moments to settle into your new posture and facial expression. After doing this, check in and see how your body feels and whether you notice any changes in your mood or thinking. Notice whether your pattern of breathing has changed.

After scanning your sensations and reactions for a few minutes, return to your breath and just focus on it, remaining in an upright posture. No-tice whether there are any residual uncomfortable feelings. If so, imagine breathing them out and breathing in bright and light air. Gradually bring yourself back to the present as you notice the contact points between your body and the chair or cushion.

CONCLUSION

THIS BOOK begins with a vignette describing work with a Vietnamese American family living on the Gulf Coast in the aftermath of Hurricane Katrina. The encounter produced more questions than answers, and I recognize that while this book has grappled with some of those questions, many still remain. Psychosocial capacity building will never be science, although it can be informed by scientific inquiry and evaluation; it always involves a certain degree of creativity and spontaneity, which is inherent in collaboration. And collaboration is at the heart of psychosocial capacity building. Questions inform such inventiveness.

The book defines the process of disaster and considers ways of conceptualizing different types of disasters, introducing the concept of the social ecology of disaster. The psychological impact and meaning of disaster can be understood only in relation to history, culture, social structures and processes, economics, and politics. While there are many important tools and strategies available to clinicians working from a disaster mental health orientation, a psychosocial capacity building approach builds on cultural traditions, is multisystemic, supports indigenous strengths and resiliency, and has the potential to continue long after clinicians from the outside have returned home. Thus, the role of clinicians when responding to disaster is not only to help people heal through professional interventions but to work alongside affected people as they reconstruct *their* communities. The book summarizes typical reactions to disaster but also stresses how suffering and recovery are culturally shaped and constructed. It argues that it is essential not only to focus on vulnerability and trauma as a consequence of disaster but to recognize and validate the impressive sources of strength and resiliency carried by individuals, families, and communities.

Emphasizing strengths and sources of resiliency does not mean that people and communities are invulnerable to the consequences of disaster; disaster causes great losses, tremendous pain, and suffering. Some groups are particularly vulnerable when disaster strikes, as is discussed in chapter 6. When there is intergroup conflict, either as a disaster in its own right or serving as part of the social ecology of other forms of disaster, suffering and vulnerability increase. However, while disasters destroy, people rebuild; while communities are shattered, community is reconstituted. There is an unending tension between the negative effects of disaster and the positive responses disaster evokes, between cycles of destruction and regeneration; they are part of the same circle.

Prevention and intervention are also part of the same circle. In southern Taiwan, cyclones strike with great regularity, causing landslides, flooding, loss of life, the destruction of homes, washed-out roads, and disrupted communication and social connections. Social workers and other professionals and volunteers in disaster stations work with affected families and communities to rebuild but also to prepare for these seasonal disasters. Using early warning systems, implementing better communication practices, and building houses in safer places are but a few examples of where prevention and intervention flow into each other. Practice and rehearsal of evacuation plans can lead to future security while deepening a sense of mastery. Safety and efficacy have been emphasized throughout the book, and engaging local people to plan for prevention helps them to feel more secure and in control of their lives. This may protect them in the future, and by knowing this, it may also help them recover from the previous disaster.

This book encourages practitioners to go beyond working with individuals, as important as this is, and to work with families, groups, and communities. There are many benefits and advantages to working in groups and using activities that can be employed particularly in cultures and societies where talk therapy is not normative. There are risks for practitioners responding to disasters, although self-care strategies, such as mindfulness exercises, help circumvent damage from these risks.

ELEVEN ESSENTIAL PRINCIPLES OF PRACTICE

Psychosocial capacity building is a complex, multifaceted way of responding to disasters. It can be challenging, therefore, to distill the complexity of psychosocial capacity building down to a simple inventory of what should be done. Yet it can be helpful for practitioners to have a set of standards to guide their work. What follows are eleven essential principles of practice that have been developed throughout the book and can serve as a framework for helping people and communities recover from a disaster.

1. Outside responders have much to offer but should be mindful of risks: do no harm.

2. The key to assessing the needs of various people and groups in the community after disaster is to understand the unique social ecology of the disaster.

3. Outside responders should work to build the capacity of local people and support systems and institutions that are part of the community; they will be there for the long haul.

4. Meaning-making is a critical task for individuals, families, and communities. It serves to integrate disasters with what came before, what follows, and what is anticipated and hoped for in the future.

5. Meaning-making is intricately linked to cultural beliefs, values, and practices, and although the desire to construct meaning after a disaster is universal, the ways that this is done and the conclusions drawn will vary considerably across cultures.

6. Social connectedness and social cohesion are essential aspects of disaster recovery; groups help foster social relations.

7. The most effective disaster responses are multisystemic, linking individual and family healing with community recovery.

8. Psychosocial healing contributes to peace and social justice, and vice versa.

9. While disasters cause harm, what most helps individuals and communities mend and make progress is encouraging them to draw on their strengths while fostering resiliency and emphasizing efficacy.

10. Self-care is critical to the well-being and effectiveness of disaster responders and should be an organizational priority—part of the preparation and support of all disaster responders.

11. Whenever possible, intervention strategies should be evidenced based—but what constitutes evidence and the design and implementation of evaluation should involve local people. Moreover, attention must be paid to the process of intervention as well as specific outcomes.

HELPING WHILE NOT HINDERING

There will always be disasters, and with population growth, shrinking and depleted natural resources, and climate change, they may occur more frequently and with greater severity. Governments, NGOs, and local communities must work together to prepare for and respond to disasters, which are an inevitable part of the human condition. There are likely to be more frequent natural disasters with profound consequences and greater competition among countries and regions for limited assets. "Natural" disasters will lead to technological disasters, as the 2011 earthquake and tsunami in Japan led to nuclear catastrophe. Countries will tighten their borders as more people seek to leave conflict areas or regions where danger is ubiquitous and jobs scarce. Insatiable appetites for energy in developed, and increasingly in developing, countries will not only fuel conflicts but also lead to increasingly risky strategies for extracting sources of energy, placing environments and economies in jeopardy. The British Petroleum catastrophe on the United States' Gulf Coast in 2010, when a deepwater accident opened up an uncontrollable oil spill, is but one example of this.

Most parts of the world are in regular communication with other parts of the world—and information and culture are spread at unprecedented speed. When a major disaster strikes anywhere, many more people around the world are aware of it than in the past. Increasingly, when disasters occur, organizations and people from many countries respond. Even the wealthiest and most powerful nations can use outside help when a catastrophic disaster occurs; Japanese relief organizations were initially overwhelmed by the scale of the 2011 earthquake/tsunami/nuclear reactor disaster and requested help from other countries. With improvements in telecommunications there are even more opportunities for international collaboration, including virtual interventions. It is now possible to offer ongoing professional support, consultation, and supervision in one country to local people on the ground in another. This is exciting and expands the possibilities for sharing knowledge and resources. It also heightens the risk of imposing cultural values and models of intervention and recovery suitable for one group but not for another.

Disasters remind us of how interconnected and interdependent we all are. We all rely on family, friends, neighbors, and community resources—government, social services, police, emergency services, hospitals, employers, religious and spiritual communities, civic organizations, and NGOs. None of us stands alone on his or her own two feet; our feet are always planted on a social platform—constructed on historical foundations—alongside the feet of others. This is not only true within our local communities but true of an increasingly interdependent world. A housing crisis in the United States affects share prices of equities in Japan. Economic contractions in one part of the world draw down industries in other regions. A war or a nuclear power plant explosion in one country affects its neighbors.

While disasters lurk in our future, legacies of the colonial past still haunt the world. As I have stressed throughout the book, disaster can happen any-where, but the poor and socially disadvantaged, marginalized, and targeted are most vulnerable and have the fewest resources to aid their recovery. This is true within developed nations but is also a worldwide pattern. It is not that developing nations are disproportionately located in disaster zones, but they are more vulnerable to the consequences of disaster, often because of colonial legacies. As a result, they have fewer resources, weaker infrastruc-tures, diminished services, and people living in dwellings and cities that offer less protection against earthquakes, floods, and fires. Many developing nations, particularly in Africa, have boundaries that are colonial creations, setting up tribes and ethnic groups to vie for power and influence, leading to wars and conflict. Western nations, and increasingly China, are still exploit-ing the natural resources of developing nations, contributing to conflicts in economically poor but mineral-rich areas, such as eastern Congo, where unending war is a colonial bequest and contemporary nightmare. Within developed nations, the legacy of colonialism and historical patterns of injus-tice are manifested by closed borders, increased economic disparities, and racism and other forms of discrimination.

As has been the case throughout history and is true today, powerful na-tions send troops into weaker countries, often at great cost to lives, local cultural practices, and social cohesion. International entities, such as the World Bank, ensure that nations with less continue to pay back loans to countries—often former colonizers—with more. Haiti is but one historical example of a country brought to its knees for centuries by Western powers through debt repayments and embargoes *before* the crippling earthquake of 2010 struck. Its inability to respond effectively to the disaster is not a histori-cal accident.

This may seem an odd place to conclude a book about how clinicians can respond to disasters. I bring up these legacies and current disparities to emphasize two points. The first is that imposing on underdeveloped non-Western nations a Western psychological approach to disaster response, however well intentioned, is a continuation of a colonial legacy. It is a softer version to be sure, but cultural domination works alongside economic, political, and military oppression. As I have emphasized, Western psychology is not inherently bad and has the potential to help many disaster survivors. But when it is imposed in an uncritical and universalistic fashion, it not only helps but subjugates.

The second point is that clinicians residing in developed nations (where most clinicians are based) have benefited from the fruits of colonialism, even though this is an abhorrent idea to most practitioners. Unexamined social and economic privilege plays an enormous role in sustaining severe worldwide inequality as well as feeding economic disparities within developed nations, re-creating colonial patterns and maintaining a neocolonial social and economic order. At the very least, those of us living in developed nations must not actively perpetuate the systems that have privileged some at the expense of many. We owe it to the people we are trying to help—whether they live within or outside of our borders. As trained professionals, we bring skills but we also carry baggage. There is a political and moral imperative for those responding to disasters to deconstruct social and economic privilege and cultural assumptions, including those that place us in the position of helper. And the responder is very much part of the contemporary social ecology of most, if not all, responses to disaster. If social justice and psychosocial healing cannot be separated, then the positioning of responders must also be subject to critical analysis.

As clinicians, we seek to alleviate suffering while helping people heal, repair, and regain a sense of their own autonomy. These are admirable aspirations and attract many dedicated, committed, and compassionate people to the helping professions. Many people are helped by clinical interventions. Poor people in developing nations who experience disaster may benefit from counseling and psychological first aid. But they will benefit more from thriving economies, infrastructure development, social networks, and democratic and functioning governments. With these structures and resources in place, the people *themselves* have the tools and capacity to prepare for and respond to disasters. In the long run, this must be the goal of disaster mental health—to help individuals and communities direct their own lives and obtain the psychosocial capacities and resources to be as protected from the consequences of disaster as those who respond to them. We are partners in this project—those who have survived and those from the outside who respond to help—and the less social distance between us the more collaborative our work together. Collaboration and connection are what protect us from catastrophe and help us heal when it occurs. Disasters remind us of our vulnerability and fragility—but also of our connections with others and shared destinies. It is to the strength and fortitude of disaster survivors, the compassion and commitment of those who try to help, and the collective response to adversity that this book is dedicated.

REFERENCES

Adams, J. (2007). Tale of two cities: Biloxi and New Orleans. MSNBC. Retrieved June 30, 2011, from http://www.cnn.com/2007/US/08/29/katrina.twocities/index .html

Adams, R. E., Boscarino, J. A., & Figley, C. R. (2006). Compassion fatigue and psychological stress among social workers: A validation study. *American Journal of Orthopsychiatry, 76*(1), 103–108.

Adams, R. E., Figley, C. R., & Boscarino, J. A. (2008). The compassion fatigue scale: Its use with social workers following urban disaster. *Research on Social Work Practice, 18,* 238–250.

Ager, A. (1997). Tensions in the psychosocial discourse: Implications for the planning of interventions with war-affected populations. *Development in Practice, 7*(4), 402–407.

Ager, A., Boothby, N., & Bremer, M. (2008). Using the "protective environment" framework to analyze children's protective needs in Darfur. *Disasters, 33*(4), 548–573.

Alexander, D. A. (2005). Early mental health intervention after disasters. *Advances in Psychiatric Treatment, 11,* 12–18.

Alexander, J. C. (2004). Toward a theory of cultural trauma. In J. C. Alexander, R. Eyerman, B. Giesen, N. J. Smelser, & P. Sztompka (Eds.), *Cultural trauma and collective identity* (pp. 1–30). Berkeley: University of California Press.

Allen, J. (2001). *Traumatic relationships and serious mental disorders.* New York: Wiley.

Allen, P. D., & Nelson, H. W. (2009). Disaster services with frail older persons: From preparation to recovery. In K. E. Cherry (Ed.), *Lifespan perspectives on natural disasters: Coping with Katrina, Rita, and other storms* (pp. 153–169). New York: Springer.

American Psychiatric Association. (1994). *Diagnostic and statistical manual of mental disorders* (4th ed.). Washington, DC: Author.

American Red Cross. (2006). *Disaster mental health services.* Washington, DC: Author.

Armstrong, K., O'Callahan, W., & Marmar, C. R. (1991). Debriefing Red Cross disaster personnel: The multiple stressor debriefing model. *Journal of Traumatic Stress, 4*(4), 581–593.

Armstrong, K., Zatzick, D., Metzler, T., Weiss, D. S., Marmar, C. R., Garma, S., Ronfeldt, H., & Roepke, L. (1998). Debriefing of American Red Cross personnel: A pilot study on participants' evaluations and case examples from the 1994 Los Angeles earthquake relief operation. *Social Work in Health Care, 27*(1), 33–50.

Atrocities against Tamils alleged in Sri Lanka's war. (2010, May 17). *The Columbus Dispatch.* Retrieved June 12, 2010, from http://www.dispatch.com/live/content/national_world/stories/2010/05/17/atrocities-against-tamils-alleged.html

Australian Centre for Posttraumatic Mental Health. (2007). *Australian guidelines for treatment of adults with acute stress disorder and posttraumatic stress disorder.* Retrieved December 9, 2009, from the Australian National Health and Medical Research Council Web site: http://www.nhmrc.gov.au/_files_nhmrc/file/publications/synopses/mh13.pdf

Baraz, J. (2010). Lighten up: Buddhism's not such a raw deal. *Tricycle.* Retrieved March 22, 2009, from http://www.tricycle.com/dharma-talk/lighten-up?page=0,2

Barboza, D. (2009, March 19). Artist defies web censors in a rebuke of China. *The New York Times.* Retrieved March 23, 2009, from http://www.nytimes.com/2009/03/20/world/asia/20quake.html?emc=tnt&tntemail1=y

Bar-Tal, D. (2007). Sociopsychological foundations of intractable conflicts. *American Behavioral Scientist, 50*(11), 1430–1453.

Benedek, D. M. (2007). Acute stress disorder and post-traumatic stress disorder in the disaster environment. In R. J. Ursano, C. S. Fullerton, L. Weisaeth, & B. Raphael (Eds.), *Textbook of disaster psychiatry* (pp. 140–163). Cambridge: Cambridge University Press.

Betancourt, T. S., & Kahn, K. T. (2007). The mental health of children affected by armed conflict: Protective processes and pathways to resilience. *International Review of Psychiatry, 20*(3), 317–328.

Bisson, J. I., McFarlane, A. C., & Rose, S. (2000). Psychological debriefing. In E. B. Foa, T. M. Keane, & M. J. Friedman (Eds.), *Effective treatments for PTSD: Practice guidelines from the International Society for Traumatic Stress Studies* (pp. 39–59). New York: Guilford.

Bolin, B. (2006). Race, class, ethnicity, and disaster vulnerability. In H. Rodriguez, E. L. Quarantelli, & R. R. Dynes (Eds.), *Handbook of disaster research* (pp. 113–129). New York: Springer.

Bonanno, G. A. (2004). Loss, trauma, and human resilience: Have we underestimated the capacity to thrive after extremely aversive events? *American Psychologist, 59*(1), 20–28.

Borland, M. (2003). The Gacaca tribunals and Rwanda after genocide: Effective community restorative justice or further abuse of human rights? *Swords and Ploughshares, 13*(2), 1–10.

Boss, P. (2006). *Loss, trauma, and resilience: Therapeutic work with ambiguous loss.* New York: W. W. Norton.

Boss, P., Beaulieu, L., Wieling, E., Turner, W., & LaCruz, S. (2003). Healing loss, ambiguity, and trauma: A community-based intervention after the 9/11 attack in New York City. *Journal of Marital and Family Therapy, 29*(4), 455–467.

Boyden, J., de Berry, J., Feeny, T., & Hart, J. (2006). Children affected by armed conflict in South Asia: A regional summary. In G. Reyes & G. A. Jacobs (Eds.), *Handbook of international disaster psychology: Vol. 4. Interventions with special needs populations* (pp. 61–76). New York: Praeger.

Brewer, M. B. (2001). Ingroup identification and intergroup conflict: When does ingroup love become outgroup hate? In R. D. Ashmore, L. Jussim, & D. Wilder (Eds.), *Social identity, intergroup conflict, and conflict resolution* (pp. 17–41). New York: Oxford University Press.

British Broadcasting Corporation. (2005, March 26). *Most tsunami dead female—Oxfam.* Retrieved June 2, 2010, from http://news.bbc.co.uk/2/hi/asia-pacific/4383573.stm

Broneus, K. (2008). Truth-telling as talking cure? Insecurity and retraumatization in the Rwandan Gacaca courts. *Security Dialogue, 39,* 55–76.

Brookings Institution Metropolitan Policy Program. (2005). *New Orleans after the storm: Lessons from the past, a plan for the future.* Washington, DC: The Brookings Institution.

Bryant-Davis, T. (2005). *Thriving in the wake of trauma: A multicultural guide.* Westport, CT: Praeger.

Canfield, J. (2005). Secondary traumatization, burnout, and vicarious traumatization: A review of the literature as it relates to therapists who treat trauma. *Smith College Studies in Social Work, 75*(2), 81–101.

Chakraborty, A. (1991). Culture, colonialism, and psychiatry. *The Lancet, 337*(8751), 1204–1207.

Chan, C. L. W., Chow, A. Y. M., Ho, S. M. Y., Tsui, Y. K. Y., Tin, A. F., Koo, B. W. K., & Koo, E. W. K. (2005). The experience of Chinese bereaved persons: A preliminary study of meaning making and continuing bonds. *Death Studies, 29,* 923–947.

Charuvastra, A., & Cloitre, M. (2008). Social bonds and posttraumatic stress disorder. *Annual Review of Psychology, 59,* 301–328.

Chemtob, C. M., Tomas, S., Law, W., & Cremniter, D. (1997). Postdisaster psychosocial intervention: A field study of the impact of debriefing on psychological stress. *American Journal of Psychiatry, 154*(3), 415–417.

Chodron, P. (2001). *Start where you are: A guide to compassionate living.* Boston: Shambhala.

Chodron, P. (2002). *When things fall apart: Heart advice for hard times.* Boston: Shambhala.

Christakis, N. A., & Fowler, J. H. (2009). *Connected: The surprising power of our social networks and how they shape our lives.* New York: Little, Brown.

Claiborne, N., & Lawson, H. A. (2005). An intervention framework for collaboration. *Families in Society: The Journal of Contemporary Social Services, 86*(1), 93–103.

Clemans, S. E. (2004). Recognizing vicarious traumatization: A single session group model for trauma workers. *Social Work with Groups, 27*(2/3), 55–74.

Clinton, W. (2006). *Lessons learned from the tsunami recovery: Build back better.* A report by the United Nations Special Envoy for Tsunami Recovery. New York: United Nations.

Cohen, J. A., Mannarino, A. P., Gibson, L. E., Cozza, S. J., Brymer, M. J., & Murray, L. (2006). Interventions for children and adolescents following disaster. In E. C. Ritchie, P. J. Watson, & M. J. Friedman (Eds.), *Interventions following mass violence and disasters: Strategies for mental health practice* (pp. 227–256). New York: Guilford.

Conroy, R. J. (1990). Critical incident stress debriefing. *FBI Law Enforcement Bulletin,* 20–22.

Corbin, J., & Miller, J. (2009). Collaborative psychosocial capacity building in Northern Uganda. *Families in Society, 90*(1), 103–109.

Corey, A., & Joireman, S. F. (2004). Retributive justice: The Gacaca courts in Rwanda. *African Affairs, 103,* 73–89.

Cox, D., & Pawar, M. (2006). *International social work: Issues, strategies and programs.* Thousand Oaks, CA: Sage.

Crocker, J., & Luhtanen, R. (1990). Collective self-esteem and ingroup bias. *Journal of Personality and Social Psychology, 58*(1), 60–67.

Cronin, M. S., Ryan, D. M., & Brier, D. (2007). Support for staff working in disaster situations: A social work perspective. *International Social Work, 50,* 370–382.

Csikszentmihalyi, M., & Rochberg-Halton, E. (1981). *The meaning of things: Domestic symbols and the self.* New York: Cambridge University Press.

Curtis, J. M. (1995). Elements of critical incident debriefing. *Psychological Reports, 77,* 91–96.

Davis, M. (2005, October 25). Gentrifying disaster: In New Orleans: Ethnic cleansing GOP-style. *Mother Jones.* Retrieved March 24, 2009, from http://www.motherjones.com/politics/2005/10/gentrifying-disaster

Deahl, M. (2000). Psychological debriefing: Controversy and challenge. *Australian and New Zealand Journal of Psychiatry, 34,* 929–939.

Deighton, R. M., Gurris, N., & Traue, H. (2007). Factors affecting burnout and compassion fatigue in psychotherapists treating torture survivors: Is the therapist's attitude to working through trauma relevant? *Journal of Traumatic Stress, 20*(1), 63–75.

de Jong, J. (Ed.). (2002). *Trauma, war, and violence: Public mental health in socio-cultural context*. New York: Springer.

de Jong, J. (2007). Nongovernmental organizations and the role of the mental health professional. In R. J. Ursano, C. S. Fullerton, L. Weisaeth, & B. Raphael (Eds.), *Textbook of disaster psychiatry* (pp. 206–224). Cambridge: Cambridge University Press.

Denham, A. R. (2008). Rethinking historical trauma: Narratives of resilience. *Transcultural Psychiatry*, 45, 391–415.

de Rivera, J., & Paez, D. (2007). Emotional climate, human security, and cultures of peace. *Journal of Social Issues*, 63(2), 233–254.

Deutsch, M. (2008). Reconciliation after destructive intergroup conflict. In A. Nadler, T. E. Malloy, & J. D. Fisher (Eds.), *The social psychology of intergroup reconciliation* (471–486). New York: Oxford University Press.

Dewane, C. (2008, September/October). The ABCs of ACT: Acceptance and commitment therapy. *Social Work Today*, 8(5), 36.

Diamond, J. (2010, January 15). A divided island: The forces working against Haiti. *The Guardian*, G2, p. 11.

Dreier, P. (2006). Katrina and power in America. *Urban Affairs Review*, 41, 528–549.

Dyregrov, A. (1997). The process in psychological debriefings. *Journal of Traumatic Stress*, 10(4), 589–605.

Dyregrov, A. (2000). Helpful and hurtful aspects of psychological debriefing groups. In G. S. Everly, Jr., & J. T. Mitchell (Eds.), *Critical incident stress management: Advanced group crisis interventions: A workbook* (pp. 47–56). Ellicott City, MD: International Critical Incident Stress Foundation.

Dyregrov, A. (2003). *Psychological debriefing: A leader's guide for small group crisis intervention*. Ellicott City, MD: Chevron.

Eagle, M. N. (1984). *Recent developments in psychoanalysis: A critical evaluation*. Cambridge, MA: Harvard University Press.

Eaton, L. (2007). In Mississippi, poor lag in Hurricane aid. *The New York Times*. Retrieved June 6, 2011, from http://www.nytimes.com/2007/11/16/us/16mississippi.html

Echterling, L. G., & Wylie, M. L. (1999). In the public arena: Disaster as a socially constructed problem. In R. Gist & B. Lubin (Eds.), *Response to disaster: Psychosocial, community and ecological approaches* (pp. 327–346). Philadelphia: Brunner/Mazel.

Elcheroth, G. (2006). Individual-level and community-level effects of war trauma on social representations related to humanitarian law. *European Journal of Social Psychology*, 36, 907–930.

Enarson, E., Fothergill, A., & Peek, L. (2006). Gender and disaster: Foundations and directions. In H. Rodriguez, E. L. Quarantelli, & R. R. Dynes (Eds.), *Handbook of disaster research* (pp. 130–146). New York: Springer.

Everly, G. S., Jr., & Mitchell, J. T. (2000). *Critical incident stress management: Advanced group crisis interventions: A workbook.* Ellicott City, MD: International Critical Incident Stress Foundation.

Everly, G. S., Jr., Phillips, S. B., Kane, D., & Feldman, D. (2006). Introduction to and overview of group psychological first aid. *Brief Treatment and Crisis Intervention, 6*(2), 130–136.

Farwell, N., & Cole, J. B. (2002). Community as a context of healing: Psychosocial recovery of children affected by war and political violence. *International Journal of Mental Health 30*(4), 19–41.

Ferks, G., & Clem, B. (Eds.). (2005). *Dealing with diversity: Sri Lankan discourses on peace and conflict.* The Hague, Netherlands: Netherlands Institute of International Relations.

Figley, C. R. (1995). Compassion fatigue as secondary traumatic stress disorder: An overview. In C. R. Figley (Ed.), *Compassion fatigue: Coping with secondary traumatic stress disorder in those who treat the traumatized* (1–20). New York: Brunner/Mazel.

Fleischman, P. (1999). *Karma and chaos: New and collected essays on Vipassana meditation.* Seattle: Vipassana Research Publications.

Flynn, B. W. (2007). A sound blueprint for building a better home. *Psychiatry, 70*(4), 366–369.

Foucault, M. (1984). Truth and power. In P. Rabinow (Ed.), *The Foucault reader* (pp. 51–75). New York: Pantheon.

Frankl, V. (1997). *Man's search for meaning* (Rev. ed.). New York: Pocket.

Fraser, T. (2010, January 20). Exploitation, racism keep Haiti in despair. *Trinidad and Tobago Guardian.* Retrieved June 6, 2011, from http://test.guardian .co.tt/?q=commentary/columnist/2010/01/20/exploitation-racism-keep-haiti-despair

Fredrickson, B. L. (2003). The value of positive emotions: The emerging science of positive psychology is coming to understand why it is good to feel good. *American Scientist, 91,* 330–335.

Fredrickson, B. L., Cohn, M. A., Coffey, K. A., Pek, J., & Finkel, S. M. (2008). Open hearts build lives: Positive emotions, induced through loving-kindness meditation, build consequential personal resources. *Journal of Personality and Social Psychology, 95*(5), 1045–1062.

Friedman, M. J., & Marsella, A. J. (1996). Posttraumatic stress disorder: An overview of the concept. In A. J. Marsella, M. J. Friedman, E. T. Gerrity, & R. M. Scurfield (Eds.), *Ethnocultural aspects of posttraumatic stress disorder: Issues, research, and clinical applications* (pp. 11–32). Washington, DC: American Psychological Association.

Friedman, M. J., Ritchie, E. C., & Watson, P. J. (2006). Overview. In E. C. Ritchie, P. J. Watson, & M. J. Friedman (Eds.), *Interventions following mass violence and disasters: Strategies for mental health practice* (pp. 3–15). New York: Guilford.

Frymer, P., Strolovitch, D. Z., & Warren, D. T. (2005). *Katrina's political roots and divisions: Race, class, and federalism in American politics.* Retrieved January 26, 2009, from Social Science Research Council Web site: http://understandingka trina.ssrc.org/FrymerStrolovitchWarren

Fujimura, N., & Nishisawa, K. (2011, March 26). Quake evacuees survive on rice balls, bread, seek to avoid contracting flu. *Bloomberg.* Retrieved May 25, 2011, from http://www.bloomberg.com/news/2011-03-26/japan-s-evacuees-battle-flu-survive-on-rice-balls-and-bread.html

Gatty, B. (2009, August 14). Disaster planning for elderly woefully inadequate. *Long-term Living Magazine,* 14–17.

Germer, C. (2009). *The mindful path to self-compassion: Freeing yourself from destructive thoughts and emotions.* New York: Guilford.

Gilliand, B. F., & James, R. K. (1996). *Crisis intervention strategies* (3rd ed.). Belmont, CA: Brooks/Cole.

Gist, R., & Lubin, B. (Eds.). (1999). *Response to disaster: Psychosocial, community and ecological approaches.* New York: Brunner/Mazel.

Gist, R., & Woodhall, R. (2000). There are no simple solutions to complex problems. In J. M. Violanti, D. Paton, & C. Dunning (Eds.), *Posttraumatic stress intervention: Challenges, issues and perspectives* (pp. 81–96). Springfield, IL: Charles Thomas Publishers.

Glasser, I. (1981). Prisoners of benevolence: Power versus liberty in the welfare state. In W. Gaylin, I. Glasser, S. Marcus, & D. J. Rothman (Eds.), *Doing good: The limits of benevolence* (97–168). New York: Pantheon.

Gobodo-Madikizela, P. (2008). Transforming trauma in the aftermath of gross human rights abuses: Making public spaces intimate through the South African Truth and Reconciliation Commission. In A. Nadler, T. Molloy, & J. D. Fisher (Eds.), *The social psychology of intergroup reconciliation: From violent conflict to peaceful co-existence* (pp. 57–75). New York: Oxford University Press.

Goldstein-Bolocan, M. (2004). Rwandan Gacaca: Experiment in transitional justice. *Journal of Dispute Resolution,* 355, 1–44.

Goleman, D. (2003). *Destructive emotions: A scientific dialogue with the Dalai Lama.* New York: Bantam.

Gordon, N. S., Faberow, N. L., & Maida, C. A. (1999). *Children & disasters.* New York: Taylor and Francis.

Gourevitch, P. (2009, May 4). The life after: A startling exercise in reconciliation. *The New Yorker,* 36–49.

Green, R., Bates, L. K., & Smyth, A. (2007). Impediments to recovery in New Orleans' Upper and Lower Ninth Ward: One year after Hurricane Katrina. *Disasters,* 31(4), 311–335.

Green Cross. (2009). Academy of traumatology. Retrieved June 6, 2011, from http://www.greencross.org

Greene, P., Kane, D., Christ, G., Lynch, S., & Corrigan, M. (2006). *FDNY crisis counseling: Innovative response to 9/11 firefighters, families, and communities.* New York: Wiley.

Halpern, J., & Tramontin, M. (2007). *Disaster mental health: Theory and practice.* Belmont, CA: Thomson Learning.

Harrison, R. L., & Westwood, M. J. (2009). Preventing vicarious traumatization of mental health therapists: Identifying protective practices. *Psychotherapy Theory, Research, Practice, Training, 46*(2), 203–219.

Henkel, K. E., Dovidio, J. F., & Gaertner, S. L. (2006). Institutional discrimination, individual racism, and Hurricane Katrina. *Analysis of Social Issues and Public Policy, 6*(1), 99–124.

Hernandez, P. (2002). Resilience in families and communities: Latin American contributions from the psychology of liberation. *The Family Journal, 10,* 334–343.

Hobfoll, S. E., Watson, P., Bell, C. C., Bryant, R. A., Brymer, M. J., Friedman, M. J., Friedman, M., Gersons, B. P. R., de Jong, J. T. V. M., Layne, C. M., Maguen, S., Neria, Y., Norwood, A. E., Pynoos, R. S., Reisman, D., Ruzek, J. I., Shalev, A. Y., Solomon, Z., Steinberg, A. M., & Ursano, R. J. (2007). Five essential elements of immediate and mid-term mass trauma intervention: Empirical evidence. *Psychiatry 70*(4), 283–315.

Hoffman, S. M. (2002). The monster and the mother: The symbolism of disaster. In S. M. Hoffman & A. Oliver-Smith (Eds.), *Catastrophe and culture: The anthropology of disaster* (pp. 113–142). Santa Fe, NM: School of American Research Press.

Hooyman, N. R., & Kramer, B. J. (2008). *Living through loss: Interventions across the life span.* New York: Columbia University Press.

Hudnall, A. C., & Lindner, E. G. (2006). Crisis and gender: Addressing the psychosocial needs of women in international disasters. In G. Reyes & G. A. Jacobs (Eds.), *Handbook of international disaster psychology: Vol. 4. Interventions with special needs populations* (pp. 1–18). New York: Praeger.

Inter-Agency Standing Committee (2007). *The IASC guidelines on mental health and psychosocial support in emergency settings.* Geneva: IASC.

Jacobs, G. A. (1995). The development of a national plan for disaster mental health. *Professional Psychology: Research and Practice, 26*(6), 543–549.

Jagodic, G. K., & Kontac, K. (2002). Normalization: A key to children's recovery. In W. N. Zubenko & J. Capozzoli (Eds.), *Children and disasters: A practical guide to healing and recovery* (159–171). New York: Oxford University Press.

Jagodic, G. K., Kontac, K., & Zubenko, W. N. (2002). Group interventions for children in crisis. In W. N. Zubenko & J. Capozzoli (Eds.), *Children and disasters: A practical guide to healing and recovery* (pp. 135–158). New York: Oxford University Press.

James, R. K., & Gilliland, B. E. (2001). *Crisis intervention strategies* (4th ed.). Belmont, CA: Thomson Learning.

Jenkins, J. H. (1996). Culture, emotion, and PTSD. In A. J. Marsella, M. J. Friedman, E. T. Gerrity, & R. M. Scurfield (Eds.), *Ethnocultural aspects of posttraumatic stress disorder: Issues, research and clinical applications* (pp. 165–182). Washington, DC: American Psychological Association.

Jones, N., Greenberg, N., & Wessley, S. (2007). No plans survive first contact with the enemy: Flexibility and improvisation in disaster mental health. *Psychiatry*, 70(4), 361–365.

Kabat-Zinn, J. (1990). *Full catastrophe living: Using the wisdom of your body and your mind to face stress, pain, and illness.* New York: Delta.

Kaniasty, K., & Norris, F. (1999). The experience of disaster: Individuals and communities sharing trauma. In R. Gist & B. Lubin (Eds.), *Response to disaster: Psychosocial, community, and ecological approaches* (pp. 25–61). Philadelphia: Brunner/Mazel.

Kanyangara, P., Rimé, B., Philippot, P., & Yzerbyt, V. (2007). Collective rituals, emotional climate, and intergroup perception: Participation in "Gacaca" tribunals and assimilation of the Rwandan genocide. *Journal of Social Issues*, 63(2), 387–404.

Karen, R. (1998). *Becoming attached: First relationships and how they shape our capacity to love.* New York: Oxford University Press.

Kates, R. W., Colten, C. E., Laska, S., & Leatherman, S. P. (2006). Reconstruction of New Orleans after Hurricane Katrina: A research perspective. *Cityscape*, 103(40), 5–22.

Katz, J. H. (1985). The sociopolitical nature of counseling. *Counseling Psychologist*, 13(4), 615–624.

Kayser, K., Wind, L., & Shankar, R. A. (2008). Disaster relief within a collectivist context. *Journal of Social Service Research*, 34(3), 87–98.

Keane, T. M., Kaloupek, D. G., & Weathers, F. W. (1996). Ethnocultural considerations in the assessment of PTSD. In A. J. Marsella, M. J. Friedman, E. T. Gerrity, & R. M. Scurfield (Eds.), *Ethnocultural aspects of posttraumatic stress disorder: Issues, research, and clinical applications* (pp. 183–205). Washington, DC: American Psychological Association.

Kelman, H. C. (2001). The role of national identity in conflict situations: Experiences from Israeli-Palestinian problem solving workshops. In R. D. Ashmore, L. Jussim, & D. Wilder (Eds.), *Social identity, intergroup conflict, and conflict resolution* (pp. 187–212). New York: Oxford University Press.

Kelman, H. C. (2008). Reconciliation from a social-psychological perspective. In A. Nadler, T. Molloy, & J. D. Fisher (Eds.), *The social psychology of intergroup reconciliation: From violent conflict to peaceful co-existence* (pp. 15–32). New York: Oxford University Press.

Kira, I. A. (2001). Taxonomy of trauma and trauma assessment. *Traumatology*, 7(2), 73–86.

Kirmayer, L. J. (1996). Confusion of the senses: Implications of ethnocultural variations in somatoform and dissociative disorders. In A. J. Marsella, M. J. Friedman, E. T. Gerrity, & R. M. Scurfield (Eds.), *Ethnocultural aspects of posttraumatic stress disorder: Issues, research, and clinical applications* (pp. 131–164). Washington, DC: American Psychological Association.

Klein, N. (2007). *The shock doctrine: The rise of disaster capitalism*. New York: Henry Holt Metropolitan Books.

Kleinman, A., & Cohen, A. (1997). Psychiatry's global challenge. *Scientific American*, 276(3), 86–92.

Klinenberg, E. (2003). *Heat wave: A social autopsy of disaster in Chicago*. Chicago: University of Chicago Press.

Kos, A. M. (2008). The pitfalls of evaluations: A critical perspective from a field worker. *Intervention*, 6(1), 57–65.

Kretzman, J. P., & McKnight, J. L. (1993). *Building communities from the inside out*. Evanston, IL: Northwestern University Press.

Kristof, N., & WuDunn, C. (2009, August 17). The women's crusade. *The New York Times Magazine*. Retrieved December 21, 2009, from http://www.nytimes .com/2009/08/23/magazine/23Women-t.html

Kwan, K. K., & Sodowsky, G. R. (1997). Internal and external ethnic identity and their correlates: A study of Chinese ethnic immigrants. *Journal of Multicultural Counseling and Development*, 25(1), 51–68.

Lacey, M. (2011, January 18). Makeshift memorials pop up in Tucson. *The New York Times*. Retrieved January 18, 2011, from http://www.nytimes.com/2011/01/18/ us/18giffords.html?src=un&feedurl=http%3A%2F%2Fjson8.nytimes.com %2Fpages%2Fnational%2Findex.jsonp

LaFraniere, S. (2009, February 5). Possible link between dam and China quake. *The New York Times*. Retrieved February 9, 2009, from http://www.nytimes.com/ 2009/02/06/world/asia/06quake.html?emc=tnt&tntemail1=y

Landau, J. (2007). Enhancing resilience: Communities and families as agents of change. *Family Process*, 41(1), 351–365.

Landau, J., Mittal, M., & Wieling, E. (2008). Linking human systems: Strengthening individuals, families, and communities in the wake of trauma. *Journal of Marital and Family Therapy*, 34(2), 193–209.

Landau, J., & Saul, J. (2004). Facilitating family and community resilience in response to major disaster. In F. Walsh & M. McGoldrick (Eds.), *Living beyond loss* (pp. 285–309). New York: W. W. Norton.

Lederach, J. P. (1997). *Building peace: Sustainable reconciliation in divided societies*. Washington, DC: United States Institute of Peace Press.

Lederach, J. P. (2005). *The moral imagination: The art and soul of building peace*. New York: Oxford University Press.

Lee, S. (2006). *When the levees broke: A requiem in four parts* [video]. HBO Productions.

Leitch, M. L., Vanslyke, J., & Allen, M. (2009). Somatic experiencing with social service workers after Hurricanes Katrina and Rita. *Social Work*, 54(1), 9–18.

Levi, P. (1961). *Survival in Auschwitz: The Nazi assault on humanity*. New York: Collier.

Levi, P. (1988). *The drowned and the saved*. New York: Summit Books.

Lystad, M. (Ed.). (1988). *Mental health response to mass emergencies: Theory and practice*. New York: Brunner/Mazel.

Macy, R. D., Behar, L., Paulson, R., Delman, J., Schmid, L., & Smith, S. L. (2004). Community based acute traumatic stress management: A description and evaluation of a psychosocial-intervention continuum. *Harvard Review of Psychiatry*, 12, 217–228.

Magnier, M. (2011, March 22). After quake, Japanese grapple with honoring the dead they can't see. *Los Angeles Times*. Retrieved May 26, 2011, from http://articles.latimes.com/2011/mar/22/world/la-fg-japan-death-20110323

Marsella, A. J., Friedman, M. J., Gerrity, E. T., & Scurfield, R. M. (1996). Preface. In A. J. Marsella, M. J. Friedman, E. T. Gerrity, & R. M. Scurfield (Eds.), *Ethnocultural aspects of posttraumatic stress disorder: Issues, research, and clinical applications* (pp. xv–xix). Washington, DC: American Psychological Association.

Marsella, A. J., Friedman, M. J., & Spain, E. H. (1996). Ethnocultural aspects of PTSD: An overview of issues and research directions. In A. J. Marsella, M. J. Friedman, E. T. Gerrity, & R. M. Scurfield (Eds.), *Ethnocultural aspects of posttraumatic stress disorder: Issues, research, and clinical applications* (pp. 105–130). Washington, DC: American Psychological Association.

Masozera, M., Bailey, M., & Kerchner, C. (2007). Distribution impacts of natural disasters across income groups: A case study of New Orleans. *Ecological Economics*, 63, 299–306.

Maynard, K. A. (1999). *Healing communities in conflict: International assistance in complex emergencies*. New York: Columbia University Press.

McKay, S. (1998). The effects of armed conflict on girls and women. *Peace and Conflict*, 4(4), 381–392.

McKnight, J. L. (1997). A 21st-century map for healthy communities and families. *Families in Society*, 78(2), 117–127.

McNally, R. J., Bryant, R. A., & Ehlers, A. (2003). Does early psychological intervention promote recovery from posttraumatic stress? *Psychological Science in the Public Interest*, 4(2), 45–79.

Miller, J. (1994). A family's sense of power in their community: Theoretical and research issues. *Smith College Studies in Social Work*, 64(3), 221–242.

Miller, J. (2000). The use of debriefings in response to disasters and traumatic events. *Professional Development: The International Journal of Continuing Social Work Education*, 3(2), 24–31.

Miller, J. (2001a). Family and community integrity. *Journal of Sociology and Social Welfare*, 28(4), 23–44.

Miller, J. (2001b). Violet's seeds. In S. L. Abels (Ed.), *Ethics in social work practice: Narratives for professional helping* (pp. 111–129). Denver: Love Publishing.

Miller, J. (2002). Affirming flames: Debriefing survivors of the World Trade Center attacks. *Brief Treatment and Crisis Intervention*, 2(1), 85–94.

Miller, J. (2003). Critical incident stress debriefing and social work: Expanding the frame. *Journal of Social Service Research, 30*(2), 7–25.

Miller, J. (2006a). Critical incident debriefings and community-based care. In A. Lightburn and P. Sessions (Eds.), *Handbook of community based practice* (pp. 529–541), New York: Oxford University Press.

Miller, J. (2006b). Waves amidst war: Intercultural challenges while training volunteers to respond to the psychosocial needs of Sri Lankan tsunami survivors. *Brief Treatment and Crisis Intervention, 6*(4), 349–365.

Miller, J., & Donner, S. (2000). More than just talk: The use of racial dialogues to combat racism. *Social Work with Groups, 23*(1), 31–53.

Miller, J., & Garran, A. (2007). *Racism in the United States: Implications for the helping professions.* Belmont, CA: Brooks/Cole.

Miller, J., Grabelsky, J., & Wagner, K. C. (2010). Psychosocial capacity building in New York: Building resiliency with construction workers assigned to Ground Zero after 9/11. *Social Work with Groups, 33*(1), 23–40.

Miller, J., & Schamess, G. (2000). The discourse of denigration and the creation of other. *Journal of Sociology and Social Welfare, 27*(3), 39–62.

Miller, K. E., Kulkarni, M., & Kushner, H. (2006). Beyond trauma-focused psychiatric epidemiology: Bridging research and practice with war-affected populations. *American Journal of Orthopsychology, 76*(4), 409–422.

Minow, M. (2002). *Breaking the cycles of hatred: Memory, law, and repair.* Princeton, NJ: Princeton University Press.

Miron, A. M., & Branscombe, N. R. (2008). Social categorization, standards of justice, and collective guilt. In A. Nadler, T. Molloy, & J. D. Fisher (Eds.), *The social psychology of intergroup reconciliation: From violent conflict to peaceful co-existence* (pp. 77–96). New York: Oxford University Press.

Mississippi's failure. (2009, September 20). *The New York Times.* Retrieved June 6, 2011, from http://www.nytimes.com/2009/09/21/opinion/21mon1.html

Mitchell, J. T. (1983). When disaster strikes: The critical incident stress debriefing process. *Journal of Emergency Medical Services, 8*(1), 36–39.

Mitchell, J. T., & Bray, G. P. (1990). *Emergency services stress: Guidelines for preserving the health and careers of emergency services personnel.* Englewood Cliffs, NJ: Prentice Hall.

Mitchell, J. T., & Everly, G. S. (2001). *The basic critical incident stress management course.* Ellicott City, MD: International Critical Incident Stress Foundation.

Mollica, R. F. (2006). *Healing invisible wounds: Paths to hope and recovery in a violent world.* New York: Harcourt.

Mollica, R., Lopes Cardozo, B., Osofsky, H. J., Raphael, B., Ager, A., & Salama, P. (2004). Mental health in complex emergencies. *The Lancet, 364,* 2058–2067.

Murphy, S. A. (2010). Women's and children's exposure to mass disaster and terrorist attacks. *Issues in Mental Health Nursing, 31,* 45–53.

Musa, S. F., & Hamid, A. A. R. M. (2008). Psychological problems among aid workers in Darfur. *Social Behavior and Personality*, 36(3), 407–416.

Nadler, A., & Shnabel, N. (2008). Instrumental and socioemotional paths to intergroup reconciliation and the needs-based model of socioemotional reconciliation. *The social psychology of intergroup reconciliation: From violent conflict to peaceful co-existence* (pp. 37–56). New York: Oxford University Press.

Nakagawa, Y., & Shaw, R. (2004). Social capital: A missing link to disaster recovery. *International Journal of Mass Emergencies and Disasters*, 22(1), 5–34.

National Child Traumatic Stress Network and National Center for PTSD. (2006). Psychological first aid: Field operations guide (2nd ed). Retrieved June 6, 2011, from http://www.nctsn.org and http://www.ncptsd.org

Nisbett, R. E. (2003). *The geography of thought: How Asians and Westerners think differently and why*. New York: Free Press.

Nishikawa, Y. (2011, March 23). Quake-ravaged Japan digs mass graves. *Reuters*. Retrieved May 26, 2011, from http://www.reuters.com/article/2011/03/23/us-japan-graves-idUSTRE72M1JE20110323

Norris, F. H., & Alegria, M. (2006). Promoting disaster recovery in ethnic-minority individuals and communities. In E. C. Ritchie, P. J. Watson, & M. J. Friedman (Eds.), *Interventions following mass violence and disasters: Strategies for mental health practice* (pp. 319–342). New York: Guilford.

Norris, F. H., & Murrell, S. A. (1988). Prior experience as a moderator of disaster impact. *American Journal of Community Psychology*, 16(5), 665–683.

Norris, F. H., & Stevens, S. P. (2007). Community resilience and the principles of mass trauma intervention. *Psychiatry*, 70(4), 320–328.

North, C. S. (2007). Epidemiology of disaster mental health. In R. J. Ursano, C. S. Fullerton, L. Weisaeth, & B. Raphael (Eds.), *Textbook of disaster psychiatry* (pp. 29–47). Cambridge: Cambridge University Press.

Ochberg, F. (Ed.). (1988). Post-traumatic therapy and victims of violence. In F. Ochberg (Ed.), *Post-traumatic therapy and victims of violence* (pp. 3–20). New York: Brunner/Mazel.

Okin, S. M. (1999). *Is multiculturalism bad for women?* Princeton, NJ: Princeton University Press.

Oliver-Smith, A. (2002). Theorizing disasters: Nature, power and culture. In S. M. Hoffman & A. Oliver-Smith (Eds.). *Catastrophe and culture: The anthropology of disaster* (pp. 23–48). Santa Fe, NM: School of American Research Press.

Orner, R. J., Kent, A. T., Pfefferbaum, B. J., Raphael, B., & Watson, P. J. (2006). The context of providing immediate postevent intervention. In E. C. Ritchie, P. J. Watson, & M. J. Friedman (Eds.), *Interventions following mass violence and disasters: Strategies for mental health practice* (pp. 121–133). New York: Guilford.

Osawa, J., Dvorak, P., Wakabayashi, D., & Sekiguchi, T. (2011, March 17). A long, painful reckoning. *The Wall Street Journal*. Retrieved May 25, 2011, from http://online.wsj.com/article/SB10001424052748703899704576204953044390300.html

Otake, K., Shimai, S., Tanaka-Matsumi, J., Otsui, K., & Fredrickson, B. L. (2006). Happy people become happier through kindness: A counting kindness intervention. *Journal of Happiness Studies, 7*, 361–375.

Paez, D., Basabe, N., Ubillos, S., & Gonzalez-Castro, J. L. (2007). Social sharing, participation in demonstrations, emotional climate, and coping with collective violence after the March 11th Madrid bombings. *Journal of Social Issues, 63*(2), 323–337.

Park, Y. (2008). Facilitating injustice: Tracing the role of social workers in the World War II internment of Japanese Americans. *Social Service Review, 82*(3), 447–484.

Park, Y., & Miller, J. (2006). The social ecology of Hurricane Katrina: Rewriting the discourse of "natural" disasters. *Smith College Studies in Social Work, 76*(3), 9–24.

Park, Y., & Miller, J. (2007). Inequitable distributions. *Journal of Intergroup Relations, 33*(1), 45–59.

Park, Y., Miller, J., & Van, B. C. (2010). Everything has changed: Narratives of the Vietnamese-American community in Biloxi, Mississippi. *Journal of Sociology and Social Welfare, 37*(3), 79–105.

Parker, C., Doctor, R. M., & Selvam, R. (2008). Somatic therapy treatment effects with tsunami survivors. *Traumatology, 14*(3), 103–109.

Pastel, R. H., & Ritchie, E. C. (2006). Mitigation of psychological effects of weapons of mass destruction. In E. C. Ritchie, P. J. Watson, & M. J. Friedman (Eds.), *Interventions following mass violence and disasters: Strategies for mental health practice* (pp. 300–318). New York: Guilford.

Patterson, J. M. (2002). Integrating family resilience and family stress theory. *Journal of Marriage and Family, 64*(2), 349–360.

Pearlman, C. A., & Saakvitne, K. W. (1995). *Trauma and the therapist: Countertransference and vicarious trauma in psychotherapy with incest survivors.* New York: W. W. Norton.

Pederson, D. (2002). Political violence, ethnic conflict, and contemporary wars: Broad implications for health and social well-being. *Social Science and Medicine, 55*, 175–190.

Perrin-Klinger, G. (2000). The integration of traumatic experiences: Culture and resources. In J. M. Violanti, D. Patton, & C. Dunning (Eds.), *Posttraumatic stress intervention.* Springfield, IL: Charles Thomas.

Prewitt Diaz, J. O., & Dayal, A. (2008). Sense of place: A model for community based psychosocial support programs. *The Australasian Journal of Disaster and Trauma Studies, 2008*(1). Retrieved December 16, 2009, from http://www.massey.ac.nz/trauma/issues/2008-1/prewitt_diaz.htm

Pupavac, C. (2004). Psychosocial interventions and the demoralization of humanitarianism. *Journal of Biosocial Science, 36*, 491–504.

Pyles, L. (2007). Community organizing for post-disaster settlement: Locating social work. *International Social Work, 50*(3), 321–333.

Pyles, L., & Cross, T. (2008). Community revitalization in post-Katrina New Orleans: A critical analysis of social capital in an African American neighborhood. *Journal of Community Practice, 16*(4), 383–401.

Pynoos, R. S., Steinberg, A. M., & Brymer, M. J. (2007). Children and disasters: Public mental health approaches. In R. J. Ursano, C. S. Fullerton, L. Weisaeth, & B. Raphael (Eds.), *Textbook of disaster psychiatry* (pp. 48–68). Cambridge: Cambridge University Press.

Quarantelli, E. L. (2006). *Emergencies, disasters, and catastrophes are different phenomena.* Retrieved April 21, 2009, from University of Delaware, Disaster Research Center Web site: http://www.udel.edu/DRC/preliminary/pp304.pdf

Radey, M., & Figley, C. R. (2007). The social psychology of compassion. *Clinical Social Work Journal, 35,* 207–214.

Rand, M. L. (2004, Spring). Vicarious trauma and the Buddhist doctrine of suffering. *Annals of the American Psychotherapy Association,* 40–41.

Rao, K. (2006). Psychosocial support in disaster-affected communities. *International Review of Psychiatry, 18*(6), 501–505.

Raphael, B. (1986). *When disaster strikes: How individuals and communities cope with catastrophe.* New York: Basic Books.

Raphael, B. (2006). Overview of the development of psychological support in emergencies. In J. O. Prewitt Diaz, R. Srinivasa Murthy, & R. Lakshminarayana (Eds.), *Advances in disaster mental health and psychological support.* New Delhi: Voluntary Health Association of India Press.

Raphael, B. (2007). The human touch and mass catastrophe. *Psychiatry, 70*(4), 329–336.

Raphael, B., Meldrum, L., & McFarlane, A. C. (1995). Does debriefing after psychological trauma work? *British Medical Journal, 310,* 1479–1480.

Raynor, C. M. (2002). The role of play in the recovery process. In W. N. Zubenko & J. Capozzoli (Eds.), *Children and disasters: A practical guide to healing and recovery* (124–134). New York: Oxford University Press.

Regehr, C., & Bober, T. (2005). *In the line of fire: Trauma in the emergency services.* New York: Oxford University Press.

Reichert, E. (2006). Human rights: An examination of universalism and cultural relativism. *Journal of Comparative Social Welfare, 22*(1), 23–36.

Reis, C., & Vann, B. (2006). Sexual violence against women and children in the context of armed conflict. In G. Reyes & G. A. Jacobs (Eds.), *Handbook of international disaster psychology: Vol. 4. Interventions with special needs populations* (pp. 19–44). New York: Praeger.

Reiss, D. (1981). *The family's construction of reality.* Cambridge, MA: Harvard University Press.

Reliefweb. (2009). South Asia tsunami fourth year report. http://www.reliefweb.int/rw/rwb.nsf/db900SID/FBUO-7MLF5P?OpenDocument

Reyes, G., & Elhai, J. D. (2004). Psychosocial interventions in the early phases of disasters. *Psychotherapy: Theory, Research, Practice, Training, 41*(4), 399–411.

Ritchie, E. C., Watson, P. J., & Friedman, M. J. (Eds.). (2006). *Interventions following mass violence and disasters: Strategies for mental health practice*. New York: Guilford.

Roberts, A. (2005). Bridging the past and present to the future of crisis intervention and crisis management. In A. Roberts (Ed.), *Crisis intervention handbook: Assessment, treatment and research* (3rd ed.) (pp. 3–34). New York: Oxford University Press.

Roberts, A. R., & Ottens, A. J. (2005). The seven-stage crisis intervention model: A road map to goal attainment, problem solving, and crisis resolution. *Brief Treatment and Crisis Intervention, 5*(4), 329–339.

Roche, D. (2006). Dimensions of restorative justice. *Journal of Social Issues, 2,* 217–238.

Roland, A. (1996). *Cultural pluralism and psychoanalysis: The Asian and North American experience*. New York: Routledge.

Romero, S. (2010, March 6). With Haitian schools in ruins, children in limbo. *The New York Times.* Retrieved March 8, 2010, from http://www.nytimes.com/2010/03/07/world/americas/07schools.html?scp=1&sq=Haiti%20schools%20&st=cse

Ronan, K. R., Finnis, K., & Johnston, D. M. (2006). Interventions with youth and families: A prevention and stepped care model. In G. Reyes & G. A. Jacobs (Eds.), *Handbook of international disaster psychology: Vol. 2. Practices and programs* (pp. 13–35). New York: Praeger.

Rosenfeld, L. B., Caye, J. S., Ayalon, O., & Lahad, M. (2005). *When their world falls apart: Helping families and children manage the effects of disasters*. Silver Springs, MD: NASW Press.

Ross, N. W. (1966). *Three ways of Asian wisdom: Hinduism, Buddhism, and Zen and their significance for the West*. New York: Clarion.

Rothschild, B. (2006). *Help for the helper: Self-care strategies for managing burnout and stress*. New York: W. W. Norton.

Ruysschaert, N. (2009). (Self) hypnosis in the prevention of burnout and compassion fatigue for caregivers: Theory and induction. *Contemporary Hypnosis, 26*(3), 159–172.

Samson, R. J., Morenoff, J. D., & Earls, F. (1999). Beyond social capital: Spatial dynamics of collective efficacy for children. *American Sociological Review, 64,* 633–660.

Samson, R. J., Raudenbush, S. W., & Earls, F. (1997, August). Neighborhoods and violent crime: A multilevel study of collective efficacy. *Science, 277,* 918–924.

Saul, J. (2000, November). Mapping trauma: A multi-systemic approach. *Psychosocial Notebook: International Organization for Migration,* 103–109.

Schabas, W. A. (2005). Genocide trials and Gacaca courts. *Journal of International Criminal Justice, 3,* 879–895.

Schlenger, W. E. (2005). Psychological impact of September 11, 2001 terrorist attacks: Summary of empirical findings in adults. In Y. Danieli, D. Brom, & J. Sills (Eds.), *The trauma of terrorism: Sharing knowledge and shared care* (pp. 97–108). Binghamton, NY: Haworth Maltreatment and Trauma Press.

Schwartz, W. (1971). On the use of groups in social work practice. In W. Schwartz & S. R. Zalba (Eds.), *The practice of group work* (pp. 3–24). New York: Columbia University Press.

The secret to better health—exercise. (2009, January 27). *HEALTHbeat.* Cambridge, MA: Harvard Medical School.

Seligman, M. E. P., Rashid, T., & Parks, A. C. (2006). Positive psychotherapy. *American Psychologist, 61,* 774–788.

Shultz, J. M., Espinel, Z., Galea, S., & Reissman, D. B. (2007). Disaster ecology: Implications for disaster psychiatry. In R. J. Ursano, C. S. Fullerton, L. Weisaeth, & B. Raphael (Eds.), *Textbook of disaster psychiatry* (pp. 69–96). Cambridge: Cambridge University Press.

Smelser, N. J. (2004). Psychological trauma and cultural trauma. In J. C. Alexander, R. Eyerman, B. Giesen, N. J. Smelser, & P. Sztompka (Eds.), *Cultural trauma and collective identity* (pp. 31–59). Berkeley: University of California Press.

Smith, P., Dyregrov, A., & Yule, W. (2002). *Children and disaster: Teaching recovery techniques.* Bergen, Norway: Children and War Foundation.

Smith, R. P., Katz, C. L., Charney, D. S., & Southwick, S. M. (2007). Neurobiology of disaster exposure: Fear, anxiety, trauma and resilience. In R. J. Ursano, C. S. Fullerton, L. Weisaeth, & B. Raphael (Eds.), *Textbook of disaster psychiatry* (pp. 97–117). Cambridge: Cambridge University Press.

Solnit, R. (2009). *A paradise built in hell: The extraordinary communities that arise in disaster.* New York: Viking.

Solomon, R. M. (1995). Critical incident stress debriefing in law enforcement. In G. Everly & J. Mitchell (Eds.), *Critical incident stress management* (123–157). Ellicott City, MD: Chevron Press.

Somasundaram, D. (2005). Short- and long-term effects of the victims of terror in Sri Lanka. In Y. Danieli, D. Brom, & J. Sills (Eds.), *The trauma of terrorism: Sharing knowledge and shared care* (pp. 215–228). Binghamton, NY: Haworth Maltreatment and Trauma Press.

Sommers, S. R., Apfelbaum, E. P., Dukes, K. N., Toosi, N., & Wang, E. J. (2006). Race and media coverage of Hurricane Katrina: Analysis, implications, and future research questions. *Analyses of Social Issues and Public Policy, 6*(1), 39–56.

Spence, P. R., Lachlan, K., Burke, J. M., & Seeger, M. W. (2007). Media use and information needs of the disabled during a natural disaster. *Journal of Health Care for the Poor and Underserved, 18,* 394–404.

Stamm, B. H. (2009). *Professional quality of life: Compassion satisfaction and fatigue version 5 (ProQOL).* Retrieved May 28, 2010, from http://www.proqol.org/uploads/ProQOL_5_English_Selfscore.pdf

Staub, E. (2001). Individual and group identities in genocide and mass killing. In R. D. Ashmore, L. Jussim, & D. Wilder (Eds.), *Social identity, intergroup conflict, and conflict resolution* (pp. 159–184). New York: Oxford University Press.

Staub, E. (2008). Promoting reconciliation after genocide and mass killing in Rwanda—and other post-conflict settings: Understanding the roots of violence, healing, shared history, and general principles. In A. Nadler, T. Molloy, & J. D. Fisher (Eds.), *The social psychology of intergroup reconciliation: From violent conflict to peaceful co-existence*, (pp. 395–422). New York: Oxford University Press.

Staub, E., & Bar-Tal, D. (2003). Genocide, mass killing, and intractable conflict: Roots, evolution, prevention, and reconciliation. In D. O. Sears, L. Huddy, & R. Jervis (Eds.), *Oxford handbook of political psychology* (710–754). New York: Oxford University Press.

Stephan, W. G. (2008). The road to reconciliation. In A. Nadler, T. Molloy, & J. D. Fisher (Eds.), *The social psychology of intergroup reconciliation: From violent conflict to peaceful co-existence*, (pp. 369–394). New York: Oxford University Press.

Strang, A. B., & Ager, A. (2003). Psychosocial interventions: Some key issues facing practitioners. *Intervention, 1*(3), 2–12.

Sue, D. W., & Sue, D. (2003). *Counseling the culturally diverse: Theory and practice.* New York: Wiley.

Summerfield, D. (1995). Assisting survivors of war and atrocity: Notes on psychosocial issues. *Development in Practice, 5*(4), 352–356.

Summerfield, D. (2000). War and mental health: A brief overview. *British Medical Journal, 321*, 232–235.

Summerfield, D. (2004). Cross-cultural perspectives on the medicalisation of human suffering. In G. Rosen (Ed.), *Posttraumatic stress disorder: Issues and controversies* (pp. 233–247). New York: Wiley.

Swiss Agency for Development and Cooperation. (2006). *Gender, conflict transformation, & the psychosocial approach toolkit.* Bern, Switzerland: Author.

Sztompka, P. (2004). The trauma of social change: The case of postcommunist societies. In J. C. Alexander, R. Eyerman, B. Giesen, N. J. Smelser, & P. Sztompka (Eds.), *Cultural trauma and collective identity* (pp. 155–195). Berkeley: University of California Press.

Tabuchi, H. (2011, May 24). Company believes 3 reactors melted down in Japan. *The New York Times.* Retrieved May 25, 2011, from http://www.nytimes.com/2011/05/25/world/asia/25nuclear.html?scp=7&sq=Fukushima%20reactor&st=cse

Tabuchi, H. (2011, May 25). Angry parents in Japan confront government over radiation levels. *The New York Times.* Retrieved June 1, 2011, from http://www.nytimes.com/2011/05/26/world/asia/26japan.html?scp=4&sq=japan&st=cse

Tabuchi, H., & Wassener, B. (2011, May 18). Earthquake and aftermath push Japan into recession. *The New York Times.* Retrieved May 25, 2011, from http://www.nytimes.com/2011/05/19/business/global/19yen.html?scp=2&sq=Japanese%20earthquake&st=cse

Tehrani, N. (2007). The cost of caring: The impact of secondary trauma on assumptions, values, beliefs. *Counseling Psychology Quarterly, 20*(4), 325–339.

Thompson, C. (2009, September 13). Is happiness catching? *The New York Times Magazine*. Retrieved September 14, 2009, from http://www.nytimes .com/2009/09/13/magazine/13contagion-t.html?emc=eta1

Tierney, J. (2011, May 16). A new gauge to see what's beyond happiness. *The New York Times*. Retrieved May 27, 2011, from http://www.nytimes.com/2011/05/17/ science/17tierney.html?n=Top%2fNews%2fScience%2fColumns%2fFindings

Torgusen, B. L., & Kosberg, J. I. (2006). Assisting older victims of disasters. *Journal of Gerontological Social Work, 47*(1), 27–44.

Tosone, C. (2007). Editor's note. *Clinical Social Work Journal, 35*, 287–288.

Tosone, C., & Bialkin, L. (2003). Mass violence and secondary trauma. In S. Straussner & N. Phillips (Eds.), *Understanding mass violence* (pp. 157–167). Boston: Pearson Press.

Triandafyllidou, A. (1998). National identity and the "other." *Ethnic and Racial Studies, 21*(4), 593–612.

Tugade, M. M., & Fredrickson, B. L. (2004). Resilient individuals use positive emotions to bounce back from negative emotional experiences. *Journal of Personality and Social Psychology, 86*(2), 320–333.

Tyiska, C. G. (2008). Working with the elderly after disaster. In S. B. Roberts & W. W. C. Ashley Sr. (Eds.), *Disaster spiritual care: Practical clergy responses to community, regional, and national tragedy* (pp. 297–314). Woodstock, VT: Sky Light Paths Publishing.

Ulman, K. H. (2008). Helping the helpers: Groups as an antidote to the isolation of mental health disaster response workers. *Group, 32*(3), 209–221.

United States Census Bureau. (2009). *Population*. Retrieved 2009 from press releases via U.S. Census Bureau: http://www.census.gov/Press-Release/www/releases/ archives/population/012242.html

Ursano, R. J., Fullerton, C. S., Weisaeth, L., & Raphael, B. (2007). Individual and community responses to disaster. In R. J. Ursano, C. S. Fullerton, L. Weisaeth, & B. Raphael (Eds.), *Textbook of disaster psychiatry* (pp. 3–28). Cambridge: Cambridge University Press.

Uvin, P., & Mironka, C. (2003). Western and local approaches to justice in Rwanda. *Global Governance, 9*, 219–231.

Van den Eynde, J., & Veno, A. (1999). Disastrous events: An empowerment model of community healing. In R. Gist & B. Lubin (Eds.), *Response to disaster: Psychosocial, community, and ecological approaches* (pp. 167–192). New York: Brunner/Mazel.

Van der Kolk, B. (2002). The assessment and treatment of complex PTSD. In R. Yehuda (Ed.), *Psychological trauma*. Washington, DC: American Psychiatric Press.

Van der Kolk, B. (2006). Clinical implications of neuroscience research in PTSD. *Annals of the New York Academy of Sciences, 40*, 1–17.

Vernberg, E. M. (1999). Children's responses to disaster: Family and systems approaches. In R. Gist & B. Lubin (Eds.), *Response to disaster: Psychosocial, community, and ecological approaches* (pp. 193–210). Philadelphia: Brunner/Mazel.

Vernberg, E. M., & Vogel, J. M. (1993). Part II: Interventions with children after disasters. *Journal of Clinical Child Psychology, 22*(4), 485–498.

Vineburgh, N. T., Gifford, R. K., Ursano, R. J., Fullerton, C. S., & Benedek, D. M. (2007). Workplace disaster preparedness and response. In R. J. Ursano, C. S. Fullerton, L. Weisaeth, & B. Raphael (Eds.), *Textbook of disaster psychiatry* (pp. 265–283). Cambridge: Cambridge University Press.

Volkan, V. D. (1988). *The need to have enemies and allies: From clinical practice to international relationships.* Northvale, NJ: Jason Aronson.

Wallace, B. A. (2007). *Hidden dimensions: The unification of physics and consciousness.* New York: Columbia.

Walsh, F. (2003). Crisis, trauma, and challenge: A relational resilience approach for healing, transformation, and growth. *Smith College Studies in Social Work, 74*(1), 49–71.

Walsh, F. (2007). Traumatic loss and major disasters: Strengthening family and community resilience. *Family Process, 46*(2), 207–227.

Watson, P. J. (2007). Early intervention for trauma-related problems following mass trauma. In R. J. Ursano, C. S. Fullerton, L. Weisaeth, & B. Raphael (Eds.), *Textbook of disaster psychiatry* (pp. 121–139). Cambridge: Cambridge University Press.

Watson, P. J., Ritchie, E. C., Demer, J., Bartone, P., & Pfefferbaum, B. J. (2006). Improving resilience trajectories following mass violence and disaster. In E. C. Ritchie, P. J. Watson, & M. J. Friedman (Eds.), *Interventions following mass violence and disasters: Strategies for mental health practice* (pp. 37–53). New York: Guilford.

Waugh, C. E., & Fredrickson, B. L. (2006). Nice to know you: Positive emotions, self-other overlap, and complex understanding in the formation of a new relationship. *The Journal of Positive Psychology, 1*(2), 93–106.

Way, I., VanDeusen, K., & Cottrell, T. (2007). Vicarious trauma: Predictors of clinician's disrupted cognitions about self-esteem and self-intimacy. *Journal of Child Sexual Abuse, 16*(4), 81–98.

Wessells, M. G. (1999). Culture, power, and community: Intercultural approaches to psychosocial healing. In K. Nader, N. Dubrow, & B. H. Stamm (Eds.), *Honoring differences: Cultural issues in the treatment of trauma and loss* (pp. 267–282). New York: Taylor and Francis.

Wessells, M. (2009, November). Do no harm: Toward contextually appropriate psychosocial support in international emergencies. *American Psychologist, 64*(8), 842–854.

Wessells, M., & Monteiro, C. (2006). Psychosocial assistance for youth: Toward reconstruction for peace in Angola. *Journal of Social Issues, 62*(1), 121–139.

Weyerman, B. (2007). Linking economics and emotions: Towards a more integrated understanding of empowerment in conflict areas. *Intervention, 5*(2), 83–96.

White, D. (2006). The hidden cost of caring: What managers need to know. *The Health Care Manager, 25*(4), 341–347.

White, M., & Epston, D. (1990). *Narrative means to therapeutic ends.* New York: W. W. Norton.

Wickramage, K. (2006). Sri Lanka's post-tsunami psychosocial playground: Lessons for future psychosocial programming and interventions. *Intervention, 4*(2), 167–172.

Wierzynska, A. (2004, November). Consolidating democracy through transitional justice: Rwanda's Gacaca courts. *NYU Law Review, 79,* 1934–1970.

Wiesel, E. (1960). *Night.* New York: Hill and Wang.

Wikan, U. (1989). Managing the heart to brighten face and soul: Emotions in Balinese morality and health care. *American Ethnologist, 16*(2), 294–312.

Wilkinson, R., & Pickett, K. (2009). *The spirit level: Why greater equality makes societies stronger.* New York: Bloomsbury Press.

Wilson, J. P. (2007). Culture, trauma, and the treatment of post-traumatic syndromes. In A. J. Marsella, J. L. Johnson, P. Watson, & J. Gryczynski (Eds.), *Ethnocultural perspectives on disaster and trauma: Foundations, issues, and applications* (pp. 351–375). New York: Springer.

Winter, D. D. N., & Cava, M. M. (2006). The psycho-ecology of armed conflict. *Journal of Social Issues, 62,* 19–40.

Within Foundation. (1998). *When helping hurts: Sustaining trauma workers* [motion picture]. Camden, ME: Within Foundation.

Worden, J. W. (2008). *Grief counseling and grief therapy: A handbook for the mental health practitioner* (4th ed.). New York: Springer.

World Health Organization. (2005, February). Asian tsunami: Death toll addiction and its downside. *Bulletin of the World Health Organization, 83*(2), 81–160. Retrieved April 22, 2009, from http://www.who.int/bulletin/volumes/83/2/editorial10205/en

Yamagawa, Y., & Shaw, R. (2004). Social capital: A missing link to disaster recovery. *International Journal of Mass Emergencies and Disasters, 22*(1), 5–34.

Yamamoto, E. (1999). *Interracial justice: Conflict and reconciliation in post-civil rights America.* New York: New York University Press.

Yassen, J. (1995). Preventing secondary traumatic stress disorder. In C. R. Figley (Ed.), *Compassion fatigue: Coping with secondary traumatic stress disorder in those who treat the traumatized* (pp. 178–208). New York: Brunner/Mazel.

Yeh, C. J., & Hwang, M. Y. (2000). Interdependence in ethnic identity and self: Implications for theory and practice. *Journal of Counseling and Development, 78,* 420–429.

Yoder, C. (2005). *The little book of trauma healing: When violence strikes and community security is threatened.* Intercourse, PA: Good Books.

Young, M. A. (1997). *The community crisis response training manual* (2nd ed.). Washington, DC: National Association of Victim Assistance.

Young, R. J. C. (2003). *Postcolonialism: A very short introduction.* New York: Oxford University Press.

Young-Eisendrath, P. (2010, March). The hidden treasure of anger. *Shambhala Sun*, 18(4), 23–26.

Yule, W., (2006). Theory, training and timing: Psychosocial interventions in complex emergencies. *International Review of Psychiatry*, 18(3), 259–264.

Zehr, H. (2002). *The little book of restorative justice*. Intercourse, PA: Good Books.

Zinner, E. S. (1999). The Challenger disaster: Group survivorship on a national landscape. In E. S. Zinner & M. B. Williams (Eds.), *When a community weeps: Case studies in group survivorship* (pp. 23–47). Philadelphia: Brunner/Mazel.

Zorbus, E. (2004). Reconciliation in post-genocide Rwanda. *African Journal of Legal Studies*, 11(1), 29–52.

Zubenko, W. N. (2002). Developmental issues in stress and crisis. In W. N. Zubenko & J. Capozzoli (Eds.), *Children and disasters: A practical guide to healing and recovery* (pp. 85–100). New York: Oxford University Press.

INDEX

Italic page numbers indicate material in tables, figures, or boxes.